Contents

Contents

Making Sense of Company Reports

(with Companies Act 1985 references and locations table)

A TEXT WITH WORKBOOKS AND ANSWERS

E. R. Farmer, MSc, FCCA, FBIM

GEE

To
R. H. K. Mogridge

First published 1983
Reprinted 1984
Second edition 1986

Published by
Van Nostrand Reinhold (UK) Co. Ltd
Molly Millars Lane, Wokingham,
Berkshire, England

Typeset in Times 10/11pt by
Columns of Reading

Printed in Great Britain by
J. W. Arrowsmith Ltd

Library of Congress Cataloging-in-Publication Data

Farmer, E. R.
     Making sense of company reports.

     Rev. and enl. ed. of: Understanding and interpreting
company reports. 1983.
     Includes index.
     1. Financial statements.   2. Corporation reports.
I. Farmer, E. R. Understanding and interpreting
company reports and accounts.   II. Title.
HF5681.B2F33   1986   657′.33   86–9268
ISBN 0–85258–244–7

British Library Cataloguing in Publication Data

Farmer, E. R.
     Making sense of company reports: (with Companies
     Act 1985 references and locations table): a text
     with workbooks and answers.—2nd ed.
     1. Financial statements   2. Corporations—Finance
     I. Title   II. Farmer, E. R. Understanding and
     interpreting company reports and accounts
     657′.33   HF5681.B2

ISBN 0–85258–244–7

Preface

This book is designed as an integrated text and workbook enabling the reader following a structured course or working alone to gain a thorough understanding of all aspects of the contemporary company report and accounts and the ability to interpret critically what he reads. Not only is every item in the balance sheet and profit and loss account considered in detail, but other main chapters deal with the sources and application of funds statement, current cost accounting statements, the directors' and auditors' reports, value added statements and employee reports.

The three workbooks provide over 250 questions and tutorial discussion topics. Answers, or pointers to the answers, are provided in the appendices. The answers to the questions in Workbook 1, testing the reader's understanding of the terminology of accounting, also double as a glossary of accounting terms. The author draws on his extensive experience as a lecturer and examiner to provide examination hints, both in his novel tutorial approach to recent questions in professional examinations and in the detailed worked example of analysis and interpretation contained in a separate chapter.

The text includes many examples and illustrations, including a number from the annual report and accounts of J. Bibby & Sons Ltd, one of the two winners of *The Accountant* and Stock Exchange Annual Awards in 1981.

Part One of the book concentrates on *understanding* as a necessary precedent to interpretation. Full tutorial commentary covering the company law, accounting, auditing and tax implications is given for each item in the statutory accounts and, where relevant, inflation and investment aspects are considered. The accounting formats follow the Companies Act 1981, the provisions of which are reflected throughout the text.

The opening chapter sets the scene for company reporting in the 1980s, noting the impact of severe inflation, the effect of Britain's entry into the European Economic Community, the growth of company groups through take-overs and mergers, the emergence of the Accounting Standards Committee, and company law reform and social change. Chapters 2 and 3 are in the form of case studies accompanied by topics for discussion. Chapter 2 considers the relative importance of cash flow and profit, and follows the development problems of a new and growing business through five successive balance sheets. Chapter 3 plots the growth of the Growstrong business from partnership to private limited company status. Chapters 4 and 5 then examine Growstrong as a public limited company and the balance sheet and profit and loss account are considered in detail. Part One concludes with chapters on the return on capital employed and 'What is *not* in a company balance sheet and profit and loss account' – an approach that is often essential to an analysis of what *is* in.

Part Two commences with an outline of the legal and accounting standards framework for company reports and accounts, including the EEC company law directives and the Stock Exchange requirements. The major features of the Companies Acts are considered.

The material changes in the directors' report and the extension of the auditor's statutory duties arising from the 1981 legislation are then covered, as are employee reports, value added statements, interim statements and statistical summaries with live illustrations, the latter as affected by the impact of inflation.

Recent failures of major companies have given increased emphasis to the importance of the liquidity and efficient funding of a company in the current environment of recession and inflation. A view of the 'funds story' of a business is available through its Statement of Sources and Application of Funds and a separate chapter deals with the preparation and analysis of these statements, with full illustrations and reference to the relevant accounting standard. As the fund statement increasingly appears in examination questions, comparative analysis exercises are included in Workbook 2, with solutions in the appendix. A full chapter considers the limitations of historic cost accounts in an inflationary period and the relevance, impact and interpretation of current cost accounts. Examples and illustrations are included.

Part Three concentrates on the analysis and interpretation of published accounts, consolidating the comment made in Part One of the book. Potential users and their special needs are considered. Trends, vertical analysis and ratios are put into the perspective of their relevance and limitations. A hierarchy of ratios is derived from the primary ratio – the return on capital. Tests of profitability, liquidity and solvency, investment ratios and inter-firm comparisons are indicated, with many examples and illustrations. A comprehensive examination question requiring ratio analysis and interpretation is used as a detailed worked example in a separate chapter which is prefaced by some 20 examination hints based on the author's experience as an examiner.

The final section comprises the three workbooks and their appendices. Workbook 1, which can be used by tutors in a variety of ways or be undertaken by the reader working alone, sets out a progress test of 150 items on understanding the terminology of accounting as well as 26 tutorial discussion topics. Workbook 2 comprises 21 graded exercises, some of which are linked sequentially, requiring classification of items in financial statements, and analysis and interpretation. Suggested answers appear in the appendix. Workbook 3 contains 35 selected examination questions on understanding and interpretation taken from past papers of professional bodies. The author has written a tutorial approach to the answers to five questions and a full model answer with tutorial comment to a sixth. At the request of reviewing lecturers, the remaining 29 questions are not provided with solutions, although their source is indicated.

In this *second edition*, a 33-question recapitulation test including some multi-choice questions has been added to Workbook 1. It is anticipated that multi-choice questions will appear in appropriate papers in the professional examinations.

EXTENDED COVERAGE IN THE SECOND EDITION

New material in the second edition includes:

- Full cross-references to the consolidated Companies Act 1985 of familiar passages within the Companies Acts 1948, 1967, 1976, 1980 and 1981.
- A locations *Table 9* in Chapter 8 to the consolidated Companies Act 1985 of major references relative to this text.
- The major changes of the Finance Act 1984 on corporate and deferred taxation.
- A material expansion of questions and answers to the workbook section including a recapitulation test, with multi-choice questions.
- Coverage of:
  SSAP 20 Accounting for exchange differences from foreign currency translation;
  SSAP 21 Accounting for leases and hire purchase accounts;
  SSAP 22 Accounting for goodwill;

SSAP 23 Accounting for acquisitions and mergers;
Revised SSAP 15 deferred tax;
Problems of accounting for depreciation leading to ED 37 and the revision of SSAP 12;
The revision of SSAP 6 (ED 36) Extraordinary items and prior year adjustments.

- The revision of Chapter 12, covering the withdrawal of the mandatory status of SSAP 16 Current Cost Accounting, the rejection of ED 35 and the debate on the future of accounting for inflation and price level changes.
- New material on:
  - (i) accounting for pension costs;
  - (ii) up-date on audit, including auditors' liability in respect of third parties and consideration of the going concern concept;
  - (iii) employee reports/participation including the Vredling directive proposals and the EEC Fifth Directive;
  - (iv) the Directors' report;
  - (v) interim statements;
  - (vi) the Unlisted Securities Market (USM);
  - (vii) the law, true and fair view concept and accounting standards;
  - (viii) changes to the standards programme, SOIs, SORPs and franked SORPS.

Acknowledgments

The author is grateful to the following professional bodies for permission to include Examination Questions:

The Chartered Association of Certified Accountants.
The Institute of Bankers.
The Institute of Chartered Accountants in England and Wales.
The Institute of Cost and Management Accountants.

He also wishes to acknowledge the many helpful suggestions of friends and colleagues and those of the publisher's reviewers, in particular Geoffrey Pitchford, FCA, FCCA, and other lecturers at Huddersfield Polytechnic, and Pat Reardon, JP, FCCA, ACIS, and Ron Webb, FCCA, of the Department of Accountancy, Slough College – the latter for material on the funds statement.

He extends his thanks to the Company Secretary, Mr S. W. Bowman, and the directors of J. Bibby & Co Ltd for permission to use and comment on material from their report and accounts which won *The Accountant* and Stock Exchange Annual Award in 1981.

He thanks the Principal of Slough College and the Royal County of Berkshire for the generous extension of research time for the preparation of this text, and his wife for her indulgence while the work was undertaken.

Many of the helpful suggestions for improvement made by college and polytechnic lecturers and in particular those contained in his generous review of the first edition by Professor Michael Harvey, City of London Polytechnic, in the Certified Students' Newsletter, have been incorporated in the text of the second edition.

Introduction

Students preparing for the increasingly demanding examinations of the professional bodies and those taking a business or accounting degree course will find this book of particular value. In both cases an essential ingredient for examination success is an ability to understand and interpret the corporate report and accounts.

The book is also intended for the non-financial manager, the non-accounting professional and the investor, to whom a better understanding of the published report and accounts is important.

For the professional student, papers in the following examinations are fully covered:

THE CHARTERED ASSOCIATION OF CERTIFIED ACCOUNTANTS

The Regulatory Framework of Accounting, which examines the ability of candidates to understand and analyse critically the current theoretical, legal and institutional influences which regulate financial statements.

Advanced Financial Accounting. Sixty per cent of the final level paper is concerned with developments in accounting practice and the presentation and analysis of financial information.
Advanced Accounting Practice (double paper). All of syllabus paragraph (E) and much of paragraphs (A) and (B).

THE INSTITUTE OF CHARTERED ACCOUNTANTS IN ENGLAND AND WALES

Financial accounting (1) examines students' ability to prepare financial statements of companies in conformity with the current legal requirements and professional standards of practice and to discuss such statements, including the provisions of SSAPs, critically. The discussion element of the paper comprises up to 35 per cent of the paper's marks.

Financial accounting (2) examines students' ability to present and interpret accounting statements and to write reports relating to the financial affairs of a business . . . and to discuss critically assumptions and conventions of current accounting practices and developments. The content includes SSAPs, current issues, the impact of international standards and EEC regulations on financial reporting, and the analysis and interpretation of accounting statements.

It is increasingly clear from professional level chartered examination results that *understanding* and *critical analysis* are the main criteria for success.

THE INSTITUTE OF CHARTERED SECRETARIES AND ADMINISTRATORS (1986 new syllabus)

Part 3 Financial Accounting examines students on:

Accounting regulations – the need for accounting standards; accounting assumptions, bases and policies, needs for disclosure; the detailed accounting requirements of the Companies Acts.

The presentation of accounts for publication – including the profit and loss account, balance sheet, sources and application of funds statements, directors' report, and the auditors' report; the treatment of taxation in accounts.

Consolidated accounts – acquisition and merger methods of consolidation; the treatment of related companies.

Interpretation of accounts. Detailed examination of accounts or other financial information regarding capital structure, asset base, liquidity, working capital levels and controls, cash flows. Use and limitations of ratio analysis. Reporting in good style, the analysis, evaluation and recommendations arising from the examination to management, investors or creditors.

Accounting policies. Questions will be set to test conceptual understanding of important topical areas such as depreciation, research and development, earnings per share, leasing, stocks and long-term contracts, foreign currency transactions, and goodwill.

Capital structure.

THE INSTITUTE OF BANKERS (This text is recommended reading)

Stage 2, Part 2 Accounting. The nature and inter-relationships of balance sheets, profit statements and funds flow statements. The distinction between working capital flows, cash flows and profit flows. Interpretation measures. Accounting ratios and rates of return.

Practice of Banking 2. The interpretation and criticism of accounting statements including balance sheets, profit and loss accounts and funds flow statements for lending purposes.

THE INSTITUTE OF COST AND MANAGEMENT ACCOUNTANTS (1986 new syllabus)

Stage 1, Foundation in Accounting: Stage I, Accounting. Accounting theory – asset valuation, research and development, capital or revenue, goodwill, stock valuation, problems of changing price levels. Objectives of financial statements – user groups and their information needs.

Stage II, Financial Accounting. Accounts of limited companies and Companies Acts requirements, treatment of shares, debentures, dividends, interest and tax, funds flow statements. Analysis of accounting statements and the use of ratios. Relevant SSAPs, accounting for changing price levels, introduction to group accounts.

Stage III, Advanced Financial Accounting. Preparation of accounts in accordance with the requirements of the Companies Acts and SSAPs, treatment of taxation, deferred taxation, acquisition and merger methods of consolidation, extraordinary and exceptional items, current cost and current purchasing power methods in practice, stocks and work in progress, investment properties, accounting for leases, recommended accounting practice for research and development and goodwill; interpretation of accounts – advanced aspects of interpretation and the use of ratios, related reports, preparation and interpretation of statements of source and application of funds, earnings per share, price earnings ratios and other stock market ratios; development of accounting standards – role of ASC, influence of IASC, EEC, Company law and Stock Exchange on financial accounting requirements, current exposure drafts and SSAPs.

THE SOCIETY OF COMPANY AND COMMERCIAL ACCOUNTANTS
THE INSTITUTE OF ADMINISTRATIVE ACCOUNTANTS
THE ASSOCIATION OF COST AND EXECUTIVE ACCOUNTANTS

Major aspects of the advanced papers.

Introduction

THE ASSOCIATION OF ACCOUNTING TECHNICIANS (This text is recommended reading – 1986 new syllabus)

Paper 5, Accounting: Accounting concepts: Accounting statements: Interpretation of financial statements. The significance and limitation of financial ratios; the definition and application of basic financial ratios and the selection and application of appropriate accounting concepts to business problems.

Paper 9, Financial Accounting: Company accounts. Accounting statements of companies, including the sources and application of funds statements, in accordance with disclosure requirements of the Companies Acts; treatment of taxation in accounts; the directors' report; application of best accounting practice to all accounting entries including an appreciation of the rules contained in SSAPs.

Analysis and evaluation. The application of financial ratios and statements of sources and application of funds to the interpretation of business situations; capital structure and gearing; working capital; appreciation of inflation on accounting statements prepared under the historic cost convention.

THE STOCK EXCHANGE examinations

Specifically the paper 'Interpretation of Company Reports and Accounts'.

FOR THE DEGREE OR DIPLOMA COURSE STUDENT IN ACCOUNTANCY OR BUSINESS STUDIES

The three parts of the book, with their related workbooks, case studies and discussion topics, have been structured as an INTEGRATED COURSE TEXT where the emphasis is on understanding and interpretation of all aspects of the corporate report and accounts in their dynamic setting. Considerable flexibility is available to tutors in their use of the graded workbook material and the depth to which they wish to take the various aspects of the subject matter.

FOR NON-ACCOUNTING PROFESSIONALS AND MANAGERS

A sound knowledge of the financial structure of business adds to their overall ability and career potential. The Certified Diploma in Accounting and Finance of the Association of Certified Accountants provides a popular post-experience qualification for management, including non-accounting professionals. In its guidance notes for tutors and candidates, emphasis is placed on "the *interpretative* aspects of accountancy and finance and on an *understanding* . . ." and not on the detailed mechanical aspects.

CERTIFIED DIPLOMA IN ACCOUNTING AND FINANCE

Paper 1, Financial Accounting specifies the regulatory framework, legal and institutional, within which financial reporting takes place; the responsibilities of the accountant, auditor, directors and others; the interpretation of financial statements and the use of performance indicators to the needs of management, employees, shareholders and others.

FOR INVESTORS

Professors Lee and Tweedie in their 1977 research report indicated the poor understanding of the corporate report and accounts by the private investor. Their subsequent 1981 study of the institutional investor showed, astonishingly, that 40% of respondents had a poor or no actual understanding of the directors' report; 64% had a poor or no actual understanding of the funds statement; 47% had only a vague understanding of what profit meant; 70% were vague on the meaning of depreciation and 73% had a poor or no understanding of the nature of a current cost statement.

PART ONE

Understanding published company accounts

1

The company reporting environment in the 1980s

The annual report and accounts is the main instrument used by companies to communicate information about their financial affairs to interested parties. It bears little resemblance to its pre-war predecessor. Its development has been a reaction to many aspects of change: economic, social and political – nationally and internationally. Summarised below and then discussed in more detail are those events which presaged change. The future appearance of the report and accounts will no doubt further reflect the dynamic nature of our times.

Take-overs and mergers

In the 1960s, particularly, companies experienced a spate of take-over and merger activities which commentators described as 'merger mania'. The growth of holding companies (the controlling company in a group) and the emergence among them of the transnational (or multinational) corporation added an international dimension to company reporting standards.

Inflation and price rises

Companies suffered chronic inflation rising to unprecedented levels in the early 1970s, adding impetus to the need for an accounting system which could measure its effect on profitability and asset values.

Companies saw profits pared to the bone by rapid cost escalation triggered, among other reasons, by the dramatic price-raising actions of the oil-producing countries and by labour unions – a powerful force in the fast-changing social and economic environment – attempting not only to protect their members against inflation, but also to gain a bigger share of the corporate cake.

Accounting causes célèbres

A series of accounting causes célèbres led to the questioning of the standing of company reports and the apparent elasticity of the principles underlying the preparation and presentation of company accounts. Among those receiving wide publicity were GEC's take-over of AEI (1967) and the enforced liquidation of the world-famous Rolls-Royce company (1971). The resulting public criticism and concern led to the formation by the accountancy profession of the Accounting Standards Committee (ASC) to undertake a programme of formulating standard guidelines to be followed in the preparation of accounting statements.

Entry to the EEC

In 1973 the UK joined the EEC and 'European accounting' assumed a new importance, providing new problems for Britain's accountants and for company reporting. Not least among these was the need to find an acceptable compromise between the 'Code Napoleon' basis adopted by the EEC, where the requirements of company reporting are set more firmly in prescriptive law or statutory regulation, and the common law background of the UK system where the state law prescribes only the basic framework, leaving the detail to be filled in by other agencies including the accountancy profession, thus permitting quicker adaptation to the needs of change.

Company law changes

The trend-setting 1948 Companies Act, which had taken post-war UK corporate reports into the top league with only the US as a serious competitor, became outmoded in the 1960s and 1970s as the volatile financial environment demanded more information and higher standards of presentation. Events which influenced the continuing trend of improvement included the initiative of the financial weekly, *The Accountant*, joined now by the Stock Exchange, in making Annual Awards to companies judged to have produced the best-presented and most informative reports and accounts; the introduction by the Stock Exchange of its own regulations setting stricter disclosure requirements for companies coming to the market for the first time or returning to raise more funds from the public by the issue of shares or debentures; and further companies' legislation enacted in 1967, 1976 and 1980. This latter flurry of new company law culminated in the Companies Act 1981, much of which originated from the requirements of the EEC Fourth Directive dealing with company accounting and disclosure procedures seen as necessary for the harmonisation of company law in the Community.

With the last consolidation as far back as 1948, company law rationalisation was long overdue and this was affected by the Companies Act 1985 (see Chapter 8 and *Table 9* thereof indexing CA 1985 locations for the subject matter of this book).

SOCIAL CHANGE

The pace of social change which saw labour move into a more dominant role in the affairs of business and industry also included a change in the nature of investment and thus of ultimate control and interest. This came through the growth and spread of the institutional investors such as investment trusts, unit trusts, insurance companies and pension funds. Bearing in mind that the source of the funds of these bodies is the body public, it is perhaps a matter for regret that the pluralistic nature of company shareholding is not more widely appreciated. The awareness of the accountancy bodies of the general impact of social change on companies led to their publication in 1975 of a discussion document 'The Corporate Report', reference to which is made later in this book.

1. Take-overs and Mergers

DEFINITIONS

A *take-over* has been defined as 'an offer to acquire company securities (voting, ordinary shares) . . . made to more than one holder . . . resulting in any person acquiring control . . .

of that company'. Usually the corporate and capital identity of the successful bidder survives the operation. This contrasts with a *merger* where there is probably a negotiated agreement between two or more parties, resulting often in the creation of a new company with a new name.

The above definition of a take-over indicates that control of a company can be obtained by purchasing 51 per cent of a company's voting equity (ordinary) shares. A sub-subsidiary company can be controlled by its ultimate holding company even though the latter has only a 13 per cent interest in the former, e.g.

Example 1.1

Ultimate Holding Company, A Plc (Public Limited Company), has an
interest of 51 per cent in B (its subsidiary company)
which has an
interest of 51 per cent in C (A's sub-subsidiary)
which has an
interest of 51 per cent in D (A's sub-subsidiary).

Ultimate Holding Company's interest in D is 51 per cent by 51 per cent by 51 per cent = 13.26 per cent.

The *minority shareholders* (those holding the balance – 49% in this case – of the ordinary shares in each company) would hope that the underlying reason which motivated the take-over of their company was in their long-term interest and that their company would survive – with the shortcomings which made it a potential candidate for take-over eliminated – and with the likely objective of the holding company of earnings growth thus increasing earnings per share and therefore achieving an increased share price.

UNDERVALUED PROPERTIES

However, there were frequently other reasons for take-overs apart from that of improving the operating efficiency and financial management of a company.

While the financial managers of bidding companies were mostly looking for those companies whose market price did not, in their view, fully discount future earnings potential and were considering the published balance sheets and accounts of the day for evidence, for example, of unused cash or excess stock holdings relative to sales, indicating poor financial management and idle capital, there were others who in the 1950s were motivated to a take-over more from what a balance sheet omitted than from what it showed.

The then practice of accounting for fixed assets (long-term assets held for use by the business, e.g. property, plant and machinery) at historical cost, resulted in undisclosed undervaluation (mainly in land and buildings) with the result that those who could assess the true market value saw the possibility of quick profit where the current price of the company's ordinary shares did not reflect that increased value. A profitable bid for the equity of the company would then be made, e.g.

Example 1.2

Summarised Balance Sheet of
Undervalued Ltd

100,000 Ordinary (equity) shares of £1 each, plus reserves	*Invested in Net Assets (Assets less liabilities) including Property at £75,000 (cost)*
£200,000	£200,000

Land and Buildings (Property) are currently worth £225,000, taking the net asset value to £350,000 and the 100,000 shares are worth £3.50 each on an assets basis. The current quoted market price of the shares is £2.25 each. A bid may be acceptable to the present shareholders if sufficiently above £2.25, and worthwhile to the bidders if sufficiently below £3.50.

LEGAL REFORM

Belatedly, the 1967 Companies Act attempted to deal with this situation where material profits were made by bidders at the expense of the owners of the companies, i.e. the ordinary shareholders. Section 16(1a) (7 Sch. 1 CA 1985) specified that where the market value of land (including property thereon) held as fixed assets differs substantially from the book amount included in the balance sheet, and the difference is, *in the opinion of the directors*, such as to require that the attention of members . . . should be drawn thereto, the difference should be indicated with such degree of precision as is practicable.

Not all directors appear to follow the spirit of the Act in using the discretion allowed them to publish or not to publish useful information. It has been observed that many such statements in company reports have been mere truisms and of doubtful value to readers, e.g.

Example 1.3

'The land and buildings of the Group are, for all practical purposes, fully utilised for manufacturing and trading operations. In view of this, the Directors are of the opinion that a market valuation of land and buildings as compared with the book value would not be of significance.'

Or, negative, e.g.

Example 1.4

'The market value of certain freehold property owned is considerably in excess of the book value, but the Directors feel it inappropriate to estimate what that surplus may be.'

ROSY PICTURE OF PROFITABILITY

Retaining historical values for properties in the balance sheet instead of the materially higher market values led, of course, to published 'return on capital employed' statistical comparisons showing a rosier picture than the reality, e.g.

Example 1.5

The Rosy Picture Co Ltd

The balance sheet (book) value of 'capital employed' in the form of the total assets – Fixed (long) and Current (short) assets – was shown as *£4 million*

The profit before tax and loan interest for the year as shown in the published profit and loss account was *£2 million*

Published form of the 'return on capital employed' = *50%*

But the value of land and property included in total assets is £3 million higher than shown in the books, thus capital employed is adjusted to: *£7 million*

and the return on capital employed falls to: *28.6%*

Also, in respect of the second quoted example (E1.4) of a published statement responding to the 1967 Act requirement, the group concerned is purported to have realised major property within a short time of its year end for £30 million more than its book value. Shareholders who had previously disposed of their (undervalued) shares had cause to feel aggrieved.

BALANCE SHEETS AS STATEMENTS OF VALUE

The once-held view that balance sheets were not statements of value, but merely the end products of the system of double entry book-keeping based on the concept of historical cost, has become outmoded principally because of the advent of high levels of inflation.

Due to inflation and take-overs resulting from the circumstances described, more and more companies have entered current estimated values of property into their accounts (increasing the value of the property on the one side of the balance sheet and increasing the value of the ordinary shareholders' funds by the same amount on its other side).

During its issuance, Statement of Standard Accounting Practice 16 (1980) requiring listed (public) and 'large' unlisted companies and nationalised industries to present a *current cost* profit and loss account and balance sheet, either as their main annual accounts or supplementary to their historical accounts, made it likely that the Stock Exchange value of a company's ordinary shares incorporated a more accurate view of the value of the underlying net assets of the company.

THE YEARS OF THE MERGERS

The property take-overs of the 1950s were followed in the 1960s by ever-increasing take-over activity, motivated by a variety of reasons, peaking in 1968 when well over one hundred take-overs, each with a value of at least £10 million, took place in the UK. In America in that year, almost 10% of independent manufacturing companies with assets of more than 10 million dollars were acquired by take-over or merger. With competition becoming increasingly international and an improvement in the structure of industry in the UK seen by many to be overdue, the increase in overall efficiency expected to be brought about by mergers was in the main welcomed. Indeed, the government of the day encouraged the independent processes of the market through its agency, the Industrial Reorganisation Corporation (new defunct), which made its presence felt through a number of notable 'marriages'.

THE WHEELER-DEALERS

However, many of the take-overs were of the type described as 'wheeler-dealing', either involving 'asset stripping' in which previously undervalued parts of a company were sold off at a substantial profit, or where the aim of the acquiring company was to increase the value of its shares through the medium of the Price-Earnings Ratio (PER). The settlement of the purchase consideration for the acquired company's shares being an exchange with those of the acquirer, it followed that the higher the PE ratio of the latter compared with the former, the cheaper the purchase price. The aim of these operations was to increase the earnings potential of the acquired company within the enlarged group and thus to increase the acquirer's PER. And so the take-over operations would continue. However, these transactions often resulted in the acquisition of a mixed bag of companies, and over time the expectation of making 3 + 3 equal 9 was not realised and the snowball melted away.

GROUP ACCOUNTS

The 1948 Companies Act introduced the requirement that the holding company must publish within its annual report to the shareholders not only its own balance sheet and profit and loss account, but also group accounts. These are normally in the form of a consolidated balance sheet and consolidated profit and loss account dealing with the state of affairs and profit or loss *of the company and its subsidiaries*.

Although this represented a major advance in the provision of financial information to interested parties, there are difficulties in comparing the performance of a conglomerate (mixed) group over time, for instance, and in determining the performance of the separate subsidiaries within the group. It is extremely rare for the full report and accounts of subsidiaries to be included with the holding company's report so that while the group may be profitable overall, analysts cannot easily identify loss-making operations. A determined researcher can make reference to the individual company's report and accounts at Companies House if it has been filed at the same time as that of the holding company, but given the number of companies within some groups the task would not be easy. And there are additional hazards, one being that of 'transfer pricing' policies within group companies – particularly multinational groups – where to take advantage of reducing overall tax, or of movements in currency exchange rates, trading transactions between companies in the group are priced differently than would be the case if the transactions concerned customers/suppliers outside the group.

2.   Inflation, Liquidity and Company Funds

The 1970s were for companies and others, years of spiralling inflation and runaway costs, with government policies unable to stem the tide. Governments concentrated on short-term, stop-go policies, attempting to deal with the latest crisis by one fiscal measure or another, and interest rates fluctuated like a see-saw. New investment in industry suffered, while the quadrupling of the price of oil in 1973–74 and subsequent further increases boosted inflation worldwide. Although the UK was cushioned to some extent by North Sea oil development, government policy was linked to high energy costs and companies were not protected.

RISING COST OF LABOUR

UK labour costs had risen during this period following pressures from strong trade unions as they bargained in an inflationary environment for higher wages and salaries. As companies went out of business or shed labour in cost-cutting exercises, unemployment rose inexorably. Demand in Britain's main markets overseas weakened and the difficulties of some key exporting companies were materially exacerbated by the strong pound which by 1980 was regarded by some commentators to be as much as 20% too high in competitive terms.

LIQUIDITY PROBLEMS

As profits fell, so did the internal cash flow of companies. The best-managed companies had in the past been able to finance their future growth almost entirely out of the profits they retained for that purpose, after paying tax and a dividend that provided a continuing incentive for the equity shareholder to maintain his confidence in the company. This growth of the profitable company was buttressed by its ability to attract low-interest, long-term loans which were invested in assets providing an adequate rate of return over and above the cost of the loan.

The fall in profitability and its effect on liquidity was compounded by the fact that companies' financial accounts were still maintained, despite rising inflation, in historic cost terms, and such profits as there were were overstated in real monetary terms. Before the government intervened to provide some relief from taxation on inflationary elements in profits, principally stock 'appreciation', the combination of historic cost accounting methods and the resulting over-taxation, meant that companies were motivated to make higher dividend distributions than was prudent, leading in some cases to reserves of capital being eroded.

The extent of the inflationary increase in stocks, as opposed to real increases, and thus the increased cost on liquid funds because of inflation of holding the same volume of stocks, is exemplified by the year 1979 when 'stock appreciation' more than doubled. Although the government's 'stock appreciation relief' meant that the company was not taxed on such appreciation, the sharply accelerated inflation put further claims on company liquidity.

INCREASED BANK LENDING

By 1981, the profitability of UK industry generally had fallen on average to levels which did not compete with those available on risk-free gilts. Many investors would have done much better with their money in a building society. Retailers performed better than manufacturers, but a number of the largest manufacturing companies in the UK were making negative returns on investors' capital.

The high cost of long-term loans made these unattainable and the lack of profit made equity investment unattractive. With industry having to fund the deficit between internal cash flow and expenditure in order to survive, company liquidations increased – rocketing in 1980 to a record 6,896; for the survivors, the banks had become the major provider of fixed-interest debt. This modification of the banks' traditional policy of short-term lending to that of medium-term lending, resulted not only from the exorbitant cost of long-term borrowing, but also because the banks were flush with funds arising from the great increase in people's personal savings. The building societies and the banks benefited from large increases in deposits, the outcome of increased pensions, wages and salaries and rapid inflation.

Following the report of the committee chaired by Sir Harold Wilson into the working of City institutions, it was clear that funds had been available for investment in industry in the 1970s, but declining profits, low growth, the high rate of inflation, and high interest rates had been among those factors which prevented enough money moving in that direction. Too large a part of the funds which might have gone to industry had gone to the government to finance its own debt, pushing up interest rates to higher levels and making industrial investment even less attractive.

MORE REALISM IN THE 1980s

The 1980s started with the banks continuing to finance companies, with short- and medium-term funds, who they judged to be reasonable risks and having growth and profit potential, helping many over the period of the recession and into improved market conditions. In 1981 sterling fell sharply below its 1980 levels and the Government continued its fight to reduce its own cash flow deficit and with it inflation. The introduction of current cost accounting for company reporting through SSAP 16 had disappointing results, becoming largely ignored as inflation diminished, but at least it had focused attention on 'real profits' and 'real cash flow'.

By mid-1985, inflation had stabilised between 5% to 7%, an outcome welcomed by all, but the connected government policies, the widespread recession, continuing high interest rates and company liquidations, then around 250 per week, saw unemployment reaching even higher levels. The volatility of exchange rates between 1981 and 1985, with the sterling/dollar rate virtually halved, had material consequences on company groups engaged in oversea operations providing export growth opportunities for them.

In 1984, with lower inflation, the Government abolished 'stock appreciation relief', phased-out first year tax allowances on plant and machinery investment and announced a reduction of corporation tax over a period of years to a low of 35% by 1987 when UK companies would enjoy one of the lowest corporation tax rates in the world. This advance notice of changes in tax rates and allowances gave a welcomed enhancement enabling companies to forward plan their financial operations.

The outcome of the year-long miners' dispute (1984–5) was a greater realism in respect of their place in corporate affairs by trade union members and their leaders. This, together with the government's employment and trade union legislation of the period and the modest spread of employee shareholding boosted by the giant 1984 British Telecom share issue, gave grounds for optimism over improved industrial relations. The success of the British Telecom issue, given its record size, again emphasised the extent of personal savings in the UK which had increased out of all proportion to the performance of the economy. Among the reasons for the increase in this huge pool of potential investment were the material increase in pension provisions, rising wages, higher incomes and the rapid inflation of recent years. It became clear that most of these monies had been channelled into banks and building societies with little going directly into companies. While by 1985, competition between societies and the banks was benefiting savers, there was an absence of the vehicle for channelling these funds into equity investment and the motivation to do so, given the comparative returns and risks involved. Meanwhile the banks indirectly assisted by continuing the large flow of savers funds to industry and commerce by way of fixed-interest finance.

The Unlisted Securities Market (USM)

One result of the Wilson enquiry into the City, and the initiative of the Stock Exchange, was the emergence of the USM in 1980. This was the Exchange's response to the recommendation that they should become more responsive to the funding needs of small and medium-sized business. The aim was to create an entirely new market in the shares of relatively new, expanding companies which were likely to be too small or too speculative to comply with the stringent standards of the Stock Exchange for a full listing.

Companies and investors came to this new market in sizeable numbers, providing funds for the former and opportunities for the latter, hoping to be in on the early development of some new ICI or Racal.

The term 'unlisted' for this secondary market is somewhat misleading. USM shares can be bought and sold through stockbrokers and bankers in the same way as with main market shares and their latest trading prices are published in the Financial Times and the Stock Exchange Official List. This new vehicle for company funding and growth has been a success story boosting many small- and medium-sized companies and providing spectacular success for others.

The main difference between a USM and a fully-listed company are:

(i) the company has only to sell 10% of its shares for a USM listing (25% for a full listing);

(ii) the USM accepts companies with a minimum of three years of trading (five years for a full listing);

(iii) the majority of USM companies have had a market capitalisation of between £1 million and £6 million (minimum £5 million full listing);

(iv) the costs of entry and the regulatory requirements are much more realistic for companies coming to the USM (likely cost from £100,000 to £200,000; full listing up to £350,000).

The US economy in the mid-1980s

The combination of high US real interest rates and the strong US economy during this period, sucked funds into America, and led to that country becoming the worlds' largest debtor nation with a huge balance of payments deficit compared to the rest of the world. One result was a strong dollar and a weakening of other currencies; its effect on sterling has been noted. Another result of the strength of this US recovery was a ripple effect which it had in starting to pull other countries' economies out of recession. UK exporters to the US benefitted as did UK leisure and other businesses from the influx of American tourists. It may be noted also that in the first half of the 1980s many major UK companies had diversified heavily overseas and derived high proportions of their earnings from the UK and Europe. Much of this investment by industry (and by financial institutions) was made in the UK at levels of over two dollars to the pound making the returns on the investment doubly attractive. Companies with subsidiaries in America were able to remit profits back to the UK at exchange rates which buoyed up their sterling receipts. What is good for exporters, however, is usually bad for importers and such companies incurred increased costs.

On balance, the benefits of the strong dollar for the UK outweighed the problems. But, at macro level, the obvious danger of the US government's huge budget deficit was the possibility of the resurgence of inflation in that country and of its export to the rest of the world. By the mid-1980s this had not happened.

3. Accounting Causes Célèbres

The traditional company report

Until comparatively recent times, the traditional report comprising the annual profit and loss account, balance sheet, directors' report and audit report was often regarded by the directors of companies as a matter of concern mainly to themselves, their current shareholders to whom it was addressed, to 'the City', including the Stock Exchange where their securities (shares/debentures) might be quoted, and to potential investors.

In respect of investment potential, there were those enlightened companies who would have accepted the conclusion of reported research that the annual report provided basic factual information on which to assess a company for forecasting future dividend levels, as well as being the main influence on the market price of the companies' shares and thus the price-earnings ratio, and as evidence for assessing liquidity, profitability and survival prospects.

Auditors saw their responsibilities as being confined to reporting to the shareholders as to whether the annual profit and loss account and balance sheet showed a 'true and fair' view, and to comment if it did not. As auditors, there was no requirement of them for a report on the financial condition of the company.

Problems concerning the traditional report and audit

While, in law, the auditors are appointed by the shareholders to report to them on the accounts and balance sheet – the financial outcome of the activities of the directors entrusted by the members with the direction of the company – in practice the appointment is usually made on the recommendation of the directors. Frequently, also, the auditors may provide financial services of one kind or another to the company. Thus there is a view that the necessary independence of the auditor in his relations with the directors is compromised.

In this respect, the draft EEC Eighth Directive contains a proposal which would prevent an auditor offering other accountancy services to his audit client. The government of the UK do not accept this proposal, believing that the wide range of accountancy expertise within one firm is one of its main sources of strength, and that such a prohibition would be bad for industry, obliging companies to employ two firms of accountants where at present one will do, leading to less satisfactory service and an increase in costs. The auditor has in law a direct contractual duty of care to the company's shareholders and an action in negligence against an auditor may be sustained on the evidence. But does an auditor have a duty to other (third) parties who relying on accounts negligently prepared and attracting a clear audit certificate, invest in it, or extend credit, and suffer loss? Following certain legal decisions (*Candler v Crane Christmas & Co*, 1951; *Hedley Byrne & Co Ltd v Heller & Partners Ltd*, 1964) it was regarded as settled law that since the annual accounts of a company might as a matter of fact be relied on for all sorts of purposes and by all sorts of people, it would be unreasonable to treat auditors as owing a duty of care to all persons dealing with the company simply by virtue of the fact that they had relied on audited accounts. A prerequisite of any liability to third parties appeared to be that the auditor *must have known*, or *ought to have known*, that the financial statements were being prepared for the specific purpose or transaction which caused the third parties' loss.

More recently, however, the decisions in the cases of *Jeb Fasteners Ltd v Marks Bloom & Co* (1981) and *Twomax Ltd & Goode v Dickson, MacFarlane, and Robinson* (1982) have clearly extended the 'proximity' of third parties to whom auditors may have responsibility in relation to their work. While, in all reason, auditors cannot be held liable to 'an indeterminate number of people for indeterminate amounts for indeterminate periods of time' (*Ultramares Corpn v Touche and others*), these recent cases show that where they should have *reasonably foreseen* in all the circumstances that a person would have relied upon their work, auditors may now be held liable for pecuniary loss caused by their negligent auditing of a company's accounts. This was despite the fact that the third parties were unknown to them at the time of their audit, nor did they have knowledge of the transaction which led to the loss (see Chapter 8, Statutory Audit).

The 'elasticity' of accounting principles

A typical report of the auditors addressed to members of a company includes the phrase 'a true and fair view', e.g.:

> 'In our opinion the financial statements give a *true and fair view* of the state of affairs of the company as at 31 December 19x1 . . . and of the profit for the year ended on that date . . .'

The implication of the use of that phrase instead of the word 'correct' is that the presentation of the content of the accounts and balance sheet involves matters of judgement on which there might be varying views. The adoption of one particular policy or principle rather than another would provide a different outcome in the accounts. The auditor has to report that, in his opinion, the outcome is true and fair, or state in what respects it is not.

Take the following example:

Example 3.1

Assume two manufacturing companies, X Ltd and Y Ltd, start business on the same day, with identical plant purchased by each on day one for £50,000. At the end of year one assume for the purposes of the illustration that each had earned the same £100,000 profit from completely identical transactions and this was the outcome shown in the profit and loss accounts of each, but before any charge had been made for the cost of depreciation of the plant.

In X Ltd the technical staff estimate a lifetime of 5 years for the plant with no residual value. The policy agreed is to charge 20% on cost for depreciation in each of the succeeding 5 years.

In Y Ltd the technical staff also indicate 5 years as the lifetime of the plant to scrap value, but give their opinion that it will be superseded in about 2 years by new technology which will make the plant obsolete. Y Ltd's management determine a policy of a 50% write off for depreciation in each of the succeeding 2 years. In year 1, therefore, the following profit is reported:

	X Ltd	Y Ltd
Profit after all expenses but before depreciation	£100,000	£100,000
Depreciation	10,000	25,000
Net profit	£ 90,000	£ 75,000

The respective auditors of X Ltd and Y Ltd will sign clear (unqualified) audit reports, quite properly, for although a different profit is reported by each from the same set of transactions, both show a 'true and fair view' based on the decisions made by the respective managements.

Accountancy practice in respect of transactions such as that exemplified, where judgement and policy might be involved, was directed by accounting rules largely empirical in nature. Besides depreciation, other areas in which there were varying degrees of flexibility (some critics would say 'elasticity') included the valuation of stock and work in progress, an item at the centre of some well known cases of fraud, and the assessment of the amount of research and development expenditure incurred in a year which should be charged against the profit for that period.

ACCOUNTING STANDARDS COMMITTEE

The equanimity of the accounting profession about its accounting rules in those areas open to judgement and to different interpretations received a series of sharp shocks resulting from the adverse publicity given in the national as well as the financial press to a series of questionable affairs where the identity of the reporting firms was often featured prominently. It is sufficient for our purpose to consider only three of these: GEC's take-over of AEI (1967); the investigation of the 1968 accounts of Pergamon Press Ltd, and the enforced liquidation of the world-famous Rolls-Royce company (1971). The first two cases were undoubtedly major factors in influencing the Institute of Chartered Accountants in England and Wales (ICAEW) to issue a Statement of Intent in December 1969 leading to the constitution of the Accounting Standards Committee (ASC) in 1970.

The Committee's basic purpose, through the publication of Accounting Standards, is to narrow the range of subjective judgement on accounting matters known to be open to a wide variety of interpretations, and thus to a variety of disclosure methods. Now, over 15 years later, 23 Statements of Standard Accounting Practice have been issued following periods of exposure to interested parties and for debate. All members of the accountancy profession, either as preparers or auditors of accounts, are expected to adhere to them, or to explain or justify departures therefrom.

The outcome has been a degree of standardization in published accounts unthought of at the beginning of the decade. Among the standards published, SSAP 13 'Accounting for

Research and Development' deals with the subject which was central to the Rolls-Royce collapse. SSAP 9 'Stocks and Work in Progress' sets out the standard accounting practice in the area which featured in the Pergamon Press and GEC/AEI affairs.

The GEC take-over of AEI (1967)

This controversial affair, which brought to public attention the extent of the difference which could emerge between two sets of figures ostensibly based on the same circumstances, was particularly concerned with the valuation of stock and work in progress.

For inexperienced readers, *Example 3.2* of the Trading Account of a retail company highlights the importance of the valuation of (closing) stock on the resulting figure of 'Gross Profit', and the effect of a fraudulent, erroneous or changed figure resulting from a 'different view' on that valuation.

The valuation of closing stock, particularly of manufacturing companies where there will be a wide range of stocks of raw material (leaving aside work in progress and finished goods which present their own valuation problems), is a difficult area in the verification work of an auditor and one in which he will place some reliance on a certification of stock sheet summaries by responsible management. Over-reliance on management has its dangers for auditors as is shown by the fraud cases referred to shortly.

Example 3.2

The Ever Improving Trading Co Ltd
TRADING ACCOUNT for the year ended 31 March 19x8

	Account 1		Account 2	
	£	£	£	£
Sales		500,000		500,000
Deduct Cost of Sales:				
being				
Opening Stock (1.4.19x7)	50,000		50,000	
Purchases for the year	350,000		350,000	
	400,000		400,000	
Less				
Closing Stock (31.3.19x8)	40,000	360,000	100,000	300,000
GROSS PROFIT for the year		140,000		200,000

Account 1 and 2 differ only because of the differing valuation of closing stock. The change in that valuation, whether through fraud, error, or a change in valuation policy, has *reduced* 'the cost of sales' by £60,000 and *increased* the 'gross profit' by 43 per cent. As the double-entry effect of the closing stock entry is to show the 'closing stock' in the balance sheet as a current asset, the result of the increase in value if from error or fraud, is to overstate the capital of the company by the amount of that increase. Further, should the remaining expenses and tax of the company to be set against 'the gross profit' be £140,000 or more, any dividends paid out of the resultant but non-existent 'net profit' will have been paid, in the absence of reserves of past profits, illegally out of capital. Similar results would occur where 'changed' figures for stocks of raw materials, work in progress and finished goods of a manufacturing company were included in the year-end accounts.

As the closing stock of one financial period becomes the opening stock of the following period, a snowballing effect is introduced and in the case of error or fraud, the inevitable effect is insolvency and the company's liquidation.

Legal actions involving stock fraud

A number of famous legal actions relate to the fraudulent over-valuation of stock. The *Kingston Cotton Mill* case (1896), well known to generations of accountancy students, had a more recent near-repeat which resulted in an action brought by the liquidator of *Thomas Gerrard and Son Ltd* against a firm of chartered accountants for breach of duty as auditors of the company. The company's managing director had over a period of years been falsifying the accounts, involving end of year stocks and concealing heavy losses. The true position on the profit and loss account as at November 1962 was an adverse balance of £272,395, whereas the accounts for the preceding year based on the falsified figures had shown a favourable balance of £152,105 – a difference of £424,504. The MD was sentenced to five years imprisonment and the auditors were found to have failed in their duty.

In 1964, the *Sunday Times* reported the 'Great Salad Oil Scandal' involving Anthony (Tino) de Angelis, president of the Allied Crude Vegetable Oil Refining Company, which had losses totalling more than 150 million dollars, involving many important banks and insurance companies in the United States as well as several in Europe, and which destroyed an imminent Wall Street brokerage house. De Angelis had attempted to corner the market in cotton seed and soya bean oils. To finance this gamble, he had been engaged in a swindle in which banks were persuaded to advance him very substantial loans against the security of his company's apparent stock in trade of salad oil held by a field warehouseman, the American Express Warehousing Company. When the scandal came to light, the books of the warehousing company showed that it was storing nearly twice as much oil as the total brimful capacity of its oil tanks, and in the event it was found there existed only one-tenth of the stated quantity of oil. The *Sunday Times* report commented that one of the factors that most great swindles have in common is the demonstration of the great gulf that exists between the world of paper and the world of things.

The importance of the verification of the existence and value of closing stock is thus well understood by accountants, as are the difficulties of so doing.

MATTERS HIGHLIGHTED BY THE GEC BID

The ASC has now issued SSAP 9 seeking to define acceptable practices in the computation of the amount at which stocks and work in progress are stated in the financial accounts in order to narrow the differences and variations in those practices and to ensure adequate disclosure in the reports and accounts. But this Standard was not available when, in 1967, as previously mentioned, the General Electric Company under Sir Arnold (now Lord) Weinstock made its bid to take over Associated Electrical Industries. It must be emphasised that there was no question of fraud involved in the production of figures which were given so much limelight.

During the bitterly-contested struggle between the two boards, the AEI directors issued a profit forecast indicating a trading profit of £10m for the company by the end of the year. That forecast was made in November 1967 shortly before the end of the accounting year, and on its estimated basis, the AEI directors recommended the rejection of GEC's bid.

In the event, the GEC bid was successful. When, however, the AEI results for 1967 were published, these disclosed a loss of £4.5 million. This staggering difference of £14.5 million needed explanation. The auditors' report on the AEI forecast of profits published in relation to the bid, said "the forecast of £10 million profit . . . has been prepared on *a fair and reasonable basis* (author's italics) and in a manner consistent with the principles followed by the company in preparing recent annual accounts".

Explaining away the difference

An explanatory statement issued at the time suggested that £5 million of the difference was attributable to matters substantially of fact and £9.5 million to matters of judgement. The matters of fact included the post-merger decision to close the AEI Woolwich factory for which a provisional charge was made against profit for anticipated extra costs. The measure of the difference of opinion of the two boards as regards the valuation of AEI's stock and work in progress was £4.3 million. This, GEC attributed to obsolescence. Even allowing for the natural tendency of the GEC directors to be conservative over the value of AEI assets taken over, this was a material factor; not so much in relation to the difference of only 4.3% in the valuation of the stocks and work in progress totalling £100 million, but when related to the forecast £10 million profit the write-off of the obsolescence factor against earnings reduced earnings by 43%. The AEI directors concluded, in respect of the shortfall of £14.5 million, "we think it incredible that such a difference could occur . . . unless there were massive changes in the management policy, and in the policies and principles of accounting, especially in relation to the valuation of stocks and work in progress". These were the circumstances which hastened the arrival of the Accounting Standards programme.

In the aftermath of the GEC/AEI affair, the City Panel on Take-overs and Mergers was formed. It quickly issued its 'City Code on Take-overs and Mergers', setting detailed rules to be followed in such situations. Rule 15 deals with profit forecasts and asset valuations.

PERGAMON PRESS (1968)

The audited profits of Pergamon Press Ltd shown in the accounts for the year ended 31 December 1968 were £2,104,000. Following events given wide publicity in the national press, a highly reputable firm of auditors, Price Waterhouse, was asked to undertake an investigation into the company's financial affairs. Their subsequent lengthy report recommended many adjustments to the accounts, resulting in a sadly diminished figure for profits of £495,000 – a net adjustment of £1,609,000. The public comment on this large difference in determined profit involving different firms of accountants and auditors did little for the reputation of the profession and cast further doubt on the flexibility of the accounting rules.

Some part of the adjustments recommended involved sales between Pergamon Press, a public company, and a private company in which the company's chairman had a family interest. Certain books included in closing stock were valued at cost, although an examination of subsequent sales statistics showed they were sold at reduced rates to libraries and students. The stock adjustment resulting amounted to £329,000. A further adjustment was required in respect of the treatment of transactions involving back issues of scientific and other learned journals. Prior to the year in question, the costs of printing these items were wholly charged against profit in the year of publication. Revenue from the sales was credited to profit and loss account when earned. No stock value was included in the accounts. In 1968, the company changed its method of accounting and brought back issues into stock at £341,000. While the investigating accountants did not dispute the inclusion of the items in stock, they were of the opinion that the same basis must be used in respect of the opening stock (nil) and recommended that the estimated value of the back issue stocks at that date (£326,000) be charged against the 1968 profit.

(*Note*: Inexperienced readers should refer to Example 3.2 of a TRADING ACCOUNT showing the importance of both Opening and Closing Stock to the determination of 'Cost of Sales' and thus of (gross) profit.)

Critical public comment

Robert Maxwell's comment as chairman to the company's shareholders that "Accountancy is not the exact science which some of us once thought it was" could perhaps, in all the circumstances, be taken as said 'tongue in cheek' nevertheless there were some stringent comments in the press.

The editorial of *Management Today* (October 1970) commented ". . . issues raised by the events at Pergamon are important, because they touch the vital nerve of the corporate system. Good management, wise investment and intelligent comment depend alike on being able to trust figures produced by the company's accountants, accepted by its directors, and approved by its auditors". And, further, "a profit which arises from an upward valuation of stocks is not a profit at all. No new money has come into the company". Pointing out that the original Pergamon accounts for 1968 showed roughly a £2 million worsening of the net *cash* position (overdrafts minus bank balance) in the year of the £2.1 million published profit, the editorial pleaded ". . . the *cash* story is the one on which management accounting is based . . . there should be a legal requirement to record the cash story for the year and explain the discrepancies between these accounts and the profit and loss statement."

(*Note*: SSAP 10 'Statements of Source and Application of Funds', designed to show the sources from which funds flowed into a company and the way in which they were used and the resultant change in the company's liquid position, was published to have effect from 1 January 1976.)

ROLLS-ROYCE DEBACLE

On 3 February 1971, British Cabinet Ministers met in special session to discuss the Rolls-Royce situation. In the course of the meeting the Prime Minister, Edward Heath, left his Ministers to confer with President Nixon on a 'hotline' to Washington. That call confirmed the decision that one of Britain's proud and most successful companies would go bankrupt – "the greatest financial disaster in Britain's history", according to the company's receiver.

Where did the company go wrong? Who was to blame? And was the public comment "but so long as company law and financial reporting requirements remain as lax as they are in Britain, disasters of the Rolls-Royce variety are bound to happen" a reasonable one? How much justification was there for the view that "the events surely complete . . . the case for much tighter control over accountancy conventions and company reporting. If Rolls-Royce had been forced to keep conservative accounts throughout the 1960s, it could never have raised the sums it did from shareholders – sums which have now evaporated into the thinnest of air. It might have been forced at a much earlier date to face up to the realities of the situation . . . and the disaster would probably never have happened"?

Economic background

The economic background to the situation was very much the same then as in the early 1980s. Profits were not keeping pace with rising costs and companies were short of cash. In 1969, the liquid assets of companies fell in the year by £308 million. In the first quarter of 1970 alone, they fell by £497 million. Rolls-Royce was among them. At the time of the crash it was estimated that £150 million was required to save the company. The appointment of a Receiver was necessary otherwise the company would have been trading (illegally) while insolvent. The alternatives were enormous subvention by the then (Conservative) government, chasing the large sums already loaned to the company by the previous government (Labour), or nationalisation. The latter appeared to be politically unacceptable, so the company was liquidated. Out of the ashes rose two companies, Rolls-Royce (Motors) and Rolls-Royce (Engines), the latter kept going by a massive infusion of taxpayers' money. Why had all this happened less than three years after the winning of the contract to build engines for Lockheed's TriStar airbus, which had been hailed as a tremendous job of salesmanship and a boon for British exports?

The main answer is that the company underestimated the cost of developing the RB 211 engine. Within a short time, the original estimates had been doubled and Rolls-Royce could not pass on these costs for it had signed fixed price contracts. And this in a period of an accelerating decline in the value of the pound. After the event, with the advantage of hindsight, the importance of a form of *cash flow accounting* was again being put forward.

Accounting cause for concern

The accounting cause for concern was the Rolls-Royce practice of carrying forward development expenditure with the intention of bringing it into charge against profit in the years when revenue from the engine sales accrued. The effect was of postponing the impact of the vast expenditures on profit results. In the meantime, of course, the money was being spent and major cash problems arose. In 1977, the ASC issued its Accounting Standard SSAP 13 'Accounting for Research and Development'. Pure and applied *research* expenditure is required to be written off against profit in the year in which it is incurred. The circumstances in which *development* expenditure may be deferred (carried forward, as did Rolls-Royce) are clearly defined and this is allowed only to the extent that its recovery can be reasonably assured.

4.   International Financial Reporting and Entry to the EEC

International investment is not a recent development, but it has increased considerably in the past few decades. One result has been the growth of transnational companies and a requirement to make common financial information available to interested parties in more than one country.

Apart from the technical problems of accountancy related to the translation of foreign currency transactions to the currency of the reporting (holding) company, there are problems of different reporting standards of the countries concerned, some of which may have been set rigidly by law, others based on law but developed by agencies of the accountancy bodies.

Legal differences may exist in respect of tax, as well as in company law and other legislation. The status and independence of the company auditor varies between countries.

While inflation has been widespread throughout the world, it has been far more rapid in some countries than in other.

Also, the regulatory authorities of countries where an enterprise's securities are quoted and traded usually insist on conformity with their own reporting standards.

INTERNATIONAL HARMONIZATION OF REPORTING STANDARDS AND PRACTICES

An ideal solution to these problems lies with the development of generally accepted international reporting standards resulting in a format of financial statements acceptable and understood in participant countries.

A significant first step forward was the establishment of the International Account
Standards Committee (IASC) composed of representatives of professional accounting bo
throughout the world. This body has issued a number of International Accounting Standa
(listed page 167) since its formation in June 1973, pursuant of its objective 'to formulate and
publish in the public interest standards to be observed in the presentation of audited financial
statements and to promote their world-wide acceptance and observance'.

Members agree to support the standards promulgated by the IASC and to try to ensure
that published financial statements comply with the standards "or that there is disclosure of
the extent to which they do not, and to persuade governments, securities markets and the
industrial and business community that financial statements should comply".

If IASC standards and domestic standards conform, then there is no problem for financial
statements issued in the domestic country. Where they conflict, then the obligations of
members of the IASC are designed to ensure that either the statements or the auditors'
report thereon will indicate in what respects the international standards have not been
observed.

In these early years of its existence, the IASC endeavours not to make the international
standards so complex that they cannot be applied effectively worldwide.

Until international standards are established on a more sophisticated level, liaison
between standard-setting bodies in different countries aimed at as much commonality and as
little conflict as possible is obviously desirable. The ASC in the United Kingdom has links
with the Financial Accounting Standards Board in the USA and the Canadian ASC for this
purpose.

Other bodies with which the ASC has links in its concern for harmonisation, apart from
the IASC, include the Organisation of Economic Co-operation and Development (OECD),
the United Nations Commission on Transnational Corporations and, within Europe, the two
accountancy organisations, the Groupe D'Etudes de la CEE (GdE), and the Union
Européenne des Experts Comptables Economiques et Financiers (UEC).

The UEC, consisting of member bodies representing the accountancy profession in a wide
range of European countries (including those within the EEC), is concerned with the
harmonization and improvement of standards of accounting and auditing, thus covering a
wider range of topics of professional practice and conduct than may happen to be involved in
the areas dealt with by EEC Directives. The demise of the UEC is likely to follow the arising
of the *Federation des Exports Comptables Européens* (FEE) in the proposed reorganisation
(1985) of the accountancy profession in Europe.

Directing its activities towards the EEC Commission and dealing primarily with EEC
Direcives and their implications for the accountancy profession is the GdE, comprising
representation from the member states of the EEC.

EEC DIRECTIVES ON COMPANY LAW

When the United Kingdom joined the EEC in 1973, a new dimension was added to the
needs of financial reporting for UK companies. The UK has to conform with the whole series
of directives (noted page 168) drafted by the European Commission and, where required,
incorporate the provisions in national legislation by a stated date. A fundamental problem
for the UK is that the Franco-German approach used by the EEC is one of legal
prescription, of codification of accounting rules by statutory regulation. In the UK, by
contrast, the law concerns itself only with a basic framework for financial reporting, leaving
the detail to be filled in by acceptable accounting standards developed over time and
modified subsequently as necessary. As the President of the Institute of Chartered
Accountants in England and Wales said when contrasting the two stems:

"this leaves us with a tremendous and valuable freedom to develop our standards, to change them if practice does not bear out the promise of the theory, and permits departures from standards when such departures are necessary to give a true and fair view."

A TRUE AND FAIR VIEW

This phrase, referred to earlier, perhaps crystallises the problem.

Section 149 of the Companies Act 1948 (S12, Companies Act 1967) required that the annual accounts should show a true and fair view of the profit or loss of the company for the year and of its financial position at the end of that year. The phrase is not closely defined and the implication is that a good deal is left to judgement. This judgement may be aided from time to time by, for example, a decision of the Court, or narrowed by accepted practice and the content of accounting standards. By contrast, early drafts of the EEC Fourth Directive concerned with the annual accounts of limited companies (excluding group accounts), their presentation, valuation rules and publication, did not include the phrase. The accounts were to be presented as prescribed. Following UK reaction and representation, the revised Fourth Directive acknowledged 'the true and fair view' base for accounting, but with little other change. As it is unlikely at present that France and Germany would be prepared to allow their accountancy professions to decide accounting standards within some EEC committee, there remains no mechanism within the Community for developing and setting EEC accounting rules outside the law.

The explicit acknowledgement that the EEC directives set only minimum requirements and that member states can add to or interpret them through their own national processes, provides the basis for current practice which falls short of idealharmony.

Introducing the Companies Bill 1981, to enact, inter alia, the Fourth Directive, the Government's Trade Secretary emphasised the likely outcome for the UK:

"The broad aim of the Bill has been to do the minimum in the form of prescriptive law and to leave the maximum room for the evolution of accounting standards and practice."

That Bill became an Act on 30 October 1981. In both S1 which governs the form and content of accounts and S2 which requires group accounts to comply with S1, the need for them to give a 'true and fair view' *over-rides* all other accounting provisions of the Companies Acts. The Act goes further in that:

(i) any additional information necessary to give such a view must be provided in the accounts, and
(ii) where, through special circumstances, compliance with the accounting requirements would not give a true and fair view and directors have to depart from a requirement, the particulars of the departure, the reasons for it and its effect must be disclosed by note to the accounts.

The true and fair view provisions are re-enacted in sections 228, 230 and 258 of the Companies Act 1985.

5. Social Change

CHANGING FACE OF THE SHAREHOLDER

Financial reports have been regarded traditionally and legally, primarily for and in the interests of shareholders. The prime objective of the company, required to report through its directors to the shareholders, has been to earn a 'sufficient level' of profit to provide, after all expenses and tax have been met, a reasonable reward to the members for their investment compared with the returns from other investment options, and a surplus for the renewal of depreciating assets and for growth.

The pace of change over recent decades affecting the organisation and attitudes of society has demanded a revision of these views. Some would argue the need for a revolutionary review. Be that as it may, there is agreement that the consequences of a company's activities affect many other parties than shareholders, and shareholders are a more pluralistic body than hitherto. They include, through the increasing impact of the financial institutions on investment, more of the public at large, as depositors in banks and building societies, membership of pension funds, subscribers of insurance premiums, investment in Unit Trusts and so on. Indirectly, through taxation, the public is again an investor, not only in nationalised industries but in companies like Rolls-Royce and British Leyland where the Government is the major stakeholder. The huge, record-breaking and highly successful British Telecom ordinary share issue of 1984 not only attracted, for the first time, a wide spectrum of the public as equity investors, which had been the government's intention, but it also saw a large proportion of BT employees taking up their special offer. Employee share ownership, not hitherto widespread in the UK, was given a material boost (see Chapter 10).

EMPLOYEES AND OTHER STAKEHOLDERS

Following the redistribution of wealth, the availability of higher education to greater numbers, the expansion and impact of information particularly through television, the desire for advertised consumer goods and travel, and the higher number of working wives, attitudes of *employees* have radically changed. The growing power of organised labour has been directed to some extent towards a greater say in the operations of 'their' company, but has concentrated mainly on taking a larger share of the corporate cake. There are other stakeholders, such as *supplying* companies. In 1981 emphasis was placed on the likely liquidation of many supplying companies and the loss of jobs which would follow if British Leyland failed to survive a loss-making period. Ten years earlier, when Rolls-Royce collapsed, it was reported that "apart from RR itself, by far the most important implication of its collapse is the effect it will have on the liquidity and survival prospects of its suppliers. In the RR December 1969 balance sheet, creditors were £62 million spread over hundreds of balance sheets of supplying companies, which must now be written off as a bad debt." Although, some time after, the Receiver was able to pay the creditors in full, the companies to survive had to solve their cash shortage problem. *Customers*, who may be individuals, institutions or other companies, are also stakeholders. The demise of the company whose products or expertise are important to the customers may cause at best inconvenience, delay and higher costs, at worst, their own end. Long and short-term *lenders* of money are stakeholders, more particularly if the loan is unsecured. The *public* is often concerned at the environmental impact of a company's product or activity. And, in total, the prosperity of the company sector is vital to the *national interest*.

THE CORPORATE REPORT

In a consideration of the relative interests of the shareholders and the various 'stakeholders' in a company's affairs, there are implications about the quality and quantity of information provided in the corporate report and of its reliability and credibility.

The Accounting Standards Committee, recognising the general impact of social change in the provision of financial information and the wider public involved, published a discussion document in 1975 entitled 'The Corporate Report'.

It was explicit on the objective of such reports:

"The fundamental objective of corporate reports is to communicate economic measurements of, and information about, the resources and performance of the reporting entity useful to those having reasonable rights to such information."

It identified areas where the reports may be of use, e.g.:

"evaluating the economic function and performance of the entity in relation to society and the national interest, and the social costs and benefits attributable to the entity"

"evaluating objectives . . . including employment, investment and profit distribution plans."

In addition to the then current requirements of law and standard accounting practice for published reports and accounts to include a profit and loss account and balance sheet, and directors' and auditors' reports (the sources and application of funds statement was added in 1976), the Corporate Report suggested six additional statements for consideration:

1. A statement of value added showing how the benefits of the efforts of the enterprise are shared between employees, providers of capital, the State and reinvestment.
2. An employment report showing the size and composition of the workforce, the work contribution of employees and the benefits earned.
3. A statement of money exchanges showing the financial relationship between the enterprise and the State.
4. A statement of transactions in foreign currency showing the direct cash dealings of the reporting entity between this country and abroad.
5. A statement of future prospects, showing likely future profit, employment and investment levels.
6. A statement of corporate objectives showing management policy and medium-term strategic targets.

It will be noted that the information currently provided is significantly concerned with the past and basically represents a stewardship report of the directors to the shareholders. Chairmen and directors are naturally cautious when forecasting the future.

The proposals which have not advanced far into reality (although Value Added statements and Employee Reports are now commonplace) are revolutionary, particularly with their emphasis on future expectations and their recognition of the wider 'public' interest. See Chapter 12 on the EEC Fifth Directive and the Vredeling proposals.

The statement in respect of funds moving across national boundaries mirrors concern over the power of multinational corporations and their potential influence on foreign exchange parities.

6. Summary

THE ENVIRONMENT OF CHANGE

A good deal may be learned about a company from a study of its annual report and accounts. There may be significant indications of its *liquidity* (its immediate ability to pay its debts as due), its *solvency* (its foreseeable cash flow status), its *profitability* (related to investment), and overall of its *likelihood to survive*. But the annual report is historic in nature, and neither the modern public corporation nor the smaller private company exist in limbo; they operate in environments where change is endemic. Environments in which there exist other organisations, some neutral, some competitive, some antagonistic, and some supportive. A thorough analysis and understanding of a company's report should therefore include an appreciation of the turbulent social, technical, economic and political climate which provides its setting. The growth of company groups, the emergence of the transnational company, Britain's entry into Europe and the international reporting dimension, as well as the problems posed by inflation – its effects on liquidity and the structure of company funds – the effects of social and other environmental change, and the impact of the accounting causes célèbres have been described and the scene for company reporting in the 1980s has been set. But the word 'set' should not be taken too literally. What we have considered can be likened to a series of 'still pictures' taken like the accounts themselves at one moment of time. More useful would be a 'moving picture' of the company and its dynamic capability.

Students and other readers should provide themselves with fresh pictures of the reporting environment through the study on a regular basis of the national and financial press, professional, economic, management and other relevant publications.

ACCOUNTING STANDARDS PROGRAMME

The Accounting Standards programme was well established in the 1970s and considerable progress has been made in a short period. The paradox that, by definition, a standard is by nature inflexible has provided difficulty and dissenting voices are heard. Some standards have been revised and these revisions can be seen as a strong point for the programme rather than a weakness in their acceptance of the need for change. While the standards were needed to *narrow* the range of acceptable accounting practice, different circumstances between industries, or changes over a period of time, do provide problems. Management is not bound to follow an accounting standard, even though the law will no doubt regard a standard in any litigation as an indication of recognised practice. Where management materially departs from a standard, this poses problems for its own accountants and for its auditors. Employee accountants and auditors, as members of the professional bodies, are bound by the standards. The employee accountant is in a difficult position and is, in practice, limited to exhorting management to adhere to the standard or explain in the annual report and accounts the reason for the departure.

The auditor's duty of reporting to the shareholders in the context of a 'true and fair view' of profitability and of a company's net assets, and his responsibilities to his professional body, require him in the absence of a management explanation, to comment on departures from an accounting standard, i.e., to qualify his audit report. There are difficulties inherent in the auditor's relationship with directors and the reality of his independence of them in circumstances where a departure from or non-compliance with a standard results, in the auditor's opinion, in the accounts showing an untrue and/or unfair view. How far should he go with his qualification? Should he annex information showing his judgement of the true position? There is an Auditing Standard on the audit report which directs the auditor in respect of varying circumstances in which a qualification is necessary and where a quantification of the financial consequences on the accounts should be given. Fundamentally, if the auditor agrees with a departure from a standard, his report must state that he concurs, i.e. the report is not qualified. If the departures are significant, even if they are disclosed in notes to the accounts, the auditor must refer to them in his report. Where auditors *disagree* with the departures, then they must qualify their report and attempt a quantification of their effect. Where, rarely, accounts which concur with a standard, do not give a true and fair view in the auditor's opinion, then they must both qualify their report and quantify the difference of opinion.

SELF-REGULATION OR A POWERFUL REGULATORY AUTHORITY?

Critics have pointed to the non-compliance of companies with accounting standards as being unacceptable where the result may be detrimental to the shareholders or to the public interest. An auditor's qualification is not regarded as a sufficient deterrent and the Stock Exchange has indicated that it is not likely to withdraw the listing of a wayward company. If a standard is widely defied, as with SSAP 16 which required a company (e.g. a listed company) to provide supplementary current cost accounting information with the historical accounts or to adopt as an alternative, current cost accounts as main accounts, the ASC can only conclude that it is not acceptable and withdraw it (see Chapter 12).

There is a view that if the self-regulation of the accountancy profession is not sufficiently strong to deal with non-compliance, then either the Government should intervene with legislation or through a UK version of the American Securities and Exchange Commission.

As far as *legal disclosure* requirements are concerned, we have noted on page 20, that the Companies Act 1981 reaffirms the importance of the 'true and fair view' formula as *over-riding all* other accounting requirements of *company law*. Where directors, in special circumstances, see the need to depart from such requirements, they must explain the reasons for it and its effect.

OVER-RIDE PRINCIPLE

The extent to which the over-ride principle may be used, can only *authoritatively* be determined by a Court. In a recent case (*Argyll Foods* (1981)), the treatment of a subsidiary acquisition by the company did not comply with the requirements of law or of SSAP 14 (the standard on 'group accounts'). The company's auditors referred in their report to the accounting method used, judging that information given with the accounts was sufficient *not* to render them misleading. Following a Department of Trade prosecution, the Court found that, in that particular case, '*economic reality*' was not shown by the accounts at the year end. The DOT's subsequent statement considered that any emphasis of '*substance over form*' in company accounts must not be at the expense of compliance with the law. It may be concluded from this case, that the discretion and judgement left to the accountancy profession and management through the over-ride principle, will see the DOT and no doubt, the financial press, vigilant to protect the public against any reversion to the 'best slant' *cause célèbre* examples of pre-standard days.

THE LAW, THE 'TRUE AND FAIR VIEW' CONCEPT AND ACCOUNTING STANDARDS

In 1983, the ASC published the opinion they had sought from Counsel on the nature of 'true and fair view', and its legal standing and relationship with the accounting standards. That opinion was regarded as having far-reaching implications for the setting of standards. The ASC stated its intention to take account of the opinion in all its future work. Important extracts of Counsels' views include:

1. True and fair view is a legal concept and the question whether accounts of companies comply can only be authoritatively decided by a court. This questions, inter alia, the relationship between the legal requirement and the SSAPs issued by ASC.
2. The value of a SSAP to a court which has to decide whether accounts are true and fair is two-fold. Firstly, it represents an important statement of professional opinion about the standards which readers may reasonably expect in accounts intended to be true and fair. The SSAP is intended to crystallise professional opinion and reduce penumbral areas in which divergent practices exist. Secondly, because accountants are professionally obliged to comply with an SSAP, it creates in the readers an expectation that accounts will be in conformity with prescribed standards . . . thus accounts which depart from the standard without adequate justification or explanation may be held *not* to be true and fair.
3. An SSAP is a declaration by the ASC on behalf of its constituent professional bodies that, save in exceptional circumstances, accounts which do *not* comply will *not* give a true and fair view.
4. Courts will treat compliance with accepted accounting principles as *prima facie* evidence that accounts *are* true and fair. Equally, deviations from accepted principles, will be *prima facie* evidence that they are not.
5. Universal acceptance of an SSAP means it is highly unlikely that a court would accept accounts drawn up according to different principles. On the other hand, if there remains a strong body of opinion which consistently opts out of applying the SSAP, giving reasons which the ASC may consider as inadequate, the *prima facie* presumption against such accounts is weakened.

The importance of these extracts is self-evident. It was concluded that a SSAP has no direct legal effect: it is simply a rule of professional conduct for accountants. But the opinion was that it is likely to have an indirect effect on the content which the Courts will give to the true and fair concept. The effect of a SSAP could be that accounts which would have previously been considered as true and fair, will no longer satisfy the law. True and fair is at once an intangible and a dynamic concept. Opinions and judgements change with time and circumstances. It follows that the accounting standards programme must react to evident changes of view over particular standards and the standards process itself. *Table 5* in Chapter 8 lists the withdrawals, revisions and changes made to standards during the 16 years of the standards programme. The needs of change motivated the ASC to review the standards process and in 1983 it published its intentions.

CHANGES TO THE STANDARDS PROGRAMME 1983

By 1983 the standards programme had covered a good deal of those matters of fundamental importance to the preparation, presentation and publication of accounts. Future *accounting standards* would only deal with matters of *major* and *fundamental* importance affecting the *generality of companies*, said the review report, and would therefore be few in number. Their other essential characteristics would be that:

  (i) they are prepared by the ASC but issued and enforced by the six members of the Consultative Committee of Accountancy Bodies (CCAB); and

  (ii) they would be applicable to all accounts which are intended to give a true and fair view.

To meet the needs of effective consultation and communication, a new form of consultative document, called '*the statement of intent*' (SOI) was announced. These would be public statements from the ASC setting out in a brief summary of how they intend to deal with a particular accounting matter. They would be much less detailed than an exposure draft (ED) and would focus on the main issues of a particular topic and the proposed accounting policies. The SOI would, hopefully, elicit public comment on the proposals more promptly than a full-length discussion paper, whilst serving to reduce problems at the exposure draft stage.

The ASC continued to believe that publication for comment by way of an entire exposure draft of a proposed standard is essential. Recognising that issues arise which, although of sufficient importance to require an authoritative pronouncement, do not meet the criteria of an accounting standard, the report announces for this purpose '*the statement of recommended practice*' (SORP). Bearing in mind the criteria for the accounting standards, it follows that SORPs will generally deal either with matters which are of widespread application but are not of fundamental importance, or matters which are of limited application, e.g. to a specific industry. SORPS of widespread application but not of fundamental importance will be prepared by the ASC. SORPs of limited application and therefore, probably of a specialised nature, will be developed by the industry itself subject to ASC review. When ASC approves this type of SORP as being the best practice, the pronouncement will be called a '*franked SORP*'. Their issue will be the responsibility of the industry concerned. It is hoped that pronouncements of the SORP type will serve as important contributions to accounting thought. Unlike the accounting standards, SORPs will not be mandatory. They will be of such quality and status as to be widely respected and compliance will be encouraged. If a company does not follow a SORP then there will be no requirement for it to disclose the reason for the departure or its effect.

Following these changes to the standards programme, there will be a hierarchy of regulation consisting of legal requirements for company reports and accounts, accounting standards, SORPs including franked SORPs, preceded as thought necessary by discussion documents, statements of intent (SOI) and exposure drafts.

Having followed the full course of such communication and consultation, the final pronouncement should bear the seal of authority and move to become established practice. While this has usually been the case in the past, there remains the possibility of the statements being rejected as has happened with some SSAPs, and changed circumstances may see the need, over a period of time, for different views.

2

Cash flow and profit

Among the post-event criticisms following the Pergamon and Rolls-Royce affairs was a call, as previously described, for a record of the 'cash story' to explain why, for example, Pergamon's net cash position 'worsened by £2 million in a year when a profit of £2.1 million was recorded'.

REASONS FOR DECREASE IN CASH

One major reason for such a decrease is the necessity to finance the purchase of long-term assets (capital expenditure), e.g. plant and machinery, *now*, with the expectation that the returns by way of sales income (revenue) will be received over a number of (*future*) profit and loss accounts.

A second major reason results from the *time lag* in the *working capital* cycle. A manufacturing company has to finance over time stocks of raw material in store, thence the raw material content included in work-in-progress, in the finished product and, when the sale is on credit, the outstanding debtor account. It is only when the debt is collected at the end of the cycle that the 'profit' is realised and costs recovered. Cash then flows in.

Labour and overhead costs similarly have to be funded within the working capital cycle. Some alleviation of the problem occurs through the purchase of the stocks of raw material on credit, but this credit period for manufacturers is usually less than the working capital cycle.

Thirdly, *inflation* exacerbates the liquidity problem as the value of money falls over time. More cash is needed to maintain the real monetary value of fixed and working capital.

Fourthly, as an enterprise increases its sales turnover, this *growth* requires additional funds to support extra plant etc., and extra working capital.

CASH CONTROL

Theoretically, *planning ahead* and detailing those plans in money terms through budgets, should result in cash flow predictions enabling management to pinpoint the need to raise medium and long-term funds and make overdraft arrangements in the short term. These plans should account for the four problems in cash management referred to, i.e. capital expenditure, working capital, inflation and growth.

In practice, the reality of the future is often different from that planned. Planning may have been less than adequate or changes may have occurred in the business environment which were not foreseen or were different from those anticipated.

Day-to-day cash management will be comparing budgeted cash flow with actual cash flow, which is part of budgetary *control*. Variances call for management action.

Some variances may have been anticipated (flexible budgeting) and action will be smooth and speedy. Others may not have been expected, may not easily be dealt with, and the outcome of plans in cash and profit terms is radically affected.

EXTERNAL FUNDS

Ideally, the on-going profitable company could finance the purchase and replacement of its fixed (capital) assets and finance working capital and growth out of the capital invested by the shareholders and the retention of its profits after paying taxation and appropriate dividends.

In practice, recent profit levels have reduced the ability of on-going companies to fund their needs in this way and external finance has been required.

Profitable companies have in any event found it advantageous to raise long-term funds from outside sources by way of loans, where the level of the interest charge (an expense reducing taxation) has been such that the use of the funds attracted a greater return, thus adding to the return of the shareholders.

Usually, for a profitable and expanding company, the long-term loans are repaid and raised again on a cyclic pattern. High interest rates have recently interfered with this policy and bank lending, traditionally meant to help fill the troughs in the working capital cycle, has extended considerably.

LIQUIDITY AND PROFITABILITY

To *survive* in the long term, a company has to be *liquid* (cash and an availability of cash) and *profitable*. In the short term, it can survive a period of falling profit or losses, but the lack of cash will be fatal.

Bridging the working capital cycle is a bigger problem for the manufacturer than the retailer, and bigger for the retailer selling on credit than the retailer selling for cash.

For Rolls-Royce, research and development expenditure of size had to precede manufacture and sale, and lengthened considerably the gap to be bridged by borrowings. And, if profitability diminishes in prospect or in actuality, in the absence of further support by lenders or shareholders, insolvency will occur.

STATEMENT OF SOURCES AND APPLICATION OF FUNDS

Most accountants accept the increasing importance of cash flow accounting as an essential *internal* control device – an integral part of budgetary planning and control.

The external analyst is restricted in his view of liquidity to the information contained in the annual report and accounts. Whilst this information is historical and therefore dated, a useful view of management's funding policy and practice and liquidity trends is available following the preparation of a Statement of Funds Flow from the two succeeding balance sheets and the intervening profit and loss account contained in the annual report.

Effective from 1 January 1976, the ASC issued SSAP 10 requiring the publication of an audited statement of funds flow during the year. The statement identifies the *movements* in assets, liabilities and capital which have taken place during the year *and the resultant effect on net liquid funds.* Net liquid funds are defined as cash at bank and in hand and cash equivalents (e.g. short-term investments) less bank overdrafts and other borrowings repayable within one year of the accounting date.

The object of the funds statement is to show the manner in which the operations of the business have been financed and in which its financial resources have been used. It should show the funds generated or absorbed by the operations of the business and the manner in which any resulting *surplus* of liquid assets has been applied, or any *deficiency* of such assets has been financed, distinguishing the long from the short term. The statement should distinguish the use of funds for the purchase of new fixed assets from funds used in increasing the working capital of the company.

These statements, considered further and illustrated in Chapter 11, provide the answer to the question posed earlier, "Why has the net cash position worsened in a period of profitability?"

Case 1.   Creditable Ltd

The illustration which follows plots the progress of a new business, CREDITABLE LTD, through five successive balance sheet 'pictures'.

The objective is to show two relationships of importance in the understanding and interpretation of accounts:

1.   Between LIQUIDITY and PROFITABILITY, as discussed in the preceding pages.
2.   Between FUNDS (long and short term) and ASSETS (long and short term).

Readers inexperienced in book-keeping will be able to follow the two entries (double entry) made for each transaction with the aid of the explanatory notes.

Following the five balance sheets, all presented in a two-sided form with FUNDS on the one side and ASSETS on the other, accompanied by comment on liquidity and profitability, the final balance sheet is re-written in the modern vertical form.

Finally, the profit and loss account for the period, dealt with as an inherent part of the successive balance sheets, is written up in detail with commentary.

Case 1. Table 1 CREDITABLE LIMITED

STARTS BUSINESS	BALANCE SHEET (1)			
	SOURCE of funds		*APPLICATION of funds*	
		£		£
Invests £3,000 *cash.*	Share Capital	3,000	Bank (Cash)	3,000

Comment: The funds are lying idle on current account in the bank. They are earning no return and if idle over time will bear the cost of inflation.

Book-keeping note: The double entry as shown is made in the *ledger* accounts named. The Balance Sheet is merely a listing of the balances remaining on ledger accounts at the end of the accounting period. While in theory, balance sheets could be prepared to show the effect of each transaction, in practice this would be costly, wasteful and unnecessary.

Case 1. Table 2   **CREDITABLE LIMITED**

	BALANCE SHEET (2)			
	SOURCE of funds	£	*APPLICATION of funds*	£
Buys stock of goods for resale *on credit.*	Share Capital (Proprietors' funds)	3,000	*Fixed Assets* Vans	8,000
			Shop Fittings	2,500
Buys Vans & Shop fittings				10,500
– bank overdraft	*Current Liabilities*	£	*Current Assets*	
negotiated.	Trade creditors	19,000	Stock	19,000
	Bank overdraft	7,500 26,500	Cash	Nil
		£29,500		£29,500

Comment: The Proprietors' funds, supported by funds from suppliers and the bank, have been invested in long-term assets (for use in the business and not for resale) and short-term assets (stock for resale) but no return has yet been earned.

       The company is *illiquid*. Its current liabilities (to be repaid in the short term) exceed its current (short term) assets by £7,500. *This is its deficit of working capital.* This deficit of working capital of £7,500 is, therefore, the amount of *short-term* funds funding *long-term* assets. Because of the double entry equation, it equals the shortage of long-term funds (here entirely from the Proprietors) compared with the investment in long-term assets. (£10,500 less £3,000.)

       More long-term capital is required.

Book-keeping note: In the ledger, Stock (Purchases) Account is debited and the individual supplier accounts (Trade Creditors) credited to a total of £19,000.

       Vans and Shop Fittings accounts are debited and the bank account credited.

Case 1. Table 3   **CREDITABLE LIMITED**

	BALANCE SHEET (3)					
	SOURCES of funds		£	*APPLICATION of funds*		£
Sells Stock costing £15,000 *on credit* for £30,000.	Share Capital		3,000	*Fixed Assets* Vans		8,000
		£		Shop Fittings		2,500
	Profit	15,000				10,500
Buys Stock costing £16,000 *on credit.*	*less* Expenses	6,000	9,000			
Pays Expenses £6,000 *cash.*	Proprietors' funds		12,000			
	Current Liabilities			*Current Assets*		
	Trade creditors	£ 35,000		Stock	£ 20,000	
	Bank overdraft	13,500	48,500	Debtors	30,000	
			£60,500	Cash	Nil	50,000
						£60,500

Comment:

The situation has improved. The business is *profitable*. But no cash has yet resulted from the sales. Its *liquidity* is still tight. Its liquid assets (those parts of its current assets in cash or near-cash form, e.g. here – debtors) total £30,000 to meet the current liabilities of £48,500 (*liquid ratio* £30,000: £48,500 = 0.62). The Proprietors' funds are still insufficient. When tax is paid on the profit, they will drop below the level of the Fixed Assets.

Note: In general, common sense suggests that the liquid ratio should be around par (1 : 1). In practice, because of the relative lengths of the working capital cycle, manufacturers operate around or a little below par (0.90+) whereas retailers (cash based) manage at lower levels. Liquidity is controlled internally through cash budgeting and day-to-day checks. The *trend* of the liquid ratio and its comparison with firms in the same business will prove informative for outside analysts. No dividend has yet been paid to the Proprietors. And no charge yet made for the use of the Fixed Assets against profit.

Book-keeping note:

Trade Creditors £19,000 (Balance sheet 2) plus £16,000 = £35,000.
Bank overdraft £ 7,500 (Balance sheet 2) plus £ 6,000 = £13,500.
Stock £19,000 (Balance sheet 2) less £15,000 (cost) sold, plus £16,000 (cost) purchased = £20,000.

The entry 'Profit' in the balance sheet is normally the profit retained, made up of the profit retained brought forward from the previous accounting period, plus the current period profit after deducting (providing) for the estimated tax due on it and after deducting (providing) for a dividend for the capital providers (here the proprietors). It DOES NOT usually represent the Profit for the period, although that happens to be the position at the interim stage here illustrated.
See Balance Sheet (5) for normal situation.

Case 1. Table 4

CREDITABLE LIMITED

BALANCE SHEET (4)

	SOURCES *of funds*	£	APPLICATION *of funds*	£
£25,000 collected from Debtors.	Share Capital	3,000	*Fixed Assets*	
	Profit	23,000	Vans	8,000
Stock costing £20,000 sold for £40,000 on credit.	*Proprietors' funds*	26,000	Shop Fittings	2,500
			Property (cost)	20,000
				30,500
Stock costing £25,000 bought *on credit.*	*Current liabilities*	£	*Current Assets*	£
	Trade creditors	45,000	Stock	25,000
Expenses £6,000 paid *cash.*	Bank overdraft	9,500	Debtors	45,000
Bank provides short-term (Bridging Loan) £20,000 for Property purchase	Bank loan	20,000 74,500	Cash	Nil 70,000
		£100,500		£100,500
£15,000 paid to Trade creditors.				

Comment: *Profitability:* the company continues to be profitable. The relationship of the long-term (Proprietors') funds to Fixed Assets is little changed from Balance Sheet 3. There is now a deficit of working capital with short-term funds funding not only the whole of the current assets, but also some part (£4,500) of the fixed (long-term) assets. Tax has still not been provided. And no charge has been made against profit for the use of the fixed assets (depreciation).

Liquidity: the deficit of working capital has been mentioned. The liquid ratio has fallen from 0.62 to 0.54.

The *continuity* of the company is over-reliant on the bank. The bank's willingness to provide a bridging loan may indicate its confidence in the business following, probably, an examination of the company's profit and cash forecasts. Other creditors will be concerned to know if the company's property is charged against the loan (as security).

The level of *profit retained* is also important to creditors. Any withdrawal of profit will worsen the already difficult liquid position.

Book-keeping   Debtors £30,000 plus £40,000 less £25,000 = £45,000.
note: Stock £20,000 plus £25,000 less £20,000 = £25,000.
            Trade Creditors £35,000 plus £25,000 less £15,000 = £45,000.
            Bank Overdraft £13,500 plus £15,000 plus £6,000 less £25,000 = £9,500.
            Profit £9,000 plus £20,000 less £6,000 = £23,000.

In each case, the first figure is that brought forward from Balance Sheet 3.

Case 1. Table 5a   **CREDITABLE LIMITED**

BALANCE SHEET (5)
as at the end of the accounting period.

	SOURCES of funds		£	APPLICATION of funds		£	£
Interest on loan and overdraft – £3,000 paid to bank.	Share capital		3,000	*Fixed Assets*			
	Retained profit		8,112	Property			20,000
	Proprietors' funds		11,112	Vans		8,000	
Long-term loan on mortgage raised – £20,000 and bank bridging loan repaid.				*less* depreciation		1,600	6,400
	Mortgage Debenture		20,000	Shop Fittings		2,500	
				less depreciation		250	2,250
	LONG-TERM FUNDS						28,650
Vans depreciated – £1,600	**EMPLOYED**		31,112				
	Current liabilities		£	*Current assets*			£
Shop fittings depreciated – £250.	Tax payable	9,438		Stock		25,000	
	Trade creditors	45,000		Debtors		45,000	
Corporation tax provided – £9,438.	Dividend payable	600		Cash		Nil	70,000
	Bank overdraft	12,500	67,538				
			£98,650				£98,650
Dividend 20% on Proprietors' share capital provided.							

Case 1. Table 5b   CREDITABLE LIMITED

	BALANCE SHEET (5) (Historical cost) at the end of the accounting period.			
		£	£	£
NET ASSETS EMPLOYED	*FIXED ASSETS* Tangible assets:			
	Property (cost)	20,000		
	Vans (net book value)	6,400		
	Shop Fittings (net book value)	2,250		28,650
	CURRENT ASSETS			
	Stock	25,000		
	Debtors (trade)	45,000		
	Cash	Nil	70,000	
	CREDITORS (amounts falling due within one year)			
	Tax payable	9,438		
	Trade creditors	45,000		
	Dividend payable	600		
	Bank overdraft	12,500	67,538	
	NET CURRENT ASSETS		2,462	2,462
LONG TERM FUNDS =	*TOTAL ASSETS less CURRENT LIABILITIES*			31,112
	CREDITORS (amounts falling due after more than one year)			
	Mortgage debenture			20,000
NET ASSETS =	ORDINARY SHAREHOLDERS' FUNDS			£11,112
	being: *CAPITAL AND RESERVES* *Called up share capital:*			
	Ordinary share capital, 3,000 shares of £1 each fully paid		3,000	
	Retained profits (reserves)		8,112	£11,112

Comment: The *financial structure* of the company has improved following the repayment of the short-term bridging loan and its replacement by a twenty-year loan secured on the property. This means that the Debenture holder has first claim on this asset in the event of the company going into liquidation.

The *long-term funds* now fully support the investment in the *long-term (fixed) assets* with the surplus £2,462 invested in *working capital* (£31,112 less £28,650).

The retention by the proprietors of a large percentage (93%) of the profits after tax (see *Table 6*) has strengthened the financial structure.

The deficit of working capital has now been erased and is positive at £2,462. The liquid ratio has improved to 0.67.

Note: Working capital is defined as either:
(i) the excess of the value of current assets over current liabilities, or

(ii) the excess of the long-term funds over long-term (fixed) assets (see Illustration 2.1 following).

Note: A *debenture* is the legal loan document setting out the terms of the loan, i.e. security (if any), interest rate and when payable, date of repayment of the loan, etc.

Book-keeping note: Profit £23,000, less interest £3,000, less depreciation £1,850, less tax £9,438, less dividend £600 (see *Table 6*) = £8,112.

The term '*fund*' used in the balance sheet is *not* represented by a fund of cash (although cash may form a part of it) but rather by a *fund of assets*.

The Balance Sheet (5a) previously shown in two-sided form, has been re-written (5b) (without any change in the figures) in the vertical form of presentation now invariably used in published versions. The Companies Act 1981 would classify CREDITABLE LIMITED as a 'small company', and the balance sheet above is set out as required by that Act. The publication of 'abridged accounts' is covered in S255 Companies Act 1985.

Notes: (i) The phrase '*Historical cost*' in the heading will now be found in the published accounts of listed companies (shares quoted and available to the public), large unlisted (classified as large in the EEC 4th Directive and Companies Act 1981) and nationalised industries who are required to submit *current cost* accounts as supplementary to, or in place of, historic cost accounts.

(ii) The description '*Net current assets*' is used as an alternative to 'working capital'.

(iii) This form of vertical balance sheet enables the working capital figure, £2,462, to be highlighted and indicates how the long-term funds, £31,112, are divided between long-term (fixed asset) investment and working capital.

Illustration 2.1

THE BOXES DIAGRAM: STRUCTURE AND WORKING CAPITAL

The following diagrammatic view of the relationship between funds and assets in an ideal setting will be found useful by students starting an analysis of the balance sheet.

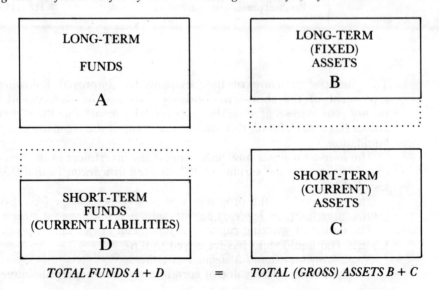

Notes:

Long-term funds: Shareholders' capital as enhanced by retained profits (reserves) plus long-term loans and other funds of a long-term character.

Working capital (dotted lines in diagram): As defined in the comment following balance sheet 5(a), i.e. the excess of A over B or, and equalling, the excess of C over D. The latter can be expressed as a ratio.

The Current Ratio: The excess of the value of current assets over current liabilities. The word 'current' means any period within the year following the balance sheet date.

An average figure has been generally regarded as a norm for the Current ratio of 2 : 1, falling in recent years following inflation, rising costs and increased bank lending to 1.5 : 1.

This ratio has obvious links with the Liquid Ratio.

The Liquid Ratio: The excess of those current assets in liquid or near-liquid form (cash, debtors, short-term investments) over current liabilities. A falling trend in these ratios from reasonable levels would be a cause for concern over liquidity.

An acceptable level of current ratio for individual companies is set by the optimum levels of the underlying items from which it is derived (see below).

Stock control procedures should determine optimum levels of stock in relation to purchases, production and sale (part of materials management).

Credit control procedures will keep debtors to the level set by sales and the credit period allowed to customers.

Cash control will set out to minimise cash holding through short-term investment, and minimise bank overdrafts.

Trade creditors will be maintained at levels appropriate to required levels of stocks and the need to maintain supplier goodwill through prompt payment.

Current liabilities are, until paid, short-term *funds* invested in the business.

Overtrading arises where sales are increasing without the needful provision of short and long-term funds. Falling levels of working capital and worsening current and liquid ratios would be an indication.

Case 1. Table 6

CREDITABLE LIMITED

	TRADING AND PROFIT AND LOSS ACCOUNT for the first accounting period			
		£	£	
	SALES (Turnover)		70,000	
Less	COST OF SALES being			
	Opening stock	Nil		TRADING
	Purchases	60,000		ACCOUNT
		60,000		
Less	Closing stock	25,000		
	COST OF SALES	35,000	35,000	
	GROSS PROFIT		35,000	
Less	Expenses	12,000		PROFIT & LOSS
	Depreciation	1,850		ACCOUNT
	Interest on overdraft and loan	3,000	16,850	
	PROFIT BEFORE TAX		18,150	
Less	Corporation tax		9,438	PROFIT & LOSS
	PROFIT AFTER TAX		8,712	APPROPRIATION
Less	Dividends (recommended) 20%		600	ACCOUNT
	RETAINED PROFITS		£8,112	

Note: This TRADING and PROFIT AND LOSS account has been derived from the transactions inherent in the preceding balance sheets.

Notes and comment:

1. *This Trading and Profit and Loss Account (sometimes called the Revenue account) is a ledger account* – part of the double entry book-keeping system. For example, the sales (all on credit here) are credited to the account of that name and debited to the same total, to individual customer (debtor) accounts.

   In this respect, it differs from the balance sheet, which is *not* a ledger account; it is a listing of the balances on all accounts (of assets, liabilities, and capital) remaining in the ledger after summarising income and expenditure entries in the profit and loss account.

2. As this was the first period of business, there is no opening stock. This period's closing stock is carried forward in the ledger and becomes the opening stock of the next period. It appears in the period-end balance sheet, *Table 5*, as a current asset.

3. Note the three divisions of the account (right-hand column). The Trading account (Retailers) is preceded for manufacturing companies by a manufacturing account from which 'the determined cost of manufactured goods' is transferred into Trading account in place of (outside) purchases. The Companies Act 1981 does *not* require the *publication* of a profit and loss account from companies designated as 'small' (see note 11).

4. Taxation is dealt with later.

5. *The percentage of gross profit to sales*, here 50%, is an important planning guide for retailers. It is also a useful comparative check for auditors and for the Inland Revenue when checking retailers' accounts for tax purposes.

   Note the relationship between *'mark-up'* and *'gross-profit'*. *Mark-up* is the relationship of gross profit to *cost of sales*, in *Table 6*, 100%. It has obvious value to the retail trade, e.g.

Sales	100			
Cost of sales	80			
Gross profit	20%	but Mark-up	25%	

6. The charge for *depreciation* against profit is an accounting *provision*. (Book-keeping: Debit profit and loss account, credit (an accumulating) fixed asset depreciation account, deducted from the relevant fixed asset in the Balance sheet.)

   It represents the *expense charged* for the *use* of the *fixed assets* in earning the profit: secondly, it *ensures* the retention of a slice of 'profit' in the business which builds up over the life of the fixed asset to a sum equal to the original cost. 'Profit' is represented by cash ONLY at the moment cash is received from the customer. The cash is then used (Cash flow) for the various purposes of the business (e.g. buying further stock, paying off creditors, or tax etc). Depreciation is *not*, therefore, a fund of cash. But profit (provided it is retained, and not subsequently lost) *is* represented by a fund of additional (general) assets (see 9 below). So, therefore, is depreciation. Depreciation has been based in this example on the widely used *Straight line method*, e.g.

	Historical cost	*Estimated life*	*Annual charge*
Vans	£8,000	5 years	£1,600
Shop Fittings	£2,500	10 years	£ 250

   Readers will appreciate the problems of depreciation and the replacement of fixed assets during a period of inflation. This is dealt with later.

   The Accounting Standard on Depreciation (SSAP 12) requires appropriate depreciation to be charged in respect of Buildings, but recognises that this will not normally be necessary in respect of land. CREDITABLE LTD has failed to do this in respect of its Property.

7. The P & L *Appropriation* Account is properly described. The *Dividend (payable)* is, of course, not an expense and clearly would not be allowed against profit for tax purposes. It is regarded as an *appropriation of (taxed) profit*. Its effect is the same as that of a provision, in so far as a 'chunk of profit' is set aside (Debit P & L appropriation Account, credit dividend payable) for payment after approval of the directors'

recommendation by the company's annual general meeting. When paid, cash is credited and dividend payable (Account) debited, and thus is cleared.

8. Competent companies plan (through budgets) the level of profit remaining after tax. The planned dividend will aim at an adequate level which will compete with other investment opportunities favourably. *The balance of the profit after tax which is retained should also have been planned.* This represents a *major source of funds*. It should not be the fortuitous residue of the profit and loss appropriation account. Plans do not, of course, always work out and directors will have the decision of balancing the needs of the present (dividends to shareholders) against the needs of the company's future (retentions).

   The figure of *Profit after tax* is the *EARNINGS* part of the *Price-Earnings (PE) ratio*, to be covered in later chapters. 'Price' is the market price of the ordinary share (of the quoted company) from day to day in the accounting year following that for which 'Earnings' was computed.

   Dividend cover is the number of times *earnings* cover *dividend*. Int he light of the exceptional level of after-tax profit earned by CREDITABLE LTD, their dividend policy is ultra-conservative. But the need to strengthen the capital structure by further shareholder funds has been largely met by the level of profit retained.

9. The company's *net assets* figure (Total assets less Total liabilities) at the *commencement* of business was (cash) £3,000

   The company's *net assets* figure at the *end* of its first accounting period was:

	£	£	£
Fixed Assets	28,650		
Current Assets	70,000		
Total Assets	98,650	98,650	
Current liabilities	67,538		
Long-term liabities	20,000		
Total liabilities	87,538	87,538	
Net assets		11,112	11,112
Increase in net assets = profit (retained) =			£ 8,112

   '*Profit*' (retained) is represented, therefore,by a *generality of additional assets*.

10. 'Retained profit' is often wholly or partly transferred to a *RESERVE account*. This has no effect on its legal status. In law the company can withdraw profit at any time. Commercial prudence and necessity will require a level of retention. A transfer to a Reserve Account is an indication of the directors' recommendation to retain the profit for use in the business as additional capital, confirmed by the shareholders (members) at the AGM. The subscribed share capital cannot be repaid to the shareholders (that would be illegal) except in a (legally) controlled liquidation or where the shares are redeemable shares (Chapter 4).

11. Prior to the Companies Act 1981, no company was required to publish information disclosing its 'cost of sales' and 'gross profit'; published profit and loss accounts, having given a figure for 'sales', usually started with a derived figure, variously described, e.g. 'trading profit' or 'operating surplus', which was effectively the 'gross profit' netted by those items of expense which were not required to be published.

   The Companies Act 1981, while requiring detailed 'cost of sales' information and the gross profit (loss) figure to be *published*, has exempted '*small companies*' from publishing any profit and loss account at all. (S255 Companies Act 1985.)

   Such a company with:

Turnover not exceeding £1.4 million* per annum,
and balance sheet total not exceeding £700,000,
and average number of employees not exceeding
50 (any two of these three conditions),

may deliver to the Registrar of Companies (publish) a modified balance sheet (see *Table 5b*), but no profit and loss account of directors' report is required, and only limited notes to the accounts.

Full accounts will need to be laid before the shareholders of such companies. The *auditor* must report to the *Registrar* that, in his opinion, the requirements of exemption have been satisfied, and reproduce the full text of his report on the accounts provided to the shareholders.

12. Published profit and loss accounts and balance sheets are required to give the requisite figures for the previous year alongside the current figures, for comparison.

13. Various *comparisons* of '*profit*' to '*capital employed*' may be derived from the CREDITABLE LTD profit and loss account and balance sheet:

   (i) Profit before tax and interest (derived from *Table 6*)   £21,150 :

      Long-term funds (*Tables 5a* and *5b*)   £31,112   =   68%

  (ii) Profit before tax and interest   £21,150 :

      Total funds (Total assets) (*Table 5a*)   £98,650   =   21%

 (iii) Profit after tax (*Table 6*)   £ 8,712 :

      Ordinary shareholders' funds (*Table 5b*)   £11,712   =   78%

The *Return on capital employed* (ROCE) in (i) and that in (iii) reflect the use of long-term loan capital to enhance the return to the shareholders (capital gearing). This subject is dealt within detail later. ROCE (ii) underlines the reliance of the company on short-term funds and the need for greater investment by the shareholders in working capital.

---

* A Department of Trade and Industry consultative document (June 1985) outlined possible changes to the accounting regulations and audit requirements for small companies and includes consideration of raising the turnover threshold for defining small companies from £1.4 million to £2.0 million per annum. Subsequently, amendments to the EEC Fourth Directive include increases in the balance sheet and turnover limits (by 55% and 60% respectively) for defining 'small' and medium companies. The DTI is consulting on their UK implementation.

3

The developing business

The objective in this chapter is to familiarise readers with the balance sheets of a business over a period of growth, commencing with Growstrong & Company as the starting partnership and leading on to Growstrong & Company Ltd as a private limited company. In the next chapter, Growstrong will be examined as a public limited company – the parent company in a group of companies.

THE BALANCE SHEET

The balance sheet is the end product of the system of double entry book-keeping (see *Illustration 3.1*). If every transaction of the business is entered in equal value to opposite sides of different ledger accounts and then, at any moment of time, after summarising profit (or loss) entries, the balances on those ledger accounts are listed in a balance sheet, it follows, given accuracy of entry, that each side of that balance sheet will balance.

Errors or omissions should be detected by an accounting control system administered internally by management, the end-stop being the checks and reports on the accounts by an external and independent auditor.

The balance sheet may be described as *a statement of affairs of a business at a given moment of time*, showing:
  (i) *the sources of its funds*, being the financial claims of persons who have funded its assets, and
  (ii) *the employment of funds*, being a tabulation of assets each given a value.

This statement regards the balance sheet as essentially a report of management's stewardship, that is, what management has done with the funds entrusted to it.

DOUBLE ENTRY BOOK-KEEPING

A diagrammatic representation of the double entry system on which much of accountancy is based is given for inexperienced readers in *Illustration 3.1*, with examples in an appendix to the illustration.
An exercise in double entry
Having considered *Illustration 3.1*, write out on your working paper the opening balance sheet of CREDITABLE LTD (Case 1, Table 1), then, noting the 'transactions' from the left-hand column of balance sheets 2 to 5, and closing the text:
  (i) Complete your versions of balance sheets 2 to 5, using the transactions.
  (ii) Write comments on each balance sheet.
  (iii) Prepare the profit and loss account for the period.
  (iv) Check with the text.
Bear in mind that, in practice, the transactions would have been entered in ledger accounts and that it is the balances on ledger accounts which form the balance sheet.

Illustration 3.1
DIAGRAMMATIC DESCRIPTION OF DOUBLE ENTRY SYSTEM
(*Experienced readers may pass on to CASE 2*)

RULE: For each transaction, without exception, a double entry is made in equal value to opposite sides of separate ledger accounts (see appendix to this illustration). Separate ledgers are usually maintained of accounts for (1) individual debtors and (2) individual creditors. These are the personal ledgers. The remaining ledger is called the General ledger (Impersonal or nominal ledgers are other descriptions). Cash transactions (one side of the double entry) are dealt with in the Cash Book, which has columns to differentiate 'cash' and 'bank' items.

Many accounting systems are nowadays mechanised or computerised to a large degree but the basic concept of double entry is followed.

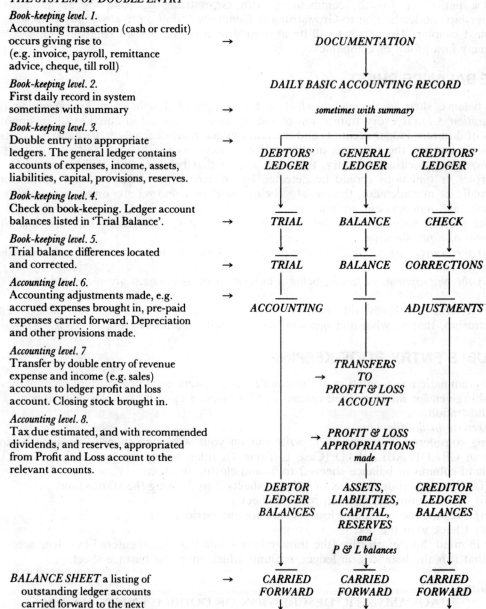

THE SYSTEM OF DOUBLE ENTRY

Book-keeping level. 1.
Accounting transaction (cash or credit) occurs giving rise to (e.g. invoice, payroll, remittance advice, cheque, till roll) → **DOCUMENTATION**

Book-keeping level. 2.
First daily record in system sometimes with summary → **DAILY BASIC ACCOUNTING RECORD**
sometimes with summary

Book-keeping level. 3.
Double entry into appropriate ledgers. The general ledger contains accounts of expenses, income, assets, liabilities, capital, provisions, reserves. → **DEBTORS' LEDGER** | **GENERAL LEDGER** | **CREDITORS' LEDGER**

Book-keeping level. 4.
Check on book-keeping. Ledger account balances listed in 'Trial Balance'. → **TRIAL BALANCE CHECK**

Book-keeping level. 5.
Trial balance differences located and corrected. → **TRIAL BALANCE CORRECTIONS**

Accounting level. 6.
Accounting adjustments made, e.g. accrued expenses brought in, pre-paid expenses carried forward. Depreciation and other provisions made. → **ACCOUNTING ADJUSTMENTS**

Accounting level. 7
Transfer by double entry of revenue expense and income (e.g. sales) accounts to ledger profit and loss account. Closing stock brought in. → **TRANSFERS TO PROFIT & LOSS ACCOUNT**

Accounting level. 8.
Tax due estimated, and with recommended dividends, and reserves, appropriated from Profit and Loss account to the relevant accounts. → **PROFIT & LOSS APPROPRIATIONS** *made*

DEBTOR LEDGER BALANCES | **ASSETS, LIABILITIES, CAPITAL, RESERVES** *and* **P & L balances** | **CREDITOR LEDGER BALANCES**

BALANCE SHEET a listing of outstanding ledger accounts carried forward to the next accounting period. → **CARRIED FORWARD** | **CARRIED FORWARD** | **CARRIED FORWARD**

Appendix to Illustration 3.1   THE DOUBLE ENTRY SYSTEM

DEBIT (left-hand side) accounts receiving value.	CREDIT (right-hand side) accounts giving value.
Cash book with cheques, cash and other remittances received. *Expense accounts* (e.g. rent, purchases, wages) with expenses paid or accrued due. *Asset accounts* with the cost of fixed assets (e.g. plant) bought. *Debtor accounts* with sale on credit. *Stock account* with end of year stock value. *Profit and loss account* with bad debts written off; provisions for known liabilities of uncertain amount; appropriation of profit to reserves; transfer of expense account debits at end of accounting period, those accounts being credited and thus closed.	*Cash book* with cash, cheque and other payments made. *Income accounts* with sales revenue whether in cash or credit; investment income received or due. *Liability accounts* e.g. trade creditors with purchases on credit; loan accounts with amount borrowed. *Capital accounts* e.g. Ordinary Share Capital Accounts with nominal value of invested capital. *Share Premium account* with amounts received as investment in Ordinary Share Capital in excess of nominal value. *Trading and Profit and Loss account* with end of year closing stock value. *Profit and loss account* Transfers of income account credits at the end of the accounting period, those accounts being debited and thus closed.
DEBIT BALANCES may indicate *expenses* (e.g. rent); *assets* (e.g. plant, debtor), or *losses* (e.g. debit balance on P & L account).	CREDIT BALANCES may include *liabilities* (e.g. creditor), *capital* (e.g. ordinary share capital), *income* (e.g. sales), *provisions* (e.g. for depreciation), *reserves* (e.g. general reserve, share premium) or *profit* (e.g. credit balance on P & L account).

CASE 2. The Growstrong Partnership

George Grow and Sam Strong enter into partnership to manufacture and sell an electronic product developed by Sam in his spare time.

George, a sales manager, has been made redundant by his company hit by the recession. He agrees to invest £10,000 of his redundancy money in the venture with Sam who gives up his job as an engineer with a large company. Sam invests all his available savings, £5,000.

They rent a small factory building and buy £3,500 of plant and equipment on credit to add to the plant which Sam brings in. They agree that this be valued at £1,500 and regarded as part of Sam's investment. They purchase a motor van for £4,000, and raw materials for £3,500, the balance of the cash invested remaining in the partnership current account with the local bank. They regard this as their starting working capital.

Their *opening balance sheet* is drawn up (*Case 2. Table 1*).

Exercise: Readers may wish to draw up their version of the partnership balance sheet before turning to Case 2, Table 1, to check.

Case 2.   Table 1   GROWSTRONG & COMPANY

		£	£	£
	BALANCE SHEET (as at the start of the partnership)			
ASSETS EMPLOYED:	*FIXED ASSETS*			
	Plant and Equipment (cost)		5,000	
	Motor Van (cost)		4,000	9,000
	NET CURRENT ASSETS (working capital)			
Current Assets:	Stock (materials) (cost)	3,500		
	Cash at bank	7,500	11,000	
	Less			
Current Liability:	Creditor (Equipment)		3,500	7,500
				£16,500
FINANCED BY:	*Capital Accounts*			
	George Grow		10,000	
	Sam Strong		6,500	£16,500

COMMENTARY ON CASE 2, TABLE 1

This starting balance sheet had been prepared by George Grow's son, James, who already has an honours business studies degree and is now studying for his accountancy finals.

Sam Strong asks George and James to discuss with him the financial position as revealed by the statement, at the start of an enterprise to which they are wholly committed and intend to be successful. George says that he had agreed with Sam that Sam's smaller investment reflected the latter's effort and skill in designing and developing the product they were to manufacture and sell. This should somehow be shown in the balance sheet. James says that human assets are not accounted for in balance sheets yet, and that research and experiment in this area have not excited accountants. However, he suggests that the problem be solved by increasing Sam's invested capital by (say) £3,500, thus equalling George's capital investment, and by bringing in an item 'Goodwill' £3,500 as an intangible asset. Sam ends the discussion on this point by declining the offer and saying that as far as he is concerned, the time to talk about 'Goodwill' will be when they have established a profitable business.

James suggests that they should plan their first year operations so as to estimate their outgoings and income, say on a monthly basis; decide on the credit period (if any) they will give their customers, plot their cash flow and using this information, speak to their bank manager to agree an overdraft level.

How much return do you want on the capital you have invested? asks James. You could get 12% (during 1986) before tax, merely by having the sum safe on deposit in the bank, plus a return, e.g. a salary, by using your personal talents elsewhere. Jobs are not that plentiful for our age group, interjects the redundant George. And, continues James, inflation is still running at around 5%. You should therefore plan a return on your investment which will cover these factors, give you an extra return for risk, pay tax on the profits and leave a residue which you can retain in the business as an additional investment for asset replacement and expansion.

Seems resonable, says Sam. We will have to discuss the selling prices of our products with this in mind, but it is what the customer will agree to pay that will finally determine the price and I suppose the quantity of our sales potential will be another factor. It would be sensible to determine a minimum level of return on capital, as well as the higher target.

Using your suppliers' credit is good sense, says James, it does not cost you anything and you will repay later in reduced real monetary terms. Yes, says George, but we must have a policy of paying our suppliers on time to maintain their goodwill. And the other side of the coin is that our customers will regard us as their suppliers and will want credit too. James nodded. You will have to finance the debt while it is outstanding. It will cost you the interest on your capital lying idle, plus the cost of inflation. I did some research for my degree on this and one current effect of inflation on credit transactions is that times fixed in contracts for payment are getting shorter. Cash transactions are much more in evidence than hitherto. And a key question for you and your suppliers is 'with transactions on credit, what payment constitutes compensation for value received?'

Your cash, he continues, lying idle in your bank current account is like stock lying idle in the stores and your uncollected debt. In double entry terms, these assets represent your invested capital. It is pretty clear you have to get these assets moving and earning a return. At this moment the idle cash represents 46% of your capital. If you foresee its immediate use, alright, but otherwise at least put it (or some part of it) on deposit account to earn a return.

Until you have turned your first sales into cash, you will have to finance your operations, stocks, work in progress, finished products, and your debtors. Your cash budget will underline this. The speedier the cycle of your operations the better. The remunerative employment of assets is yours as owner/managers. At least you will look at your business with an owner's eye. Some people have seen the divorce of managership from ownership, post-war, as a reason for less than maximum profitability. Remember that when . . . Yes, I know, says Sam, . . . when our business gets too big for George and me to handle!

DISCUSSION TOPICS ON CASE 2, TABLE 1

The problems of starting a business – particularly a small business – are very relevant at the present time, and the *starting balance sheet* forms a fertile base for a discussion of financial management considerations, requiring little technical accounting expertise.

Readers, with or without their tutors, may want to assume the mantle of George, James and Sam, and pursue the discussion further.

Four discussion areas are suggested, as follows, and others will no doubt occur to the reader:
1. Discuss the view that Goodwill is directly related to profitability and that Sam's decision to refuse the offered increase in his capital was correct.
2. Assume you are the bank manager to whom the partners are looking for finance. Discuss the bank's view of the starting balance sheet and its likely requirements before granting an overdraft.
3. Discuss the views of James and Sam in respect of the target return on their capital employed.
4. Discuss the control of working capital as an essential prerequisite to the survival and growth of the business, considering policies for credit control, stock control and cash control.

CASE 2. Growstrong & Co Ltd (a private limited company)

In balance sheet terms, when profit is earned it results in the arising of additional assets. At one moment of time, the profit will be realised in cash, but this cash keeps flowing (cash flow) in and out of the business. It is soon turned into some other form when used with or without further invested share or loan capital, e.g. purchase of buildings, machinery, extra stock, work in progress, debtors, or invested in other companies to the extent that they become associates or subsidiaries. It is also used to pay off liabilities, thus increasing the net assets.

On the sources side of the balance sheet, after-tax profits, to the extent that they have been retained and not distributed as dividends, are stipulated as reserves (including any balance on the profit and loss account). These reserves of undistributed profits increase the investment of the (ordinary) shareholders.

The business prospers

After several years of operations, having formed themselves into a private limited company, with George and Sam holding almost all the controlling ordinary shares, they meet to discuss the balance sheet and accounts for the year just ended. James has passed his qualifying accountancy examinations and will shortly be admitted to membership of his professional body. He is needed in the business as the problems of growth start to weigh with our entrepreneurs.

COMMENTARY ON CASE 2, TABLE 2

Problems of growth

George and Sam meet in May 19x1 to discuss the balance sheet and accounts recently received from their local accountant.

Sam's inventive mind has produced a number of winning ideas and George's marketing and sales skills have turned these into a growing order book. Business is booming. The flood of orders since the end of the financial year lead them to realise the need for an immediate increase in their productive capacity.

A bigger factory building is required, with more plant and equipment and stocks of raw material. Staff will be needed in the factory and office to cope with the extra business. Expenses of all kinds are on the increase, leaving aside the costs of inflation. It is evident they will need more funds to finance extra capital purchases and additional working capital.

Their accountant, whom they meet tomorrow to discuss the funding problem and matters arising from their appraisal of the accounts and balance sheet, had emphasised that this is the common concern in growing businesses. What you want to avoid, he had said, is OVERTRADING, in other words, allowing your sales to grow beyond your ability to finance that growth. You can go so far, by stretching your supplier's credit and the bank manager's goodwill to the limit, but in the end you have to come to terms with the need to plan your financial future properly.

Return on capital

I see we earned £12,000 after tax, says George, looking at the summary page of their profit and loss account:

GROWSTRONG LTD
Summary Profit and Loss Account
for the year ended 31 March 19x1

	£
Profit before loan interest and taxation	24,000
Loan interest	7,000
Profit before tax	17,000
Taxation	5,000
Profit after tax	12,000
Dividends payable	8,000
Profit retained (included in balance sheet reserves)	£4,000

That's more than we expected, and on top of our management salaries it is quite good. Let's see, you and I have £50,000 invested in the business, so that's a 24% return. Have you noticed that this balance sheet is laid out differently from those of our partnership days. Which is best, I wonder? (See Case 2, Table 2.)

To come back to our *profitability*, didn't James say we should plan to earn a return on the total funds available to us including the short-term funds? Should we use as the figure of capital employed,

    (i) £50,000 owners' funds, or
    (ii) £85,000 long-term funds, or
    (iii) £128,000 book value of total funds?

The balance sheet which is being discussed reads:

Case 2. Table 2

GROWSTRONG & COMPANY LIMITED

	BALANCE SHEET* as at 31 March 19x1.	£	£	£
NET ASSETS *EMPLOYED*	*FIXED ASSETS* Tangible assets: Freehold factory property (cost less depreciation of buildings) Plant & Equipment (cost less depreciation) Vehicles (cost less depreciation) Office furniture (cost less depreciation)	 40,000 35,000 6,000 1,500	 	 82,500
	CURRENT ASSETS Stocks Debtors (Trade) Cash	 35,150 10,000 350	 45,500	
	CREDITORS (amounts falling due within one year) Taxation (due to the Inland Revenue) Trade creditors (due to suppliers) Expense creditors (light, heat etc) Dividend payable (to shareholders) Bank overdraft	 5,000 18,500 3,250 8,000 8,250	 43,000	
	NET CURRENT ASSETS		*2,500*	*2,500*
LONG TERM FUNDS =	*TOTAL ASSETS LESS CURRENT LIABILITIES* *CREDITORS* (amounts falling due after more than one year) Bank loan (secured on property)			85,000 35,000
NET ASSETS =	*ORDINARY SHAREHOLDERS' FUNDS*			50,000
	being: *CAPITAL AND RESERVES* Called up share capital: Ordinary share capital in £1 shares fully paid Reserves (profit & loss account balances retained)		 40,000 10,000	 50,000

* The balance sheet incorporates the format required by the Companies Act 1981. (Sections 227(1), 228, 245, 742 and 4 Sch. 1–5 Companies Act 1985. 'Modified' Balance Sheet, 8 Sch. 1, 2, CA 1985.)

Didn't the accountant say that 'book value' indicates that the balance sheet is not a statement of value, certainly not the value we would get if we sold the business as a going concern, or if the assets were sold piecemeal?

Remember, too, we expect to get £60,000 for the factory property when we move shortly. If we brought that value into the balance sheet, our investment would increase by £20,000 to £70,000 and on that basis, the profit after tax of £12,000 works out at about a 17% return.

I suppose we should compare the profit before tax and interest £24,000 with the long-term funds employed which include the bank loan of £85,000. That's about 28%. Seems OK as we are paying the bank interest of about 20%. At least we are making good use of their funds.

On the other hand, if you follow James' advice and relate the £24,000 before tax and interest figure to the total book value of the assets we are using, £128,000, the return is only 17% – less if you add in the appreciation in the property value. I wonder what is a 'sufficient return'? We'll have to discuss it tomorrow.

Liquidity cover

Yes, says Sam. I am reasonably happy with our *profitability*. It's our *liquidity* I am concerned about, particularly as we expand with costs rising all round as they are at present.

We have to remain solvent, which means having sufficient assets of all kinds to cover all our liabilities. That's no problem, says George. But our immediate ability to pay – our liquidity – is worrying.

Our working capital is only £2,500 and our current ratio just over par (1.06). And our liquid ratio is really bad. Our debtors and cash (£10,350) are nowhere near enough to meet our short-term liabilities (£43,000). That's a *liquid ratio* of 0.24, he says, tapping the buttons of his calculator.

We shall have to see our Bank Manager about our overdraft ceiling; we agreed £15,000 and we'll soon reach that. Perhaps we should forego our £8,000 dividends and leave them in the business as extra capital? These ratio indications are useful pointers to our problem . . . and to the bank and suppliers too, interjected Sam . . . but it's our cash budget which will provide us with information in advance of the problem.

And that tells me that if we expand as we plan, we'll be moving into a new financial league!

DISCUSSION TOPICS ON CASE 2, TABLE 2

The *financial problems of growth* need to be well understood by business managers. Growstrong & Co Ltd, are in the midst of these.

Readers, with or without their tutors, should cast themselves in the role of either Sam or George who have both invested all their savings and an immense amount of personal effort towards business success and then with the sharp edge of risk as a spur, consider the whole range of extra expenditure which growth will bring, and the likely solutions in funding arrangements.

Three formal discussion topics are listed:

1. Make a list of likely financial problems associated with growth and of the likely balance sheet indications of overtrading.
2. Discuss the relationship of liquidity and profitability to business survival in the growth situation in which Growstrong & Co Ltd are presently placed.
3. Are the various bases for capital employed mentioned by George for use in return on capital (ROCE) computations realistic? From what point of view could each be used?

4

Balance sheet

Growstrong becomes a Public Limited Company

The Growstrong business did in fact expand rapidly. Its products did exceptionally well. Then, on the advice of its London merchant bankers, the company 'went public' and obtained a quotation for its ordinary shares.

The business had grown to a size of net asset value and profitability which, together with the integrated budget of all the operations of the company mirroring expansion, warranted the decision to apply for Stock Exchange listing. Besides its shares, the company's debentures were also included in the Stock Exchange's Official List. Thus access was provided to funds from the public and the institutions.

The company had issued a prospectus (as an Offer for Sale) complying with the requirements of both company law and the Stock Exchange. The ordinary shares had been issued at a premium of 20 pence per share on top of the nominal value of 50 pence. The price of 70 pence per share was attractive to investors and the shares were fully subscribed.

The company's growth included the acquisition of, as well as investment in, other companies.

At the end of its most recent year, the balance sheet in the consolidated form of a public holding company and its subsidiaries appeared as in *Table 3* (page 52).

ACCOUNTING POLICIES

An essential preliminary to the understanding and interpretation of the statutory accounts is a review of the main assumptions on which they are based and the explanations of the accounting policies adopted. One of the earliest accounting standards, SSAP 2, Disclosure of Accounting Policies, set out four fundamental concepts underlying the accounts with an obligation on companies to explain any departure from them, as well as the disclosure of their adopted policies.

Importance of Statement of Standard Accounting Practice No. 2 to the understanding and interpretation of financial accounts
The preamble to the standard justified its need as follows:

> "It is fundamental to the understanding and interpretation of financial accounts that those who use them should be aware of the main assumptions on which they are based.

The purpose of this statement . . . is to assist such understanding by promoting improvement in the quality of the information disclosed. It seeks to achieve this by establishing as standard accounting practice the disclosure in the financial accounts of clear explanations of the accounting policies followed in so far as these are significant for the purpose of giving a *true and fair view*."

The four fundamental accounting concepts which underlie the periodic financial accounts of business enterprises were listed:

1. The *going concern* concept is the assumption that the accounts have been compiled on that basis with no intention or need to go into liquidation.
2. The *accruals concept*, also known as the *matching* concept, follows the practice of charging expenses in the same accounting period in which the related revenue is recognised. It is *not* therefore the timing of cash receipts and payments which is important. Where an expense is accrued due, it is brought into the applicable accounting period. Similarly, that proportion of a cash payment which relates to a subsequent accounting period is carried forward.
3. The *consistency* concept implies that the accounting treatment of the same transaction is the same from period to period. Where a change is judged needful, it follows that an explanation of this should appear with the published accounts setting out the effect thereof.
4. The *prudence* concept implies that no profit or income is anticipated but that all known liabilities (expenses/losses) are brought into account.

These concepts have such general acceptance that they call for no explanation in published accounts and their observance is presumed unless otherwise stated.

However, the Companies Act 1985 (Sch. 4) specifies that they should be followed, requiring that where any of them have not been observed, particulars of the departure, the reasons and the effect must be disclosed.

Disclosure requirement

The standard requires that the accounting policies, i.e. the specific accounting bases judged by the reporting company as most appropriate to their circumstances and adopted by them in the preparation of their accounts, should be disclosed. The importance of this requirement is exemplified by the affairs of Rolls-Royce (policy on accounting for research and development expenditure) and of GEC/AEI (valuation of stock and work in progress) considered in Chapter 1. It is not surprising, therefore, to find that it has become common practice for a company's accounting policies to be stated as the *earliest note* to the accounts.

Among significant matters listed in SSAP 2 as examples of items whose accounting treatment could have a material effect on the reported results and the financial position, and in respect of which accounting policies should be disclosed, are:

1. Depreciation of fixed assets (SSAP 12).
2. Treatment and amortisation of intangibles such as research and development expenditure (SSAP 13).
3. Leasing and rental transactions (SSAP 21).
4. Hire purchase or instalment transactions (SSAP 21).
5. Conversion of foreign currencies (SSAP 20).
6. Consolidation policies (SSAP 14).
7. Deferred Taxation (SSAP 15).
8. Stocks and Work in Progress (SSAP 9).

It will be noted that all these matters are now subject to their own accounting standard.

The content of the 'Accounting Policies' section of the published report of companies varies greatly in practice, some providing detailed information and others a bare minimum.

And because most of the significant matters exemplified in SSAP 2 and noted above, have themselves since become the subject of specific standards, this has led to more information being given in their respect. An example of the more informative statement which illustrates the best practice is given in the accounts of J. Bibby & Sons Ltd, one of the two winning companies in 1981 of *The Accountant* and Stock Exchange Annual Awards:

STATEMENT OF ACCOUNTING POLICIES
Fixed Assets
Fixed assets acquired through the purchase of a subsidiary are included in the consolidated balance sheet at the amounts at which they are stated in subsidiaries' accounts. Investment and regional development grants receivable in respect of expenditure in the UK on fixed assets are credited to an investment grants account. Equal annual instalments, determined by the life of the asset on which the grant was received, are then transferred to the credit of the profit and loss account. Depreciation is calculated to write off the cost of fixed assets by equal annual instalments over their estimated lives. Freehold land and a long leasehold property held as an investment are not depreciated.

The estimated lives of the assets are:

	Years
Freehold buildings	10–50
Leasehold buildings	50*
Plant and machinery	3–20
Vehicles – trailers	10
Vehicles – others	3– 8

*or the period of the lease, if less.

A note to this company's *current cost* balance sheet amplified the above policy relating to the historic accounts:

'Fixed assets are included in the current cost balance sheet at their depreciated replacement current cost at balance sheet date. Those assets which were fully written off under the historical cost convention have been reinstated at their depreciated replacement cost using revised residual lives. Fixed assets which it is not intended to replace have been included at their estimated residual value.'

This gives a great deal more information to the analyst than the following generalised and not very helpful note on the accounting treatment of 'stocks' taken from another company's report:

'Stock is valued at the lower of cost and net realisable value.'

Companies Act 1981. The CA 1981 requirements (4 Sch. 36 CA 1985) that the 'Statement of Accounting Policies' including depreciation (also required by SSAP 12) *must be included as a note to the accounts* gives legal emphasis to the importance of these statements to the understanding of the published accounting information.

The Growstrong plc consolidated balance sheet

The Growstrong plc balance sheet which follows, *Table 3*, although more complicated in detail, is in essence the same document as previously illustrated in *Tables 1* and *2* covering the start and earlier growth years of the enterprise.

A value for capital employed has to be determined and a target planned for return on capital. Operations based on the plan must proceed.

Responsibilities of management

The major difference now from the days when Grow and Strong both owned and managed the business is its size: the fact that it is a public company with a wide range of shareholders

– individual and institutional – and that the managers are not committed as owners.

Is it possible for the management of a large diversified business to see their responsibilities with 'an owner's eye' so that their involvement in its affairs will be sharpened?

Samuel and Wilkes[1] see management responsibility as much wider than merely to their own company:

"It is perfectly possible for successful divisions within a company to subsidise the less successful operations, and with limited disclosure required, these facts need not be known to anyone outside the company. This means that the managers of a large company are responsible not simply to their own shareholders, but to the whole economy which is inevitably influenced by the ability of central management to control the performance of its divisions. The management of the large diversified company has in many areas taken over from the stock market the responsibility of measuring performance, and it is the managers who now have to take the necessary remedial action."

Who are the 'owners'?

Whether or not there is any truth in the assertion that the post-war divorce of ownership from management has had anything to do with the decline in the efficiency of some businesses, perhaps the greater emphasis should be on the analysis of ownership.

Apart from the obvious interest in the nationalised industries, in today's pluralistic society most of us, managers and other employees alike, are owners in one way or another, either as taxpayers, members of pension funds, holders of insurance policies, depositors in banks, holders of government securities, etc. The institutions and the government who channel these funds into industry are the agents in this way of the investing public. Wider awareness of this spread of ownership base (a near-majority of ordinary shares of public companies and the highest share of debentures in them are held by the institutions) could provide some motivation for an improvement in the return on the nation's capital employed.

Growstrong plc and subsidiaries

EXPLANATORY INTRODUCTION TO THE CONSOLIDATED BALANCE SHEET

The balance sheet shown in *Table 3* typifies that of a listed (public) company with subsidiary and associated companies. It is in the *consolidated form* of a holding (parent) company and its subsidiaries. It would be published accompanied, inter alia, by notes to the accounts and the *separate* balance sheet of the holding company (not illustrated). The previous accounting year's figures are given in the consolidated balance sheet and would also be shown in the notes to the accounts which amplify them. These notes contain information either mandatorily required by company law, or seen as desirable by the directors.

The *format* follows that required by the Companies Act 1985. GROWSTRONG's status as a public limited company makes it ineligible for certain accounting exemptions to which it might otherwise have been entitled as a 'medium-sized' company under that Act.

Although the EEC Fourth Directive does not cover group accounting, its provisions in respect of the accounts of large single entities, first enacted in the 1981 legislation, apply equally to those of groups. These provisions will eventually be supplemented by future

[1] J. M. Samuels and F. M. Wilkes, 'Management of Company Finance' 4th edn, Van Nostrand Reinhold 1986.

legislation when the EEC Seventh Directive in respect of group accounts is introduced.

   Note: While this chapter and Chapter 5 deal with legal requirements for published accounts, including the detail first set out in the Companies Act 1981 (now CA 1985), the text is not intended to be exhaustive in respect of matters of law. For detail of the 1981 Act, readers are referred to the two publications: Companies Act 1981 (i) Guide to requirements and (ii) Model reports and accounts, published by Gee & Co for the Institute of Chartered Accountants of Scotland. For details of the Companies Act 1985, refer to the publication by Van Nostrand Reinhold.

What is in a Balance Sheet?

4.1   SHARE CAPITAL

The notes to the consolidated balance sheet are required to show the number of shares and their aggregate nominal value comprising the *allotted* and *paid up* share capital of the parent company.

   The number and aggregate value in respect of the *authorised share capital* is also given, distinguished from the *allotted* share capital as required by the Companies Act 1981, which followed the CA 1967 with the substitution of "*allotted* share capital" for "*issued* share capital". The 1981 Act also stipulated that "the amount of the *allotted* share capital and the amount of the *called up* share capital which has been *paid up* shall be shown separately".

   Among other legal requirements in respect of shares, *notes to the accounts* (replacing disclosure in the directors' report) must give information in respect of shares allotted during the financial year:

   (a) reasons for allotment;
   (b) classes of shares allotted; and
   (c) for each class, the number allotted, their aggregate value and the consideration received. (Sch. 1, CA 1981.)

The legal provisions regarding share capital, debentures and financial statements are now contained in 4 Sch. 37–41 CA 1985.

Authorised share capital

The authorised share capital written into the company's Memorandum of Association (the document forming the constitution of the company and defining its objects and powers) sets the limit to which the directors may issue shares of the specified types. The Articles of Association (the rules for the company's operation; they define the rights of the members and the powers and duties of the directors) will state how the authorised limit may be changed. This is usually by a simple majority of the voting shareholders on an ordinary resolution at a general meeting. The authorised share capital as stated in the note to the balance sheet does *not* form part of the double entry system. The issued (or allotted) capital does. Specimen 'articles' (Table 'A') may be adopted instead of a company's own set. Previously appended to the Companies Act, it is now contained in separate regulations (SI 1985/805) to facilitate subsequent amendment.

Allotted share capital

The allotted share capital is the *nominal* value of the total number of shares *allotted*, for cash or other consideration, and whether paid up or not.

   GROWSTRONG plc has on issue 1 million ordinary shares of *nominal* value 50p each, priced at 70p each and fully paid. Thus its issued (allotted) and fully paid capital is £500,000. The premium of 20p per share, £200,000, is credited to a *Share Premium Account* (see 4.2 RESERVES) as required by company law.

Table 3

GROWSTRONG plc & SUBSIDIARIES
CONSOLIDATED BALANCE SHEET
(historic cost)
as at the end of its most recent financial year

	NOTE	THIS YEAR £'000	£'000	LAST YEAR £'000	£'000
FIXED ASSETS					
Intangible assets	6	60		70	
Tangible assets	6	916		789	
Investments	7	134	1,110	100	959
CURRENT ASSETS					
Stocks	8	490		360	
Debtors	8	425		430	
Cash at bank and in hand	8	50		70	
		965		860	
CREDITORS: amounts falling due within one year	9	600		440	
NET CURRENT ASSETS		365	365	420	420
TOTAL ASSETS LESS CURRENT LIABILITIES			1,475		1,379
CREDITORS: amounts falling due after more than one year					
Debenture loans	4	250		300	
Bank loans	4	40	290	50	350
PROVISION FOR LIABILITIES & CHARGES					
Deferred taxation	5	30		25	
Minority interests	3	133	163	97	122
SHAREHOLDERS' FUNDS			1,022		907
being:					
CAPITAL AND RESERVES					
Called up share capital	1		500		500
Share premium account	1 & 2		200		200
Revaluation reserve	2		50		40
Profit and loss account	2		272		167
			1,022		907

Signed *   G Grow, Director.   S Strong, Director.

Tutorial notes
* 1.   The group balance sheet is not required to be signed, but it is good practice to do so.
2.   Published balance sheets will not necessarily contain amplification notes in respect of each item.
3.   The information which would be contained in the notes to this balance sheet is discussed in the text of this chapter.

Called up capital

The called up capital is that part of the issued capital which the company has called up. A company is not bound to require the full nominal amount of each share to be paid immediately. If the funds are required for a costly development over time, it may issue partly paid shares for the amounts needed immediately and defer the balance to be called later. The holders of partly paid shares have an obligation in law to subscribe the balance if the company's liquidation intervenes.

Paid up capital

The paid up capital is that sum received in cash or other consideration by the company. When calls remain unpaid, the difference between the called up and paid up capital is designated *'Calls in Arrear'*. In this event, the balance sheet entry will show the nominal amount of capital called, with the 'calls in arrear' deducted therefrom, the balance being the cash or consideration actually received.

If authorised by its articles, a company may receive 'Calls in Advance' which will be so designated in the balance sheet.

Ordinary share capital

Ordinary shares usually form the largest part of a company's share capital. Commonly called *'equities'*, they carry controlling voting rights, through the ability of their holders to elect the company directors. The ordinary shareholders have an entitlement to all the company's profit after tax and after the provision of a dividend to (any) *preference* shareholders.

Where, as is usual, only a proportion of the profit after tax attributable to the ordinary shareholder (*'Earnings'*) is paid as a dividend, it follows that the balance, retained as additional capital, adds to his investment in the company. The amount, whether remaining as a credit balance on profit and loss account or transferred to reserves, forms part, therefore, of the *ordinary shareholders' interest*. Ordinary shares without voting rights are possible, but rare because of the difficulty of attracting new capital on that basis.

In a liquidation, i.e. when the company is 'wound up', the ordinary shareholder is not entitled to a return of any part of his capital until *all* liabilities and the capital of (any) preference shareholders has been covered.

Equities, therefore, accept the highest risk in return for the potential of the highest share of profit.

Ordinary shares and the Companies Act 1981

This Act empowered companies under certain conditions to issue *redeemable equity shares* (CA 1985, S159), an extension of their power to issue redeemable preference shares under the 1948 Act. More significantly, companies may now purchase their own shares (CA 1985, S162, 170–2).

Both these innovations are more logically dealt with later in this Chapter following the sections on 'limited liability' and 'redeemable preference shares'.

Dividends

Dividends to ordinary shareholders are declared as a percentage of the nominal value of the share, but usually expressed in the published profit and loss account as, e.g. 7p per share.

Under the present imputation system of tax, the recipient of the dividend is imputed to have suffered income tax at the basic tax rate on that sum, which with the deduction of the basic rate of tax thereon, equals the amount of his dividend cheque. That is, the tax credit is $x/(100-x)$ of the dividend paid, where x is the basic rate of income tax.

Example 4.1.1

Given a basic rate of income tax of 30%, the ordinary shareholder receives a dividend warrant for 7 pence per ordinary share (nominal value 50 pence), for which this shareholder paid 80 pence.
The current market price of the share is 100 pence.
The shareholder's tax credit per share = $30/(100-30) = 3/7\text{ths} \times 7p = 3p$.

The shareholder will declare income of 10p per share for his personal tax purposes, but claim relief of the tax, 3p, already (imputed to have been) paid. The *gross dividend percentage on the nominal value of the share is 10/50 × 100 = 20%.*

The *gross dividend yield* expressing the dividend as a return on the current market price = 10/100 × 100 = 10%; it is this figure which appears in the financial press. The gross dividend yield may alternatively be computed:

$$= \text{Gross dividend* rate} \times \frac{\text{nominal value of share}}{\text{market price of the share}}$$

$$= 20 \times 50/100 = 10\%$$

*Dividend paid plus tax credit.

For this particular shareholder who paid 80p for his ordinary share, his personal gross dividend yield

$$= 20 \times 50/80 = 12.5\%$$

Notes:

(i) Dividends are further covered in Chapter 5, dealing with the GROWSTRONG plc profit and loss account.

(ii) The imputation tax system is also described in that Chapter. Its basic philosophy is that the company having suffered corporation tax on its profits, the shareholder should not be taxed again on his dividend; indeed, he should be given credit within his personal tax computations for the tax imputed to have been paid.

Rights issues

These are issues of ordinary shares to *existing shareholders* at a price somewhat less than the market price and the expected ex-rights price. The rights are offered to members in proportion to their existing holdings. The discount allowed them will vary in relation to the proportion of shares required to be taken up. A rights issue of 1 share for every 5 shares presently held would require a larger discount than an issue of 1 for 10. If the share price to be paid is above par (the nominal value) as is usually the case, then the par or nominal value is credited to the ordinary share capital account and the excess, less any expenses of the new issue, credited to share premium account. Cash account would, of course, be debited.

The object of rights issues is to attract current shareholders, among them often being the institutional shareholders, to add to their investment in the company.

Bonus issues

Bonus issues of shares regarded as fully paid to ordinary shareholders are merely tidying-up operations; by implication, management regard the amount of the bonus as representing a permanent part of the company's capital which can no longer be regarded as free for distribution to the shareholders as dividends. It is a general misconception that a bonus issue adds to the value of a shareholders' investment. It does not. The bonus issue (also called 'scrip' or 'capitalisation' issue) is provided for by transfer from the company's reserves.

Example 4.1.2

Extract from the balance sheet of XY company
BEFORE A 2 for 1 BONUS ISSUE

	£
400,000 ordinary shares of 50p each fully paid	*200,000*
Reserves	*600,000*
Book value of ordinary shareholders' interest	£800,000

Every 50p (nominal) share has a *book value* of £2.00, i.e. £800,000/400,000.
THE COMPANY MAKES A BONUS ISSUE OF 2 ORDINARY SHARES REGARDED AS FULLY PAID, FOR EVERY 1 HELD BY MEMBERS. THE ISSUE IS MADE BY CAPITALIZING RESERVES.

Extract from the balance sheet of XY company
AFTER a 2 for 1 BONUS ISSUE

	£
1,200,000 ordinary shares of 50p each fully paid	600,000
Reserves	200,000
Book value of ordinary shareholders' interest	£800,000

The *book value* of the shareholders' interest is unchanged at £800,000. Every 50p (nominal) share now has a book value of only £0.66p, i.e. £800,000/1,200,000, but members now have 3 shares for every 1 previously held with a total book value as before the bonus issue of £2.00. (3 × £0.66p.)

The *market price* of the share should adjust in like manner, i.e. if priced at £2.55 *before* the bonus issue, it should settle to around £0.85p.

Preference shares

Subject to the company's Articles of Association, the preference shareholder has the right to a fixed percentage dividend in priority to a dividend to the ordinary shareholder. The dividend may be paid only out of profit which remains after the company has met all its expenses and liabilities, including any loan interest. If no profit arises and there are no reserves of past profits, no dividend can be paid. The Companies Acts make it illegal to pay a dividend to any type of shareholder out of capital. (*Note:* The Companies Act 1980 introduced new rules on 'distributable profit' and these are covered in Chapter 5.) If no preference dividend is paid in an accounting period, no other dividend can be paid in that period. And preference shareholders normally have voting rights only on the non-payment of their dividend.

Preference shareholders usually have priority rights over ordinary shareholders as to a return of their capital in a liquidation. These rights, naturally, are subordinate to those of all types of *creditors* – preferential, secured or unsecured. If the preference shares are of the *non-cumulative* type (they will be, if not prefaced in their description by the word 'cumulative'), a dividend not paid in the current year cannot be carried forward to be paid out of future years' profits. It is lost to the shareholders.

If the shares are *cumulative preference shares* and the dividend of one year is unpaid, then it is carried forward for future payment. No book-keeping entry is made for preference dividends in arrear, but a note is required to the published accounts.

Participating preference shareholders have the right to a dividend additional to their fixed preference dividend; this is usually a proportion of any ordinary dividend declared.

Convertible preference shareholders have an option to convert their preference shares into ordinary shares within a specified time, normally on a nominal value basis.

Preference dividends are paid 'net' (of tax) and carry an associated tax credit as described for ordinary dividends. The dividend *yield*, the relationship between the dividend paid and the market price of the share, is calculated:

Example 4.1.3

Gross dividend yield =

$$\text{Gross dividend rate} \times \frac{\text{nominal value of share}}{\text{market value of share}}$$

A 10% (now 7% net plus tax credit*) £1 preference share has a quoted market price of 0.80p.

$$Dividend\ yield = 10 \times \frac{100p}{80p} = 12.5\%$$

*Basic tax rate of 30% assumed.

In addition to the yield, preference shareholders (including potential ones) would be interested in the *preference dividend cover*. As the preference dividend is payable in priority to the ordinary dividend, this cover, a measure of risk in the investment, could be calculated:

Cover = Profit after tax/preference dividend (paid and or payable).

Preference dividends are normally paid half-yearly.

Limited liability

No consideration of the meaning of 'share capital' in a corporate report is complete without reference to the concept of 'limited liability'.

Most companies are incorporated under the Companies Acts as *limited by shares*. If a member's shares are *fully paid*, then that amount states the limit of his personal liability. If the company runs into difficulties and is compulsorily liquidated, the member's loss is limited to the amount of his fully paid share and there can be no further recourse to him for liabilities of the company not covered by the value of its liquidated assets. This contrasts with the position of a sole trader or partnership business, where in a bankruptcy of the business, creditors can look not only to the business assets for compensation, but also to the personal assets of the business owners.

Where shares are *partly paid*, the member is liable in law to pay the balance when 'called' to do so, or in a liquidation.

The potentially increased market for funds available is a clear advantage for limited liability companies. *Private* companies are prohibited from inviting the public at large to subscribe for their shares or debentures, but nevertheless can raise funds by share issues and loans through personal contacts or professional recommendation. Investors who may be unwilling to undertake the wider liability of partnership, may be willing to subscribe to the share capital of a limited liability company.

Limitation of liability is of greatest advantage when, having outgrown its 'private' status, the company goes 'public', its shares and debentures are 'listed' by a recognised Stock Exchange, and it can make a public offer of its securities, in which potentially, there is a ready market.

Given limited liability for shareholders, it logically follows that trade creditors, bankers, debenture-holders (long-term lenders) and others dealing with the company expect that there shall be no return of subscribed capital to the shareholders of a going concern, although it is recognised that capital can be lost in trading. Thus the law provides that the share capital must be maintained, and no dividend may be paid out of capital. Although, as will be considered shortly, the Companies Act 1981 breached this fundamental rule by authorising a *private company* to make a *payment out of capital* for the redemption or purchase of *its own shares*, there are significant safeguards imposed to protect the shareholders and persons dealing with the company, e.g. creditors, bankers. Lenders, of course, can and do secure their loans on the assets of the company. A bank overdraft to a private company is often covered by the personal guarantee of a controlling shareholder/ director. The guarantor would be responsible personally, but with the right to reimburse himself from the assets of the company. However, where a bank had to take up such a personal guarantee, it would be unlikely that the company would have sufficient assets for the reimbursement.

Charitable and kindred organisations are usually *limited by guarantee*. No shares are issued and members undertake a personal guarantee which fixes the limit of their liability in the event of a liquidation.

Professional firms are often incorporated with *unlimited liability*. This effectively means what it says and members have joint and several liability as in a partnership.

Redeemable preference and redeemable equity shares

Until the advent of the Companies Act 1981, the redeemable preference share was the only form of share capital which could be repaid during the lifetime of the company. The capital would be repaid either at a stated date or within a given period, often at par, but sometimes at a premium.

Although S58 of the Companies Act 1948, which empowered the issue of these shares and the conditions of their redemption, has now been repealed, S45 of the 1981 Act in essence re-enacted these provisions, at the same time extending them to redeemable equity shares; (now S159(1)(2) CA 1985).

How then, in these circumstances, is the basic rule preserved which requires that share capital be maintained in the interests of those dealing with the company whose shareholders are protected by 'limited liability'?

The answer is that the law requires that the capital redeemed must be replaced:

either (i) by a new issue of shares of like amount, the proceeds whereof are used for the redemption,

or   (ii) where the shares are *redeemed* wholly or partly out of profits, then a transfer must be made to a non-distributable reserve, entitled '*capital redemption reserve*' from profits equal to the nominal value of the shares redeemed less the proceeds of any fresh issue (S53, CA 1981 now S170 CA 1985).

Note: These provisions apply to the new power given to companies under the 1981 Act to *purchase* either out of distributable profits, or out of the proceeds of a new issue, their own fully paid shares for·cancellation. This is dealt with in the next section. Do not confuse this power with the additional provision of the 1981 Act which allows *private* companies only to redeem or purchase their own shares out of *capital*. This, too, is covered later.

In the circumstances outlined above, the *capital redemption reserve* (the word 'fund' which used to be appended to this reserve has been dropped) has one allowable use under the 1981 Act, and that is its application in allotting bonus shares regarded as fully paid, thus completing the cycle of replacing the repaid capital.

Example 4.1.4

Example of a company redeeming its preference shares at par, wholly out of profit.

*XYZ plc balance sheet extract BEFORE the
redemption of its preference share capital*

		£	£
1,000,000 ordinary shares of 50p each, fully paid			500,000
Non-distributable reserve	Share premium account		150,000
Distributable reserves	General reserve	300,000	
	Profit & Loss account	50,000	350,000
Ordinary shareholders' funds			1,000,000
Redeemable preference shares 200,000 £1 shares fully paid			200,000
			£1,200,000

Note: At this point, BEFORE the redemption, the capital of the company which must not be reduced, totals £850,000, i.e.

	£
Ordinary share capital	500,000
Share premium account	150,000
Redeemable preference shares	200,000

XYZ plc balance sheet extract AFTER the redemption of its preference share capital at par out of profits

		£	£
1,000,000 ordinary shares of 50p each, fully paid			500,000
*Non-distributable reserves**	Share premium account	150,000	
	Capital redemption reserve	200,000	350,000
			850,000
*Distributable reserves**	General reserve	100,000	
	Profit & Loss account	50,000	150,000
			£1,000,000

It can be seen that the non-distributable capital is intact at £850,000 after the redemption.

*Reserves are dealt with later in this chapter, section 4.2.

Shares redeemed at a premium

It has been a view that where under the 1948 Act (S58) – S130 CA 1985 –, new shares are issued at a premium to provide for the redemption of preference shares, that the whole of the proceeds could be applied for that purpose. This could have led to a reduction of capital.

Example 4.1.5

A Ltd balance sheet extract BEFORE the redemption of its preference share capital issued at par, out of the proceeds of a new issue of shares

		£
200,000 ordinary shares of £1 each fully paid		*200,000*
Non-distributable reserve – share premium account		50,000
Redeemable preference shares of £1 fully paid		100,000
	(C)	350,000
Distributable reserves		150,000
		£500,000

The preference shares are to be redeemed at a premium of 10% and the funds for this purpose are provided by a new issue of 80,000 £1 shares at a premium of £20,000.

A Ltd balance sheet extract AFTER the redemption of its preference share capital based on the 1948 Act which allowed the premium on redemption to be provided out of the share premium account

	£
280,000 ordinary shares of £1 each fully paid	*280,000*
Share premium account £50,000 above less £10,000 premium on	
redemption, plus £20,000 premium on new issue of shares	*60,000*
	(C) 340,000
Distributable reserves (unchanged)	150,000
	£490,000

It will be seen that if this view was correct the non-distributable capital has been reduced by £10,000 (C).

In any event, S58, CA 1948, permitted the premium on redemption of preference shares to be provided out of an existing share premium account. This effectively permitted a reduction of capital as the share premium account could be reduced without any corresponding replacement of capital.

SECTION 45 of the CA 1981 Act, now S159(1)(2) CA 1985 ensures that the capital will be replaced.

Power to issue redeemable shares, Companies Act 1985 S159(1)(2)

A company may issue shares which are to be redeemed or may be redeemed at the option of the company or the shareholder. It must be authorised by its own articles to do so. 'Redeemable shares' includes both equity and preference shares. No redeemable shares may be issued, unless there are shares in issue which are not redeemable.

Redeemed shares must be cancelled on redemption.

No redemption may take place unless:
- (i) the shares are fully paid;
- (ii) the shares are redeemed out of distributable profits or out of the proceeds of a fresh issue; and
- (iii) any premium payable on redemption must be paid out of distributable profits of the company except where it is paid out of the proceeds and the shares redeemed were *issued* at a premium. In this case the premium on redemption may be provided out of share premium account to the extent that it does not exceed the *lesser* of: (i) premiums received on the *issue* of the shares being redeemed; and (ii) the balance on the share premium account.

Clause (iii) ensures that in circumstances such as in *Example 4.1.5*, the reduction of capital previously thought to be possible cannot now take place.

Example 4.1.6

A Ltd balance sheet extract AFTER the redemption of its preference share capital based on the current law, S159, CA 1985

	£
280,000 £1 ordinary shares fully paid	280,000
Non-distributable reserve – share premium account, £50,000 opening	
balance, plus £20,000 premium on the new issue of shares	70,000
	(C) 350,000
Distributable reserves – £150,000 opening balance less £10,000	
premium on redemption	140,000
	£490,000

It will be seen that the non-distributable capital is intact at £350,000 (C).

As the A Ltd redeemable shares were *not issued* at a premium, clause (iii) above does not allow the premium on redemption to be taken from share premium, but requires that it should come from distributable reserves

Whatever the level of premium received when the redeemable shares were *issued*, that level sets the maximum premium allowable on redemption, and that will not be allowed if the balance on share premium account is less, when the latter will be the limit (S45; S46 CA 1981 – see next section).

Section 45 (redemption) (now S159, 160 CA 1985) and Section 46 (purchase) CA 1981, (now S162, 170–2 CA 1985)

This section deals with the position where the shares being redeemed (or purchased), were themselves *issued at a premium* and reads:

"Where the redeemable shares were issued at a premium, any premium payable on their redemption *may* be paid out of the proceeds of a fresh issue of shares made for the purposes of the redemption, up to an amount equal to:

"(a) the aggregate of the premiums received by the company on the *issue* of the shares redeemed; *or*

"(b) the current amount of the company's share premium account (including any sum transferred to that account in respect of premiums on the new shares), *whichever is the less*; and in any such case, the amount of the company's share premium account shall be reduced by a sum corresponding (or by sums in the aggregate corresponding) to the amount of any payment made by virtue of this subsection out of the proceeds of the issue of the new shares."

Example 4.1.7

X plc had issued 500,000 10% redeemable preference shares of £1 per share at a premium of 50 pence per share redeemable at £1.80 per share. The company issue 100,000 ordinary shares of £1 per share at a premium of 20 pence per share as partial financial for the redemption of 100,000 of the redeemable preference shares. The balance on share premium account before the redemption and new issue transactions was £90,000 as indicated in the balance sheet extract:

*X plc before the redemption of the preference
shares and before the new issue*

	£'000s
1 million £1 ordinary shares fully-paid up	*1,000*
Non-distributable reserve – share premium account	90
Redeemable preference shares of £1 fully-paid up	500
Capital and non-distributable reserve	1,590
Distributable reserves	410
Net assets	2,000

After the new issue and the redemption transactions the balance sheet extract would read:

*X plc after the new issue of ordinary shares and
the redemption of the preference shares*

	£'000s
1.1 million of £1 ordinary shares fully-paid up	1,100
Non-distributable reserve – share premium account (see note 1 below)	60
Redeemable preference shares of £1 fully-paid up	400
Capital redemption reserve (see Note 2)	30
Capital and non-distributable reserve	1,590
Distributable profit (see Notes 1 and 2)	350
Net assets	1,940

It will be observed that the non-distributable capital has been maintained at £1,590,000.

Note 1
(a) the aggregate of the premiums received by the company on the *issue* of the shares redeemed = £50,000
(b) the current amount of the company's share premium account including the sum transferred to it in respect of premiums on the new issue of shares £90,000 + £20,000 = £110,000
As (a) is *less* than (b) on the wording of Section 45 (above), £50,000 is the maximum amount which can be provided out of the proceeds of the new issue and charged to share premium account. Therefore the share premium balance is:
$$£90,000 + £20,000 - £50,000 = £60,000$$
The premium required on redemption is £80,000 and deducting the maximum amount of £50,000 allowed as a charge against the share premium account, leaves the balance to come from profit, i.e. *£30,000*.

Note 2
S53(2) CA 1981 (S170 CA 1985) is relevant to the transfer of £30,000 from distributable profit to the capital redemption reserve. It reads:

". . . where in pursuance of S45 or S46, any shares of a company are redeemed or purchased wholly or partly out of the proceeds of a fresh issue and the aggregate amount of those proceeds is less than the aggregate *nominal* value of the shares redeemed or purchased, the amount of the difference shall be transferred to capital redemption reserve."

A look at the balance sheets of X plc before and after the transactions will show that if the £30,000 transfer was *not* made to the capital redemption reserve, the total of capital and non-distributable reserves would have been reduced by that amount. The transfer is therefore necessary in maintaining capital.

Therefore, nominal value of shares redeemed –	£100,000
Proceeds of new issue – £120,000	
less (note 1) applied as share premium on new issue – *£50,000*	*£70,000*
Required transfer to capital redemption reserve	*£30,000*

Power of a company to purchase its own shares, CA 1985 S162, 170–2

A company may purchase its own shares, including redeemable shares. It must be authorised by its own articles to do so.

The conditions set out above in respect of redemption of shares also apply to purchases of its own shares. No purchase of such shares may take place if the result would be that there would no longer be any member of the company holding shares other than redeemable shares.

Both public and private companies may *purchase* their own fully paid shares for cancellation either out of the proceeds of a fresh issue of shares, or out of distributable profits.

As one would expect, the members of the company must have an adequate control over such purchases and legal conditions are laid down in the 1985 Act which include the passing of a special resolution of members in respect of off-market purchases and an ordinary resolution for an authority to make a market purchase of its own shares. In the case of listed companies, it is likely that the Stock Exchange will require additional safeguards and disclosures, through its listing agreement.

Where shares are *purchased* wholly or partly out of profits, then the same transfer as in the case of redemption is required to the *capital redemption reserve* of a sum equal to the nominal value of the shares purchased less the proceeds of any fresh issue. Disclosure to the Registrar of Companies of particulars of shares purchased is required within 28 days.

Only a private company is given power to redeem or purchase its own shares out of *capital*.

Redemption or purchase by a private company of its own shares out of capital

A private company may, subject to the authority of its own articles, make a payment out of *capital* for the redemption or purchase of its own shares (S171, CA 1985). The purchases must be authorised by the company in general meeting by a special resolution approving the payment. The shares, the subject of the authorisation, are not voted for the purpose of the resolution.

Furthermore, the directors must give a statutory declaration of the continuing solvency of the company to which must be attached a report by the auditors of the company to the directors.

The *directors' statutory declaration* must specify the amount of the permissible capital payment and state that, having made full enquiries into the affairs and prospects of the company, they are of the opinion that:
  (a) there will be no ground on which the company could be found unable to pay its debts immediately after the payment is due to take place; *and*
  (b) the company will be able to continue its business as a going concern throughout the year immediately following the payment and will thus be able to pay its debts as they fall due.

The *auditors' report* attached to the directors' statutory declaration must state that:
  (a) they have inquired into the company's state of affairs;
  (b) the *permissible capital payment* as specified in the declaration has in their view been properly determined in accordance with the Act (CA 1981, S54) now S171(3) CA 1985; and
  (c) they are not aware of anything to indicate that the opinion expressed by the directors in the declaration is unreasonable.

The permissible capital payment

The amount which may be paid out of capital is equal to the price of redemption or purchase after deducting the *distributable profits* of the company *and* the proceeds of any fresh issue of shares made for the purposes of redemption or purchase.

Therefore, *before any payment out of capital made me made*, distributable profits* must first be *exhausted*.

Note: 'Distributable profits' are to be determined in accordance with Part 111 of the

Companies Act 1980 (see Chapter 5, GROWSTRONG plc Profit and Loss Account). Accounts sufficient to enable a reasonable judgement of the amount of the company's distributable profit must be prepared within the period of three months before the date of the directors' statutory declaration.

Example 4.1.8

ABC Ltd, a private limited company, having its balance sheet as under, makes a new issue of 10,000 ordinary £1 shares at £1.20p each to provide partly for the redemption of its redeemable share capital at a premium of 10%:

ABC Limited balance sheet
BEFORE REDEMPTION *(Extract)*

	£
Ordinary share capital of £1 each fully paid	50,000
Redeemable share capital, fully paid	20,000
Non-distributable reserve – share premium	10,000
	80,000
Distributable profit	3,000
Shareholders' funds	£83,000

Calculation of permissible capital payment:

	£	£
Price of redemption		22,000
Less: Proceeds of fresh issue	12,000	
Distributable profit	3,000	15,000
Permissible capital payment		£7,000

ABC Limited balance sheet
AFTER REDEMPTION *(Extract)*

	£
Ordinary share capital of £1 each fully paid (£50,000 plus nominal value of new issue £10,000)	60,000
Non-distributable reserve – share premium (£10,000 plus premium on new issue £2,000)	12,000
Capital redemption reserve*	1,000
Shareholders' funds	£73,000

*Note: The £83,000 shareholders' funds before redemption are increased by the capital proceeds of the new issue £12,000 to £95,000. When the cost of redemption is set against this, i.e. £22,000, the shareholders' funds fall to £73,000. As distributable profit must be exhausted, this gives rise to a non-distributable amount of £1,000 after accounting for the new issue of ordinary shares.

S54, CA 1981 (S171(3) CA 1985) indicates that once the purchase or redemption and any fresh issue have been made, the share capital and non-distributable reserves (share premium, capital redemption reserve and revaluation reserve) will be reduced by the permissible capital payment.

This means that if the premium (and any incidental costs) on redemption or purchase is less than distributable profits, then the difference must be transferred to capital redemption reserve, so that distributable profits are exhausted. In *Example 4.1.8* Distributable profits £3,000 less premium on redemption £2,000 = £1,000 to be transferred to capital redemption reserve.

Example 4.1.9

Assume the same starting balance sheet of ABC Limited as in *Example 4.1.8*, but that the redeemable share capital is redeemed at a premium of 20%; the same new issue of ordinary shares being made.

Calculation of permissible capital payment:

	£	£
Price of redemption		24,000
Less: Proceeds of fresh issue	12,000	
Distributable profit	3,000	15,000
Permissible capital payment		£9,000

ABC Limited balance sheet
AFTER REDEMPTION *(Extract)*

	£
Ordinary share capital of £1 each fully paid	60,000
Non-distributable reserve – share premium (£10,000 plus premium on new issue £2,000 less £1,000*)	11,000
Shareholders' funds	£71,000

Note: £83,000 original shareholders' funds plus £12,000 proceeds of new issue less cost of redemption £24,000 = £71,000. The distributable reserve is eliminated.

Following S171, CA 1985, when the premium on redemption (and any incidental costs) is greater than distributable profits, then the difference should be debited to fully paid share capital, capital redemption reserve, share premium account or revaluation reserve.

Safeguards for shareholders and creditors

Within a week following the passing of the resolution for payment out of capital for the redemption or purchase of its own shares, the company must publish a notice in the Gazette:

(a) stating the fact that such a resolution has been approved;
(b) specifying the amount of the permissible capital payment, together with the date of the resolution;
(c) stating that the directors' statutory declaration and related auditors' report (see above) can be inspected at its registered office, and
(d) that any creditor of the company may apply to the court within the five weeks immediately following the resolution for an order prohibiting the payment.

This notice must also be published in a national newspaper or given in writing to each of the company's creditors.

Members of the company who did not consent to, or vote in favour of, the resolution may also apply to the court in the same time span as creditors, for its cancellation. If the winding up of the company commences within one year of a payment out of capital for the redemption or purchase of its own shares, then the members whose shares were redeemed or purchased *and* the directors of the company who signed the statutory declaration may be liable to contribute to the assets of the company where these and all other contributions are insufficient to meet its liabilities.

The member whose shares were purchased or redeemed is liable to the extent that the payment out of capital relates to his shares.

Objectives and benefits of the power granted to companies to purchase their own shares (CA 1981)

These changes in company law were made by the Government with the principal objective of increasing investment in companies and thereby assisting their maintenance and development. In their consultative paper (1980) which presaged the changes they stated:

"For private companies, the changes . . . should make investment and participation in such companies more attractive, by providing shareholders with a further means of disposing of their shares and by permitting the remaining members to maintain control and ownership of the business.

Different considerations apply to a company whose shares are dealt in on a market. Public companies with surplus cash resources could find it useful to be able to buy their own shares and thus return surplus resources to shareholders, thereby removing the pressure on such companies to employ those surplus resources in uneconomic ways, and enabling shareholders to deploy their resources to better effect."

Potential benefits which will arise from the ability of a company to purchase or redeem its own shares include:

Private companies
1. Investment/participation in such companies is more attractive.
2. Shareholders have a further means of disposing of their shares while remaining members maintain ownership and control.
3. Holders of unquoted shares can more easily realise their value for whatever reason, e.g. family shareholders' representatives who need cash to pay capital transfer tax arising on death.
4. Dissident or apathetic shareholders can be bought-out contributing to more efficient management.
5. Family-owned companies may maintain control when a family shareholder with a significant holding dies or retires.
6. Employee share schemes in unlisted companies are boosted through the provision of this 'market'.
7. Easier for proprietors to seek equity investment from others.

Public companies
1. Companies over-capitalised, e.g. with surplus cash, can distribute the cash and at the same time contract their capital base of funds attributable to the shareholders; thus –
2. This could remove pressure on such companies to employ surplus funds uneconomically and enable shareholders to employ those funds to better effect.
3. A re-purchase may improve earnings and assets per share perhaps alleviating a weakness in the share price.
4. Capital structure is more flexible. Shares of one class can be bought out and shares of another class issued.

The related tax question

These changes in company law allow companies to purchase/redeem their own shares, with private companies being able to do this out of their capital, and were made with the principal objective of increasing investment in and thereby assisting with the maintenance and development of business. The related tax issue was whether, and to what extent, proceeds attributable to the purchase or redemption of shares would be recognised as 'capital' or 'income'.

The following summary sets out the general tax position following the *Finance Act 1982* and the Inland Revenue guidance. While company law legislation is aimed at the objective set out above, and is concerned that creditors and those dealing with the company are protected, tax legislation aims to complement company law but also has to minimise the possibility of tax avoidance.

The basic rule in these matters to which the *exceptions* of the Finance Act 1982 apply is given in the Income Tax Act 1970:

> "where a company buys its own shares and give consideration in excess of the amount originally subscribed for the shares, the excess is treated as a distribution so that:
> (i) the vendor is subject to income tax, and
> (ii) the company is required to pay ACT (Advance Corporation Tax – see Chapter 5) on the excess of the issue price over the average price."

The *exceptions* to the above basic rule apply mainly to *unquoted shares* in *trading companies* being:
  (i) shares *needed to be sold* (by personal representatives, legatees) to meet a capital transfer tax demand;
  (ii) shares purchased/redeemed by the company, *wholly or mainly* for the *benefit of the company's trade* and which do not form part of a tax-avoidance scheme. The shares must have been held for five years (three years in exceptional cases) by UK residents.

Noting that the last paragraph relates to the exceptions to *unquoted shares* in trading companies, the following types of companies could benefit:
  (i) private companies;
  (ii) unquoted public companies;
  (iii) public companies trading on the Unlisted Securities Market (USM) (see page 10) where the transaction is off-market, e.g. where the company makes a direct agreement with a vendor.

Where the exceptions apply and the Finance Act conditions are met:
  (i) the vendor is subject only to capital gains tax; and
  (ii) the company is not required to pay ACT.

On market purchase by a quoted company or a company whose shares are traded on the USM will attract (CGT) but not income tax in the hands of the vendor.

Some problems in relation to purchase/redemption of own shares by companies

The five-year shareholding period of potential vendors is a defect of the now freer market.

The requirement of a quoted company to pay ACT as well as the purchase price for the shares.

For all companies, where cash is the consideration and is borrowed for the purpose, there is a double-adverse effect on the capital gearing ratio which increases the risk for the remaining shareholders. It may be noted that given the Revenue's agreement on value, cash need not be the consideration, thus property, a division or a subsidiary, could be exchanged for shares if this was seen to enhance re-organisation schemes. Re-purchase may reduce a company's size to affect adversely its market standing. It will be weaker if the asset used as consideration was earning attractive income; stronger if the purchase price was, e.g. a loss-making division. The transaction must 'benefit the company's trade' if the tax advantages are to apply, pure tax-avoidance schemes are not acceptable.

4.2 RESERVES

The notes to the three categories of reserves in the GROWSTRONG consolidated balance sheet show the movements on them during the year, stating the source of any increase and the application of any decrease. Although there is no longer any legal need to distinguish reserves as either 'capital reserves' or 'revenue reserves', many companies have continued to do so and may choose to elaborate the permitted formats of balance sheets under the Companies Act 1981 accordingly.

The distinction informs shareholders and others dealing with the company of those reserves which are available for distribution (revenue reserves) and those which are not (capital reserves).

Of GROWSTRONG's reserves, the share premium account and the revaluation reserve are *statutory* capital reserves, i.e. required by law, while the profit and loss account balance, being the retained after-tax profits of the group are, by nature, revenue.

The descriptions 'non-distributable reserves' and 'distributable reserves' are displacing those of 'capital' and 'revenue' reserves.

Share premium account

Section 56, Companies Act 1948 (S130(1)–(3) CA 1985), requires that where shares are issued in excess of their nominal value, the excess must be credited to a share premium account.* GROWSTRONG's shares, of a nominal value of 50p each, were issued at 70p. 20p per share was therefore credited to share premium account.

The uses of this account are set out in the Act. It cannot be distributed to the shareholders of a going concern. It may be used:

(i) to provide for the paying up of shares for distribution to the shareholders as a bonus issue (as previously described), or

(ii) to write off the expenses of forming a company (preliminary expenses), the expenses and commissions of issuing share or loan capital, or to provide for a premium on the redemption of redeemable shares or loan capital.

(iii) as it has been shown (*Example 4.1.9*), where a private company purchases or redeems its own shares out of capital, the share capital and undistributable reserves (share premium account, capital redemption reserve and revaluation reserve) will be reduced by the permissible capital payment. (CA 1985 S171(3), 181.)

The share premium account is therefore regarded effectively as part of the paid up share capital of the company which is a going concern and would be so regarded by the Court in any scheme for the reduction of the company's capital. These legal provisions preclude the use of the share premium account for the immediate write off of goodwill (SSAP 22).

Capital redemption reserve

The uses of this second example of a *statutory* capital reserve have been described and exemplified in the previous section (4.1).

Revaluation reserve

Apart from the statutory reserves, a company may decide to designate other reserves as non-distributable. For example, some companies recognising the inadequacy of their depreciation

---

* Shares may be issued for cash, or other consideration (e.g. in acquisitions or mergers where shares in one company are exchanged for shares in another). The effect of a recent tax case, *Shearer v. Bercain* (1980) on the need to establish a non-distributable share premium account following mergers of companies by way of share exchange, has been resolved by the CA 1981. This is dealt with later in a section on acquisitions and mergers.

provisions based on the historical cost of certain fixed assets (e.g. plant) in an inflationary period, have appropriated additional (after tax) profits to a non-distributable reserve (*plant replacement reserve*) to provide for the enhanced cost of replacement.

As the source of this reserve is profit (revenue) there is no *legal* bar to the use of this reserve for dividend purposes: however, so long as inflation pertains, it would be imprudent so to do and thus the reserve is recognised and often labelled as a capital (non-distributable) one.

Companies can, if they wish, restrict the distribution of non-statutory 'capital' reserves through their Articles of Association.

GROWSTRONG's *Revaluation Reserve* is the surplus arising from its periodic upward revaluation of its properties. The fixed asset – property – account is debited and this reserve credited. As these surpluses are unrealised amounts and clearly have no place in the profit and loss account, this transaction is a major exception to the requirement of SSAP 6 (see below) banning 'reserve accounting', in that all profits (and losses) be dealt with through the profit and loss account.

The Companies Act 1981, by introducing valuation rules other than the use of historical cost accounting, had given statutory recognition to the above practice, and thus to the Revaluation Reserve. The Act required that this reserve must be disclosed in the place indicated in the balance sheet formats (as in *Table 3*) although it need not be shown under that name. This presumably means that although the fundamental nature of the reserve is that of a revaluation reserve, it may have a different description, (see 4 Sch. 34 CA 1985).

The Act bans any transfer from the reserve to profit and loss account unless:

(a) it was previously charged to that account (see comment above re plant replacement reserve); or

(b) it represents *realised* profit.

Note: The 1981 Act (para 91 4 Sch. CA 1985) has made it clear that its use of the expression 'realised profits' in relation to a company's accounts "is in reference to such profits . . . (derived from) . . . accounts (based on) . . . principles generally accepted".

This important legal statement meets the concern of professional bodies that the term 'realised profits' should not be interpreted in a narrow legal sense. It may be seen as increasing the need for, and importance of, accounting standards.

The tax implications of amounts credited or debited to the revaluation reserve must be explained in a note to the accounts (see also Chapter 5.6 (ED 36)).

The above comments on the CA 1981 valuation rules and the revaluation reserve do not apply to supplementary current cost accounts which were governed solely by SSAP 16.

The DTI has indicated (subject to the Court ruling otherwise) its belief that it would not be legal to use the Revaluation reserve to write off goodwill (see SSAP 22) either in the company's accounts or on consolidation.

Revenue reserves

These represent *undistributed profits*, retained after providing for all expenses, interest, taxation and (any) preference dividend. They accrue to the *ordinary shareholders* and effectively increase their investment in the company.

The CA 1981 balance sheet formats require that the balance of profit retained within the *profit and loss account* be separately distinguished under that heading, as in the GROWSTRONG balance sheet.

Companies may and do appropriate after-tax profits to variously designated reserve accounts. One example, already given in this section, is the plant replacement reserve, created for a particular non-distributable purpose.

Another example would be a 'general revenue reserve' which in essence would be no different from the profit and loss account balance. Both are revenue reserves and available for distribution as dividends to shareholders. A further example would be a 'dividend equalisation reserve' created to smooth dividends through periods of fluctuating profitability.

Such reserves will be shown under the heading 'Other Reserves' within the CA 1981 balance sheet format. GROWSTRONG's balance sheet entry under the heading 'Profit and Loss account' represents the credit balance at the start of the year increased by the retained profit of the parent company and its share of the retained profit of subsidiary and associated companies for the year.

Movements on reserves

The CA 1981 reinforced previous company law requiring publication of information with the accounts showing the movements on various reserves, including to and from profit and loss account (which have to be shown on the face of that account), stating the source of any increase and the application of any decrease. This is to ensure that there should be little doubt in the minds of readers of the corporate report as to the level of profitability for the year and the source of dividends. In a poor year for profitability, it is quite proper to decide to draw on reserves of past profit in order to maintain dividends. The purpose of the Act is to require information to be published showing that this has been done (see also Chapter 5.6, ED 36).

SSAP 6 – Extraordinary items and prior year adjustments

The publication of this Standard enhances this rule, by requiring that, with few exceptions, all profits and losses, whether normal operating items of extraordinary items, be dealt with through the profit and loss account. Thus was outlawed the practice of 'reserve accounting', where adjustments were made directly against reserves in an attempt to conceal the true operating results.

Company law further states that reserves must be distinguished from provisions for known liabilities including depreciation provisions and amounts set aside to prevent undue fluctuations in charges for taxation, each of these items needing to be separately dealt with. A review of SSAP 6 resulted in the issue of a new draft standard – ED 36 – in January 1985. This left the fundamental principles of SSAP·6 unchanged. See Chapter 5.6 for detailed commentary.

4.3 MINORITY INTERESTS

This entry in the GROWSTRONG consolidated balance sheet arises because its interest in a subsidiary company results from holding a majority, but less than all of the equity share capital of that company, i.e. the subsidiary is partly and not wholly owned.

In these circumstances, it is the practice to bring ALL the net assets of the subsidiary into the consolidated balance sheet, balanced by an entry on the funds (or liabilities) side, recognising the extent of the Minority shareholders' interest in them.

Similarly, in the consolidated profit and loss account (*Table 4* for that of GROW-STRONG), the whole of the subsidiary's profit (or loss) for the year is brought in, subject to a transfer therefrom, to the Minority Interest account of their proportion of their company's profit after tax.

Example 4.3.1

Company X acquires 60% of the ordinary shares of Company Y for £100,000. On the date when Y became a *partly owned* subsidiary of X, their respective balance sheets were summarised as follows:

Balance sheet of Company X as at the date
of acquisition of control in Company Y

	£		£
Share capital and reserves	1,000,000	Net Assets (Gross Assets less all liabilities)	900,000
		Investment in Y at cost (60% interest)	100,000
	£1,000,000		£1,000,000

Balance sheet of Company Y at date of
acquisition of control by Company X

	£		£
Ordinary share capital and reserves	150,000	Net Assets	150,000

The consolidated balance sheet of the parent (X) company and subsidiary (Y) would appear:

Balance sheet (consolidated) of companies
X and Y at the date of acquisition

	£		£
Share capital and reserves (X)	1,000,000	Net assets (X)	900,000
		Net assets (Y)	150,000
			1,050,000
Minority Interest**	60,000	Goodwill*	10,000
	£1,060,000		£1,060,000

*Goodwill = Purchase price paid for the shares less the value of the net assets acquired
= £100,000 less 60% × £150,000 = *£10,000*
(Goodwill is discussed further in this Chapter at 4.6.)
**Minority Interest = 40% of the net assets of Y = 40% of Y's ordinary share capital and reserves
= 40% × £150,000 = £60,000.

Note: Since the EEC Fourth Directive does not specifically deal with group accounts, the entry 'Minority Interest' is an example of an item which is not covered by the CA 1981 balance sheet formats.

4.4 LOAN CAPITAL

The heading "Creditors: amounts falling due after more than one year", is a mandatory requirement of the CA 1981 balance sheet format. The note 4 to the GROWSTRONG plc consolidated balance sheet (*Table 3*) gives the detail of the debenture loan and bank loan required by the Companies Acts 1967 and 1981 and the Stock Exchange listing agreement. It discloses that the £250,000 outstanding represents:

10% debentures, secured by a floating charge, redeemable in annual instalments of £50,000 commencing with a first instalment on the first day of the current accounting year.

The CA 1981 required 'current instalments due on loans' to be quantified under the heading "Creditors: amounts falling due within one year", and a perusal of GROWSTRONG's note 9 to its end of year balance sheet shows the debenture instalment of £50,000, payable on the day following the balance sheet date, i.e. the first day of the next accounting year.

Similarly, the amount of the bank loan outstanding at balance sheet date is shown as to £40,000 under heading note 4, and £10,000 due as a current liability under note 9.

These distinctions are helpful to an analyst considering the group's liquidity position, who would note that no new loan or share capital having been raised for the purpose, both loans are being paid out of internal resources.

The Companies Act 1967 required, inter alia, separate information to be disclosed on:

Bank loans and overdrafts, in aggregate.
Other loans repayable wholly or in part, more than 5 years from the date of the balance sheet, in aggregate.
Other loans, wholly repayable within 5 years, in aggregate.

The *Stock Exchange Listing Agreement* requires disclosure of information separately for bank loans and 'other borrowings', e.g. debentures, showing amounts due between 'one and two' years, between 'two and five years' and 'after five years'.

GROWSTRONG shows this information.

The CA 1981 required that information which was given in the directors' report, detailing debentures allotted or issued during the year, be given now as a note to the accounts.

(*Note:* Sch. 4 CA 1985 S228 individual accounts S230 group accounts now incorporates the legislation governing the form and content of accounts.)

Charges on assets

A company's *power to borrow* must be stated in its Memorandum of Association and *the limit of that borrowing* in its Articles of Association. This is a protection to creditors and lenders, apart from any security afforded the latter under the loan contract. That security may be by way of a *fixed charge* or a *floating charge* on a company's assets.

The *fixed charge* identifies specified assets (e.g. property) as security for the loan. The company is then precluded from disposing of the asset without the consent of the lender. In default of paying the due interest or in repaying the capital, the lender can, subject to the contract, foreclose on the property (i.e. sell it, repaying himself from the proceeds, accounting to the company for any surplus, or if a deficit, ranking for that amount as an unsecured creditor in a winding up of the company) or appoint a receiver to manage the assets in the interests of the lender.

The *floating charge* does not specify particular assets for security, but 'floats over' them, as it were, as they change from day-to-day in the normal operation of the business. The lender has no legal interest in them, and thus more conveniently than with the fixed charge, the company can deal with them in the ordinary course of business. The floating charge crystallises into a fixed charge on the happening of events specified in the loan contract, e.g. failure to pay interest or to repay capital, or the company exceeding its borrowing powers or going into liquidation.

Debentures

While the description '*Debenture loan*' is sometimes used generally to indicate longer term loans to companies, it usually connotes that the loan is *secured. Unsecured loan stock* is the description of loans not secured (sometimes the secured debenture is referred to as a '*Mortgage debenture*' and the unsecured loan as 'Unsecured notes'). Unsecured loan stock would probably be successfully issued only by large companies, with the added risk to the lenders recognised in the higher level of interest required. The inherent asset strength of the company and the lenders' priority over the shareholders in respect of these assets being regarded as sufficient security in itself.

Trustee for debenture holders

Where the debenture or loan stock is to be issued publicly, and is to be listed on the Stock Exchange, a trustee or trustees are appointed to act for the wide spread of lenders and a trust deed is entered into in place of the loan contract. In these circumstances, one of the trustees must be a trust corporation completely independent of the borrowing company. Among other conditions, the trust deed may restrict or preclude a company from further borrowing.

Debentures or loan stock are usually issued in larger units than shares, often in £100 units.

Convertible debentures

These and the more usual convertible loan stock provide the holders with the right to choose to take shares of the company at repayment dates instead of cash. For the lenders there is thus a combination of the security of a reasonably safe return, with in due course, the potential advantage of equity holding. The investor comes in with the status of creditor and retains that relationship with the company until redemption when, depending on his view of the standing of the ordinary shares, he can opt for a cash repayment or an equivalent value of shares.

Institutional lenders

A high proportion of the debentures and loan stock of listed companies is held by the institutional investors, e.g. pension funds. The convertible unsecured loan stock which usually carries a lower interest coupon than other unsecured loan stock, has proved particularly attractive to them because of its deferred equity status.

Loan interest – an expense

It should be noted that the fixed debenture/loan interest is a contractual expense which must be paid whether or not profits are earned. This contrasts with the fixed preference dividend which may only be paid out of profits.

The loan interest is a *charge* against the company's income and an allowable expense for tax purposes, whereas the preference dividend is an *appropriation* of taxed profit and a distribution of income to a member of the company.

The debenture holder is, of course, a creditor of the company, secured or unsecured. In a liquidation of the company secured creditors and unsecured creditors rank before any class of shareholder, including preference shareholders.

The tax factor is attractive to a company wishing to raise long-term loan capital. GROWSTRONG's 10% Debenture, with corporation tax at 35% would only cost 6.5% (10% × 65% = 6.5%). And, in an inflationary period, a further gain accrues to the company as it will repay the fixed monetary loan at some future time in reduced real monetary terms. An equal 10% gross return to a preference shareholder would, with a tax credit equal to the basic rate of tax (30%), require a 7% dividend payment.

The objective of borrowing is to provide long-term funds for use in the business. If this use brings a return on capital which exceeds the cost of borrowing, then this will provide an increase in the profit available to the ordinary shareholders. This practice is sometimes called *'trading on the equity'*.

Limitations to borrowing

There are limitations, however, to the amount that a company can or will want to borrow. As already mentioned, a limit is fixed by the Articles of Association and a limit is set by current lenders in the trust deed covering their loan. Limitations from the lenders' and company's viewpoints are:

From the lenders' viewpoint: The 'cover' available for the loan interest. The 'cover' available for the loan capital. The loans already made to the company and the ranking of those loans against the security of the assets available (prior claims). The company's current and future prospects linked to environmental factors, e.g. level of inflation, and level of interest rates generally.

From the company's viewpoint: The volatility of the environment of business and the related levels of profitability and interest rates and the company's likely ability to meet the loan interest and provide for the repayment of the loans.

While the loans are commonly 'rolled over', i.e. a new loan, or issue of shares, is intended to 'fund' the repayment of the old, the ability of the company to raise new funds will depend on its ability to meet new loan terms and on the lenders' view of that factor.

Capital gearing

From the company shareholders' point of view, borrowing introduces a further element in the assessment of the degree of risk involved in the investment in ordinary shares. This is because the loan interest is a prior charge on profits.

Capital gearing is the relationship of a company's borrowed capital (debentures, unsecured loan stock, preference shares) to the ordinary shareholders' interest or equity (nominal share capital plus reserves).

This *Gearing Ratio* is commonly expressed as:

$$D : DE$$

where D represents 'Debt' or Loan capital and E represents Equity.

Where the company's bank overdraft is of material significance and continues year after year despite its 'current liability' status, it would be included in 'D'.

The *Debt/Equity ratio* is commonly expressed as:

$$D : E$$

The latter is a more significant measure of the risk for the lenders and the risk/potential gains for the equity. The Americans use the word *'leverage'* to describe the Debt/Equity ratio.

While reserves are included in 'equity', it is usual for any 'Goodwill' included as an asset in the accounts to be deducted therefrom.

Where the company's securities (shares and loan capital) are quoted on the Stock Exchange, an alternative assessment of gearing can be made using the relative market values.

The *fixed interest lender* is concerned with the security of his investment, i.e. the *cover for his interest* by the profits of the company, and the *cover for his capital* by that of the company, as well as the *yield* from his investment.

Interest cover is expressed as:

$$\frac{\text{Profit before interest and tax}}{\text{interest}}$$

Interest is stated 'gross'.

This calculation gives the number of times the interest is covered by profit available.

If there are loans with prior security to the loan in question, then the interest cover can be calculated on a *rolled over* basis, and the interest cover would be the number of times its interest plus the interest on the priority loans is covered by profits before all interest and taxation.

Loan capital cover is expressed as:

$$\frac{\text{Total Long-term capital (D plus E)}}{\text{Loan capital}}$$

Preference share capital would be included in the numerator but not in the denominator, because of the prior status of the loan capital (as creditor) over the (Preference) shareholders.

If there are different ranking loans, e.g. unsecured loan stock and debentures (secured), the more conservative 'rolled over' basis of cover is usually used:

$$\frac{\text{Total Long-term capital (D plus E)}}{\text{Loan stock capital in question plus all PRIOR ranking loans}}$$

Again, preference share capital would be included in the numerator but not in the denominator.

Preference share capital cover is expressed as:

$$\frac{\text{Ordinary share capital plus reserves plus preference capital}}{\text{Preference Share Capital}}$$

based on the Preference shareholders' priority to a return of capital in a liquidation of their company.

For *Preference dividend cover and yields*, see page 55.

Loan interest yields

The *basic yield* is the return represented by the annual income, expressed as a percentage of the price paid for the investment.

As a general rule all investors must expect to pay for a higher degree of security of capital by accepting a lower yield. If a high yield is required, the investor must expect to run a greater risk of loss or depreciation of capital. The possibility of capital gain by selling the stock (net of expenses) at a price higher than paid must also enter the investment consideration.

The 8% Debenture Holder (see *Example 4.4.1* following) who bought his £100 stock at £95 has a yield of 8.42% (i.e. 8%/0.95). This is *the basic or running yield* as would apply if no redemption date was set for the security (i.e. it would be an *irredeemable debenture, and would need to be quoted). Where the debenture is redeemable at a fixed date or within a given period, the gross redemption yield* can be calculated taking into account the stream of future income plus/minus any capital gain/loss on redemption in relation to the present market price for the security (or the particular price paid by the lender).

Highly geared capital structure

A company is said to be *highly geared* when it has a high ratio of fixed return capital to equity.

The ordinary shares in a highly geared capital structure are more speculative than in other cases. Any rise or fall in the profit before interest and tax wil result in a larger percentage alteration in the return for equity. Consequently the rate of dividend may be subject to wide fluctuations.

Lowly geared capital structure

A company with such a structure would be predominantly financed by equity.

Example 4.4.1

Examples of differing long-term capital structures

Each company, X, Y and Z has long-term capital of £100,000 structured as follows:

Companies		X £	Y £	Z £
Ordinary shares of £1		60,000	50,000	30,000
Reserves		40,000	30,000	10,000
Equity	E	100,000	80,000	40,000
6% preference shares ⎱	D	—	20,000	20,000
8% debentures ⎰		—	—	40,000
Total long-term capital		100,000	100,000	100,000
Gearing description		None	Low	High
Gearing ratio D : DE		Nil	20%	60%
Debt: Equity ratio D : E		Nil	25%	150%

It will be seen that D : E is the sharper indication of capital structure. In general, a D : E of 50% (Gearing 33%) would be regarded as reasonable. The actual gearing of a particular company will be the outcome of the views of prospective lenders on the level of risk/security and return involved, and of the borrowers of their ability to utilise successfully the long-term loans to the advantage of the ordinary shareholder. For example, a property company with a high level of fixed assets, steady income and small working capital requirements will readily attract fixed interest capital and will probably be highly geared.

Example 4.4.1 (continued)

Capital cover

	Y	Z
Preference share capital cover	5 times	3 times
	(100/20)	(60/20)
Debenture loan cover		2.5 times
		(100/40)

The debentures (creditors) rank before preference shareholders in any liquidation of the company.

The preference shareholders in Y would regard themselves as well covered, but accept a higher risk in company Z.

The debenture holders' (Z) cover is on the low side compared with normal expectations if the security is by a 'floating charge', but much would depend on the realisability of the 'floating assets' in a liquidation. If the security is a fixed charge, say on property, then the cover would be ample. Prospective lenders will, of course, compare covers (of interest and capital) of alternative investments before committing themselves.

Assuming that each company earns 30% before interest and tax on the capital of £100,000, the profit and loss accounts would be:

	X £	Y £	Z £
Profit (Earnings) before interest and tax (EBIT)	30,000	30,000	30,000
Debenture interest	—	—	3,200
Profit before tax	30,000	30,000	26,800
Corporation tax (assumed 50%)	15,000	15,000	13,400
Profit after tax	15,000	15,000	13,400
Preference dividend	—	1,200	1,200
Profit after tax attributable to Equity (Earnings-members)	£15,000	£13,800	£12,200
Earnings per ordinary share (EPS)	25p	27.6p	40.7p
Return on the book value of the ordinary shareholders' interest	15%	17.25%	30.5%

The earnings per (ordinary) share and the percentage return on the book value of equity rise in each case (of Y and Z compared with X) because of the increasing use of debt. This is because the earnings before interest and tax (EBIT) exceed the weighted cost of fixed capital before tax.

Example 4.4.1 (continued)

Use of debt to increase 'Earnings'

	X	Y	Z
Earnings before interest and tax (EBIT) on £100,000 capital	30%	30%	30%
Weighted cost of fixed capital before tax	—	12%*	9.3%**
Excess of EBIT over weighted cost of fixed capital before tax	—	18%	20.66%

*Company Y.   Cost of preference dividend *before* corporation tax (50%) =
  $6 \times 100/50 \times £20,000 = £2,400$.
  Weighted cost of fixed capital = £2,400/£20,000 = 12%
**Company Z.   Cost of preference dividend before
      corporation tax (50%)   =   £2,400 (above Y)
      Cost of debenture interest before
      corporation tax (50%)   =   £3,200
      Total of fixed capital cost before tax   =   £5,600
      Total of fixed capital   =   £60,000
  Weighted cost of fixed capital = £5,600/£60,000   =   9.3%

Proof: In *Company X*, because there is no gearing, the 30% EBIT is accrued entirely to the ordinary shareholders' capital £100,000, i.e. £30,000 before tax, and after tax of 50% = *£15,000.*
  Earnings per share (EPS) 25p (£15,000/60,000).

In *Company Y* the 30% EBIT on the ordinary shareholders' capital £80,000 equals £24,000 before tax, to which must be added the excess of EBIT over the weighted cost of fixed capital before tax, 18% (above) on £20,000 equals *£3,600* before tax. Thus the total earnings for Equity before tax equals *£27,600* being *£13,800* after tax.
  Earnings per share (EPS) 27.6p (£13,800/50,000).

In *Company Z*, the weighted cost of fixed capital 9.33% is appreciably less than that of Company Y, and with the same EBIT, the EPS for the ordinary shareholder is even higher.

The 30% EBIT on the ordinary shareholders' capital £40,000 equals £12,000 before tax to which must be added the excess of EBIT over the weighted cost of fixed capital before tax, 20.66% (above) on £60,000 equals *£12,400* before tax. Thus the total earnings for Equity before tax equals *£24,400 being £12,200* after tax.

Earnings per share (EPS) 40.7p (£12,200/30,000).

Effect of a material fall in earnings

Assuming that Earnings before interest and tax (EBIT) for each company fall by 60% from £30,000 to £12,000, i.e. to 12% on the total long-term capital of £100,000 each employs. What is the effect on Equity?

Example 4.4.2

Companies	X	Y	Z
	£	£	£
Earnings before interest and tax (EBIT)	12,000	12,000	12,000
Debenture interest	—	—	3,200
Profit before tax	12,000	12,000	8,800
Tax (assumed 50%)	6,000	6,000	4,400
Profit after tax	6,000	6,000	4,400
Preference dividend	—	1,200	1,200
Profit after tax attributable to Equity (EARNINGS)	6,000	4,800	3,200
Earnings per ordinary share (EPS)	10p	9.6p	10.7p
Return on Equity	6%	6%	8%
Percentage fall in return on Equity (Fall in EBIT = 60%)	60%	65.2%	73.8%

For *Company X*, having no gearing, the 60% fall in EBIT results also in a 60% fall in Earnings per share, and a 60% fall in the return on equity. For *Company Y*, where EBIT on the total long-term capital employed and the cost of fixed capital (before tax) are the same, 12%, there is no gain or loss on the borrowed capital, so that the return on equity is also 12% (6% after tax). Because Y is effectively now earning on a smaller capital base (on equity of £80,000 only), the 60% fall in EBIT results in a higher fall in the return on equity, i.e. by 65.2%, and this is reflected in the fall in EPS.

For *Company Z*, the *highly geared company*, the percentage fall in the return on equity is more drastic, the 60% fall in EBIT resulting in a fall of 73.8%, which is also the fall in the EPS.

Risk to Equity of a highly geared structure

The percentage fall in the return on equity in the three companies, 60%, 65.2% and 73.8% respectively from the same 60% fall in EBIT, demonstrates the more speculative nature of ordinary shares in a highly geared company. In the recent depression it has led to the liquidation of many, debt-ridden companies. And some survivors have had to forego payments of, or reduce the level of, the payment of dividends. It should also be noted that, in profitable times, a high proportion of the after-tax equity profit is retained in the company

77

as additional investment, and this policy, too, is eroded by falling profits, more particularly for highly geared ones. When these (historic) profits are further reduced by inflationary costs, the position becomes more critical.

It may be concluded that high gearing of capital is increasingly advantageous to Equity as profits rise above the weighted cost of fixed capital, but equally it is dangerous when the trend reverses and profits fall drastically and continuously.

Preference dividend cover		
Companies	Y	Z
(Profit after tax/preference dividend)		
When EBIT was £30,000	12.5 times	11.2 times
When EBIT was £12,000	5.0 times	3.7 times
Interest cover		
(Profit before interest and tax/interest)	Y	Z
When EBIT was £30,000	—	9.4 times
When EBIT was £12,000	—	3.8 times

The covers are ample when EBIT is £30,000, but in company Z both preference shareholders and the debenture holders would be concerned, particularly if the fall in profitability was to continue. Although at 3.7 times and 3.8 times covered respectively the cover for the preference shares and debentures appears to be on a par, the position of the former is worse, as their dividend may be passed (not recommended by the directors) and as their shares are non-cumulative, would be lost. The interest to the debenture holder is a contractual expense which the company must meet, or suffer the penalty laid down in the contract or deed.

4.5 DEFERRED TAXATION

Presentation of 'Deferred tax' in the balance sheet

Statement of Standard Accounting Practice 15 'Accounting for deferred taxation' requires that deferred taxation account balances should be shown separately in the balance sheet notes, described as 'deferred taxation' and should *not* be shown as part of the shareholders' funds. A note in the financial statements should indicate the *nature* and amount of the *major elements* of which the net balance is composed, a description of the method of calculation adopted, and the period or periods of time within which it is likely to crystallise. Transfers to and from deferred tax should be declared in the note.

Provision made for deferred tax

Note 5 to the GROWSTRONG plc balance sheet (*Table 3*) shows the balance of the deferred taxation account under the heading 'Provision for liabilities and charges' (CA 1981) and explains that the *provision made* and shown is in respect of miscellaneous *timing differences accounted for* at the balance sheet date, less *advance corporation tax recoverable* (ACT).

Note to the accounts in respect of POTENTIAL liability

The note goes on to state the figure of deferred taxation for which *no provision* has been made in the accounts because, in the opinion of the directors, no liability will arise in the *foreseeable future*. This is because they believe that levels of capital expenditure are expected to be adequate enough to ensure that corporation tax deferred by *accelerated capital allowances* will continue in the present form. They base their decision upon the provisions of SSAP 15.

They identify the *potential* amounts for which *no provision* has been made, as required by the standard, as:

Deferred charges – Deferments due to accelerated capital allowances.
– Corporation tax on capital gains arising should the revaluation surplus on properties be realised.

Note: Following the Finance Act 1981, *stock appreciation relief* was no longer regarded as a *reversible timing difference* (as defined by SSAP 15) and would not normally enter into the potential liability requiring disclosure in the accounts. The relief was finally abolished in the 1984 budget.

Tutorial Notes
The tutorial notes which follow set out explanations of items included in the above note to the GROWSTRONG balance sheet.

Timing differences

The main reason for a company to operate a system of accounting for deferred taxation is to enable fluctuations in the *profit after tax figure* (P & L account), caused by *timing differences*, to be eliminated.

As the 'Earnings' figure (profit after tax attributable to Equity) is used to provide the significant 'earnings per share' (EPS) indicator, it is important to ensure that these fluctuations should not be allowed to impair the proper appreciation of the year's profit. Deferred taxation is, in essence, the taxation attributable to timing differences. These are differences between profits as computed for *taxation* purposes and profits computed for and stated in *financial statements*, because of items which are included in the financial statements of a period different from that in which they are dealt with for taxation.

These items are *capable of reversal* in one or more subsequent periods. A main category of timing difference is:

'the availability of capital allowances in taxation computations which are in excess of the related depreciation charges (on fixed assets) in the financial statements.'

Differences due to capital allowances

The *capital allowance* is the statutory amount allowed by the Inland Revenue for depreciation. The depreciation policy of the company is ignored for tax purposes and the depreciation charged in the accounts is added back by the Revenue in the calculation of *taxable profits*. The actual capital and other allowances change from time to time depending on the political and economic objectives of government policies.

In respect of plant and machinery, for example, purchased since March 1972, there was available a 'first year capital allowance' of 100%. Its intention was obviously to encourage capital investment. (See page 83 on the gradual withdrawal of FYA.)

A company whose depreciation policy is to write off capital expenditure on plant over 5 years at 20% per annum, for which it claimed the 100% first year allowance (FYA) will, unless it operates a system of deferred taxation, show a much greater 'profit after tax' (Earnings) figure in the first year, than in the subsequent four years, and none of the five years will show 'the true and fair view' of the financial accounts based on the company's depreciation policy.

Example 4.5.1

Company X with 1 million ordinary shares of £1 in issue and fully paid, earns £600,000 before charging depreciation and taxation for each of the first five years of its operations. It purchased plant and machinery in year 1 for £500,000 which it intends to write off over 5 years on 'the straight line' base of 20% per annum. It claims the 100% FYA on the purchase. Corporation tax is taken at 50%.

The true trading position

The company's *true* trading position is unchanged in each of the five years and given that the depreciation charge and the capital allowance were the same, would properly be reported as:

(A) Profit before tax	£500,000
Corporation tax (50%)	25,000*
Profit after tax	£250,000
Earnings per share	25p

*£600,000 less £100,000 depreciation = £500,000 × 50%
(*Note:* The total tax payable in the five years is £1.25 million.)

Example 4.5.1 (continued)

The company's position for the five years based on the actual corporation tax payable in each year, based on the receipt of the 100% FYA on capital expenditure would be as follows:

(B) *First year*	Profit before tax	£500,000
	Corporation tax	50,000*
	Profit after tax	£450,000
	Earnings per share	45p
Second to fifth year inclusive	Profit before tax	£500,000
	Corporation tax	300,000**
	Profit after tax	£200,000
	Earnings per share	20p

*£600,000 profit before tax (depreciation £100,000 added back) less FYA £500,000 = £100,000 taxable profit × 50% = £50,000.
**£600,000 profit before tax with no capital allowances (all given in FYA) × 50% = £300,000.
(*Note:* The total tax payable in the five years is unchanged (from A) at £1.25 million.)

Example 4.5.1 (continued)

The Deferred tax account

To bridge the gap between the true version needed to be reported in each of the five years (A) and the materially different versions (B), the Deferred tax account is operated.

The difference between the corporation tax actually payable (B) and that which would have been paid if the capital allowances were in line with the company's depreciation policy (A), is transferred (credited) in the year of the expenditure to the deferred tax account.

In this example, this difference is £200,000.

Example 4.5.1 (continued)

Entries in the published accounts

In *year 1*, the extract from the profit and loss account would be published as in (A). The note to the accounts would state:

Corporation tax payable	£ 50,000
Credit to Deferred tax	£200,000*
Taxation charged in P & L	£250,000

*And shown in the balance sheet.

In *years 2 to 5*, the extract from the profit and loss account would be published as in (A). The note to the accounts would reflect the *reversal of the timing differences* between the greater amount of corporation tax required to be paid (B) in the second to fifth years – £300,000, and the corporation tax charge shown in the published accounts (A) £250,000, i.e. £50,000. It would read:

Corporation tax payable	£300,000
Less (debit) from deferred tax	50,000
Taxation charged in P & L	£250,000

At the end of the fifth year, the deferred tax account would be reduced to a NIL balance, the £200,000 credit in the first year being offset by the annual debits of £50,000 in years two to five.

Although not affecting the principle of deferred tax as illustrated in *Example 4.5.1*, the Finance Act 1984 major tax changes (see end of this section) includes the phasing out of 100% first year allowances and provide a fresh impact on accounting for it.

Other timing differences

(1) *Short-term timing differences* arise from the use of the cash (receipts and payments) basis for computing tax and the accruals (income and expenditure) basis used in accounting. These differences normally reverse in the next accounting period and deferred taxation is accounted for on all of them.

(2) *Revaluations and disposals of fixed assets.* Tax does *not* arise when a fixed asset (e.g. property) is revalued. It normally arises on the *disposal* of the asset at a price exceeding original cost or tax written down value where *no roll-over relief* is available. No tax, current or deferred, is necessary until the company decides to sell the asset. Until that decision, the whole revaluation surplus may be credited to revaluation reserve.

(*Note:* CA 1981 required that the tax implications of amounts credited or debited to revaluation reserve must be explained in a note to the accounts.)

Roll-over relief arises when a company sells an asset at a profit and replaces it by purchasing another asset and elects to have the profit on disposal deducted from the cost price of the new asset, instead of paying tax on it.

Provision for taxation payable on the disposal of a fixed asset whch has been revalued is not made as a charge on profit and loss account, but out of the revaluation surplus credited to a reserve account. The tax provided in this way is credited to Deferred Tax account at the time the company decides to dispose of the asset (but only in the absence of roll-over relief).

Example 4.5.2

Company X revalues property from its original cost of £150,000 to £200,000. Assuming that the tax payable on the gain (when the asset is sold) is £15,000 (30% × £50,000), then the following entries would be made in the accounts (assuming no roll-over):

	£
Debit (add to value) Property)	50,000
Credit, Deferred Tax account	15,000
Credit, Revaluation reserve	35,000

Advance corporation tax recoverable

Companies are charged to corporation tax at a single rate on their taxable income, whether the income is distributed or not. In the absence of a dividend, the whole of the tax is payable on a date which may be a year or more after the end of the relevant accounting period. When a company makes a distribution (e.g. pays a dividend) it is required to make an *advance payment of corporation tax* (ACT) to the Inland Revenue. This ACT will normally be set off against the company's total liability for corporation tax on its income of the same accounting period. The resultant net liability is known as the *mainstream corporation tax*. The charge for corporation tax, therefore, comprises the mainstream corporation tax and the ACT.

ACT on *dividends paid* will either have been paid by the balance sheet date, or will be due for payment shortly afterwards. Where the ACT is regarded as recoverable, then it will normally be deducted from the full corporation tax charge based on the profit of the period in arriving at the mainstream corporation tax liability *shown in the balance sheet*.

In the case of *dividends proposed* but not paid at balance sheet date, the related ACT will become due for payment at the end of the quarter in which the dividend is paid and is shown in the balance sheet as a current liability (CA 1981: Creditors, amounts falling due within one year).

The right of set-off, however (assuming the ACT is recoverable) will not arise for at least 21 months from the balance sheet date, being given against the corporation tax on the profits of the accounting period in which the dividend is paid.

Where there exists a deferred tax account credit balance, the recoverable ACT can be deducted therefrom, as here with the GROWSTRONG accounts. This deduction properly reflects the difference in timing of payments brought about by ACT.

Where there is no deferred taxation account, the right to recover the ACT is in the nature of a *deferred asset*. The CA 1981 balance sheet format requires that where assets are not fixed assets as defined by the Act (intended for use on a continuing basis in the company's activities), they shall be taken as current assets. Para 75 of Schedule 1 of the Act, however, noted that although such assets have to be included within the heading of 'net current assets', if they represent non-current amounts they should be disclosed separately.

(*Note:* Further commentary on 'Taxation in company accounts' appears in Chapter 5, GROWSTRONG Profit and Loss Account.)

Stock appreciation relief

Stock relief was introduced effectively at the end of 1974 (Finance Acts 1975, 1976) to counter the inequity of companies being taxed on the increase in value of stocks caused by inflation. The original scheme attracted a good deal of criticism and was superseded under the Finance Act 1981 by a new method for calculating the relief and changing the rules regarding clawback of relief. The relief was abolished by the Finance Act 1984 with none being given for periods beginning after 12 March 1984.

Material effect of Finance Act 1984 on Corporate and Deferred Taxation

Example 4.5.1 demonstrated the operation of the deferred tax account for timing differences arising as a result of 100% first year allowance in respect of capital expenditure on plant. It will be appreciated that many concerns operate a stable or growing investment policy in depreciable assets which result in tax relief arising year by year of an amount which equals or exceeds the additional tax which would otherwise have been payable as a result of the reversal of the original timing differences.

In these circumstances, the *foreseeable concept* outlined in SSAP 15 allowed for a provision for deferred taxation becoming unnecessary where a company, a going concern, reasonably foresaw little likelihood of tax having to be paid for some considerable time ahead (at least three years) following the reversal of timing differences. It became commonplace for companies to reduce or omit the provision for deferred tax. J. Bibby & Sons Ltd, one of the two winners of *The Accountant* and Stock Exchange awards in 1981 for the best reports and accounts of public companies, judged that *no* provision was required. Their policy was stated as follows:

'The directors are of the opinion that no provision for deferred taxation is necessary because, based on the projected levels of inventories and capital expenditure and the continuing business use of properties, there is reasonable probability that tax deferral will continue for the foreseeable future.'

With this statement of policy on deferred taxation, the company gave a detailed note of its *potential liability* based on a full provision calculated under the *liability method.*

The liability method of accounting for deferred taxation requires the balances on that account to be maintained at the *rate of corporation tax current in the year of account.* Adjustments are therefore necessary through the profit and loss account (separately noted in the make up of the tax charge) when the rate is changed. On the issue of a *revised SSAP 15 (1985)* 'Accounting for deferred tax', the liability method became the *prescribed* method. It was considered to be more consistent with the aims of *partial provision* for deferred tax and would provide comparability between companies following the corporation tax changes announced in the 1984 budget. This, incidentally, brought the UK standard into line with the international standard (IAS 12) which had withdrawn the option of using the alternative *deferral method.* That method involved the recording of deferred taxation applicable to original timing differences at the current rate of tax and their reversal at the *same* rate.

The full rate of corporation tax in the UK had been stable at 52% since 1973, and the distinction between the deferral and liability methods had little practical relevance. The major changes of the Finance Act 1984 not only underlined the merit of the latter method, but they also established that what were previously seen as potential tax liabilities to be dealt with by way of note, were now liabilities which would crystallise, necessitating the establishment of a deferred tax account where it had not previously existed, and the recalculation of liability by all.

Corporate tax changes, Finance Act 1984

The significant changes in tax law required companies to take a new look at their deferred tax policies and practices, these were:
1. The *rate of corporation tax* for the year ending 31 March 1984 was reduced to 50% followed by a phased reduction through 45% (1985), 40% (1986) to 35% for the year to 31 March 1987.
2. *First year allowance* on plant and machinery remained at 100% only on purchases incurred before 14 March 1984. They were reduced to 75% (expenditure to 31 March 1985), 50% (to 31 March 1986) and to *nil* for expenditure on or after 1 April 1986. Relief for qualifying capital expenditure is available in the form of 25% annual writing down allowances (WDA) calculated on a reducing balance basis. *Initial allowances* on industrial buildings were also to be phased out by 1986.
3. *Stock relief* on inflationary profits in stockholdings was abolished.

Effects of these changes

1. The eventual move to a corporation tax rate of 35% will be profound. The UK will enjoy one of the lowest corporate tax rates in the world.
2. The advance notice of the changes in rate and allowances will considerably enhance the effectiveness of corporate financial planning.

3. In general, retail and service sectors where capital allowances are of less importance, will have major benefit from the corporation tax rate reduction, relative to manufacturing and other capital intensive sectors.

4. These latter sectors may find that the loss of their first year capital allowances is insufficiently compensated for by the reduction in the tax rate. Their unrelieved allowances at the date of the change may run out well before the prospective stable regime of a rate of 35% with 25% WDA eventuates.

5. Companies previously using the foreseeable concept of SSAP 15 in conjunction with stable or rising amounts of capital expenditure, to follow a policy of non-provision for deferred tax, need to recreate deferred tax accounts following recalculations of their potential liability and its timing (see *Example 4.5.3*).

6. The major leasing activities of banks based on the 100% first year allowance was judged likely to abate materially. Very substantial increases were required in their deferred tax provisions.

7. In a statement of intent (SOI) following the 1984 budget, the ASC ruled that companies must immediately provide in their accounts for any deferred liabilities likely to arise. *Significant* adjustments to the deferred tax account were to be treated as *extraordinary* items (SSAP 6) through the profit and loss account, thus not affecting the earnings per share figure.

8. The build-up of writing down allowances will, in the long run, provide substantial compensation for the loss of the first year allowance of 100%, but only if inflation remains low, for the real value of these allowances, being based on historical cost, falls with inflation.

Example 4.5.3

Illustration of the effects of the corporation tax rate and capital allowances changes of the Finance Act 1984 on a company operating a stable plant investment programme.

X Ltd purchases plant each year for £15,000, with an estimated life of six years, a nil scrap value and written down in the accounts on a straight-line basis. Each purchase of plant produces an annual profit of £25,000. By 1983, the company has a constant stock of six assets and a profit before tax of £150,000 per annum. it had no deferred tax account balance at the end of that year, operating the foreseeable concept, anticipating under the then tax rules that timing differences would not reverse.

	1983 £	1984 £	1985 £	1986 £	1987 £	1988 £
Accounting profit	150,000	150,000	150,000	150,000	150,000	150,000
Tax *charge* (%)	(52) 78,000	(50) 75,000	(45) 67,500	(40) 60,000	(35) 52,500	(35) 52,500
Profit after tax	72,000	75,000	82,500	90,000	97,500	97,500
Capital expenditure – first year allowance (FYA) (rate)						
First year allowances	(100) 15,000	(100) 15,000	(75) 11,250	(75) 7,500	Nil	Nil
Writing down allowance	—	—	—	938	6,328	8,496
	15,000	15,000	11,250	8,438	6,328	8,496
Depreciation	15,000	15,000	15,000	15,000	15,000	15,000

	1983 £	1984 £	1985 £	1986 £	1987 £	1988 £
Reversing timing differences (RTD)	—	—	(3,750)	(6,562)	(8,672)	(6,504)
RTD times tax rate	—	— (45)	1,688 (40)	2,625 (35)	3,035 (35)	2,276
Tax *charge* (above)	78,000	75,000	67,500	60,000	52,500	52,500
Tax *payable*	78,000	75,000	69,188	62,625	55,535	54,776

Note: The company which started with a zero balance on deferred tax account is required in 1984 to create a provision as an extraordinary item through the profit and loss account on an amount equal to the excess of the assets book value over the zero value of the assets for tax purposes. This amount of £37,500* is the value of the timing differences which will reverse each year, consequent upon the changed tax system from 1984.

Year of purchase	Cost £	Depreciation to 31.3.84 £	Written down value 31.3.84 £
1	15,000	15,000	—
2	15,000	12,500	2,500
3	15,000	10,000	5,000
4	15,000	7,500	7,500
5	15,000	5,000	10,000
6	15,000	2,500	12,500
	90,000	52,500	37,500

[In 1984, ICI reported that they had provided £100 million for deferred tax consequent upon the 1984 Finance Act's tax changes.]

The 1984 provision is calculated as the amount of the liability crystallising at the rates of tax applicable at the time of the reverse timing differences:

				£	£	
	1985	45%	RTD	3,750 =	1,688	
	1986	40%	RTD	6,562 =	2,625	} = £13,829
Balance	1987 *et seq*	35%	RTD	27,188 =	9,516	

By 1988, £25,488 of the timing differences will have been reversed, being charged annually against the created deferred tax account, so that the tax charge shown in the profit and loss account is the product of the trading profit times the current annual rate of corporation tax. If the pre-1984 corporation tax of 52% and 100% FYA had continued, this company would have paid £78,000 tax per annum, which would have been the charge in the profit and loss account. Over the period, and in the particular circumstances of this illustration, the combination of the lower tax rates and changed capital allowances, reduce both tax charged and tax paid. The earnings figure is enhanced. The writing down allowance gradually increases annually, the reverse timing differences reducing correspondingly. By 1992 they will be fully-reversed.

Deferred tax and earnings per share

The importance of the earnings (attributable to ordinary shareholders) figure and the associated earnings per share has been emphasised. Prior to the 1984 tax changes, analysts would have to consider that the decision not to provide deferred tax, while based on the best judgement of the directors, did have the result of maintaining the profit after-tax figure at a level higher than would have otherwise been the case. They were concerned as to whether the company's distribution policy (i.e. how much of the 'earnings' were distributed and how much retained) was sufficiently conservative in recognising the potential tax liability.

The general effect of the 1984 legislation will be that deferred tax will cease to be a significant accounting problem, in the long-term, as differences between depreciation rates and tax rates narrow. Taken together with the mandatory requirement of the revised SSAP 15 for companies when computing their deferred tax to use *partial provision* and the liability method, comparability of 'earnings' between companies will be enhanced.

Partial provision and the revised SSAP

The revised accounting standard, SSAP 15 (1985), replaces with more flexible criteria, the rather mechanistic test of a minimum three year period within which a tax liability is expected to crystallise. This period had tended in practice to become a maximum period. The new rules require that deferred tax should be provided in respect of *all* timing differences (the previous distinction between short- and long-term timing differences is now less meaningful) of material amount, to the extent that a liability may crystallise, otherwise provision is not necessary.

Deferred tax assets (debit balances)

The effect of the 1984 tax changes on many companies will be that deferred tax ceases to be a material matter, but for others it will mean that a deferred tax asset will arise. The revised SSAP 15 requires that such debit balances arising on separate categories of timing differences, be first offset against any overall provision for deferred tax liabilities. Where, however, the balance on the deferred tax account becomes a net debit, the standard allows this to be carried forward *only* where it is expected to be recoverable without replacement by equivalent debit balances. This will evidently not be the case for capital intensive companies whose investment programmes will lead to continuous deferred tax debits. These will be required to be written off by the standard and will lead to the companies paying a higher rate of corporation tax than the intended standard rate of 35%. The deferred tax asset will arise when companies write off their assets for accounting purposes at a faster, straight-line, depreciation rate than allowed by the reducing balance rate available for tax purposes.

4.6   INTANGIBLE FIXED ASSETS

The amount shown under this heading in the GROWSTRONG consolidated balance sheet (*Table 3*) represents *cost of control goodwill* which is being systematically written off over a short period of time, in accordance with the alternative treatment allowed by SSAP 22 (see following).

Cost of control goodwill

This item in a consolidated balance sheet represents the excess of the cost of the investment in a *subsidiary* company (purchase price) over the fair value of the net assets of the subsidiary thus acquired. It results from the inclusion in the consolidated balance sheet of the various assets and liabilities of the subsidiary and the exclusion of the entry showing the cost of acquiring the shares in the subsidiary.

Example 4.6.1

Company X acquires *all* the ordinary shares of Company Y for £100,000 cash. On the date Y becomes a *wholly owned subsidiary* of X, their respective balance sheets are summarised as:

Company X balance sheet as at date of acquisition of Y

Share capital plus reserves	£1 million	Net Assets	£900,000
		Investment in Y at cost	£100,000
	£1 million		£1 million

Company Y balance sheet as at date of acquisition by X

Share capital plus reserves	£ 80,000	Net Assets (current values)	£ 80,000

In the preparation of the consolidated balance sheet, the account 'Investment in Y' (the purchase price) is set against the Y Company accounts 'Ordinary share capital' and 'Reserves' (equating to the value of the net assets acquired), all being eliminated in a 'Cost of Control' account which nets to a balance of £20,000 representing 'goodwill':

Cost of Control Account X in Y

	£		£
Investment in Y at cost	100,000	Share capital Y ⎫	
		Reserves of Y ⎬	80,000
		Balance carried down	20,000
	£100,000		£100,000
Balance brought down	20,000		

The balances on the accounts remaining in the respective balance sheets together with that of the cost of control account are entered in the consolidated balance sheet, thus:

Consolidated balance sheet of X and its subsidiary Y at acquisition

Share capital plus reserves	£1 million	Net assets X	£900,000
(of X)		Net assets Y	80,000
		Goodwill	20,000
	£1 million		£1 million

Minority interests

Where a majority, but less than all, of the equity share capital of a subsidiary is acquired, then goodwill represents the excess of the purchase price of the shares over the *relevant proportion* of the current value of the net assets.

Nevertheless *all* of the net assets of the subsidiary are brought into the consolidated balance sheet, balanced by an entry 'Minority interests' recognising the extent of the interest of these outside shareholders in them (*see Example 4.3.1*).

Write off of cost of control goodwill

Where a company pays more for the shares of a subsidiary than the value of the attributable net assets acquired, it does so presumably in the expectation that profits over and above those expected to be earned on the investment in the net tangible assets will be received. To the extent, over time, that the actual profit earned differs more or less from expectations, the value of goodwill will vary. According to market circumstances, it will increase or decrease with the passage of time. However, because of the difficulty in determining over a period of time the changing value of *inherent goodwill* (or non-purchased goodwill), i.e. that generated internally through the attainment of super-profitability (earnings above those normally expected from the employment of tangible capital), it has not been the practice to recognise it by varying the figure of purchased goodwill shown in the balance sheet or introducing it where no purchased goodwill is involved.

SSAP 22 'Accounting for Goodwill' (1984) follows this established practice, specifying that "no amount should be attributed to non-purchased goodwill in the balance sheets of companies or groups". This standard accepts the previous conservative practice of write off of positive purchased goodwill (e.g. cost of control goodwill) as quickly as possible. Indeed, it goes much further, emphasising that the *normal* and *preferred practice* is for its *elimination* from the accounts *immediately* on acquisition against *reserves*. The rational for the immediate write off to be against the reserves and not against the profit and loss account is because:

    (i) this is seen as a matter of accounting policy to achieve consistency of treatment with non-purchased goodwill, rather than because it has suffered a permanent diminution in value; and

    (ii) the immediate write off is not related to the results of the year in which the acquisition was made.

The standard does allow for the *alternative* of *amortisation* of purchased goodwill through the profit and loss account in arriving at the profit on ordinary activities on a systematic basis over its economic life. The expectation is that this alternative practice will be followed by a minority of companies, who could include, for example, those which are part of foreign groups whose policy is amortisation, or certain service industries typically acquired at high prices in relation to the value of the net assets, because of the material effect that immediate write off would have on reserves.

Companies Acts requirements

These *standard* treatments conform with those of the Companies Act 1981 (4 Sch. 21, 66 and note 3 balance sheet format CA 1985), although that Act is restricted to the treatment of purchased goodwill in the *unconsolidated* accounts of a *single* company. The Act permits, but does not require, that purchased goodwill be treated as an asset. It confirms the practice of non-recognition of inherent goodwill, goodwill only to be included if it was acquired for valuable consideration. The Act requires that goodwill should be written off systematically over a period not exceeding its useful economic life. The period for write off and the reasons for choosing that period must be disclosed. The EEC Seventh Directive (group accounts) proposes to follow the same course but has yet to be enacted in the UK.

Whichever of the two standard treatments is followed, either the preferred immediate write off to reserves or the amortisation of goodwill against profits, the policy must be disclosed (CA 1948, 8 Sch. 36) as must the movements on the goodwill account, as well as other fixed assets (CA 1948, 8 Sch. 42). These provisions now appear in the 4 Sch. CA 1985. The Department of Trade and Industry has indicated its belief that it would be illegal for goodwill to be written off against the revaluation reserve either in individual or consolidated accounts. S56 CA 1948 – S130(1)–(3) CA 1985 – prohibits the write off of goodwill against the Share Premium account of an individual company and this would almost certainly apply on consolidation.

Goodwill write off, realised and distributable profit

Amortising goodwill over its economic life (CA 1981 – unconsolidated accounts) reduces distributable profit but the effect is spread over a number of accounting periods, and given the new rules on distribution (CA 1980 and see Chapter 5) appears to be a practical and expedient solution. SSAP 22 is based on the concept in the UK Companies Acts that *purchased* goodwill has a limited useful life, so that ultimately its elimination *must* constitute a *realised loss* for any individual company. However, it should be remembered that distributions are made by individual companies, not by groups. It follows that the elimination of consolidation cost of control goodwill has no effect on the *distributable profit* of any company.

Interpretative aspects

Financial, investment and other analysts of company reports, including those lending to companies, have tended to ignore any amount standing against goodwill in the balance sheets. The preferred treatment of SSAP 22 of immediate write off will aid this process. Gearing ratios and security cover calculations will exclude it. When comparisons are made between the 'earnings per share' of immediate write off companies and those whose policy is amortisation, then the charge against profit of the latter will usually be excluded. Conversely, return on capital-employed ratios shown in published company reports, or used internally for profit planning purposes, will have to be considered carefully where a material investment of resources has been written off against reserves, if a too rosy picture is not to be seen, or too soft a target set.

ACCOUNTING FOR ACQUISITIONS AND MERGERS

The method of consolidating the separate accounts of a holding company and its subsidiary (or subsidiaries), illustrated in the above discussion on goodwill, is known as the *acquisition method*. This method applies where there is a take-over by a company purchasing a majority of the shares of another, usually above market price, and where the purchase price is settled by the issue of the take-over company shares so requiring the setting up of a share premium account and the locking up of pre-acquisition reserves.

A second method that has been used, known as the *merger method*, where shares in one company were exchanged for those in a second in a merger desired by both companies, and where it was felt that no share premium account need be opened, had the advantage that subsequent dividends paid by the subsidiary out of pre-acquisition profits need not be regarded as capital in the hands of the holding company.

An exposure draft (ED 3) on 'Accounting for acquisitions and mergers' was issued as long ago as 1971 but did not emerge as a standard because of various criticisms made against it. Although there were doubts about the legality of the 'merger' method, it was not regarded as unacceptable until the case of *Shearer v Bercain* (1980). Mr Justice Walton stated in respect of S56, CA 1948, dealing with the share premium account (see this Chapter (4.2)):

> "S56 is mandatory and requires the excess of the value of assets, whether cash or not, over the nominal value of shares issued in exchange to be carried to a share premium account in the books of the acquiring company."

Share premium account relief

The Companies Act 1981 has dealt with the problem that has arisen for companies who had used the merger accounting method which was ruled against in the above law case. It introduces relief in certain cases from the obligation under S56 of the CA 1948 (see S130–134, CA 1985) to create a share premium account and effectively legalises merger accounting where a holding in another company is increased to ninety per cent or more *by issuing shares*. This relief applies retrospectively in certain circumstances where the shares were issued before February 4, 1981 and no share premium account was created.

Example 4.6.2

This example illustrates the use of the ACQUISITION and the MERGER methods.

X plc whose £1 ordinary shares are listed on the Stock Exchange at £3 each, makes an offer for the whole of the ordinary share capital of Y plc. The offer of one X ordinary share for one Y ordinary share was accepted and the whole transaction completed on 31 March 19x1 when the summarised balance sheets of the two companies were as follows:

(A)   *Balance sheet X plc as at 31 March 19x1 before the issue of its ordinary shares to Y plc shareholders for the acquisition of that company*

	£		£
3 million ordinary shares of		Fixed assets	6,000,000
£1 each fully paid	3,000,000	Net current assets	2,000,000
Reserves	5,000,000		
	8,000,000		8,000,000

Under the ACQUISITION method, the purchase consideration for Y plc would be based on the market value of X ordinary shares, i.e. 2 million X shares issued (one-for-one exchange) at £3 each equals a purchase price of £6 million. Following S56, CA 1948, the shares (nominal value £1) were issued at a premium (£2 per share) of £4 million.

Entry in X's books is Debit: Investment in Y account £6 million
Credit: Ordinary Share Capital £2 million
Credit: Share Premium account £4 million

The Share Premium account is subject to the legal restrictions of the CA 1985 (this chapter (4.2)).

(B)   *Balance sheet X plc after the issue of shares to Y shareholders (ACQUISITION METHOD)*

	£		£
5 million ordinary shares of		Fixed assets	6,000,000
£1 each fully paid	5,000,000	Net current assets	2,000,000
Share Premium account	4,000,000	Investment in Y	6,000,000
Reserves	5,000,000		
	£14,000,000		£14,000,000

(C)   *Balance sheet Y plc as at 31 March 19x1*

	£		£
2 million ordinary shares of		Fixed assets	2,000,000
£1 each fully paid	2,000,000	Net current assets	3,000,000
Reserves	3,000,000		
	5,000,000		5,000,000

In this example, Y plc remains a separate legal entity after the merger but its former shareholders are now shareholders of X plc which wholly owns Y.

On consolidation (ACQUISITION method) the 'Investment in Y' account in X's books is eliminated (for consolidated balance sheet purposes) against the net assets of Y (at the date of acquisition) represented by Y's share capital account and reserves. The excess of the former (the purchase price) over the latter (net assets acquired) represents a payment for goodwill, i.e.:

Cost of control X in Y (wholly owned subsidiary)

	£		£
Investment in Y	6,000,000	Share capital Y	2,000,000
		Reserves	3,000,000
		Balance c/d	1,000,000
	6,000,000		6,000,000
Balance b/d (Goodwill)	1,000,000		

(D)   The remaining items in the separate balance sheets of X and Y together with the goodwill of £1 million form the consolidated balance sheet:

*Consolidated balance sheet of X and its subsidiary Y
as at 31 March 19x1 (ACQUISITION METHOD)*

	£		£
5 million ordinary shares of		Fixed assets	8,000,000
£1 each fully paid	5,000,000	Goodwill	1,000,000
Share Premium account	4,000,000	Net current assets	5,000,000
Reserves	5,000,000		
	£14,000,000		£14,000,000

Three items should be noted in connection with this method of consolidation:

1. The pre-acquisition reserves of Y, £3m, which were free for distribution have effectively been capitalised and any dividend paid thereout, necessarily to X, will be regarded as capital in that company's hands.
2. An asset account – goodwill – of £1 million has arisen in the process.
3. A non-distributable share premium account of £4 million also appears.

The merger method

ED 3 considered that where a 'merger' had taken place, the restrictions governing the distributions of pre-acquisition profits, the share premium and the unnecessary arising of the goodwill figure, could be eradicated using the MERGER METHOD of consolidation.

Problems arose over the definition of a 'merger' and its different character from other acquisitions, but in essence the concept underlying a merger is one of continuity of the amalgamating businesses, no new capital having been subscribed. The only change that has taken place is in the separate ownerships which are considered to have been *pooled* into one common ownership (giving rise to the alternative description used in the USA of 'the pooling of interests' method). For practical purposes, this means that there is no change in the amounts at which assets, liabilities, reserves and undistributed profits of the amalgamating companies are recorded.

Under the merger method, accumulated profits (reserves) at the date of the merger are not treated as pre-acquisition profits and remain available for distribution. No goodwill arises or share premium, for the shares issued in exchange are regarded as issued at nominal value and are so recorded:

(E) *Balance sheet X plc after the issue of shares to Y shareholders (MERGER METHOD)*

		£		£
Contrast with	5 million ordinary shares			
(B) under the	of £1 each fully paid	5,000,000	Fixed assets	6,000,000
Acquisition	Reserves	5,000,000	Net current assets	2,000,000
method			Investment in Y	2,000,000
			(nominal value)	
		10,000,000		10,000,000

(F) *Consolidated balance sheet X and subsidiary Y as at 31 March 19x1 (MERGER METHOD)*

		£		£
Contrast with	5 million ordinary shares			
(D) under the	of £1 each fully paid	5,000,000	Fixed assets	8,000,000
Acquisition	Reserves	8,000,000	Net current assets	5,000,000
method				
		13,000,000		13,000,000

The merger method clearly has advantages in the limited circumstances exemplified. The CA 1981 granted retrospective relief in certain cases (page 89) from the need to set up a share premium account in accordance with the 1948 Act. Where no share premium account was set up, there is now no need to do so and the decision of *Shearer v Bercain* does not apply. It has been said that the sections 36–41 of the CA 1981 (S130–4 and 255 Sch. CA 1985) were drawn up in broad terms with a specific understanding that the ASC would produce an accounting standard which would clearly differentiate 'acquisitions' from 'genuine mergers and internal reorganisations'. This it set out to do, issuing exposure draft ED 31 late in 1982, followed in April 1984 by a statement of intent, a precursor for the full standard *SSAP 23 'Accounting for acquisitions and mergers' published in 1985*. But as we shall note, a new method of financing an acquisition known as '*vendor rights*' was being publicised as the standard was issued. Its aim was to have 'take-overs' accounted for as 'mergers' in order to gain the attendent benefits of the latter method.

SSAP 23 Accounting for acquisitions and mergers

The *objective test* contained in the standard determine whether or not a business combination may be treated as a merger is – whether or not material resources have left one or other of the combining companies. Broadly, if an acquisition involves a material cash payment by the acquiring company (more than 10%), the conditions for merger accounting have *not* been met because resources have left that company. If, on the other hand, the acquirer issues its own shares of not less than 90% of the *fair value* of the total consideration, only limited resources will have left the company and merger accounting is appropriate. Working to the SSAP 23 ensures compliance with the *International Standard 22 'Accounting for business combinations'*, both relate to each other in all material respects. IAS 22 refers to 'merger accounting' as the pooling of interests method. That standard sees a merger as a 'uniting of interests' where

(a) the basis of the transaction is principally an exchange of voting common (equity) shares of the enterprises concerned; and

(b) the whole, or effectively the whole, of the net assets and operations of the enterprises are combined as one entity.

The differences between acquisition accounting and merger accounting, earlier described and illustrated, are materially unchanged under SSAP 23. In merger accounting, the standard does not see any need to revalue the net assets of the subsidiary to fair value, either in its own books or on consolidation. It does, however, accept that appropriate adjustments should be made to ensure uniformity of accounting policies between the combining companies. The third method of accounting for business combinations, the so-called *'new entity method'*, which in essence is the *merger method with revaluation* is therefore virtually excluded, as it is by IAS 22. SSAP 23 confirms that the normal treatment of the 'investment in the new subsidiary' in the accounts of the holding company, under the merger method, would be the recording of the shares it issues at nominal value. To this would be added any additional consideration in form other than equity shares. On consolidation, under the merger method, any difference whether debit or credit, between the carrying value of the investment in the subsidiary and the nominal value of the shares transferred to the issuing company is to be set against reserves. A debit balance arising is not to be regarded as goodwill because the difference is not based on the fair values of the consideration given and the separable net assets acquired.

The standard requires the *disclosure* of information with the financial state-ments of the year covering the identity of the combining companies, details of the securities issued and of any other consideration; the accounting treatment adopted whether acquisition or merger, and the nature and amount of significant accounting adjustments made to achieve consistency of accounting policies. As required by SSAP 14 – 'Group accounts' – the consolidated financial statements have to contain sufficient information of the acquired results of the subsidiaries to enable shareholders to appreciate the effect on the consolidated results. Certain additional information is required where merger accounting is adopted, which includes the amount of the fair value of the purchase consideration, and an analysis of the profits of the acquisition year as between pre- and post-merger periods, of extraordinary items and of relativities with the previous year.

SSAP 23 and the proposed EEC Seventh Directive on group accounts

The UK is required to enact the provisions of the EEC Seventh Directive by 1 January 1988 to apply to accounting periods beginning on or after 1 January 1990. The Directive requires, for merger accounting to be available, that the combination arrangement should not include a cash payment exceeding 10% of the *nominal* value of the shares issued. This differs materially from SSAP 23, which as we have noted, relates the 10% cash consideration to *fair values* of the total consideration. The ASC propose to review SSAP 23 following the enactment of the Directive.

Financing acquisitions by vendor rights

Under this financing technique, the acquiring company's shares are offered to the shareholders of the company being taken over. But, by agreement, those shareholders can then offer the shares back, via a vendor rights placing, to the acquiring company's existing shareholders. The cash to finance the purchase is thus raised indirectly from the acquiring company. As merger accounting is permitted provided cash consideration is less than 10%, this method, which was adopted to gain the benefits of 'mergers', constitutes a loophole in SSAP 23. In the actual transaction publicised, accounting for the take-over as a merger avoided the need to show the difference between the net assets acquired and the purchase price as goodwill. This was important in this case for the company had insufficient reserves to allow it to write off goodwill immediately, and amortisation under SSAP 22 'Accounting for goodwill' would have reduced its future earnings per share. And, under the merger method adopted, there was no need to adjust asset values from book value to fair value, thus the increased depreciation charges likely under acquisition accounting were avoided. The merger treatment also allowed pre-acquisition profits to be available to the acquiring company's shareholders.

Vendor placing is a variable to vendor rights and is available to companies aiming to merge accounts on a take-over. This method involves the shares on offer being accompanied by a placing arrangement with an institution so that the shares can be subsequently sold for cash. In the US, the accounting statement on business combinations specify vendor placings as 'acquisitions'.

The ASC took the view that these abuses should not delay the publication of SSAP 23 which had been so long in gestation. Should these take place on any scale, they can be rectified with the implementation of the Seventh Directive.

Intangible fixed assets – CA 1981 (45 Sch. CA 85)

Other items accepted to be shown under this heading by the CA 1981, include: '*Concessions, patents, licences, trade marks and similar rights and assets*', subject to the assets having been acquired for valuable consideration, or the assets in question were created by the company itself.

Development costs

The 1981 Act – 4 Sch. 20 CA 1985 – states that these may only be shown as an asset in a company's balance sheet in *special circumstances* and a note to the accounts must state:
  (a) the period over which the capitalised costs are being, or are due to be, written off; and
  (b) the reasons for the capitalisation.
The phrase 'special circumstances' remains undefined but the stringent requirements set out in SSAP 13 'Accounting for Research and Development' for treating development expenditure as an asset would appear to apply (see page 95).

Expenditure falls into three categories when considering the proper accounting treatment. Two of these are relatively clear-cut, i.e. revenue expenditure and capital expenditure. The third – deferred expenditure – is a 'grey' decision area.

Revenue expenditure defined as expenditure incurred in *maintaining* fixed assets, in acquiring assets for conversion into cash, in producing such assets, and in selling, distribution and administration, contributes only once to the earning of profit and (except for unsold stock and payments in advance at balance sheet date) is wholly exhausted and written off immediately.

Capital expenditure defined as expenditure incurred in the *purchase* of fixed assets (for use in the business and not for sale) or in *increasing* the earnings capacity of those assets, results in longer term benefit to the business and is written off proportionately over the estimated useful life of the assets. The residual net book value is carried forward as part of capital employed.

Expenditure which is clearly not capital expenditure, but is revenue in character and considered not to be wholly exhausted within the current accounting period, is categorised, to the extent that it is carried forward, as *deferred revenue expenditure*. Examples are abnormal advertising expenses on the launch of a new product and research and development costs.

In making the decision on whether development costs should be written off immediately or over a number of accounting periods, consideration will be given to the fundamental *concept of prudence* which requires that all known liabilities (expenses/losses) be brought into immediate account, and the *accruals* (matching) concept which requires that revenue and profit must not be anticipated and that expenditure should be written off in the period in which it arises, unless its relationship to the revenue of a future period can be established with *some certainty*.

SSAP 13 Accounting for Research and Development

Although there is always an element of 'the crystal ball' about future outcomes, and some managements may wish to boost current earnings per share by deferring such expenditure, the phrases 'with some certainty' and 'special circumstances', together with the restrictions of SSAP 13, should ensure that the concept of prudence determines the true and fair outcome.

Indeed, the accounting standard requires that pure and applied *research* costs be written off in the year of expenditure. The CA 1981 (4 Sch. 20 CA 85) stipulates that research costs may not be treated as an asset.

Development expenditure may be deferred to future periods only in stated stringent circumstances:

(a) there is a clearly defined project, and
(b) the related expenditure is separately identifiable, and
(c) the outcome of such a project has been assessed with reasonable certainty as to:
    (i) its technical feasibility and
    (ii) its ultimate commercial viability (in the light of stated factors)
(d) if further development costs are to be incurred on the same project, the aggregate of such costs together with related production, selling and administration costs are reasonably expected to be more than covered by related future revenues, and
(e) adequate resources exist, or are reasonably expected to be available, to enable the project to be completed and to provide any consequential increases in working capital.

The note to the accounts must show the movement on such expenditure during the year (SSAP 13) and the accounting policy should be stated.

Distributable profits and deferred expenditure

The CA 1981 (S269 and 11 Sch. CA 85) provides that where *development costs* are shown as an asset in a company's accounts, any amount shown in respect of these costs shall be treated as a realised loss for the purpose of calculating 'distributable profits' under the CA 1980 (see Chapter 5). This section does not apply, however, provided that the note to the accounts giving the reason for capitalisation justifies the directors' decision not to regard the amount as a realised loss. This extra legal requirement puts emphasis on the stringent conditions (above) of SSAP 13 for carry-forward. The grounds of any such justification must be included in the notes to the accounts (para 20(2) 4 Sch. CA 1985).

4.6   TANGIBLE FIXED ASSETS

The figure shown in the GROWSTRONG plc consolidated balance sheet (*Table 3*) against tangible fixed assets is the *net book value* of the total tangible fixed assets of the group at balance sheet date.

Note 6 to the accounts breaks down this figure over the constituent groups of such assets, e.g. freehold properties, leasehold properties (differentiating long and short leases) under an overall heading 'land and buildings'; plant and machinery including leased plant (see Chapter 5), fixtures and fittings; motor vehicles, etc. Under each of these heads, to the cost/valuation at the beginning of the year is added the cost of 'additions' and deducted the cost-value of disposals during the year, to arrive at the cost/valuation of tangible fixed assets in use at the end of the year. In respect of the accumulated depreciation, the opening total under each head is increased by the depreciation provided from profit for the year and decreased by the accumulated depreciation on disposals. The resultant accumulated depreciation at the end of the year is deducted from the cost/valuation of the particular asset group to give its *net book value*. The summation of the net book value for each type gives the one figure shown in the balance sheet.

Companies Act 1981

For the purposes of Sch. 1 of this Act – 4 Sch. 77 CA 85 – assets of a company are to be regarded as *fixed assets* if they are intended for use on a continuing basis in the company's activities.

Fixed assets include tangible assets, intangible assets and investments. Tangible assets include leased assets (see Chapter 5).

Where the fixed assets are accounted for under the historical cost convention, they must be stated at their purchase price or production cost less any provision for depreciation or diminution in value.

Depreciation must be calculated to write off the purchase prior or production cost less any estimated residual value over the useful economic life of the asset.

Note: These requirements do not apply to cost of control goodwill (see previous section) for which there are at present no statutory valuation rules.

Government grants, SSAP 4

Either of the two methods set out in SSAP 4 for the accounting treatment of such grants in respect of capital expenditure are acceptable under the CA 1981. The simplest method of deducting the grant from the cost of the additions during the year will spread the benefit of the grant over the life of the asset as each year's depreciation charge is correspondingly reduced. Where the alternative method of regarding the grant as deferred income to be credited to profit and loss account over the life of the asset is adopted, the credit has to be shown under the heading of 'Accruals and deferred income' in the CA 1981 balance sheet format, and may not be deducted from 'fixed assets.'

The net effect on the profit and loss account is, of course, the same whichever treatment is adopted.

Alternative accounting rules

In general, as regards methods of accounting, Sch. 1 of CA 1981 – 4 Sch. 29–34 CA 85 – gives companies a choice; they can use either historical cost or current cost information (see Chapter 12). Where current cost accounting is used, historic cost statements must be published as well.

The 1981 Act allows tangible fixed assets, as an alternative to purchase price or production cost, to be shown at market value (at the date of their last valuation), or at current cost.

The depreciation rules stated earlier as applying under historic cost accounting, apply equally to revalued fixed assets.

Where assets have been revalued (except in the case of stocks) additional information is to be disclosed in respect of each balance sheet type, showing *either*:

(a) the comparable historical cost information both as to cost and depreciation; *or*

(b) the difference between those amounts and the corresponding amounts actually shown in the balance sheet.

The amount of any revaluation must be credited (or debited) to a 'revaluation reserve' (see this chapter (4.2)).

Accounting policy on fixed assets

The accounting policy adopted in respect of fixed assets (SSAP 2) would typically give information on the valuation rules adopted, estimated lives of asset groups, depreciation method, the treatment of government grants, together with any special comment, e.g. the accounting treatment adopted for land and buildings held as an investment (see J. Bibby example, page 49).

SSAP 19 Accounting for Investment Properties

This standard, applicable in respect of financial statements for accounting periods starting on or after 1 July 1981, states that investment properties should *not* be subject to periodic charges for depreciation except for property held on a lease with an unexpired term of 20 years or less.

The application of this standard rule for the overriding purpose of giving a true and fair view is a departure from the statutory requirement of the law to provide depreciation on any fixed asset having a limited useful economic life. In these circumstances, CA 1985 requires a note to the accounts giving particulars of the departure, the reasons for it and its effect.

Note: An investment property is an interest in land and/or buildings: (a) in respect of which construction work and development have been completed; and (b) which is held for its investment potential, any rental income being negotiated at arm's length.

A property owned and occupied by a company for its own purposes or let to and occupied by another group company, is not an investment property. Changes in the value of investment properties will normally be dealt with as a movement on (investment) revaluation reserve.

Investment properties are to be included in the balance sheet at their current open market value, with information about the valuers and the basis of their valuation.

Problems of accounting for depreciation

SSAP 12 'Accounting for Depreciation' (1977, revised 1981), and the Companies Act 1981 'Prescriptions for accounting for the tangible fixed assets of limited companies', both under section B – HCA rules and section C – alternative accounting rules, together with SSAP 19, 'Accounting for Investment Properties', provide a codification of much-established practice in relation to depreciation. But problems were apparent in the application of the rules, particularly in the revaluation of assets, current cost accounting and the alternative accounting rules. The ASC issued a discussion document on these matters in 1983 without any pre-supposition that SSAP 12 would again be revised. However, in March 1985, it published *ED 37 'Accounting for Depreciation'* which followed on swiftly from a statement of intent issued late in 1984. The aim of these documents was the discouragement of inconsistent depreciation practices. Meanwhile the inflation accounting exposure draft ED 35, 'Accounting for the Effects of Changing Prices', which related to and had preceded the depreciation SOI, was running into trouble (see Chapter 12).

Main points of ED 37 'Accounting For Depreciation'

The basic *underlying principle* of the proposed new standard is unchanged, namely that the cost or revalued amount of fixed assets (other than investment properties, goodwill, development costs and investments) less their estimated residual value should be written off systematically over their useful economic lifes. Related to this principle:

(i) companies are encouraged to incorporate fixed assets in historical cost accounts at revalued amounts, the valuations to be 'relatively recent', i.e. kept up-to-date;

(ii) 'useful economic life' being the period over which an asset is depreciated should be the realistic judgement of the present owner and not its *total* economic life;

(iii) estimates of residual values should not take into account future inflation; residual value is defined as the realisable value of the asset at the end of its useful economic life based on prices prevailing at the date of acquisition or revaluation, realisation costs being deducted;

(iv) the depreciation charge in the profit and loss account must be based on the carrying amount of the asset in the balance sheet whether it is a historic cost or a revalued figure. No part of the depreciation charge should be set directly against reserves. This requirement followed the 'novel' method adopted by Woolworth's of revaluing properties in the balance sheet while leaving the profit and loss account on an historic basis. The exposure draft required consistent treatment in these statements, and this was confirmed in the revised standard;

(v) assets fully depreciated, but still in use, should be reinstated where this might otherwise lead to a failure to give a true and fair view;

(vi) the practice of some companies in taking the movement in value of certain assets off the depreciation charge is categorically disallowed – 'the difference between the book amount and the revalued amount should be transferred to revaluation reserve'.

The *revised SSAP 12* was published in April 1986 effective from 1 January 1986 subject to CCAB approval. Coincidentally, the DTI issued a consultative document on depreciation which is likely to provide legal backing for the new standard. The current legal requirement to charge depreciation on any fixed asset with a limited useful life is briefly set out in 4 Sch. CA 85.

Disclosure requirements of the new standard

Disclosures required in the financial statements in respect of each major class of depreciable assets are:

(i) depreciation methods used;

(ii) the useful economic lives or the depreciation rates used;

(iii) the total depreciation charged for that period; and

(iv) the gross amount of depreciable assets and the related accumulated depreciation.

Where there is a change in the depreciation method used, the effect must be disclosed in the year in which it was changed. Where assets have been revalued, the effect on the depreciation charge in that year must be stated.

4.7 FIXED ASSETS – INVESTMENTS

The figure shown in the GROWSTRONG plc consolidated balance sheet against this heading is the net book value at balance sheet date of investments in an *associated company* and of *other listed* and *unlisted investments*.

Associated companies

SSAP 1 'Accounting for the Results of Associated Companies' was published in January 1971. Although the standard was at that time innovative, its principles have since been incorporated into recommendations in several other countries. In 1982, ASC having reviewed the working experience of SSAP 1, issued a revision of it containing several refinements but essentially continuing with the basic principles of the original.

An explanatory note of SSAP 1 gave the reasons for differentiating the treatment in the accounts of investments in associates, investments in subsidiaries and other investments:

"It is accepted accounting practice for a company not to take credit in its own (i.e. non-consolidated) profit and loss account and balance sheet for its share of the profits of other companies (subsidiary or otherwise) *which have not been distributed*. The view is taken that the inclusion of undistributed profits would ignore the separate legal entities of the companies concerned and, as regards the investing company, be in breach of the principle that credit should not be taken for investment income until it is received or receivable (prudence concept).

"However, where a company conducts an important part of its business through the medium of other companies, whether more or less than 50 per cent owned, the mere disclosure of dividend income is unlikely to be sufficient to give shareholders adequate information regarding the sources of their income and the manner in which their funds are being employed.

"At one time such operations were usually carried out through the medium of subsidiary companies. It was for this reason that the Companies Act 1948 required the preparation of group accounts, normally in the form of consolidated accounts. At the time of the issue of SSAP 1, there had been two important developments. One was the growing practice of companies to conduct parts of their business through other companies (frequently consortium or joint venture companies) in which they had a substantial but not a controlling interest. The other was the importance which investors have come to attach to earnings per share (EPS) and the price-earnings ratio (PER). To ensure that the investing company's accounts as a whole gave adequate information and provided a total of earnings from which the most meaningful ratios could be calculated, it was considered necessary that the coverage of *consolidated accounts* should be extended to include . . . the share of earnings or losses of companies . . . described in the Standard as associated companies.

"This approach recognises a difference in principle between the nature of investments in associated companies and other forms of trade investment. The *essence of the distinction is that the investing company actively participates in the commercial and policy decisions* of its associated companies; it thus has a measure of direct responsibility for the return on its investment, and should account for its stewardship accordingly, whereas it will not normally seek to exert direct management influence over the operating policy of other companies in which it invests and should continue to deal with them in accordance with traditional accounting methods.

"The broad concept underlying the accounting treatment of the results of associated companies . . . was the adoption in modified form of the consolidation procedures used for subsidiaries. It followed from this that the investing group's share of associated companies' profits and losses would be reflected in its consolidated profit and loss account and *its share of their post-acquisition retained profits* would be reflected in its *consolidated balance sheet*, though not in its own balance sheet as a legal entity."

Associated company – consolidated balance sheet entry

Following SSAP 1, the entry 'investment in associated company' represents an interest of the group in a company which is not a subsidiary, and in which the investment is long term and substantial (e.g. between 20% and 50%) and on whose management a *significant influence* can be exercised. The appropriate share of the current year's profit (or loss) and the related tax of such a company is included in the consolidated profit and loss account. In the *balance sheet*, the investment in the associate may be shown at a value, but more usually at the cost of the investment less any amounts written off, plus the investing group's share of the post-acquisition *retained* profits and reserves of the associate. The assets and liabilities of the associate are *not* allocated between categories in the investing company's consolidated balance sheet, as has been shown happens in the case of subsidiaries. SSAP 1s standard method of accounting for associates is labelled '*equity accounting*'.

Note 7 to the GROWSTRONG plc consolidated balance sheet in respect of its associated company shows the balance at the beginning of the year differentiating the cost of the investment and its share of the associate's post-acquisition reserves at that date; to this is added the share of the retained profit for the year to give the net book value at the end of the year.

COMPANIES ACT 1981 – RELATED COMPANY

For the purposes of the CA 1981 (4 Sch. 92 CA 85), a *related company* is one in which the investing company holds on a long-term basis a 'qualifying capital interest' for the purpose of securing a contribution to its own activities by the exercise of any control or influence arising from that interest. 'Qualifying capital interest' means the holding of equity share capital with the right to vote. Where that interest is equal to twenty per cent or more of the nominal value of all equity shares carrying voting rights, there is a presumption that the company in question is a related company. For practical purposes, therefore, a related company may be regarded as an associate. The revised SSAP 1 (1982) indicates that the term 'related company' need not be used on the face of the accounts so long as notes to the accounts make it clear that there are no related companies other than associate ones.

Besides the investment in subsidiaries which is replaced in the consolidated balance sheet by the net assets of the subsidiaries representing that investment, with any excess of the purchase price of the investment over the net assets being shown as goodwill, and the investment in associated companies dealt with in the consolidated balance sheet as described above, the investing company is required to give statutory information regarding 'other investments'.

OTHER INVESTMENTS

Such investments will be either fixed assets or current assets; and they may be 'listed' or 'unlisted investments'.

The CA 1981 (4 Sch. 77 CA 85) regards all assets intended for use on a continuing basis in the company's business as 'fixed'; all other assets are 'current'. There are no in-between categories. Investments in subsidiaries and in associated companies clearly fall into the category 'fixed'. 'Short-term' investments, e.g. of surplus seasonal cash, would normally be realised within one year from balance sheet date which was the traditional definition of a current asset. Presumably investments held for a short term in excess of one year ahead which did not fall within the category definition 'fixed' would be shown as current assets. For both fixed and current asset investments, the following information must be disclosed (CA 1981):

    (a) total (book value) listed investments, differentiating

        (i) investments listed on a recognised stock exchange; and

        (ii) other listed investments; and

(b) the market value of listed investments where different from book value and stock exchange value if less than market value.

SSAP 15 requires that the amount of tax payable on the capital gain arising if the investments were sold at valuation should be disclosed.

Additionally, for all investments in which the investing company holds more than 10% of any class of equity share capital, or more than 10% of all allotted share capital, or share capital having a total book value exceeding ten per cent of its own net assets, it is required to disclose:

(a) the name of body corporate;
(b) country of incorporation if outside Great Britain or country of registration if incorporated in Great Britain and different from country of registration of reporting company; and
(c) description and proportion of the nominal value of the allotted shares of each class held. (CA 1967 as amended by CA 1981.)

Note 7 to the GROWSTRONG plc consolidated balance sheet shows the movement during the year of its 'other investments', i.e. to their cost at the beginning of the year is added 'additions' and deducted 'disposals' to give the cost figure at the end of the year. GROWSTRONG had written off amounts during the year leaving the net book value at its end. This figure, together with that for investments in associates, gives the figure shown in the balance sheet. The required statutory information is noted. Directors' valuation for unlisted investments is no longer required.

4.8   CURRENT ASSETS

The amounts shown under the heading 'Current Assets' in the GROWSTRONG plc consolidated balance sheet and detailed in Note 8, indicate the book value of the assets which are *not* held for use in the business on a continuing basis, but which are in process of conversion into cash.

The excess of the total book value of current assets over current liabilities measures the *working capital* of the business, alternatively labelled 'net current assets' (see *Table 3*).

Since the CA 1981 (4 Sch. 77 CA 85) requires all assets which are not fixed assets, as defined, to be entered as current assets, there is a need to differentiate those amounts which although shown under that head, are in fact 'non-current items'. Prepayments, e.g. rates paid during the current accounting period, but due in respect of a succeeding period, and e.g. debtor accounts not due within the year following balance sheet date, are required to be disclosed separately.

Valuation of current assets

The 1981 Act required that current assets must be valued at the *lower* of purchase price or production cost and net realisable value.

The purchase price of *any* asset is to be determined by adding to the actual price paid any costs incidental to its acquisition.

To explain 'purchase price' in relation to assets such as 'debtors' which have no such price as normally understood, the Act states that 'references to purchase price include references to any consideration (whether in cash or otherwise) given by the company in respect of the asset in question'.

The production cost of an asset is determined by adding to the purchase price of the raw materials and consumables used in its production, the amount of any costs directly attributable to its production. Reasonable indirect costs and interest on capital borrowed to finance the production may also be included. Distribution costs are not allowed in the computation.

Where interest on capital is included in production cost, the fact and the amount of the interest must be disclosed in a note to the accounts.

CA 1981 Balance Sheet Formats (227(1), 228, 245, 742 and 4 Sch. 1–5, CA 1985)

The Act specifies four mandatory sub-headings of 'current asset', three of which – stocks, debtors and cash – must be separately disclosed *on the face of the balance sheet*.

Stocks

The figure stated in the consolidated balance sheet (*Table 3*) is the aggregate of the book value of stocks of raw materials and consumables, work in progress, and stocks of finished goods and goods for resale – sub-headings of the CA 1981 formats.

The importance of the valuation of 'closing stock' to the determination of profit has been considered, as has its prominent part of the GEC/AEI and Pergamon Press affairs (see Chapter 1).

The problems arising in its valuation have been compounded by the effect of rapid inflation on prices. And, obviously, the Inland Revenue are concerned by its effect on 'taxable profit'.

SSAP 9 Stocks and Work in Progress

This standard is deceptively short at six paragraphs. But recognising that:

'the majority of problems which arise in practice in determining both the cost and net realizable value of stocks and work in progress result from considerations which are relevant to particular businesses and are not of such universal application that they can be the subject of a statement of standard practice'

it prefaces the six 'standard paragraphs' with twenty-four paragraphs of explanatory notes, and follows with a twenty-seven paragraph appendix of further practical considerations, a glossary of terms and an Inland Revenue statement.

SSAP 9 perhaps exemplifies the difficulties of providing a standard, by definition of an inflexible nature, which can reasonably apply to a wide variety of business circumstances, even when inflation is excluded.

Valuation of 'stocks'

SSAP 9 requires that:

'the amount at which stocks and work in progress, other than long-term contract work in progress, are stated in periodic published accounts, should be the total of the *lower* of cost and net realizable value of the separate items of stock and work in progress, or of groups of similar items.'

This does not differ in substance from the overriding legal definition of the CA 1981 (4 Sch. 77 CA 85) for current assets quoted earlier, except that the Act specifies 'cost' as purchase price or production cost. This may be determined using any of the methods for assets of the same class, either 'first in, first out' (FIFO); 'last in, first out' (LIFO); 'weighted average price' or 'any other method similar to the above'. The cardinal principle is that the method adopted must be one which appears to the directors to be appropriate to the company. The Act requires that where the amount shown in respect of such assets differs materially from 'the relative alternative amount', then the difference must be disclosed in a note to the accounts. It indicates that 'relative alternative amount' means *replacement cost* at balance sheet date. The most recent actual purchase price or production cost before that date may be used, but only if it appears to the directors to constitute the more appropriate standard of comparison for each type of asset under consideration.

SSAP 9 docs not regard replacement cost where this is lower than net realisable value to be an acceptable alternative as it is regarded as unreasonable in its effect of taking account of a loss greater than that which is expected to be incurred.

SSAP 9 does not consider the LIFO method to be a normally acceptable basis for valuation; if the directors consider that its use is necessary to meet the 'true and fair' view requirement, this could be regarded as a departure necessitating a note to the accounts giving the directors' reasons for so doing, and its effect on the accounts.

Long-term contract work in progress

SSAP 9 requires that long-term contract work in progress should be at cost plus any attributable profit, less any foreseeable losses and progress payments received and receivable. If, however, anticipated losses on individual contracts exceed cost incurred to date less progress payments received and receivable, such excesses should be shown separately as provisions. This valuation rule is therefore an exception to the prudence concept of accounting that profit should not be anticipated. SSAP 2 would require a note to the accounts disclosing the departure from the basic principle and this is normally given under the heading of 'Accounting Policies'.

The CA 1985 goes further; its valuation rules do not permit the inclusion of profit in the valuation of a current asset. As this would be regarded by the directors as a needful departure from the rules so as to meet the overriding true and fair view formula, particulars of the departure, the reasons for it and its effect must be disclosed in a note to the accounts. In 1984, the Department of Trade and Industry confirmed the need for such a disclosure when noting the acknowledged conflict between the requirements of SSAP 9 and the Companies Acts relating to the inclusion of attributable profit in stocks and work in progress. The Department insisted that companies should not 'casually depart' from the requirements of company law; but where they did see this as necessary, then they were bound to disclose information essential to a true and fair view. *Example 4.8.1* reproduces the note given with its 1983 accounts by construction industry giant, Taylor Woodrow. In 1983 and again in 1985, the ASC told the construction industry that it would not amend SSAP 9 because the issue of supplemental interpretation of standards was not a desirable policy to follow. However in 1985, the Committee announced that it was to review all accounting standards in the light of the 1980 and 1981 company legislation.

Example 4.8.1

Extract from notes to the published 1983 accounts of Taylor Woodrow.
The inclusion of profit in contract work in progress is in accordance with SSAP 9 and is required by S149(3) of the Companies Act 1948* to enable the accounts to give a true and fair view. This constitutes a departure from the valuation rules of the Companies Act 1981. As payments received on account cannot be allocated meaningfully between cost and profit, it is not practicable to state the effect of this departure on the balance sheet.
* *Now contained in S228(1)–(6) Companies Act 1985.*

The determination of 'attributable profit' is a matter involving subjective judgement – an important and difficult area where 'prudence' is a key word. The difficulties of inflation in this context can, perhaps, be contained by relevant contract terms, nevertheless some companies prudently do not take any profit into account until the long-term contract is completed; some going further and waiting until the profit is realised.

Stock profits

The increase in the monetary value of stocks in inflationary periods lead in the historic accounts to the arising of so-called stock profits. It has been noted (4.5, Deferred taxation) that the government provided a 'stock relief' so as to reduce tax on profit. This operated from 1974 through periods of high inflation until withdrawn in 1984.

In supplementary current cost accounts (Chapter 12) 'a cost of sales adjustment' (COSA) together with an indexing adjustment of 'closing stock' value deals with the problems arising in the historic accounts.

CA 1985 allows stocks in historic cost accounts to be valued at 'current cost'. Where current cost equates to replacement cost at balance sheet date and is materially different in amount from that used in the balance sheet, the difference must be disclosed.

Debtors

The amount shown in the GROWSTRONG plc consolidated balance sheet against 'Debtors' is the aggregate of the amount due from individual debtors less a provision for those debts regarded as doubtful of recovery. The valuation rule of the lower of 'purchase price' (see valuation of current assets earlier) and realisable value is therefore met.

Note 8 shows the aggregate total split among the sub-heads required by the CA 1985. The 1985 Act requires 'Debtors' to be split between trade debtors, other debtors and prepayments. Amounts owing to and from associated companies are to be shown separately. Debtors (or creditors) falling due after more than one year are to be distinguished from current debtors.

The information required by the CA 1980 – 232–4 and 6 Sch. CA 85 – in respect of loans to officers of the company, whereof the aggregate amount will be included among 'other debtors', will need to be disclosed. These loans to directors include loans made by the company or its subsidiaries. 'Loans' includes quasi-loans and credit transactions, and 'directors' means directors of the company or its holding company or persons connected with such directors.

Prepayments and accrued income may be included with the aggregate book value of debtors, distinguished as a separate sub-head, or shown apart from debtors as a main balance sheet heading (CA 1985, balance sheet formats).

Cash at bank and in hand

This is the amount of cash balances of the GROWSTRONG plc group at balance sheet date. Analysts would expect that for a manufacturing group these balances would be the minimum required for day-to-day needs. Obviously, cash on current account earns no return; indeed, in an inflationary period its purchasing power falls over time. Transactions between companies within the group which are shown as debtor or creditor accounts in each company's separate balance sheet are set off against each other in the consolidated accounts, any balances remaining representing value (e.g. cash or stock) in transit. These balances would be included in the aggregate of the stock or cash balances.

4.9 CREDITORS – AMOUNTS DUE WITHIN ONE YEAR

The aggregate amount shown against this CA 1985 heading is that formerly described as 'current liabilities', although this is still a proper description as creditors due after more than one year (section 4.4 of this chapter) have to be shown separately.

Whereas the CA 1985 requires the main sub-heads of current assets to be shown on the face of the balance sheet, the amount of current liabilities can be shown in aggregate with the necessary detail given by way of note.

GROWSTRONG plc adopts this practice and against note 9 shows separate amounts against debenture loans (amount to be repaid in the succeeding year); bank loans (current instalment due) and overdrafts; trade creditors; amounts owed to associate (related) companies; other creditors, including (current) taxation and social security; accruals and deferred income (this may be shown on the face of the balance sheet as its own separate head); and proposed dividends.

The Act requires that the amount for creditors in respect of taxation and social security shall be shown separately from the amount for 'other creditors'.

Current taxation is that due within the succeeding twelve months. Taxation, including the dates of due payment, is dealt with in Chapter 5.

The amount shown as 'proposed dividends' is the amount recommended by the GROWSTRONG directors to be paid as a final dividend to its ordinary shareholders. A dividend is not legally due to members until declared by the company in general meeting, but the CA 1967 (4 Sch. CA 85) gives statutory authority for its inclusion as a current liability even though the liability might not materialise if the company does not declare or reduces the proposed dividend.

The nature of any securities given in respect of creditors must be disclosed as a note to the accounts (4 Sch. CA 85).

Where there are debit (asset) and credit (liability) bank balances with no legal right of set off the full amounts of bank loans and overdrafts and of bank balances (CA 1967) should be shown. The CA 1981 (4 Sch. CA 85), in any case, denies the right to set off – 'assets or income may not be set off against liabilities or expenditure, and vice-versa'.

Contingent Liabilities

SSAP 18 Accounting for Contingencies defines a contingency as:

'a condition in existence at balance sheet date where the outcome is dependent upon the happening, or failure to happen, of an uncertain future event or events'.

Clearly the board of directors have to consider the accounting treatment necessary and in circumstances where:
   (i) the future event is probable,
   (ii) it will result in a loss,
   (iii) the amount can be assessed with reasonable accuracy, and
   (iv) it is material
the contingent liability *should be brought into the accounts*. This will usually mean a charge in the profit and loss account and a corresponding creditor in the balance sheet.

If the contingent liability does not satisfy the foregoing criteria, it must be disclosed by way of note if the likely amount is material and the contingency is other than remote.

Contingent *gains,* following the prudence concept, are not to be brought into account. They should be noted if the gain is material and has a probability of being realised.

The disclosure note for contingent gains and losses should give, where possible, a prudent estimate of the net pre-tax financial effect. The CA 1985 requires disclosure of the legal nature of, and any securities given, in respect of contingent liabilities. An example would be a guarantee given by a company secured on the company's assets.

Guarantees and financial commitments

The information required by the CA 1967, extended by the CA 1981, is now contained in CA 1985 4 Sch. 37, 50. Apart from the above requirements, detail must be disclosed of:
   (i) *future capital expenditure*, differentiating expenditure already *contracted* but not provided for in the accounts, and amounts authorised by the company but not yet contracted;

    (ii) *pension commitments* included under any balance sheet item, and any such commitments for which no provision has been made, giving separate detail relating to pension commitments to past directors of the company (see Chapter 5 – Disclosure of pension information in company accounts);

    (iii) *any other financial commitments* not provided for and relevant to assessing the company's state of affairs.

The above disclosure requirements extend to commitments undertaken on behalf of any subsidiary of the reporting company which must be given separately.

Post balance sheet events

SSAP 17 Accounting for Post Balance Sheet Events deals with the arising of information and the happening of events which either give need to adjust the prepared accounts or to prevent such accounts being misleading require disclosure of information about them. Material '*adjusting events*' up to the date that the accounts are formally approved by the directors, must be included. Examples of adjusting events are: the insolvency of a debtor, receipt of information regarding changed rates of taxation, and the discovery of errors or frauds which show the financial statements as incorrect.

For '*non-adjusting events*', the nature of the event, an estimate of the financial effect, or a statement that it is not practicable to make such an estimate, must be disclosed.

The tax implications of the event must be disclosed where necessary for a proper understanding of the financial position.

Examples of post balance sheet events which would normally be regarded as 'non-adjusting' are: mergers and acquisitions, the issue of shares or debentures, changes in the rates of foreign exchange, and strikes or other labour disputes.

Information on contingencies, financial commitments and events occurring post balance sheet is obviously necessary for analysts, current shareholders, potential investors and others dealing with or considering dealing with a company.

As an example, the ICI group, under the heading 'Commitments and contingent liabilities' in a recent balance sheet, showed:

'contracts placed for capital expenditure of £320m, and expenditure sanctioned but not contracted £540m.'

It noted: 'Guarantees and uncalled capital relating to subsidiary and other companies £122m, and guarantees relating to Pension Funds, currency exchange arrangements in respect of which losses (or gains) could arise and other contingencies £161m.'

Section 235 Sch. 7 Companies Act 1985 requires the disclosure of 'important events affecting the company . . . which have occurred since the end of the period either in the 'Directors' report or by note to the financial statement' (see Directors' Report', Chapter 9).

5

Profit and loss account

Introduction

The balance sheet, as we have seen in the previous chapter, provides information on the structure and book value of the total capital employed by the enterprise. Analysts can thus consider the relationship between owners' capital and borrowed capital and that between this long-term capital and its investment in long-term fixed assets, with, as a corollary, the adequacy and source of working capital giving pointers to the liquidity position.

But the assessment of the efficiency with which capital is employed requires further information, much of which is contained in the company's *profit and loss account* for the accounting period of which the balance sheet ends.

Table 4 shows the GROWSTRONG plc profit and loss (or revenue) account. It is presented in the consolidated form of a holding company with its subsidiaries. A holding company is exempt from presenting its *own* profit and loss account where it publishes a consolidated statement (CA 1985, S228(7), 245(2)). Where it relies on this exemption, the fact must be stated together with the amount of the consolidated profit or loss for the financial year which is dealt with in its own accounts.

The S228 and 4 Sch. 1–5 CA 85 offers four choices of profit and loss format. It is likely that most large and listed companies will choose format 1 which is that followed in *Table 4*. The principal change and additional information resulting from the 1981 legislation is the requirement to include expense headings and amounts between turnover and operating profit before tax. Thus the 'cost of sales' and 'gross profit' need to be disclosed for the first time in UK published accounts. The remainder of the profit and loss account format is little changed.

What is in a Profit and Loss Account?

5.1 TURNOVER

The figure shown by GROWSTRONG for 'turnover' includes sales made by subsidiary companies to customers outside the group. Sales made by associated companies are not required to be included, but this information has been published where the directors considered it to be material in total.

Sales between companies in the GROWSTRONG group are excluded, as is the profit thereon in determining the 'operating profit' (see 5.2).

The CA 1985 required all companies, except banking or discounting companies, to declare 'turnover'. Certain information needing to be disclosed under that legislation in the directors' report must now be given in the notes to the accounts. The exemption from disclosure if the turnover required to be stated did not reach a stipulated sum (£1 million. SI 1979) has been withdrawn.

Current legal requirements for disclosure

Note 1 to the GROWSTRONG plc consolidated profit and loss account gives the following statutory information:

    (a) In respect of each class of business (as defined by the directors) carried on by the group during the financial year:
      (i) the turnover attributable to that class, and
      (ii) the profit before taxation attributable to each class.
    (b) The amount of turnover attributable to each market (geographically bounded and as defined by the directors) supplied by the group (e.g. United Kingdom, Europe, USA).

Notes: Item (b) is a Stock Exchange disclosure requirement for listed companies, which is now extended to other companies (CA 1985).

    Information on exports need no longer be given.

    Where in the opinion of the directors, disclosures (a) and (b) above would seriously prejudice the interests of the company (group), the information may be omitted. The fact of omission must be stated.

There is no legal definition of turnover. It is generally considered to include the sale of goods and the provision of services in the ordinary course of business.

The turnover information is shown net of value added tax (SSAP 5. Accounting for VAT).

Augmenting the statutory information

The statutory information is often augmented by other valuable data for analysis. A typical ICI directors' report before the CA 1981 contained:

> Example 5.1.1
>
>   A 10 year bar chart of sales distinguishing UK from overseas.
>
>   A quarterly analysis of sales for the current and previous year with related quarterly profit before tax.
>
>   The sales for each class of business for the current and previous year with the related 'Trading Profit'.
>
>   A territorial analysis of sales for the current and previous year differentiating for UK sales between home and export sales, with related profit.
>
>   A 10 year bar chart of exports from the UK.

Much of this information needs now to be given as notes to the accounts.

5.2   OPERATING PROFIT

The *internal* books of account deal with the double (accounting) entry resulting from *all* transactions. At the end of the accounting year, the balances of the income and expenditure

Table 4   GROWSTRONG plc & SUBSIDIARIES
                    CONSOLIDATED PROFIT AND LOSS ACCOUNT
                              (historic cost)
                      for its most recent financial year

	NOTE	THIS YEAR £'000	LAST YEAR £'000
TURNOVER	1	4,520	3,990
Cost of sales	2	3,640	3,186
Gross profit	2	880	804
Distribution and administrative expenses	2	522	479
		358	325
Share of profit of associated company	2	15	10
OPERATING PROFIT	2	373	335
Income from fixed asset investment	2	10	8
		383	343
Interest payable	2	42	47
PROFIT ON ORDINARY ACTIVITIES BEFORE TAX	1	341	296
Tax on profit on ordinary activities	3	120	97
PROFIT ON ORDINARY ACTIVITIES AFTER TAX		221	199
Minority interest	4	26	15
PROFIT APPLICABLE TO HOLDING COMPANY SHAREHOLDERS BEFORE EXTRAORDINARY ITEMS	5	195	184
Extraordinary items less tax	6	15	9
PROFIT APPLICABLE TO HOLDING COMPANY SHAREHOLDERS	7	180	175
Appropriations of profit			
Dividends	7	75	75
Retained profit for the year	7	105	100
		180	175
Earnings per ordinary share	5	19.5p	18.4p

Tutorial notes
1. The related consolidated balance sheet (*Table 3*) is shown on page 52.
2. Published profit and loss accounts will not necessarily contain amplification notes in respect of each item.
3. The information which would be contained in the notes to this profit and loss account is discussed in the text of this chapter.
4. Disclosure of movements on reserves as required by the revised Schedule 4 CA 1985, SSAP 6 and its revision, ED 36, may be shown immediately following the profit and loss account, and form a separate statement within the financial statements or as a note to the latter (see Section 5.6 following).

accounts are transferred into a manufacturing, trading and profit and loss account.

The manufacturing account determines the aggregate cost of manufactured goods, inclusive of materials, labour and overhead costs, the latter including depreciation of plant etc., wages and management salaries. Adjustments are made in arriving at the cost of manufactured goods for opening and closing stocks of raw materials, work in progress and finished goods, and the final figure is transferred into the trading and profit and loss account.

The summarised trading and profit and loss account of the GROWSTRONG group assuming the figures of the subsidiaries were merged with those of the holding company would be:

GROWSTRONG group Trading and profit and loss account

	£'000s	£'000s
Sales		4,520
less *Cost of Sales:*		
Opening stock of finished goods	180	
plus Cost of manufactured goods	3,700	
	3,880	
less Closing stock of finished goods	240	3,640
Gross Profit		880
less Distribution and administrative expenses		522
Group *operating profit* before accounting for its share of associated company profit, and *before taxation*		358

Prior to the operation of the CA 1981, the *published* GROWSTRONG plc consolidated profit and loss account would have stated the turnover figure of £4.52 million at its head, but started the account with the group operating profit of £358,000 – the end figure in the above summarised internal revenue account. Recognising a need for some confidentiality, the CA 1948 and the CA 1967 required only limited disclosure of some of the items making up the difference between these figures of £4.16 million. As will be seen from *Table 4*, the CA 1985 requires the disclosure of the figures for *cost of sales, gross profit*, and *distribution and administrative expenses*, supplemented in the notes to the profit and loss account with the information required by the previous legislation, largely unchanged.

Other formats of the CA 85 than format 1 on which *Table 4* is based include some of this supplementary information on the face of the profit and loss account.

The statutory information

Note 2 to the GROWSTRONG plc consolidated profit and loss account sets out this information and the major items showing the movement between turnover and operating profit before tax are:

> *Depreciation* charged against profit for the year in respect of the use of fixed assets (see Chapter 4), and the diminution of intangible assets (including goodwill).
>
> *The Chairman's emoluments, the directors' emoluments* in aggregate, distinguishing fees, other emoluments, pensions and compensation for loss of office; in group accounts disclosure applies only to directors of the holding company, but includes all emoluments of these persons in respect of their services to the group; the number of directors falling within brackets of a scale in multiples of £5,000; the aggregate emoluments of the highest paid director if these exceed those of the Chairman; and the number of directors who have waived emoluments and the aggregate amount waived.
>
> Interestingly, ICI give information of the income tax and assumed take home pay of its directors based on a married person without children and with no other income source.
>
> *Employees:* the number of employees (other than directors and persons working mainly outside the UK) receiving more than a stipulated sum per annum (£20,000 from 1979, changeable by Statutory Instrument) and numbers within rising bands of £5,000; the average number of persons employed during the financial year (previously given in the directors' report); the average number of persons employed within each category of employees (as defined by the directors); and in respect of the persons employed, the aggregate amounts of:
>   (i) wages and salaries paid or payable in respect of the financial year;

(ii) social security costs incurred and

(iii) other pension costs, see below.

The information in respect of highly paid employees need only deal with holding company employees in group accounts, but groups may choose to extend the information to include subsidiary company senior employees.

Pension costs: as yet there is no standard guidance on meeting the requirements of the Companies Act 1985 to disclose 'pension costs' in the profit and loss account and commitments (see Chapter 4) in the balance sheet, but the subject has been well-aired. Despite the significance of pension costs as a proportion of a company's total employment costs, UK companies typically provide little information about their pension arrangements in their financial statements. The ascertainment of pension costs involves long-term actuarial estimates of a number of inter-linking factors, such as projected pay levels, general inflation and future return rates on pension fund investments. Following prolonged study by its working party which gave emphasis to the difficulty of calculating and allocating the costs to particular accounting periods, the ASC decided that the first stage of an accounting standard on pension information should limit its requirements to certain *disclosures* which would assist the users of financial statements to understand the basis on which provision was being made and the significance of these costs for a particular company. This was the purport of *Exposure Draft 32* issued in May 1983.

Considering responses to ED 32 and its own further consideration of the complex problems involved, the ASC issued a *Statement of Intent (SOI)* in November 1984 within which the disclosure recommendations of the exposure draft were substantially reproduced. A comprehensive exposure draft is to be developed from the SOI, although ASC appears confident that most employers already calculate their contributions in accordance with their latest statements.

The *summary conclusions* of the SOI are:

(i) the *emphasis* in accounting for pension costs should be on the *profit and loss account charge*;

(ii) the *accounting objective* should be to charge systematically the cost of pensions against profits over the service lives of the group of employees;

(iii) in meeting this objective, a *periodic pension cost* will be produced which is a substantially level percentage of the current and expected future pensionable payroll based on current actuarial assumptions;

(iv) variations from regular costs should be allocated on a prudent basis over a period not exceeding the average remaining service lives of the employees;

(v) as long as they are consistent with the basic accounting objectives, no limitation on the actuarial valuation methods and assumptions is foreseen;

(vi) the basic principles apply to all types of scheme, including those which are funded or unfunded, and to those where the employer's strict legal commitments may be limited, but where the commitment arises out of customary practice;

(vii) no single distinct method of accounting is suggested but companies, e.g. who do not make assumptions about future salary levels when estimating their contribution or who pay directly on a pay-as-you go basis, without provisions in the profit and loss account would have to change their approach.

With the emphasis in accounting for pension costs on the profit and loss account charge, any balance sheet entry would be limited to any net pension liability relating to the cumulative cost charged to the profit and loss account, but not yet discharged through payment of contributions, or directly paid pensions.

Although the employer has a general commitment to support the pension scheme, and would disclose this commitment, his specific liability is for the costs relating to the accounting period. The indeterminate costs in future periods are not a present liability, although it may be necessary to disclose by way of note any commitment to make *additional* contributions, now or in the future.

Apart from the above noted *disclosures*, the SOI lists others which are seen as essential to a readers understanding of pension costs and commitments. These include: the nature of the pension scheme, its funding and legal obligations; the accounting and funding policies including the basis of allocating pension costs to accounting periods; detail of the actuarial service; explanations of changes to regular costs charged to revenue; total pension cost as a percentage of pensionable payroll; detail of provisions or pre-payments in the balance sheet arising from differences between accounting policy and funding policy; expected significant effects on future financial statements of changes in any of the above matters are the subject of disclosure.

Pension costs are at present of the order of tens of billions of pounds per annum in the UK. These SOI recommendations represent a needed progress in accounting for them.

Auditors' remuneration including expenses. Any amounts paid to the auditor in a non-audit capacity, e.g. as an accountant or consultant, do not have to be disclosed.

Charge for hire of plant and machinery. This requirement of the CA 1967 for some years cloaked the size of potential liabilities for non-cancellable future rental obligations as fixed assets were acquired by the leasing method known as financial or capital leasing. In 1973, for example, the ill-fated company, Court Line, published accounts which gave no hint of its leasing obligations of aircraft and equipment costing £40 million. Clearly all persons dealing with a company, not least unsecured creditors (trade and loan), would want to know of such a liability. The write off of the rental expense in the profit and loss account as part of its 'cost of sales' was clearly an insufficient disclosure. Given the boom in leasing – by 1980, the Equipment Leasing Association, representing the major leasing companies, reported that assets acquired by leasing represented some 12.4% of all new capital investment in plant and machinery – the ASC was under pressure to recommend standard practice. But the problems were not straightforward. It was not until 1981 that an exposure draft ED 29 was issued, and it was a further three years before the issue of *SSAP 21 Accounting for leases and hire purchase contracts.* In that year, the Finance Act (1984) introduced changes which included the abolition of first year capital allowances (see Chapter 4 (4.5)), this materially eroded the tax advantages of leasing to the lessor companies.

Financial leases, funding and tax advantages

The key reasons for the growth of leasing were:
  (i) the tax advantages available; and
  (ii) its availability as a major source of medium-term finance for industry.

The tax advantages followed the introduction of the first year capital allowances which eventually reached 100%. Although these first year allowances were available to industrial *purchasers* of plant and machinery, many companies because of a combination of tax stock relief and first year allowances already available, did not have sufficient taxable profit to obtain immediate benefit from new allowances. This led to the decision by many industrial companies to lease in order to obtain a tax advantage – an indirect advantage, through the leasing companies as owners getting the allowances together with in some cases, regional development grants, and passing them on by way of lower rentals to the lessee – and a direct advantage as the rent or hire charge is deductible by the lessee for tax purposes.

Leasing became an attractive major source of medium-term finance. Short-term loans on overdrafts were readily available from the clearing banks and long-term finance was available from the financial institutions (e.g. insurance companies and pension funds), but until the banks moved from a policy of short, to a policy of short and medium-term lending, there was a gap in funding sources. Leasing helped significantly to fill it.

The lessors were, in the main, financial institutions who still had sufficient mainstream tax liabilities to utilise the tax advantage and the boost to their business. They were followed by some industrial groups who formed their own leasing subsidiaries as a sales aid to their products and others seeking to employ surplus funds or for tax reasons.

There is little doubt that the loss of the 100% first year allowance will make a considerable impact on the size and operations of the leasing industry, although the phased reduction over three years gave time for adjustment. It is expected that there will be a switch back to hire-purchase with more emphasis on operating leases. Whatever the outcome, the requirements of SSAP 21 cover hire-purchase, operating leases and financial leases both in the lessor and the lessee accounts.

SSAP 21 Accounting leases and hire purchase contracts

The significant requirement of this standard is for lessee companies to capitalise material *finance leases* – which treatment many companies were already following, given the long discussion period preceding the issue of SSAP 21. No longer would the write off of the 'rental charge' in the profit and loss account be sufficient. The lessees' balance sheets will reflect both the 'leased asset', so described to differentiate from 'owned assets', and the total liability to the lessor. The amount at which both the asset and the obligation to pay future rentals is recorded, is the present value of the minimum lease payments derived by discounting them at the interest rate implicit in the lease. In practice 'the fair value of the asset' may be an acceptable substitute. The 'asset' is *depreciated* over the term of the lease or the useful life of the asset whichever is the shorter and charged annually to the profit and loss account of the lessee. The *finance charges* are debited to profit and loss account as a constant periodic amount of the outstanding balance of the 'obligation' to the lessor. After the first year, the capital element of the amounts due to the lessor will be separately shown under the headings 'creditors due in less than one year' and 'creditors due in more than one year'. In respect of the latter amount, information must be given showing separately 'the amounts payable in the second to fifth years inclusive from the balance sheet date' and 'the aggregate amounts payable thereafter'.

The *finance lease* to which these standard requirements apply, is defined as one 'that transfers substantially all the risks and rewards of ownership of an asset to the lessee'. What is being capitalised in the lessee's accounts is not the asset itself, but the rights in the asset.

The *hire purchase* contract is differentiated from the finance lease as the former is a contract for the hire of the asset which contains a provision giving the hirer an option to acquire legal title (ownership) to the asset upon fulfilment of certain conditions stated in the contract. The accounting and disclosure requirements of the standard are substantially the same for hire purchase contracts as for finance leases.

An *operating lease* defined in the standard as 'a lease other than a finance lease' is a short-term lease of some physical asset, usually cancellable at short notice and without material penalty. The lessor maintains substantive ownership with obligations of maintenance, depreciation and insurance. In the lessee's account, the rental under an operating lease is charged to the profit and loss account on a straight-line basis over the lease term, even if the payments are not made on such a basis, although the standard allows other appropriate, systematic and rational bases.

In respect of finance leases including hire purchase contracts, the balance sheet of the lessee company must include a note of *commitments* at balance sheet date, i.e. leases entered into but whose inception incurs after the year end. Because of their importance finance leases in the lessee books have been emphasised. Previously, they were often treated as an '*off-balance sheet*' item, an expression which speaks for itself, but now they are subject to effective standard accounting and disclosure requirements. External users of accounts making investment or credit decisions will be more readily informed. Return on capital employed targets and outcomes can more certainly be set and measured.

In the lessors accounts, assets held for use under *operating leases* are recorded as fixed assets and depreciated over their useful life. For *finance leases*, lessors will show amounts due from lessees as debtors, and credit gross earnings to profit and loss accounts to give a constant periodic rate of return in respect of each contract. Both lessors and lessees are required to disclose the accounting policies they have adopted.

Tax-free regional development grants received by the lessor are to be spread over the period of the lease, and brought into periodic profit and loss accounts *either* as non-taxable income, *or* by grossing up the grant for inclusion in the profit before tax figure, and increasing the tax charge disclosing the amount of the enhancement to both figures.

In addition to the foregoing information, GROWSTRONG show:

(i) the amount written off as goodwill as required by SSAP 22 (see Chapter 4 (4.6); and

(ii) the separate totals of distribution and administrative costs,

in arriving at the profit and loss sub-total of £358,000.

Cost of sales and gross profit

This additional information, hitherto undisclosed, will be useful to analysts in their comparisons of the profitability of separate companies and groups and of the trends within one enterprise or group. While companies who take part in inter-firm comparison exercises have been able to compare their rating against those of other companies over a range of ratios, it has been on a confidential basis.

The disclosure of cost of sales and gross profit figures will lead to open comparison between competing companies and will be particularly revealing for the retail trade where this information has been closely guarded. Hopefully, the disclosures should lead to improved all round efficiency.

Exceptional items of income or charges

SSAP 6 – Accounting for Extraordinary Items and Prior Year Adjustments, and the draft new standard ED 36 (January 1985) are dealt with later in this chapter (5.6). Exceptional items are those of an unusual nature, incidence or size arising from the *ordinary activities* of the business, e.g. the failure of a customer company giving rise to a substantial and exceptional bad debt. Extraordinary items are those which derive from events or transactions *outside* the ordinary activities. The CA 1985 requires that details of extraordinary or exceptional income or charges arising during the year should be given as a note to the profit and loss account. As *exceptional* items arise from the ordinary operating activities of the business, they should be included in that part of the profit and loss account under discussion leading to the determination of the group operating profit of £358,000. They should be separately designated where this is necessary for a true and fair view, whether on the face of the profit or loss account or in a separate note.

Profit on ordinary activities before tax

In arriving at this important sub-total from the figure of £358,000, three items are accounted for on the face of the GROWSTRONG consolidated profit and loss account, i.e.

(i) its share of the profit before tax of its associated company (see Chapter 4 (4.7)),

(ii) its income from fixed asset investments, and

(iii) interest on its debenture and bank loans.

'Other operating income' (e.g. rents from land) and 'Other interest receivable and similar income' are examples of other headings in the CA 85 profit and loss account formats which would be dealt with at this point.

Income from fixed asset investments

Within note 2, GROWSTRONG give the make-up of the amount shown separately on the face of the consolidated profit and loss account against this heading. As required by the CA

1985, they distinguish the income from listed investments.

Although no longer legally required so to do, the note states the income from unlisted investments as this is obviously identifiable as the balance of the investment income credited to the profit and loss account.

Tutorial Comment

These amounts do not include income from associated companies or from subsidiaries. The former, as will be seen from *Table 4*, is included in the consolidated profit and loss account as an inclusive part of the entry 'share of profit of associated company' stated before tax. The tax on the share of the associate's profit is deducted as part of the group's overall tax charge (5.3).

On consolidation, dividends received *from* a subsidiary in the holding company's and any co-subsidiary company's separate profit and loss account cancel against dividends paid *by* any subsidiary. In the consolidated profit and loss account all the levels of profit (from gross profit to profit on ordinary activities after tax) include all subsidiary profits and therefore the dividends paid or payable by them.

Accounting for investment income

The investment income that is included here is shown gross, i.e. at the net sum received plus the attributable tax credit. An amount equal to the tax credit is then included in the overall tax charge (see 5.3). This is the standard accounting practice (SSAP 8) for incoming dividends from UK resident companies. thus the double entry would be:

	£		£
Debit: cash (received)	70	Credit: Investment income	100
Debit: Tax on investment income	30		

for every £100 of investment income where the basic rate of income tax is 30%.

For *corporation tax* purposes (see 5.3) investment income is distinguished as either *franked investment income* (i.e. dividends from other UK companies arising from profits which have already suffered corporation tax), or *unfranked investment income*. The important point is that the recipient company does not have to pay corporation tax on *franked* income.

Where a company or group has investments which are categorised as current asset investments, the income if material will be included in the profit and loss account against the CA 1985 format heading 'Other interest receivable and similar income' or a more suitable heading determined by the directors, but it is probable that the head 'income from fixed asset investment' would be extended to include such income, the separate amounts being distinguished in the note.

Interest payable

The statutory information required by the CA 1985 is show1 in *Note 2* to the GROWSTRONG plc consolidated profit and loss account distinguishing:
   (i) Interest on bank loans, overdrafts and loans (other than bank loans or overdrafts) repayable within five years; and
   (ii) Interest on all other loans.

Tutorial Comment
Chapter 4 (4.4) – Loan capital, noted that loan interest as a pre-corporation tax item is chargeable by a company as an expense so as to reduce its taxation burden. The use of capital gearing by companies so as to increase the return on the ordinary shareholders' investment, and interest and capital covers are dealt with in that chapter.

The 'earnings before interest and tax' (EBIT) of the GROWSTRONG group are £383,000 and on a group basis amply cover the interest charged. The extent, however, of the liability of the *group* as opposed to the liability of the *borrowing company* within the group will depend on the legal loan document, and in addition, within total borrowings, may be those with prior ranking to others so that individual loan interest covers would be more appropriate.

Accounting for interest expense

Apart from being an allowable expense so as to reduce corporation tax – bank loan interest excepted – debenture and other loan interest payable are, generally, '*annual charges*' for income tax purposes. The paying company is required to deduct income tax at the basic rate from the gross interest payable, paying the net interest to the lender and accounting to the Inland Revenue for the tax. In this respect, the paying company merely acts as an agent of the Revenue. Thus the double (accounting) entry would be:

	£		£
Debit: Loan interest payable	100	Credit: Cash (paid)	70
		Credit: Tax on loan interest	30

for every £100 of loan interest payable, where the basic rate of income tax is 30%.

As the gross loan interest is an expense reducing the *corporation tax* payable by a company and has not, therefore, suffered corporation tax, it is an example of an *unfranked payment* (i.e. unfranked for corporation tax purposes). If the recipient of the interest is a company, its receipt would represent unfranked investment income (see page 115).

The interest-paying company has to account to the Inland Revenue for the tax deducted from the gross interest. Where it both receives and pays unfranked items, the tax on the one can be offset against the tax on the other. Net balances of income tax due to the Revenue will be paid to them within 14 days of the calendar quarter in which they occurred. Any net balance of income tax owed *by* the Revenue is deductible from the mainstream corporation tax payable in that accounting year (see 5.3).

Profit on ordinary activities before tax

This single figure shows the return earned by the group from all its activities before taxation. Its apportionment over each class of business carried on must be shown by way of note (page 108).

The remainder of the consolidated profit and loss account (*Table 4*), subject to the 'minority interest' and any 'extraordinary items', shows how this profit is APPROPRIATED:
  (i) by the government in taxation;
  (ii) to the shareholders in dividends, and
  (iii) the residue being retained by the group for its maintenance and growth.

5.3 TAXATION

GROWSTRONG, which has no overseas taxation liabilities, explains in note 3 the make up of the £120,000 charged in the consolidated profit and loss account against 'tax on profit on ordinary activities':

	£'000s
TAXATION Based on the results for the year –	
United Kingdom corporation tax at 52%:	
Parent and subsidiary companies	122
Associate company	6
	128

Overprovision in previous year   8

Tax charged in consolidated profit and loss account   120

The corporation tax charge on the results for the year has been reduced by £56,000 by reason of accelerated capital allowances and stock appreciation relief.*

(*Note:* Tax, as it is affected by 'extraordinary items', is dealt with as a composite part of that entry – see 5.6.)

*Tutorial Comment
Note 3 confirmed that GROWSTRONG was one of the large number of companies which prior to the 1984 budget operated a policy of non-provision of deferred taxation arising out of its fixed asset investment, taking the view that its level of capital expenditure would not require the recovery of deferred corporation tax in the foreseeable future. In 1984 it had to re-assess its position on deferred taxation following that year's Finance Act tax changes (see 4.5 Finance Act 1984 and corporate and deferred taxation).

Legal and Standard requirements of disclosure

The CA 1985 requirements are:
> *Disclose:*   (a) the basis for computing UK corporation and income tax;
>   (b) detail of any special circumstances affecting the liability in respect of taxation of profits, income or capital gains for the financial year or for succeeding financial years;
>   (c)   (i) the charge for UK corporation tax;
>   (ii) if that amount would have been greater but for double taxation relief, the amount it would have been;
>   (iii) the charge for UK income tax; and
>   (iv) the charge for taxation imposed outside the UK on profits, income and (so far as charged to revenue) capital gains.

SSAP 1 requires that the tax attributable to the share of the profit of associated companies credited to the profit and loss account should be disclosed separately within the group tax charge.

SSAP 8 – The Treatment of Taxation under the Imputation System in the Accounts of Companies – specifies the following for inclusion in the detail note of the taxation charge, to be shown separately, if *material*:

Profit and loss account
1. (a) UK corporation tax specifying transfers between the deferred taxation account and the profit and loss account, if material.
   (b) Tax attributable to franked investment income.
   (c) Irrecoverable advanced corporation tax (see later).
   (d) The relief for overseas taxation (a reduction of the charge) to UK taxation (see later).
2. Overseas taxation (in total, relieved and unrelieved, but specifying in relation to the latter that part which arises from dividend distribution) (see later).

Note: The concept of materiality
This concept allows a company to judge whether an item needs to be separately specified or be included with other items undisclosed. The relative size of the amount involved is most often the criterion on which the judgement is based, although occasionally a transaction may arise which although insignificant in amount, is such that disclosure would be the proper course. The phrase 'if material' is often used (see above) within legal and standard disclosure requirements.

GROWSTRONG has decided that the amount it has transferred to Deferred Tax account in respect of short-term timing differences (see page 81) and the tax attributable to its franked investment income was not sufficiently material to necessitate its separate disclosure outside the stated £122,000 within the note explaining it tax charge in the consolidated profit and loss account.

Why the accounting pre-tax profit and taxable profit differ

There are two main reasons why profit for tax purposes differs from the accounting pre-tax profit:

1. The fact that certain types of income may be tax free or that certain expenditure incurred is disallowable for tax purposes. The tax suffered or relieved in this way is a fixed or permanent loss or gain. They are not reversible in future periods and cannot, therefore, be offset by provisions for deferred tax. Logically these are labelled *permanent differences*.
2. The existence of items which are included in the financial statements of a period different from that in which they are dealt with for taxation, known as *timing differences*.

Short-term timing differences normally reverse in the next accounting period to that under consideration and require the operation of deferred taxation.

Other timing differences (see 4.5 Deferred taxation and SSAP 15) are such that the company *may* be liable to pay the full tax at some time. It has been shown why some companies chose not to operate a deferred tax account in respect of these, and how this decision was affected by the Finance Act 1984.

Example 4.5.1 showed that if there were *only* timing differences and these were provided in a deferred tax account, the sum of the deferred tax provided plus the corporation tax payable should always equal the corporation tax rate times the pre-tax profit.

Permanent differences

Other differences arising between tax based on accounting profit and taxable profit which, NOT being timing differences, can be bracketed as permanent differences, include:

1. *Income tax imputed to have been suffered on franked investment income received* (see 5.2). This is included in the overall tax charge.

   While this income tax is charged and the grossed up franked investment income is credited to profit and loss account, there arises an associated *tax credit* which may be used by a company to reduce any liability to advance corporation tax (see page 82 and later in this chapter).

   Example 5.3.1
     (Assumes a basic income tax rate of 30%.)
       Company X receives franked investment income of £14,000 on which income tax of 3/7ths, i.e. £6,000, has been incurred.
       Company X shows the gross franked investment income £20,000 as a credit in its profit and loss account and includes the £6,000 within the tax charge in that account as tax attributable to franked income. Subsequent to the receipt of this income, Company X pays its own shareholders a dividend of £70,000. Under the imputation system, it is required to pay advance corporation tax to the Inland Revenue of 3/7ths thereof, i.e. £30,000. However, the actual payment is reduced by the tax credit of £6,000 on the investment income received and the balance only is payable.
       This example shows that companies receiving dividends can pass them on to their own shareholders, without incurring tax. Therefore, the grossed up *value*

of received dividends to the company because they are franked (i.e. not liable for corporation tax purposes), is the net amount grossed up at the *corporation tax rate* and not the income tax rate.

2. *Adjustment for over- and under-provisions of tax for prior years*
   The charge entered in the profit and loss account for corporation tax is the estimated figure computed by the company. The subsequent agreed assessment of the Inland Revenue gives rise to over and under provision which has to be adjusted as a 'prior year' item in a later revenue account.

3. *Taxation on capital gains*
   Where an asset is sold at an amount in excess of its original cost, tax is payable on the excess at the capital gains rate and unless the transaction is regarded as an 'extraordinary' one (see 5.6) it will be included in the corporation tax charge. Corporation tax (balancing charges) would be recovered on the capital allowances previously given.

4. *Taxable losses*
   Companies can use taxable losses to obtain repayment of corporation tax levied in the previous two years, or carry them forward against future profits without restriction.

   Offsetting of losses against profits within the group may take place for corporation tax purposes given that the subsidiary is wholly or mainly (75% plus) owned, otherwise the losses are carried forward within the individual company for future recovery, and this latter regulation applies to all overseas subsidiaries.

THE IMPUTATION TAX SYSTEM IN THE ACCOUNTS OF COMPANIES

The introduction of corporation tax in the UK in 1965 and its significant change to the 'imputation system' in 1973, are examples of external influences to which companies have had to adapt. While, no doubt, introduced for macro-economic reasons, both had political overtones.

Some would say that when Mr Callaghan, the then Labour Chancellor, introduced the 1965 Corporation Tax, he deliberately and unashamedly taxed profits companies paid out as dividends, not once but twice. Whether or not that was the purpose, that was the result.

Under that system, a company was liable to pay (then) 40% of its profits in corporation tax. In addition, from the dividends it paid out of its after-tax profits, it was required to deduct income tax at the (then) standard (now basic) rate, and account for it to the Inland Revenue. Shareholders received a net payment, i.e. the 'gross dividend' declared by the company less income tax deducted at the source. Thus profits distributed as dividends were taxed twice.

The Conservatives promised to stop this form of (as they saw it) Socialist discrimination and to go further by adopting a system that would positively encourage companies to pay out more of their profits in dividends, not less as the 1965 system encouraged.

They favoured the German 'two-rate' system under which distributed profits were taxed at a lower rate than profits retained. But the Germans changed to favour the French 'imputation' method, and the UK then joined the EEC and followed suit.

Under the imputation system, a company pays corporation tax on its taxable profit at the rate prescribed by a Finance Act, for the purpose of this example 50%, irrespective of the amount, if any, it chooses to pay out in dividends.

Example 5.3.2

Company X earns £1 million pre-tax profits, and distributes 35% of its after-tax profits.

Company Y earns £1 million pre-tax profits, and distributes 70% of its after-tax profits.

Pre-imputation corporation tax rate is 40%

Imputation corporation tax rate is taken as 50%

Standard (basic) income tax rate is 30%

Pre-imputation corporation tax system		X	Y
Profit		£1,000,000	£1,000,000
40% Corporation tax		400,000	400,000
Profit after tax (PAT)		600,000	600,000
Dividend 35% (X) 70% (Y) of PAT		210,000	420,000
Paid by the company to:			
Shareholder	£147,000		£294,000
Inland Revenue	63,000		126,000
Retained by the company		£390,000	£180,000
Total tax bill		£463,000	£526,000

Present imputation tax system

Note: The rate of corporation tax was raised by the Government with the intention of maintaining the cash flow to them under the changed system.

		X	Y
Profit		£1,000,000	£1,000,000
50% (say) Corporation tax		500,000	500,000
Profit after tax (PAT)		500,000	500,000
Dividend 35% (X) 70% (Y) of PAT		175,000	350,000
Paid by the company to:			
Shareholder	£175,000		£350,000
Inland Revenue	Nil		Nil
Retained by the company		£325,000	£150,000
Total tax bill		£500,000	£500,000

Under the present system, the shareholders of X and Y will, for the purposes of their personal tax return, 'gross up' the dividend received multiplying its amount by 10/7 (basic rate 30%). The difference between the two amounts will be the imputed tax which is assumed as paid tax for the purpose of determining their personal tax liability. Where, for example, their total income was such that no tax liability arose, the imputed tax could be reclaimed. Thus, the imputed tax is a tax credit for the shareholder.

It will be observed from the example that the total tax bill of X and Y is the same under the present system despite the variance in the level of dividends.

Secondly, the shareholders of both companies receive considerably more (19%) under the present system than the previous one from the same percentage of after-tax profit.

Company Y, with the more generous dividend policy, receives the greater tax benefit from the new system in comparison with the old.

With the phased reduction of Corporation Tax rates to 35% (1986/7) announced in the Finance Act 1984 (page 83) these advantages of the imputation system were further enhanced.

ADVANCE CORPORATION TAX (ACT) (see also page 82)

When, in an accounting period, a company makes a distribution (e.g. a dividend) to its shareholders, although it is not required to withhold income tax from the payment, it is required to make a payment on account of corporation tax in advance of the normal due date of payment of corporation tax (ACT).

This ACT is payable within fourteen days of the end of the calendar quarter in which the distribution is made.

ACT is normally set off against a company's total liability for corporation tax on its income (but not its chargeable gains) of the same accounting period.

The resultant net liability is known as *mainstream corporation tax*.

Example 5.3.3

ACT payable by companies X and Y
Basic income tax rate = 30%.

	X £	Y £
ACT = x(100 − x) times the dividend paid where x = the basic rate of tax.		
= 30(100 − 30) = 3/7ths times £175,000 =	75,000	
= 3/7ths times £350,000 =		150,000
The mainstream corporation tax is then –		
£500,000 less £ 75,000	425,000	
£500,000 less £150,000		350,000

Due dates of payment of corporation tax

The required early payment of ACT (linked to dividend payment) speeds the flow of corporation tax to the Government and offsets some of the delay in the receipt of the mainstream tax.

While for companies commencing business after March 1965, when corporation tax was introduced, payment of mainstream tax is due nine months after the end of a company's year, for those operating before that date the tax is payable on 1 January of the financial year (financial year 1985 is from 1 April to 31 March 1986) following the financial year in which the company's accounting period ended.

These provisions lead to intervals from 9 to 21 months after the end of an accounting year for the payment of mainstream tax.

Example 5.3.4

Old-established company X, accounting year ended 31 March 1985, would pay its mainstream corporation tax on the profits of that year on 1 January 1986, an interval of 9 months.

Old-established company Y, accounting year ended 31 May 1985, would pay its mainstream corporation tax on the profits of that year on 1 January 1987, an interval of 19 months.

New company Z, accounting year ended 31 May 1985, would pay its mainstream corporation tax on the profits of that year on 1 March 1986, an interval of 9 months. Payments due within the 12 months after balance sheet date would be shown therein as Current Liabilities (Creditors: amounts falling due within one year). Payments due outside the period of the next accounting year would be included as deferred taxation. In either case, the appropriate ACT would be deducted from the full corporation tax payable.

Irrecoverable ACT

It will be noted that the advance corporation tax payable and the shareholders' tax credit link a company's corporation tax and the shareholder' own tax liability, and this is a key to the system.

Example 5.3.2 showed that a company, with no overseas earnings and tax, incurs no extra corporation or other tax burden because of the level of its dividend payments. Because the ACT payments are *deducted* from the corporation tax and are not additional levies on top of that tax, it matters not, *from a tax viewpoint*, whether it pays out all its after-tax profits as dividends, some of them, or none at all.

From the Inland Revenue point of view, although they are not concerned with the level of dividends a company might pay, they do need to receive the *minimum rate of mainstream tax* on the pre-tax profits, which is the excess of the corporation tax rate in force over the basic rate of income tax, say 52% less 30% = 22%.*

To avoid a situation where a company was paying dividends out of profits which were bearing corporation tax at only the ACT rate and not the corporation tax rate, the following rule is enforced:

Example 5.3.5

The rule for offsetting ACT: ACT may be offset only against the corporation tax on trading and unfranked investment income and the *maximum amount* cannot exceed that amount which, together with the *minimum rate of mainstream tax* on that income, equals the corporation tax payable on the pre-tax profit.

Company X has pre-tax income, subject to corporation tax, of £100,000. Corporation tax rate is 52% and the basic rate of income tax 30%.

	£			£
Profit before tax	100,000	*Minimum* mainstream tax		
Corporation tax 52%	52,000	must be 22%	=	22,000
Profit after tax	48,000	Therefore, the *maximum*		
		ACT set off	=	30,000
		Corporation tax on		
		pre-tax profit		52,000

The maximum dividend which allows maximum ACT set off is therefore, 7/3 × £30,000 = £70,000.

If Company X decides to pay a dividend of £84,000, *unrelieved ACT of £6,000* will arise:

	£		£
Profit before tax	100,000	Dividends paid	84,000
Corporation tax 52%	52,000	ACT paid 3/7ths × £84,000	36,000
Profit after tax	48,000	Minimum mainstream tax	22,000
		Act set off restricted to	30,000
		Unrelieved ACT paid	£6,000

* This principle is unchanged by the reduction of the Corporation Tax rate to, e.g., 35%.

Accounting for unrelieved ACT

Where ACT cannot be fully recovered by set off against corporation tax on the income of the year in which the related dividend is *paid*, the taxable income of the six previous years*

* For accounting periods ending after 31 March 1984.

can be used to absorb the amount unrelieved. In the case of a *proposed* dividend to be paid in the following accounting year, then the related ACT falls to be set off against the corporation tax on the taxable income of the year of payment of the dividend, and in default of that, against the taxable income of the current year or the year previous to that. In both cases, any unrelieved ACT can be carried forward indefinitely, subject to the overriding restriction on recovery illustrated above.

SSAP 8 – The Treatment of Taxation under the Imputation System in the Accounts of Companies – requires that where the recovery of unrelieved ACT is not foreseeable as reasonably certain, *it should be written off* in the profit and loss account *as irrecoverable ACT*; such a write off would be the extra cost of paying dividends. Where it is judged as recoverable, and in practice this is always likely to be so, unrelieved ACT can be debited to deferred tax account to be offset against future available excess of minimum mainstream corporation tax.

Taxation on overseas earnings

Liability to UK taxation arises only on that part of the earnings of overseas subsidiaries which is remitted to the UK. And so that tax is not payable twice, *double tax relief* is given where foreign tax has been borne at a rate equal to or higher than the rate for UK corporation tax. If the foreign tax rate is lower, then the difference must be met in the UK. Some countries (e.g. the USA) impose a further 'withholding' tax on dividends remitted overseas.

The *total* overseas taxation is required to be shown in the published profit and loss account, with the double taxation relief shown as a deduction from the charge for UK corporation tax (see page 85).

Double taxation relief and advance corporation tax (ACT)

The basic rule in regard to the recovery of ACT (*Example 5.3.5*) where UK dividends are paid out, or partly paid out of overseas earnings, still applies, i.e. the Inland Revenue will not begin to allow a company to offset ACT based on dividends to its shareholders against its final mainstream corporation tax until it gets the basic minimum, which at 1984 tax rates was 20% (50% corporation tax less 30% basic income tax rate).

Following the Finance Act 1984, double-tax relief became available to set against a company's mainstream corporation tax liability *before* any deduction for ACT set off is taken into account. The limit of the ACT that can then be deducted, is calculated by splitting the company's income between that for which there is double-tax relief and that where there is none. The ACT, in respect of double-tax relievable income, is limited to the mainstream corporation tax left in to be charged after double-tax relief.

Example 5.3.6 (General principle)

The earnings of Company X (*Example 5.3.5*) were £50,000 in the UK, and £50,000 overseas taxed at the same rate as in the UK (50%) and remitted here, with a dividend of £42,000 being paid in the UK.

	£			£
Profit before tax			UK Corporation tax	£50,000
UK	£50,000		Double tax relief	£25,000
Overseas	£50,000	100,000		
Corporation tax (50%)		50,000	Balance of corporation tax	
			available for ACT set off	£25,000
Profit after tax (UK)		50,000		

123

ACT = 3/7 × £42,000	=	£18,000	Minimum of mainstream tax must be 20% (50% less			
ACT unrelieved	=	£3,000	30%) × £50,000	=	£10,000	
			Therefore, maximum ACT offset	=	£15,000	

Accounting treatment of unrelieved overseas tax

SSAP 8 requires that *unrelieved overseas tax* which arises from an outgoing dividend should be treated as part of the tax charge to be deducted in arriving at the profits after tax, with the amount to be separately disclosed, if material (page 117).

Accounting treatment of Government grants (SSAP 4)

As an incentive to investment, various grants are available against the cost of fixed assets. The accounting standard, seeking reasonable uniformity of the accounting treatment, requires that grants be credited to profit and loss account over the life of the asset. This can be accomplished using either of the two acceptable methods.

In the first, the grant is deducted from the cost of the fixed asset, and depreciation is charged to profit and loss account over the lifetime of the asset on the net cost. In the second method, the grant is regarded as a deferred credit, a Government grants account is opened to receive the credit, and a proportion is credited to each profit and loss account over the lifetime of the asset, depreciation being charged on the gross cost of the asset.

ICI change their accounting treatment of Goverment grants

Until their traumatic 1980 experience when profits fell from £613 million to £284 million, with losses in the final six months, and a cut in dividend for the first time since 1938, ICI were among a minority who chose a variation on the second method of accounting for grants.

A credit item of £157 million for 'Government grants not yet credited to profit' appeared in the 1979 group balance sheet below the line of shareholders' funds. The profit and loss account took the annual credit for grants as a *deduction from taxation*, and stated:

Profit before taxation and grants	£560 million
Taxation less grants	£104 million

This treatment had the same final effect on the 'profit after tax', but avoided any increase to pre-tax profit. In 1980, there was a change in policy with this note to the accounts:

> "Government grants receivable, which are spread over the lives of the relevant assets, are included in trading profit, instead of being deducted from taxation. The change in presentation increases profit before tax by £21 million (1979, £19 million) but does not alter the profit attributable to the parent company."

Treatment *not* allowable by the standard for these capital-based grants, is to take full credit to profit and loss account in the year it arises, or full credit to a non-distributable reserve, where it would remain.

5.4 MINORITY INTERESTS

As explained in Chapter 4 (4.3) in respect of the consolidated balance sheet entry for Minority Interests, where some of the ordinary or other shares of a subsidiary are not owned by the holding company, a 'Minority interest' account arises in the consolidated balance sheet reflecting the extent of the group's liability to these outside shareholders, or to put it another way, the interest of the minority shareholders in the net assets of the group.

Theoretically, only that proportion of the subsidiary's net assets applicable to the holding company's shareholding need be brought into the consolidated balance sheet. However it is obviously impracticable to split the assets and liabilities into relevant proportions; so it is that the *whole* of the subsidiary's net assets are brought into the consolidated accounts, although in a partly-owned subsidiary this overstates the group's interest. The excess represents the Minority Interest.

It has been shown that profit equals additional assets. The entry for Minority Interests in the balance sheet at the end of the financial year includes their proportion of the subsidiary's profit after tax for the year. This latter amount is that shown in the GROWSTRONG consolidated profit and loss account, separately after 'Profit on ordinary activities after tax' but before extraordinary items, as required by SSAP 14, the standard on group accounts.

The *whole* of the subsidiary's profit for the year is included in the GROWSTRONG consolidated profit and loss account, as part of each relevant item from 'turnover' through to 'profit on ordinary activities before tax' inclusive. The *whole* of the subsidiary's tax is included in the group's tax charge. From the resulting balance, 'profit on ordinary activities after tax', the transfer of the minority interest net of tax (£26 million) leaves the AFTER TAX PROFIT OF THE GROUP APPLICABLE TO HOLDING COMPANY SHARE-HOLDERS ON ORDINARY TRANSACTIONS (assuming all group accounts are consolidated).

In the absence of preference shares and therefore of preference dividends, this line of profit is the EARNINGS base (see 5.5 following) for the calculation of the important stock market indicators – the EARNINGS PER SHARE (EPS) and the PRICE-EARNINGS RATIO (PER).

5.5 EARNINGS PER SHARE AND PRICE-EARNINGS RATIO

EARNINGS is common to both of these ratios. It is obviously important that it should be calculated and disclosed on a comparable basis between companies and over successive financial periods as far as this is possible.

In SSAP 3, *Earnings per share* (EPS) is defined as:

"The profit in pence attributable to each equity share based on the consolidated profit of the period after tax and after deducting minority interests, but before taking into account extraordinary items, divided by the number of equity shares in issue and ranking for dividend in respect of the period."

Thus, extraordinary transactions are ignored (see 5.6) and the basic calculation determines how much of the 'pure' profit remaining after all expenses, tax and outside interests have been satisfied, is applicable to one of the holding company's ordinary shares.

Example 5.5.1

GROWSTRONG's profit after tax but before extraordinary items, applicable to holding company ordinary shareholders (it has no preference shares) is £195,000. The number of ordinary shares in issue at the beginning and the end of its financial year is 1 million.

Therefore its EARNINGS PER SHARE (EPS) = *19.5 pence.*

This basis of calculating EPS is called *the net basis.* The calculation of the net basis EPS is made after deduction of *all the elements making up the tax charge.* The standard considers that listed companies should report EPS on the net basis and that the figure should be disclosed on the face of the profit and loss account.

The NET and NIL calculations of EPS

The use of the EPS as a comparative ratio was somewhat complicated by the introduction of the imputation system of taxation (1973) already described. *Examples 5.3.5* and *5.3.6* showed that the *decision to pay a particular level of dividend* can give rise to *additional taxation*.

As the EPS is calculated after tax, it follows that if all elements of tax (including the *variable* ones of 'irrecoverable ACT' and 'unrelieved overseas tax' exemplified) are deducted, the EPS of two companies with the *same pre-tax earnings* will have different figures of EPS only because the particular dividend policy of one brought additional tax charges.

In these circumstances, the standard allows the computation and disclosure of what is called the NIL BASIS EPS, a short form for a 'nil distribution basis', i.e. the 'Earnings' figure used in the calculation would be that which would apply if no ordinary dividend was paid and, therefore, no variable tax arose. Preference dividends, if any, would still be deducted.

Example 5.5.2

GROWSTRONG has, in fact, incurred no variable tax charges, but assuming that of the tax charge of £120,000 there was included £30,000 irrecoverable ACT: EPS (NIL BASIS) = £195,000 plus £30,000 divided by 1 million ordinary shares = *22.5 pence per share.*

The standard requires the disclosure of the basis of the calculation of EPS in the profit and loss account or in a note thereto, together with the amount of 'earnings' and 'the number of shares'.

As it can be expected that most companies, in normal circumstances, will not incur either of the variable elements of taxation, the calculation for them of EPS on either the NET or the NIL basis will produce the same result. Where there is, however, a material difference between the EPS calculated using both bases, suitable disclosure is recommended.

Fully diluted earnings per share

Where a company has at balance sheet date contracted to issue further shares after the end of the accounting period, or where it has already issued shares which will rank for dividend later, the effect may be to dilute the EPS.

In these circumstances, SSAP 8 requires that in addition to the basic EPS (already exemplified), the fully diluted EPs should also be stated.

Example 5.5.3

Assuming that GROWSTRONG's loan capital of £300,000 was in fact 10% convertible loan stock and that each £100 of loan stock (nominal) is convertible into 80 ordinary shares at any time between 19x5 and 19x9; and that the end of the current financial year on which the accounts are based falls in 19x2:

Calculation of fully diluted earnings per share

		19x2
		£
Earnings (*Table 4*)		195,000
Add back interest on convertible loan stock	£30,000	
Less corporation tax 52% (say)	15,600	14,400

Adjusted earnings	£209,400
Number of shares in issue	1,000,000
plus maximum number of shares after conversion	240,000
Adjusted number of shares	1,240,000

The published accounts would show both the basic and the fully diluted earnings per share for the current and previous year.

Fully diluted EPS £209,400/1,240,000   *= 16.9 pence*

Basic EPS (net basis) (Table 4)   *19.5 pence*

New shares issued during the accounting year

In these circumstances, the number of shares used in the denominator of the calculation is based on a time weighted average.

Example 5.5.4

Assuming that GROWSTRONG started the year with only 750,000 ordinary shares and that on the first day of the tenth month of its accounting year it acquired a subsidiary company and settled the purchase price by issuing a further 250,000 of its ordinary shares as fully paid. The profit of the subsidiary for the period since acquisition applicable to GROWSTRONG's interest is assumed to be included in the earnings figure of £195,000:

Basic EPS = £195,000 divided by 750,000 plus ($\frac{1}{4}$ × 250,000)

= £195,000 divided by 812,500 = *24.0 pence.*

THE PRICE-EARNINGS RATIO (PER)

This INVESTMENT RATIO derives from the stock market *daily* price of the listed company's ordinary share and its EPS.

Example 5.5.5

GROWSTRONG's ordinary share is quoted today at 137.0p. The EPS based on the published accounts for the last financial year (*Table 4*) is 19.5p.

GROWSTRONG's *historical* PE ratio TODAY is therefore, 137.0p : 19.5p = 7.0 to 1 or more simply as would be quoted in the *Financial Times*, 7.

It will be noted that one side of this ratio is static, i.e. 'Earnings', but that the share price moves freely, reflecting many factors crystallised into the decision of investors to hold, buy or sell shares.

The theoretical value of the share is the present value of the stream of FUTURE earnings. The historic PER is the share price expressed as a number of years of the HISTORIC earnings. But the share price is in reality an assessment of FUTURE prospects – of growth potential, income potential, capital appreciation and relative risks. It will react to moods of optimism and pessimism, not only of the company and its industrial or other environment, but also of the stock market as a whole.

EPS is therefore a more certain investment indicator than PER. EPS enables analysts, investment advisers and other interested parties to assess the efficiency of a company's directors in utilising the company's equity capital and measures its progress year by year. But it is historic.

If through any number of indications, increased earnings per share are anticipated, then the share price will move ahead and with 'earnings' static, the PER will rise. To counter this problem of static E's in PE ratios, investment analysts will make recalculations including estimates of forward EPS, using this figure in relation to the market price to produce a *prospective PER* in place of the historic PER.

The *Financial Times* share information service gives relevant investment information in respect of the equity shares of listed companies:

Example 5.5.6

Financial Times, March 12, 1981

Sector: DRAPERY AND STORES.

| 1980–81 | | | | | Div | | Yield | |
High	Low	Stock	Price	± or	Net	Cover	Gross	PE
266	190	Mothercare	214	− 12	5.0	3.4	3.3	12.7
126	77	Marks and Spencer	110	− 6	3.4	2.0	4.4	16.6

The *Financial Times* actuaries share indices table publishes the PER and other investment information for industrial and other equity groups and sub-sections:

Example 5.5.6 (continued)

Financial Times actuaries table, March 12, 1981

| PER — Stores | 10.57 |
| PER — 500 Share Index | 6.62 |

The fall of 12 pence and 6 pence respectively in the share price of these market leaders is an example of the stock market reacting to information which they believed made the investment in these equity shares less attractive. March 12, 1981 was two days after the presentation of a deflationary budget and fears that its proposals would lead to a substantial reduction in consumer spending prompted these examples of marked weakness among shares in the 'Stores sector'.

Nevertheless, the PE ratios show that the shares of these companies were highly valued, Mothercare being nearly twice and Marks and Spencer more than twice the average PER of the 500 Share index. It was still a matter of judgement for the investor, private or institutional, whether the shares were keenly or under or overvalued at that time. Nine months late, December 17,1981, Mothercare shares had fallen to 174p and Marks and Spencer shares had risen to 125p. By 1985, Mothercare was part of the Habitat/Mothercare group and in July of that year, Marks and Spencers shares stood at *circa* 140 pence.

Dividend policy (see 5.7) affects the PE ratio. While many investors look for capital gains following the sale of shares bought at a lower price, others, particularly the institutional shareholders now holding a high proportion of equity shares, are more concerned with a strong and certain income flow. It will often be the case, therefore, that a company with high profit retentions has a lower PER than others which are distributing a higher proportion of their after-tax profit as dividend.

But this comparison may be short term, for the company paying higher dividends, and following demand for its shares, having a higher PER than others, may find itself short of capital, exacerbated by its low retention policy. Raising new capital, adding to the number of shares in issue, will lower EPS and PER. The company with high retentions may avoid this dilution of shares and end up with a higher PER, and the relative positions are reversed.

PE ratios and take-overs

In the late 1960s, the so-called 'years of the mergers', the PE ratio was the pivot point for those who entered the stock market, as they put it, to 'manage money'.

Companies were bought into a group with the object of increasing overall earnings. The shares of the acquired companies were purchased with the shares of the acquiring company. The higher the PER of the latter compared with the former, the cheaper was the purchase price.

This type of take-over, illustrated in *Example 5.5.7*, was regarded as an alternative investment decision. If the other company is under-utilising its assets, then went the argument, it could be acquired to increase its and the group's earning power. Thus growth of earnings, higher prices, higher PER, and the cycle as before, resulting in available capital gains.

Example 5.5.7

The wheeler-dealer operation

The operation would start with the finance company vehicle holding the lowest possible equity both in price and number of shares (a).

Our whizz-kid directed company would aim to bring in profits, mainly by purchase of under-utilised assets. The purchase price would be settled, not by cash, but by the issue of his shares in exchange. Efforts to avoid or delay the dilution of the original equity would be effected wherever possible. The EPS of the whizz-kid company would rise quickly over a period of time (b).

Leaving aside any change in the price due to the demand for his shares, the price in the PER would rise relative to the rise in earnings (c).

Inevitably, however, market demand would see an increase in the PER (d), leading to a dramatic upward swing in the price (e).

(a) Price is 10e (e = earnings; PER = 10e to e, or 10)

(b) Over a period of time, earnings per share rise threefold.

(c) Price becomes 30e (with the PER still at 10, i.e. 30 : 3)

(d) But with demand for the shares, the PER rises in fact to 25, so that

(e) the price rises to $25 \times 3e = 75e$.

Where these acquisitions were based on sound policies, e.g. to acquire a company in the same line of business, but nearer the customer, or to acquire a supplying or manufacturing company with common interests, or acquiring a competing company to increase market share, these operations may have proved successful. Many were, however, based on financial astuteness, operating in bull markets (markets full of investors looking for quick capital gains) having little long-term concern for the viability of group operations, but merely manipulating a changing and mixed bag of companies. Their end was inevitable. It may be concluded that share prices and PER are created by the stock market aiming to relate price to future potential. Actual growth of earnings is effected by a company's management and other employees and will reflect its financial and operating efficiency.

Market price, PER and net assets per share

There is an element of risk involved in the investment decision (hold, buy, sell) which is higher with some investments compared with others. An investment in a blue chip (first class industrial or commercial security) company like British Petroleum (PE 3.2 : March 1981) carries a quite different risk from an investment in a little known North Sea Oil company (PER 71.0). And the risk will vary over time as the price of the share changes in response to varying influences on the company's future prospects.

One useful comparison in the judgement of risk is that of the market price of the ordinary share with its net asset value per share as determined from the company's published accounts.

Example 5.5.8

*Comparison of market price and net asset value
of a company's ordinary share*

GROWSTRONG's ordinary share has a market value of *137.0 pence.*

The book value of GROWSTRONG's shareholders' funds (*Table 3*, it has no preference shares) is £1,022,000.

This is the net asset value of the ordinary shareholders' interest based on the historical accounts.

Divided by the number of ordinary shares, 1 million, the net asset value per share is *102.2 pence.*

Where preference shares are included in the total of shareholders' funds, their book value needs to be deducted to determine the ordinary shareholders' interest. The prospective investor in GROWSTRONG ordinary shares knows that any investment at 137.0 pence will have a backing of 102.2 pence worth of net assets. The difference between the two figures measures the added risk related to the market view of the level of future earnings prospects.

The NAV would be an important guide to a prospective acquiring company. In so far as purchased goodwill (see Chapter 4) is defined as the excess of the purchase price paid for a business over the current value of the net assets, it may be considered that for GROWSTRONG the difference between market price and NAV of the ordinary share multiplied by the number of shares would give some indication of the value of its goodwill, i.e.,

$$34.8p \times 1 \text{ million} = £348,000$$

This would be no more than a useful indicator to negotiators in a merger situation. As 'future earning potential' will vary with time, with environmental change and in the view of interested parties, its 'value' will also vary. This 'value' is determined only at the point of the purchase of a business and equates then to cost. The requirement for listed (and other) companies to produce and publish *current cost accounts* (see Chapter 12) enabled a current cost NAV to be calculated to supplement that derived from the historic cost balance sheet, until SSAP 16 became defunct.

Earnings yield

The 'Earnings yield' is the reciprocal of the price-earnings ratio:

GROWSTRONG's PER is 7.0 : its Earnings yield is $1/7 \times 100 = 14.3\%$

This is sometimes called the capitalization rate, the rate at which the stock market is apparently capitalizing the value of current earnings.

Earnings yield has been superseded in stock exchange statistics for some time by PER.

The relationship of 'Earnings yield' and 'net dividend yield' (see 5.7 following) is the same as that of 'Earnings' : 'net dividend' in normal circumstances. The Earnings-Dividend (E/D) ratio is one measure of the risk in holding or investing in a company's share. The higher the E/D ratio, or *dividend cover*, the smaller the risk. And probably a smaller PE ratio (page 128).

5.6   EXTRAORDINARY ITEMS

The make up of the £15,000 which GROWSTRONG has deducted at this stage in its consolidated profit and loss account would be detailed.

Tutorial Comment

The adjustment for *Extraordinary Expenditure or Income* is made *after* the determination of 'Earnings' used for 'Earnings per share' and the 'Price-earnings ratio', the important stock market indicators.

The object of the adjustment at this stage in the revenue account is obviously to ensure that *earnings* are not clouded in any way with items which *derive from events or transactions outside the company's ordinary activities*. A second aim is to require that these items which could have a material impact on the investment decision are *disclosed* and not hidden from view by adjusting reserves brought forward and carried forward. The basis of the judgement as to whether an item is 'Extraordinary' for the purpose of being shown below the line of 'earnings' is whether or not it arose *outside* the *ordinary* activities of the company.

For example, a substantial loss arising on the bankruptcy of a major customer is *not* an extraordinary item as by definition, it falls within ordinary business. If the loss was regarded as abnormal because of its amount, it would be disclosed as an *exceptional item* of operating profit. It would need to be separately designated (either in the profit or loss account or in a note thereto) where this is necessary for a true and fair view.

Examples of extraordinary items could be profits or losses arising from:
  (i) the discontinuance of a significant segment of a business either through termination or disposal;
  (ii) the sale of an investment not acquired with the intention of resale such as investments in subsidiary or associated companies.

Any taxation payable or recoverable because of an extraordinary item is netted against the item and not included in the overall charge to profits for taxation. The tax attributable to extraordinary items, and the minority share of extraordinary items, are required to be shown separately on the face of the profit and loss account, or in a note thereto.

In group accounts, an extraordinary item relating to a subsidiary should be stated net of minority interests (SSAP 14); where the item relates to an associate, the group's share should be included in the aggregate extraordinary items in the consolidated profit and loss account (SSAP 1).

Example 5.6.1

From the annual accounts of J. Bibby & Sons Ltd,
Winner of *The Accountant and Stock Exchange Award* in 1981

EXTRAORDINARY ITEMS	£'000
Release of provision against investment in quoted associated company	243
Profit on cancellation of debenture stock	24
Profits and losses on disposal of subsidiary companies and fixed, other and intangible assets	(670)
	(403)
Taxation	162
	(241)

Analysts will pay particular attention to 'Extraordinary items' and their classification. Treatment as 'Extraordinary' rather than as 'Exceptional' could make an appreciable difference to EPS and PER.

The write off by J. Bibby & Son Ltd (*Example 5.6.1*) of £241,000 represents nearly 10p per share and although there is no suggestion that the items were other than extraordinary, if assumedly they had been charged above the line of tax, their reported EPS of 32.68p would have dropped drastically.

SSAP 6 'Extraordinary items and prior year adjustments' (1974) set out to achieve the aims stated at the commencement of this tutorial comment and to ensure that these transactions were accounted for through the profit and loss account and not through reserves.

There are a few special instances where items of a *revenue* or *expense nature* are permitted or required by law to be taken to reserves. For example, section 56 of the CA 1948 – S130(1–3) CA 85 – permits the preliminary expenses of a company or the expenses of, or commission paid or discount allowed on, any issue of its shares or debentures to be written off against the share premium account. This section and section 45(6) of the CA 1981 – S160 CA 85 – permit the share premium account to be used in certain circumstances in providing for the premium payable on redemption of redeemable shares or debentures of the company. Similarly section 46(1) of the CA 1981 – S162 CA 85 – allow for the purchase by a company of its own shares (see Chapter 4). These transactions should be dealt with as movements on reserves.

Accounting adjustments to reserves also arise which are *not* of a revenue nature where it would be inappropriate to include them in the determination of the year's profit. One such example is indicated in the following section dealing with exchange differences arising from foreign currency translation where specified exchange differences are required to be taken to reserves (*SSAP 20 'Foreign Currency Translation'*), and another is the immediate write off against reserves of goodwill which is not treated as an asset permitted by *SSAP 22 'Accounting for Goodwill'* (see Chapter 4.6).

SSAP 20 and SSAP 22 were not in issue clearly when SSAP 6 appeared in 1974. The recent intensive review of SSAP 6 through a discussion paper and culminating with a *new draft standard – ED 36* – in January 1985 has embraced SSAP 20 and SSAP 22 but its main aim has been to deal with *inconsistencies* in the determination of transactions, either as extraordinary or as exceptional, while still accepting that what is extraordinary for one company will not necessarily be extraordinary in another. The new proposals do not greatly affect the way in which companies have been accounting for these transactions as they do not differ fundamentally from the SSAP 6 principles set out in the tutorial note at the start of this section. A definition of *'ordinary activities'* has been added as this phrase is a key determinant in the differentiation between extraordinary items and exceptional items.

Extraordinary items continue to be those items derived from events or transactions which fall *outside* the *outside activities* of the company, while being both material and not expected to recur regularly.

Exceptional items continue to be those items derived from events or transactions which fall *within* the *ordinary activities* of the company and need to be disclosed separately by virtue of their size or incidence if the financial statements are to give a true and fair view.

In these contexts, ED 36 defines *ordinary activities* as those which are usually undertaken by the company and any related activities in which the company engages in furtherance of, incidental to, or arising from those activities. They include, but are not confined to, the trading transactions of the company.

One problem which has been highlighted by the review of SSAP 6 concerns the treatment of *terminated activities* particularly following the many reorganisations and reconstructions which have happened during the recent recession. It was evident that there was inconsistency over the treatment of similar transactions by different companies. ED 36 exemplifies 'the discontinuance of a *significant business segment*, either through termination or disposal' as being an *extraordinary item*. It defines a *business segment* as a separately identifiable component of a company whose activities, assets and results can be clearly distinguished from those of the company as a whole. It may be in the form of a subsidiary or associated company, a joint venture, a division, a plant or department and will normally have its own separate product lines or markets. Where programmes of *reorganisation* do *not* amount to the discontinuance of a business segment, these are *not* to be treated as extraordinary items.

The subsequently revised SSAP 6 effective from 1 January 1986 subject to CCAP approval, confirmed that *reorganisations* do *not* amount to a discontinuance of part of a business. Related costs are to be charged to profit and loss account as an ordinary activity, disclosed as an exceptional item by way of note, if material.

The revised standard could not deal with the knotty problem of the measurement of and accounting for profits and losses on the *disposal* of revalued assets. An ASC working party is to look at this again.

Accounting for exchange differences from foreign currency translation (SSAP 20)

SSAP 20 was published in 1983 to come into effect from April of that year. This standard is based on exposure draft 27 (1980) and responses to it. The thorny problems of foreign currency exchange movements and their translation in accounts have been the subject of a number of exposure drafts by the ASC and accounting statements in other countries. The publication of the *International Accounting Standard 21 'Accounting for the effects of changes in foreign exchange rates'* shortly after the domestic standard to come into effect from January 1985, provided considerable harmony not only with the UK, but also with the comparable statements in the United States (FAS 52) and Canada (s 1650).

The UK standard follows the exposure draft in respect of consolidated (group) financial statements being based on 'the net investment concept'. This approach recognises that the investment of a holding company is in the *net worth* of a *foreign business enterprise* rather than a direct investment in its individual assets and liabilities. The standard recognises that exchange differences resulting from the restatement in sterling of the net investment of a holding company in a foreign subsidiary do not represent or measure changes in cash flows to the holding company and are, therefore, different in kind from those resulting from trading and financing operations. The standard concludes that it is inappropriate to regard them as profits or losses and they should be dealt with as *adjustments to reserves*. This standard practice represents a further exception to the general rule of SSAP 6 which outlaws 'reserve accounting'.

Volatility of exchange rates

The volatility of exchange rates can have material effects on groups engaged in foreign operations whether as importers or exporters, through foreign subsidiaries or otherwise. It is generally an environmental factor outside their control, although its effects may be mitigated or anticipated in the short-term. The dramatic surge of the US dollar in 1984 could hardly have been anticipated. In the period between the writing of the first edition of this book in 1981 and the second edition in 1985, the sterling/dollar rate has virtually halved. *Example 5.6.2* notes recent UK/US exchange rates alongside the dramatic turn-round of ICI profits 1980–84, together with the exacerbation of its 1980 losses by exchange losses, and the enhancement of 1984 profits by exchange gains.

Example 5.6.2

Sterling/US dollar exchange rates
1974 US$2.34   1977 US$1.75   1980 US$2.33   1983 US$1.56   1985 (March) US$1.08*
* At this point, where parity between the pound and the dollar was expected, confidence in the dollar was eroded and the value of the pound began to rise.*

In 1980, ICI suffered losses in the final six months of the year in which profits fell by some £330 million. The group's position had been worsened by exchange losses. Anticipating SSAP 20, following the publication of ED 37 in 1980, they noted a change in their presentation policy:

'Following the publication of ED 27, the exchange loss of translating the net

> *current assets of overseas subsidiaries into sterling is charged against reserves instead of against profit for the year. This . . . increases profit before tax by £37 million and profit attributable to the parent company before extraordinary items by £33 million.'*

This was a material adjustment for them, where the last stated profit level was only £97 million before the adjustment. It exemplifies the importance of standard accounting treatment and full disclosure of material information for readers of published accounts.

By 1984, this remarkable group were able to publish profits which exceeded £1 billion at the pre-tax level, the first British industrial business to do so. The fall in the US/UK dollar to near parity, had with other currency changes boosted pre-tax profits by £100 million, based on their export business.

Standard treatment – individual companies and groups differentiated

The accounts of the separate companies within a group are drawn up in the currency in which each subsidiary reports and for the UK holding company its results are, of course, stated in sterling. For the separate companies all exchange gains and losses, representing for example, differences on debtors and creditors payable or receivable in foreign currencies and differences on foreign bank balances and loans, are all cash flows, i.e. realised gains and losses. The standard requires that these be brought into the profit and loss account as profits or losses on ordinary activities. Hence the ICI treatment of its 1984 exchange profits.

At the consolidation stage, i.e. consolidating the accounts of the subsidiaries with those of the holding company into the latter's domestic currency, in this instance sterling, the net investment concept is used and the exchange differences arising from this – essentially a revaluation process – are treated as movements on reserves, as in the ICI 1980 example.

The cover concept

The standard provides for the sensible arrangement where foreign currency *borrowings* have been used to finance, or provide a hedge against, group *equity investment* in foreign investments. Obviously if UK Company X borrows US$15 million for the acquisition of a new subsidiary's equity in the USA, any movement in the US/UK exchange rates will effect the loan in the opposite way to the investment, so that the net result in sterling is zero. The standard allows in these circumstances for the exchange gains or losses on the borrowings, which otherwise would have to be taken into the profit and loss account, to be offset as reserve movements against exchange differences arising from the retranslation of the net investment.

Prior year adjustments

Routine and regular annual estimates made in the accounts usually differ from the actual amounts when they become known in the next accounting period. For example, an estimate of £10,500 is made of the amount accrued due at balance sheet date for electric power used. This amount is included in the expense account total charged to the profit and loss account for the year, and shown in the balance sheet as a current liability due to the Electricity Board. When the bill is received, it amounts to £10,650. The marginal underestimate is not such that this item should be regarded and treated as a prior-year item. It and others of like routine are merely adjusted through the charge to profit and loss account for the expense in the succeeding year.

SSAP 6 regards 'prior year adjustments' as those prior year items which are the result of:

Changes in accounting policies, and/or the correction of fundamental errors.

Changes in accounting policies would need special consideration by analysts because of the fundamental accounting concept that there should be *consistency* of treatment from one period to the next. Such changes should only occur when they result in a fairer presentation of the results and of the financial position of the business. Changes should be seen as *not* made for the purpose of showing improved results.

Restatement of prior years' results when adjustments are made
Where such a change is seen as necessary, e.g. a change in the method of valuing stocks and work in progress, so that all production overheads are now included, being previously excluded, SSAP 6 requires that it should be made *as far as the prior years are concerned* in the profit and loss appropriation account by adjusting the opening balance of retained profits or reserves, and appropriately detailed in a note *which should immediately follow* the profit and loss account showing movements on retained profits/reserves. The effect of the new policy on the current year will, of course, arise from the normal entries (e.g. the deduction of the value of closing stocks in the determination of 'cost of sales') in the profit and loss account.

The review of SSAP 6 (ED 36 1985) considered the question as to whether there should always be a statement of retained profits/reserves, or only when prior year adjustments were involved. Because of the possible significance to analysts of reserve movements (including unrealised revaluation surpluses, certain exchange differences (SSAP 20), immediate write off of goodwill (SSAP 22), as well as prior year adjustments), ASC propose the inclusion in financial statements of *a single statement showing all movements on reserves*. This *may* either immediately follow the profit and loss account, or appear separately within the financial statements, or as a note thereto (see end of this Chapter). Prior year adjustments need not necessarily appear immediately after the profit and loss account.

Appropriations of profit

The profit remaining after adjusting for extraordinary items is the pure profit applicable to the holding company shareholders, and after payment of any fixed e.g. preference dividend, is that available to the ordinary or risk-bearing shareholders.

It is the duty of the directors to make a recommendation as to the proportion of this profit which should be paid as ordinary dividends and thus determine the amount to be retained as an added investment of equity shareholders for the company's maintenance and growth.

5.7 DIVIDENDS AND DISTRIBUTABLE PROFIT

The note to the GROWSTRONG consolidated profit and loss account distinguishes the *interim dividend* already *paid* to the ordinary shareholders and the *final dividend proposed* by the directors, the latter being reflected as a current liability (within: creditors, amounts falling due within one year) in the consolidated balance sheet. It details the information in pence per share

		£
Dividends – Ordinary – interim paid 2.5p		25,000
– final proposed 5.0p		50,000
		£75,000

As with other notes to the accounts, last year's figures are given for comparison.
The *CA 1985* specifies that every profit and loss account must show:
   (i) the company's profit or loss on ordinary activities before tax, and must also show
   (ii) transfers and proposed transfers to and from reserves, and

(iii) the aggregate amount of dividends paid and proposed.

Remarkably, the EEC 4th Directive did not contain these headings and they are not included in the profit and loss account formats.

Tutorial Comment

Most companies having articles of their own (as an alternative to adopting the set contained in the Companies Acts) empower the directors to *pay interim* dividends. Articles usually empower directors to declare and pay final dividends on preference shares, but not on ordinary shares. They usually *recommend* the level of *final* ordinary dividends, the payment being authorised by the members themselves in general meeting.

The model set of articles which companies may adopt, restricts the level of dividends which members may authorise to that recommended by the directors. They also stipulate that 'no dividend may be paid otherwise than out of profits'.

Dividend policy

In exercising their judgement on the division of available profits between dividends and retentions, directors will be concerned:

(i) to ensure that dividends are paid only out of profits *legally* available for distribution,

(ii) to satisfy current and prospective shareholders' expectations and thus maintain or improve the share price,

(iii) to maintain the operating capacity of the business intact in real terms, and to

(iv) provide funds for future growth.

Distributable profit

The concept of limited liability (see Chapter 4, page 56) requires that capital is maintained intact, and although it may be lost in the ordinary course of trading, it cannot, generally, be distributed as a dividend. Any dividend paid out of the capital fund contributed by the shareholders would deplete the assets which form the security for debenture holders, and if the remaining assets are insufficient to provide for the payment of ordinary creditors their interests would obviously be affected.

Although the Companies Act 1981 – S171–77 CA 85 – breaches this fundamental rule by authorising a *private* company to make a *payment out of capital* for the redemption or purchase of its own shares, there are significant safeguards imposed to protect the shareholders and persons dealing with the company (Chapter 4, page 62 et seq.).

And, directors may make themselves personally liable for any dividends considered to be an illegal distribution. They might be held to have misapplied the company's funds, and consequently be liable to the company to account for them; there could be penalties under the terms of debenture trust deeds if the company had long-term borrowings.

Where a company makes a distribution which is not permitted by the Companies Act 1985 (see below), that legislation provides for a member of a company to repay the illegal distribution made to him, if he knows or has reasonable grounds for believing that it was made in contravention of the Act.

In any consideration of the legality of a dividend payment, the answer to the question "what is, in law, capital?" or its reciprocal "what is in law, profit?" is important.

Profits available for distribution – Companies Act 1980 [S255, 263, 265, 268–277 CA 85 11 Sch.]

Until this Act, there had been no legal definition of 'profit' and recourse was necessary to the decisions in a number of Court cases arising in this respect, some reaching back into the nineteenth century, so that in the absence of a contemporary view, there were doubts as to their current applicability.

Definition in law of 'realised profits'

It has already been noted that the importance of accounting standards has been enhanced by the inclusion in the Companies Act 1981 (para 91 4 Sch. CA 85) of a definition of *realised profits*:

"... references ... to realised profits, in relation to a company's accounts, are references to such profits of the company as fall to be treated as realised profits for the purposes of those accounts *in accordance with principles generally accepted* ... for *accounting purposes*, at the time when those accounts were prepared" (author's italics).

The precise determination of accounting principles and therefore of profits is left to the accounting profession. What is regarded as acceptable accounting practice will be acceptable in law.

Realised profits for the purposes of references hereto in the 1985 legislation are accounting realised profits and not as interpreted in any narrow legal sense.

The Companies Act 1980 laid down definitive rules to be applied in general when distributing profits and in particular in respect of investment and insurance companies.

The essential point in respect of the rules, which follow, is that the profits be realised profits and only these shall be distributed.

CA 1980 (S263(2) CA 85). Rules in respect of distributable profits
A company (public or private) may not make a distribution except out of profits available for the purpose.

These are its accumulated, *realised* profits, not previously *distributed* or capitalised, less its accumulated *realised* losses, so far as not written off in a reduction or reorganisation of capital. The word '*distribution*' covers every description of distribution of a company's assets to members (in cash or otherwise) *except*:
1. An issue of shares as fully or partly paid bonus shares.
2. The redemption or purchase of any of the Company's shares (Part V. CA 1985).
3. A reduction of share capital by repayment or extinguishment of unpaid capital; and
4. A distribution of assets to members in a winding up.

The last two of these four exemptions from these new legal restrictions on distributions are tightly controlled by law in the interests of all parties involved – shareholders and creditors.

CA 1980 (S264 CA 85). Further restrictions on the distributions of a PUBLIC company
A PUBLIC company may only make a distribution provided this does not reduce the *net assets* to less than the aggregate of its called up share capital and *undistributable reserves*.

The *undistributable reserves* are:
The Share premium account.
The Capital Redemption Reserve Fund.*
The excess of the current *unrealised* profits, less *unrealised* losses.
Any reserve, distribution of which is prohibited by the company's memorandum or articles, or by statute.
Net assets are defined as total assets less liabilities and provisions.

* See Chapter 4: The word *fund* has been dropped by the current legislation; this capital reserve is now 'the capital redemption reserve'.

Auditors' responsibility in respect of distributions

The relevant accounts which reflect the distributable profits are the most recent *audited* annual accounts. If the auditors qualify their report on the accounts, they are required to state whether, in their opinion, a proposed distribution would contravene the Act.

Example 5.7.1

Distributable profits (CA 1980)

	Private company XYZ Ltd £'000	Listed company ABC plc £'000
Share capital	60	60
Share premium	20	20
Capital reserve	10	10
Unrealised deficit on property revaluation	(5)	(5)
Realised profits	60	60
SHAREHOLDERS' FUNDS	145	145

(Share capital plus reserves)

The figures for purpose of illustration are identical. The capital reserve in each case has been set aside to meet the enhanced inflationary cost of replacing fixed assets, but only ABC, the listed (public) company, has prohibited its distribution in its articles.

The maximum legally distributable profit is:

XYZ Ltd	£70,000
ABC plc	£55,000

ABC plc has chosen to prohibit the distribution of its capital reserve, and as a *listed* company has the further restriction in respect of the *unrealised* deficit.

While the CA 1980 did not define the meaning of *realised* (or *unrealised*) profit (or loss), an omission rectified by the CA 1981 (S275 CA 85) (see page 137), it did lay down the following rules:

  (i) any provision is a realised loss, the only exception being a provision in respect of any diminution in value of a fixed asset resulting from a revaluation of *all* the fixed assets;

 (ii) if a fixed asset is revalued, and depreciation is calculated on the revalued amount, the excess of this depreciation over the depreciation based on cost need not be deducted when calculating realised profits;

(iii) if the directors are unable to determine whether a profit or loss made before the appointed day was realised or unrealised, they may treat the profit as realised and the loss as unrealised.

The S269(1) CA 1985 provides that where *development costs* are shown as an asset in a company's accounts (see Chapter 4), any amount in respect of these costs shall be treated for the purposes of the CA 1980 rules on profits available for distribution, as a realised loss.

For companies with ample realised revenue reserves (profits) these *legal* restrictions will be of little concern. They will, nevertheless, need to give consideration to the amounts that can *prudently* be distributed.

CA 1980, Distributable profits – preference shares

The Act did not differentiate preference and ordinary dividends and the rules on distributions apply to both. In circumstances of a company making losses and having arrears of preference dividends, the law presumably prohibits payment of dividends to preference shareholders until the company's accumulated losses are cleared.

Amounts that can be PRUDENTLY distributed

While the CA 1980 ruled on the legal maximum which can be distributed to shareholders, prudence, the availability of cash (or borrowing capability) and judgement as to the effect on share price will be determinants of the actual amount paid.

Neither the private nor the public company in *Example 5.7.1* could *prudently* distribute the legal amounts determined.

In exercising their judgement as to the level of dividends within the legal maximum, the directors will need to balance both sides of the decision coin. For obviously, the more distributed, the less retained, and vice versa. Presumably in a well-manage company, the last line in the profit and loss account, i.e. the retained profit, was planned as a major source of funds to meet the needs of maintenance and growth. But, of course, budgeted plans do not always come to fruition and the dividend decision may have to be made against poor current profits or even losses (see *Example 5.7.3* following). In these circumstances, strong reserves are essential to the maintenance of dividends.

Shareholders and the stock market will be looking for steadily increasing dividends, a key factor in the determination of share price. A cut in dividend undermines confidence and will damage the share price.

Example 5.7.2

Financial press comment following ICI's cut in dividend (1981) based on the 1980 profits, "for the first time since 1938":

"On the Stock Exchange, the news of a sharp reduction in the dividend, from 23p per share to 17p per share, came as a shock. Standing at 296p before the announcement, the share price fell as low as 266p, but finally rallied to close at 268p."

In assessing the dividend decision, the level of reserves, the level of current profits, the company's liquidity position, its foreseeable future and its financial planning for that future will all need to be weighed. And the effect of inflation should not be overlooked (see Chapter 12).

Example 5.7.3

ICI Profit and loss appropriation accounts 1980

	Historic cost £m	Current cost £m
Profit attributable to the parent company before extraordinary items	130	− 61
Extraordinary items	− 150	− 173
Profit after extraordinary items	− 20	− 234
Dividends	− 101	− 101
Loss (retained) – deficit reducing reserves	− 121	− 335

In relation to ICI's liquidity, it should be noted that the decision to pay a reduced dividend, whatever its merits, required cash (or a borrowing facility) of £101 million. ICI's strong reserves provide security to lenders, but do not, of course, provide the cash. And borrowed money carries an interest cost.

The *reduced* dividend is just covered by 'earnings' (£130m : £101m) on an historical cost accounting basis. But after meeting the extraordinary costs, shareholders are left with a deficit which is pushed to £121 million by the dividend. On a current cost accounting basis, ICI's final line deficit is £335 million.

In deciding between dividends and the maintenance of reserves, given these results, the ICI directors clearly assessed the importance of the former. The compromise of reducing, rather than not paying any dividend, was criticised, particularly because of the company's need to borrow for the purpose.

Dividend yields

Dividends are paid to shareholders net of tax at the basic income tax rate and carry an associated tax credit (see *Example 4.1.1*, page 53).

The *gross dividend yield* for the individual investor is the gross dividend related to the *market price* which he paid for his share. The gross dividend yield quoted in the *Financial Times* is the gross dividend related to the *current market price* of the share (*Example 5.5.6*, page 128, showed the yield for 'Mothercare' at 3.3% gross).

Example 5.7.4

GROWSTRONG's net dividends are grossed up, with basic rate at 30%, as follows:

Dividend paid $\quad$ 2.5p $\quad = \dfrac{2.5}{0.70} = \quad$ 3.56p gross

Dividend proposed $\quad$ 5.0p $\quad = \dfrac{5.0}{0.70} = \quad$ 7.14p gross

Total dividend $\qquad$ $\underline{7.5p}$ $\qquad\qquad$ $\underline{10.70p}$ gross

Note: the grossing up of the *proposed* dividend will be at the basic rate of tax current when the dividend is *paid*, assumed to be unchanged.

$$\textit{Gross dividend yield} = \frac{\text{gross dividend}}{\text{market price of the share}} \times 100$$

$$= \frac{10.70p}{137.00p} \times 100 = 7.8\%$$

Note: Alternatively,

$$\textit{Gross dividend yield} = \frac{\text{NOMINAL value of share}}{\text{MARKET value of share}} \times \frac{\text{gross dividend}}{\text{PERCENTAGE}}$$

$$\text{Net dividend } \textit{percentage} = \frac{\text{dividend per share net}}{\text{nominal value of share}} \times 100$$

$$= \frac{7.5p}{50.0p} \times 100 = 15\% \quad \begin{array}{l}\text{net dividend}\\ \text{percentage}\end{array} \quad = \frac{15.0}{0.70} = 21.4\% \quad \begin{array}{l}\text{gross dividend}\\ \text{percentage.}\end{array}$$

$$\textit{Gross dividend yield} = \frac{50.0p}{137.0p} \times 21.4\% = 7.8\%$$

Dividend cover

This ratio, also known as the E/D (Earnings: dividend) ratio (see page 130) is a measure of risk in relation to the receipt of income. It compares EARNINGS, i.e. earnings after tax but before extraordinary items attributable to the ordinary shareholders, with the dividends (*net*) paid and proposed to be paid to them.

Example 5.7.5

		£
GROWSTRONG's *Earnings*		195,000
GROWSTRONG's Dividends paid and proposed for ordinary	shareholders (net)	75,000

Dividend cover 195 : 75 = 2.6 *times*.

Alternatively, Earnings per share = 19.5p
Dividend per share = 7.5p

Dividend cover 19.5 : 7.5p = 2.6 *times*.

The dividend cover results from the directors' decision on the dividend to be paid and the proportion of 'earnings' to be retained. If planned profits eventuate, then the planned dividend can be paid and the planned residual funds used for maintaining and developing the business.

GROWSTRONG's cover of 2.6 times, or to put it another way, the retention of 62% of 'earnings' (before extraordinary items) would be regarded as a strong point for the group by analysts.

It should be noted, however, that it is based on the historic cost accounts. Given a material level of inflation, the dividend cover based on available current cost accounts would provide a finer yardstick. Witness *Example 5.7.3* and the ICI 1980 figures.

Comparative investment ratios

Example 5.7.6

GROWSTRONG's *investment ratios,* set alongside those of *Mothercare* (see *Example 5.5.6*) (Drapery and Stores) and *Boots* (Industrials) from the *Financial Times* (1981) are:

Stock	Price	EPS*	Divd(net)	Cover	Gross divd yield	PER
GROWSTRONG	137	19.5	7.5p	2.6	7.8%	7.0
Mothercare	214	16.9	5.0p	3.4	3.3%	12.7
Boots	219	21.7	7.0p	2.8	4.6%	10.1

*EPS – Earnings per share is not quoted in the *Financial Times* but can be calculated, i.e. Price divided by PER.

Mothercare and Boots were among market leaders. Given GROWSTRONG's EPS and dividend, the market after consideration of the *trend* of the group's figures over a number of years, information on its prospects from the directors' report and other sources, and the likely environment in which it would operate, may feel that the share was underpriced.

Profit retained

It has been shown that the profit retained and transferred to reserves depends on the level of earnings attained and remaining after tax, preference dividends (if any) and extraordinary items, and the dividend policy adopted for the ordinary shares.

In theory, the amount of profit retained should not be a fortuitous residue remaining, but an amount planned in relation to the future of the enterprise as far as foreseen by the directors and detailed in budgets. In practice, unforeseen events occur, outcomes are different from those planned, so that amounts transferred to reserves are different from those budgeted, and in difficult times transfers are needed *from* reserves to enable dividends to be paid (*Example 5.7.3*). It has been noted that SSAP 6 and its revision ED 36 have virtually outlawed the practice known as 'reserve accounting' whereby profits were boosted by adjustment of some transactions against reserves. SSAP 6 required that a statement of the movements on the various reserve accounts, including those retained on the profit and loss account, should immediately follow the published profit and loss account for the year when *prior year* adjustments arise. Because of the statement's enhanced importance on the movement of reserves the revised draft standard amends this requirement (see page 135). With the latter two options, the *single statement of movements in reserves* proposed, would be referenced on the face of the profit and loss account.

In practice, in the absence of prior year items, as the movements on the various reserves are reflected in balance sheet changes between one year and the next, a *balance sheet note* usually incorporates the information including that on retained profit. Disclosure of the movement on reserves is required by the revised Schedule 8 (CA 1948) as inserted by section 1. CA 1981 (4 Sch. CA 1985).

Example 5.7.7

Statement showing the movements on reserves, including retained profit, taken from the Award-winning accounts of J. Bibby & Sons Ltd.

RESERVES Consolidated	Share premium account £'000	Debenture redemption reserve £'000	Surplus on property valuation £'000	Premium on acquisition of subsidiaries £'000	Retained profit £'000	TOTAL £'000
OPENING BALANCE	72	2,291	7,749	(2,083)	20,133	28,162
Capitalisation	(8)				(4,097)	(4,105)
Retained profit for the year					6,029	6,029
Appropriation to debenture redemption reserve		227				227
Surplus realised			(107)		107	—
Valuation adjustment			(26)			(26)
CLOSING BALANCE	64	2,518	7,616	(2,083)	22,172	30,287

Comment on the J. Bibby statement:
The opening total balance of £28,162 and the closing total balance of £30,287 are the figures shown on the face of the balance sheets for the previous and current years. The profit and loss appropriation account shows the appropriation of £6,029 'transfer to reserve' as retained profit, and £227 to increase the debenture redemption reserve to £2,518. This latter reserve represents retention of profits to replace redeemed loans and nearly equates to borrowings 'repayable within 5 years' of the company.

The entry 'capitalisation' indicates the transfer to share capital account of an amount of £4,097 to effect a bonus issue of shares of one ordinary share for every two held (see Chapter 4 on bonus shares).

The £8 transferred from share premium account was used to write off the expenses of the issue, an approved use of that account by law (see Chapter 4 on share premiums).

The debit 'premium on the acquisition of subsidiaries' represents a payment which exceeded the value of the subsidiaries' net assets acquired, i.. for 'goodwill', and is effectively here deducted from reserve (but not actually written off) – a treatment referred to as 'the dangling debit' (see Chapter 4 on goodwill).*

A surplus *realised* on the sale of properties is transferred to retained profits (£107), and the overall surplus on revaluations is reduced by a valuation downwards (£26).*

All figures are in £'000s.

Note: SSAP 22 'Accounting for goodwill', effective from January 1985, does not allow purchased goodwill to be carried as a permanent item on balance sheets. The goodwill must be written off immediately against reserves on acquisition or amortised over a period of time against profit (see Chapter 4 on goodwill). The CA 1985 balance sheet formats also require that such goodwill, to the extent that it is not yet fully written off, be shown under the heading of goodwill as an intangible fixed asset.

Profit attributable to members of the holding company

In accordance with the requirement of the CA 1985, GROWSTRONG disclose how much of the above level of profit (before dividends), £180,000 (*Table 4*) is dealt with in the *accounts of the holding company*; and following the requirement of SSAP 1, how much of it represents the group's share of the retained net profit of its associated company. The balance which is noted, is the profit attributable to holding company shareholders retained by its subsidiaries.

6

Return on capital employed

Growstrong's Results Reviewed

At the conclusion of the consideration of the GROWSTRONG plc consolidated balance sheet (*Table 3*), it was noted that although more complicated, it was in essence the same document as those produced for the start and earlier years of the enterprise. A value for the capital employed in the group needed to be determined and a return on that capital planned.

What options are there to represent the group's capital employed and what profit levels should be related thereto? What are the outcomes of its operations as disclosed by its published accounts and related notes (Chapters 4 and 5) for the latest financial year?

If the starting assumption is that the directors are responsible for the efficient use of the group's TOTAL ASSETS so that the outcome is the best return for the ordinary shareholders (*SHAREHOLDERS' FUNDS*), a progression of returns on capital employed linking these two levels is as shown in *Example 6.1* (page 145).

Comment on Example 6.1
1. Instead of using the end of the year balance sheet figures for the various levels of capital employed, the average of the last two years could be taken. ROCE(E) would then be 20%, i.e. 'earnings' £195 on average shareholders' funds of £964.
2. GROWSTRONG's capital structure is lowly-geared, nevertheless the low net cost of interest (C), raises the return on shareholders' funds (D) by 2.4% from that obtained on the long-term funds (B). The group has scope for further borrowing.
3. The progressive relationships of these returns could be extended to take in the dividend yield and cover shown in *Example 5.7.5* (page 141) ending with the percentage of profit retained.
4. Where inflation is a material factor, it is likely that for most companies ROCE based on historic accounts is overstated. Where current cost accounts (see later chapter) are available, alternative calculations can be made for comparison.
5. Variants on the determination of capital employed include the deduction of the book value of intangibles from its total (ROCE A and B). This would increase the ROCE. Purchased goodwill to the extent not yet written off is often a material item in a consolidated balance sheet. It could be argued that having paid that extra sum over the value of the net assets for the acquisition of the subsidiary, it is an amount invested on which a return should be earned. On the other hand, if it had been written off – a conservative and recommended treatment – then the capital employed would have been reduced.
6. Another variant is to include the bank overdraft in ROCE (B). Bank overdrafts

Example 6.1

	GROWSTRONG plc RETURNS ON CAPITAL EMPLOYED		
	(figures in £'000s)		
	CAPITAL EMPLOYED *(Table 3)*	RETURN THEREON *(Table 4)*	ROCE
	£2,075 *TOTAL ASSETS* (Fixed plus current)	£383 PROFIT before interest and tax	18.5% A
	£1,475 *LONG TERM FUNDS* (Total assets less current liabilities)	£239 PROFIT after tax (£221) but before loan interest net*	16.2% B
less	£290 *LONG TERM LOANS*	£18 LOAN INTEREST net*	6.2% C Net cost to group
	£1,185 *SHAREHOLDERS' FUNDS* including minority interest and deferred tax	£221 PROFIT after tax but before minority interest	18.6% D
	£1,022 *SHAREHOLDERS' FUNDS* Equity: the group has no preference capital	£195 EARNINGS – Profit after tax but before extraordinary items	19.0% E
=	1 million ordinary shares	£195	19.5p F Earnings per share
=	Market value – 137p per share	19.5p EPS	7.0 G Price earnings ratio

*Long-term loan interest included in the total interest payable of £42,000, i.e. interest on debentures (10%) and bank loan interest (average 15%) is £37,500 gross. With corporation tax at 52%, the net cost to the GROWSTRONG group is £37,500 × 48% = £18,000.

appear for many companies as a permanent feature of 'current liabilities' in the balance sheet. Although legally current liabilities, they often in practice take the form of 'long-term funds'. For a proper comparison with the returns of other companies which include loans which are both legally and factually long-term, bank overdraft should, so the argument goes, be included in ROCE (B). A sub-variant where bank overdraft is included is to deduct any 'cash in hand' therefrom. This seems illogical, for should a company choose to hold cash, for whatever reason, then the nil return on it in historical terms and the negative return in inflationary terms should be accepted and included in ROCE.

RETURN ON TRADING/OPERATING

It is useful to consider what return GROWSTRONG has earned on its trading/operating activities and to link it with a hierarchy of ratios (see *Example 6.2* below). For this purpose, investments including investment in the associated company, together with the attributable investment income, are excluded from the ROCE calculation.

Example 6.2

Primary and Secondary ratios

The ROCE or *PRIMARY RATIO* used for internal management purposes and for inter-firm comparisons when measuring the efficiency of the employment of operating assets is:

$$\frac{\text{Operating profit}}{\text{Operating assets}}$$

As *Primary ratio* = Sales margin × turnover of assets, the ROCE will vary with the increase/decrease in the two secondary ratios. A hierarchy of ratios can be developed from these ratios and this is illustrated and considered in PART 3 of this book – Interpretation of company accounts.

For GROWSTRONG, the figures at the apex of the pyramid are:

$\dfrac{\text{Operating profit}}{\text{Operating assets}}$	=	$\dfrac{\text{Operating profit}}{\text{Sales}}$	×	$\dfrac{\text{Sales}}{\text{Operating assets}}$
Primary ratio		Secondary ratio		Secondary ratio
$\dfrac{358}{1,881}$	=	$\dfrac{358}{4,520}$	×	$\dfrac{4,520}{1,881}$
19%	=	7.9%	×	2.4 times

Notes: Net operating profit (£358) is before tax, loan interest and investment income as shown in *Table 4*, page 109.

Operating assets are total assets £2,075 (ROCE A, *Example 6.1*) less investments £134 and less intangible fixed assets £60.

Sales are as shown in *Table 4*.

GROWSTRONG has earned 19.0% before tax on its OPERATING capital. This can be compared with the budgeted figure, with its own previous performance and with available comparative figures of companies in the industrial sector.

These comparative analyses will cover the secondary and subsequent ratios in the hierarchy to pinpoint comparative strengths and weaknesses and areas for enquiry. Much of such analyses is available also to external appraisers.

FUNDS, PROFIT AND CAPITAL STRUCTURE

The first objective of a company is to survive. To survive, it has to earn a sufficient profit on its invested capital to meet the needs of its investing shareholders for income and/or appreciation of share value – needs based on the risk contemplated, the level of current interest rates and on current monetary values.

Three major external sources of long-term funds derive from the issue of ordinary shares including rights issues, loan capital including debentures, and from preference shares, although the latter have not recently been an attractive force. The individuals or institutions within these groups have their own different measures of risk, yield on investment and possible capital growth. The sum total of their outlook at a time when a company requires funds may not be immediately compatible with the capital structure envisaged by the directors, who may then have to adopt some compromise.

The business must compete in the market for its external funds. Thus its planned profit will have to be based not only on an adequate return on its capital employed to be achieved by its workforce led by management, but also related to the long-term return (dividend and capital growth) considered desirable by its equity shareholders.

It may be concluded that capital structure and its gearing; profit and return on capital employed targets set by the company, together with the individual investors' criteria, are inter-connected factors.

This connection between the various levels of capital employed, through to the equity shareholders' investment ratios, has been demonstrated in *Example 6.1*.

7

What is *not* in a balance sheet?

A company's earnings related to its invested ordinary share capital, the level of its paid dividends, and the amount of profit retained and 'ploughed back' to add to its financial strength, are important factors in the determination of the public standing of a listed company as reflected by the market value of its ordinary shares.

Dividend per share, earnings per share, dividend cover and the price-earnings ratios have been shown to be used in this respect.

Analysts will keep in perspective other information available to them within the company report (e.g. directors' report, statistical information, see PART 2) and from other sources when considering the meaning of such ratios. And they will know that there are certain items of expenditure which management can choose to incur or not to incur, which could make the results of one company seen through its accounts seem quite irrational when compared with another, the problem being compounded by the statutory need to report within the time span of one year.

Let us take the example of the ALPHA and BETA public limited companies to make the important point that an approach based "What is *not* in a company balance sheet or profit and loss account?" is often essential to an analysis of what *is* in it.

CASE 3. Alpha plc and Beta plc

Objective: 1. To encourage the search for and use of all other available information, besides the 'accounting figures', and to keep this in perspective.
2. To show the derivation of earnings per share, dividend per share, dividend cover and the price-earnings ratio.

Within the company report there will be available (as shown in Chapters 4 and 5) the detailed notes to the accounts required either by law or the accounting standards, or given additionally by progressive companies, plus the further information covered in PART 2 of this book. Obviously important are the 'accounting policies' followed by the company and required to be disclosed by SSAP 2.

Table 1 shows summarised extracts of the profit and loss accounts of the two companies, Alpha and Beta, which for our purposes can be considered to be in the same line of business.

The item TOTAL EXPENDITURE has been summarised into one figure. Chapter 5 has detailed the minimum disclosure requirements by law and the accounting standards which

Case 3. Table 1

	ALPHA plc £m	BETA plc £m
SALES	20.0	20.0
less TOTAL EXPENDITURE, being cost of sales including all operating and other expenses, plus corporation tax	18.0	19.0
Profit after tax – EARNINGS (there are only ordinary shareholders)	2.0	1.0
Transfer FROM reserves (Beta only)		0.5
		1.5
Dividend to ordinary shareholders	1.5	1.5
Retentions of profit	0.5	Nil
Market value of 10 million ordinary shares before the publication of these results	£m 15	£m 15

Case 3. Table 2

The investment ratios derived from these summarised figures:

			ALPHA plc	BETA plc
Dividend per share	(150/10)		15p	15p
Earnings per share	(200/10)	(100/10)	20p	10p
Dividend cover	(2.0/1.5)	(1.0/1.5)	1.33 times	0.66 times
Price earnings ratio	(15/2)	(15/1)	7.5	15

include cost of sales, detail of depreciation and capital expenditure, exceptional and extraordinary items, loan interest, directors' emoluments, taxation etc., all being information available to the analyst.

Comment: It is reasonable to expect that the difference of £1 million in the earnings after tax between the companies will be a material factor in the market adjustment of the price of Alpha plc shares in relation to those of Beta plc.

But what is the reason for this difference in expenditure from which all other figures flow? It could be that Alpha management is more cost conscious and cost effective. It could be, in part, a tax adjustment. It could be many things, but this is what is found on investigation of other information in the companies' reports. Beta plc has newer, more up to date plant. It has recently purchased new equipment which is expected to increase productivity significantly in the near future. It believes in, and plans, a first class progressive capital investment programme. It is writing off the capital cost of the plant (depreciation policy) against profit at a far quicker – thus higher – rate than Alpha plc. In addition, there are three major areas of expenditure charged against profits by Beta plc which are not in evidence in the case of Alpha plc to anything like the same extent:

(i) Research and development expenditure.
(ii) Development expenses in building up a better marketing, including market research, function.
(iii) Material expenditure on a management development programme.

Alpha plc is spending on research and development, though not on the same scale as Beta plc. Furthermore, Beta's policy is to write off its R & D expenditure in the year in which it is incurred. Alpha carries forward a proportion of its development expenditure in an endeavour to 'match' the expenditure with income derived from it in future years.

Clearly there may be found much information of importance behind the immediate figures in the published accounts, which may or may not be given emphasis in the notes to those accounts, or in the directors' report.

No one can be certain about the future, but it could well be the case that the policies which Beta plc is following will result in a better future for that company than for Alpha – a reversal of the impression gained from the reported figures. The additional information has put these in perspective.

Note: It is assumed that Alpha's R & D policy is acceptable within the terms of SSAP 13, Accounting for Research and Development, and that the expenditure carried forward is judged to meet the stringent criteria set out in the standard, which allows the amounts carried forward to be amortized over the period expected to benefit.

Beta's policy is of prudence. They disclose this policy as required by SSAP 2, saying that their board has consistently argued that R & D expenditure should be charged against current income, and not capitalized. The reality, they say, is that money has been paid out, but that no tangible asset has been created as a result. They take the view that if the R & D leads to profit in the future, and they expect that it will, then that profit should be taken when it is made – in the future.

The matters covered in Part One of this book are the subject of work and discussion assignments in WORKBOOK 1 which commences at page 263.

PART TWO

Information in the Company Report

8

Legal and accounting standards framework for company reports and accounts

In publishing their report and accounts, directors will have considered the minimum disclosure requirements of company law as well as domestic and, where applicable, international accounting standards, and for listed companies the requirements of the Stock Exchange. EEC Directives on company law awaiting UK legislation and Exposure Drafts of proposed Accounting Standards will need review in the light of the directors' duty to present accounts showing 'a true and fair view'.

It is beyond the scope of this book to give detailed information on these requirements. Instead, the legal and accounting standard requirements are considered or noted in context, particularly in respect of the balance sheet (Chapter 4) and the profit and loss account (Chapter 5). In this chapter, the legal and accounting standards framework and the more recent influences of the EEC Directives on UK company law will be considered.

At the end of the chapter are listed the UK and international accounting standards issued to date, together with the information requirements of the Stock Exchange.

UK Company Law – the Companies Act 1985

With the Companies Act 1981 receiving the Royal Assent on 30 October 1981, it became necessary to refer to no less than five Acts, plus relevant statutory instruments, to determine the law applying to companies. The other Acts were the Companies Act 1948, referred to as the principal Act, and those of 1967, 1976 and 1980.

The long overdue *consolidation* of company law was effected by the *Companies Act 1985*, which came into force on 1 July of that year. This main Act was supported by three others:
   (i) *the Business Names Act 1985* which controls the use of trading names;
  (ii) *the Companies Securities (Insider Dealing) Act 1985*; and
 (iii) *the Companies Consolidation (Consequential Provisions) Act 1985* which deals with the technical minutiae of consolidation.

This package was seen by the Government as a means of encouraging greater investor protection and hence wider participation in share ownership.

Table 9, at the end of this Chapter, sets out the location within the Companies Act 1985 for all references to previous legislation contained in this book.

THE CA 1948 AND GROUP ACCOUNTS

The last *consolidated* Companies Act prior to 1985, was that of 1948 – a trend-setting landmark for company reporting and the disclosure of accounting information. Required to be published for the first time in the UK were:
   (i) a detailed profit and loss account, and
   (ii) group accounts in consolidated or other form.
Readers may be surprised to learn that detailed profit and loss accounts were not required to be published before 1948; undoubtedly, the adverse publicity which followed the famous Royal Mail Steam Packet Co case of 1931 (*Rex v Kylsant and Morland*) had much to do with this. The case will be referred to later in this chapter in the context of the CA 1981.

The need for *group accounts* to be published was a major step forward, to be compared with the more recent requirement of SSAP 16 to publish current cost accounts.

Group accounts are required where a company (the holding, or parent company):
   (i) has a subsidiary at the end of its financial year, and
   (ii) is not itself a wholly-owned subsidiary of another company incorporated in Great
     Britain (S229, CA 1985).
Group accounts are normally synonymous with *consolidated accounts*, where these comprise a consolidated balance sheet and a consolidated profit and loss account dealing with the affairs of the holding company and *all* its subsidiaries, such as the GROWSTRONG accounts, *Table 3* and *Table 4*.

The directors may, if they believe it to be in the interests of members, present group accounts in alternative form, providing consolidated accounts for some part of the group and separate information regarding others.

Subsidiaries may be omitted from group accounts in certain circumstances, e.g.
   (i) where consolidation is impracticable, or
   (ii) the amounts are insignificant, and are of no real value, or
   (iii) the expense or delay involved is out of proportion to value, or
   (iv) the result would be misleading or harmful, or
   (v) it is undesirable because the businesses of the holding company and the subsidiary
     are so different that they cannot reasonably be treated as a single undertaking.
In the last two noted circumstances, Department of Trade approval is necessary.

Where subsidiaries are omitted from group or consolidated accounts, then the holding company must annex to its own balance sheet:
   (i) an explanation of the reasons for exclusion,
   (ii) any audit qualification in the accounts of the omitted subsidiary, and
   (iii) information on the valuation of the investment in the omitted company.
Subsequent legislation has not substantially changed these requirements. Group accounts must comply with Schedule 4, CA 1985 (replacing Schedule 8 of the CA 1981) so far as applicable to group accounts, and as with individual company accounts, the requirement for them to give a true and fair view overrides the detailed accounting requirements of the Companies Acts (S230, CA 1985).

The Accounting Standard on Group Accounts, SSAP 14, makes no major change to the well established procedure of preparing such accounts. It was made desirable by the publication of International Accounting Standard 3, which differed from UK practice on minor matters.

Future legislation to take account of the Seventh EEC Directive on group accounts (not yet adopted) is not expected to affect radically current practice and law.

THE CA 1967 AND THE STRUCTURE OF CAPITAL

Two important aspects of the 1967 Act were:

    (i) the amendment of the 1948 Act's Schedule 8 and the detailing of accounting provisions in its Sch. 2. This subsequently became Sch. 8 of the CA 1985.

   (ii) the abolition of the category of 'exempt private company' created by the 1948 Act, with the result that ALL limited companies were required to file copies of their profit and loss account and balance sheet together with other documents,including the auditors' and directors' reports, with their Annual Return to the Registrar of Companies, where they are available for public reference.

Note: The CA 1981 made changes in respect of the publication of accounts by its category of 'small company'. This is referred to later in the context of the Royal Mail Steam Packet case.

A major section of the CA 1967 was introduced to deal with the operations of cut-price insurance companies and is of interest in the context of a consideration of the adequacy of the capital structure of a company in relation to a growth in the level of its operations.

The operations of established insurance companies, like those of banks and pension funds, are based on the trust and confidence of the public or the subscribers that these 'institutions' are sound and reliable. While the lay public would not express it so, the general expectation is that their financial strucure is inviolable.

It was a matter for public concern, therefore, when certain insurance companies failed in the mid-1960s, leaving some of their customers without payment of claims and all without insurance cover.

It is a sound principle of finance in a free enterprise system that the primary source of capital in a business conducted for profit should be the proprietors. Ideally, this and other long-term borrowed funds should amply cover not only the long-term investment in fixed assets, but a good proportion of the working capital as well. In addition, it is essential to ensure that as business increases, extra funds necessary to sustain additional long-term investment and growing working capital needs are provided. In this way, the often fatal phenomenon known as overtrading is avoided.

While the investment of long-term funds by insurance companies differs from that of manufacturing companies, these basic precepts still apply. They were ignored, however, by the cut-price companies who invested very little of their own capital, relying mainly on premium income as their main source of funds. Naturally this source expanded rapidly as news of its relative cheapness spread. The customer was happy to have his mandatorily-required insurance cover so cheaply and drove away in his car or on his motor cycle giving scant regard to the insurance companies' ability to meet claims.

The premium income – the main source of funds – was also, of course, a liability in so far as it represented potential claims of policyholders. Claims were low in the early months of operations but, over time, they and the attaching liability increased.

Concurrently, the counter operations of the established companies and the birth of other cut-price companies encroached on the premium income. The day inevitably arrived when these new, unsoundly financed companies failed to meet claims, and the subsequent publicity was fatal for them. The basic reason for their failure was the growth of business was an inadequate capital structure.

The consequent public outcry led to the rush through Parliament of the insurance company provisions of the CA 1967. Section 62 thereof is a rare case of the law trying to ensure an adequate framework of capital in such companies, a normal responsibility of any sound board of directors. The section sets out provisions for securing the sufficiency of assets and capital of insurance companies. It stipulated not only a required basic share capital, but also an increasing capital requirement to be maintained in line with an increasing premium income. The Act empowered the Government to impose a ban on a company taking on new business or renewing existing policies where the capital is inadequate in terms of the Act, in relation to expanding business. These legal provisions affecting Insurance Companies were subsequently replaced by the Insurance Companies Act 1974 2 Sch.

ACCOUNTING REFERENCE PERIODS

Features of the CA 1976 relating to the preparation and publication of accounts were the introduction of accounting reference periods, and the shortening of the period which may elapse between the end of a company's financial year and the preparation and filing of accounts.

Normally a company's accounting reference period will end on 31 March, but there is provision for established companies at that time and for new companies since that time to specify a different date.

The accounts must be laid before the company in general meeting, with a copy to the Registrar of Companies, by a private company within ten months and by any other company within seven months after the end of its accounting reference period.

A further three months is allowed if the company has interests abroad. The accounting reference date may only be altered by notice to the Registrar of Companies and subject to certain conditions being met. (S3, CA 1976.) Accounting reference periods are now dealt with in sections 224 and 225 Companies Act 1985.

EEC DIRECTIVES AND UK COMPANY LAW

Both the Companies Act 1980 and the Companies Act 1981 dealt, *inter alia*, with EEC Directives. The former with the Second Directive and the latter with the Fourth. They represented major first steps in the process of harmonising UK company law with that of other member states of the Community.

Harmonisation of company law is seen as a practical necessity in the process of making the EEC work. In the diverse community involved, such harmonisation is likely to be a long and complex matter, but the programme is gathering momentum (see *Table 8*).

The EEC Treaty sees the need to 'provide safeguards equivalent throughout the Community which, for the protection of the interests of members and others, are required by Member States of companies or firms . . .' *Article 189* of the Treaty provides that:

"In order to carry out their task, the Council and the Commission shall, in accordance with the provisions of this Treaty, make Regulations, issue Directives, take decisions, make recommendations or deliver opinions. A *Directive shall be binding, as to the result to be achieved, but shall leave to the national authorities the choice of forms and methods.*"

From the definition of a Directive given in the Treaty, it can be seen why Companies Acts may be required to implement them and why the statutory language used in those Acts may sometimes differ from the language used in the Directives themselves.

In summary, a Directive is binding as to the result to be achieved. It sets a minimum standard which must be reached. The national authority has a choice of forms and methods.

COMPANIES ACT 1980

Intended to meet the requirements of the EEC Second Directive (classification and capital of public and private companies; restrictions on distributions) approved by the Council of Ministers in 1976, the CA 1980 was extended to deal with aspects of directors' duties and with 'insider dealing'.

A *public company* is one:

(i) whose memorandum states that it is a public company;

(ii) whose name ends with the words 'public limited company' or its Welsh equivalent. The abbreviation PLC or (Welsh) CCC may be used;

(iii) whose authorised and allotted share capital is not less than £5,000. The Secretary of State can alter this figure by statutory instrument;

(iv) which has not less than *two* members (previously seven);

(v) where at least one-quarter of the nominal share value and the whole of any premium has been paid on allotment.

A *public* company may not (but a *private* company may) do business or exercise borrowing powers until the Registrar has issued it with a certificate that the requirements as to share capital have been complied with. A *private* company is one which has not been registered as a public company and is subject to the restriction that it may not offer its shares or debentures to the public for cash or otherwise.

Issue of new capital

Implementing Article 29 of the Second Directive, the Act gives statutory rights to *existing* shareholders (private or public companies) to subscribe to new issues in proportion to their present holdings on the same or more favourable terms under which offers are made to third parties. The memorandum or articles of a *private* company may exclude these pre-emption rights.

Maintenance of the capital of a public company

An extraordinary general meeting of shareholders must be called in the event of a serious loss of capital (when the net assets of the company are half or less of the company's called up share capital) for the purpose of determining what measures should be taken to deal with the situation.

Restrictions on the distribution of profits and assets

The 1980 Act provided a statutory basis for deciding whether a distribution is legal (Section 43). Readers are referred to its consideration in the discussion on divisible profit (page 135 *et seq*).

In summary, a *private* company may distribute its *realised* profits without accounting for any unrealised losses. A *public* company may only distribute the excess of its profits over any unrealised losses.

Directors' loans

The provisions of the 1948 Act in respect of loans to directors were replaced by more stringent provisions in the CA 1980 (SS49-53). A company may not make a loan to a director or to a director of a holding company or enter into credit transactions (quasi loans) on their behalf (guarantees or securities for a loan). The defined exceptions cover loans incurred 'in the normal course of business' and loans which do not exceed £2,500. (SIII, CA 1981). Regulations on director's loans are now within CA 1985 (see *Table 9*).

Information in respect of transactions or arrangements involving a director, as well as loans, quasi loans or credit arrangements made for officers other than directors, must be *disclosed in the accounts*.

Employees

Directors are required by the 1980 Act to have regard to the *interests of the company's employees*. The words 'in general' are used in this respect. The extent of this obligation, which is enforceable in the same way as any other fiduciary duty *owed to a company* by its directors, will have to await the tests of future court actions. The interests of employees in the liquidation of a business are strengthened following the overturning by the Act of the decision in *Parke v Daily News Ltd* (1962). In that case, the directors' intention to set aside part of the surplus arising from the proceeds of the sale of the major part of the company's assets to provide redundancy payments and pensions for employees was held by the Court not to be in the interests of the company's shareholders. The CA 1980 – now S309 CA 85 – imposes an obligation on the directors to have regard to the interests of the employees in general and the company has the power to make some provision for employees on cessation or transfer of the whole or part of the business even if it is not in the best interests of the company. Note, again, the general implication. And see Chapter 10 on the proposed EEC Fifth Directive, the related Vredeling proposals and employee interests.

Insider dealing

The object of the provisions of the CA 1980 on insider dealing is to prohibit persons having 'inside information' about a company from obtaining unfair advantage through dealing in the company's securities. The Act does not, however, use the phrase 'inside information' but the expression 'price-sensitive information', which is then closely defined (S73(2)). The statutory language thus attempts to state the generally understood requirement in a manner which is likely to achieve that object. Only time will tell of its success. Insider dealing is a criminal offence with the liability of imprisonment and/or an unlimited fine. The Companies Securities (Insider dealing) Act 1985 now consolidates the law related to this subject.

CA 1981 AND ACCOUNTING EXEMPTIONS FOR SMALL AND MEDIUM-SIZED COMPANIES

The CA 1981 – SS247–50 CA 85 – allows small and medium-sized companies to file accounts which are exempt from the full legal requirements for published accounts.

In order to establish itself for these exemptions, a company must satisfy two of the three qualifying conditions during the current and immediately preceding financial years.

Qualifying conditions	*Small company*	*Medium-sized company*
*Turnover not exceeding	£1.4 million	£5.75 million
*Balance sheet total not exceeding	£700,000	£2.8 million
Average number of employees not exceeding	50	250

* See note page 38.

A public company, whatever its size, is ineligible for these exemptions.

It is important to note that although, as a result of the exemptions, a company may file modified accounts with the Registrar of Companies, it must still present unmodified accounts to its shareholders.

Medium-sized companies are permitted to submit a *modified profit and loss account* which need not include details of turnover and gross profit margins.

Small companies are permitted to *file only an abridged balance sheet.* No profit and loss account or directors' report is required to be filed. The notes to the accounts, which must be given, result from a consideration of the needs of those who deal with the company: information is required on accounting policies, share capital, substantial investments in other corporate bodies, aggregate creditors falling due after more than five years, secured creditors, ultimate holding company, loans to directors and officers, aggregate of debtors falling due after more than one year, and the aggregate of creditors falling due within one year and the aggregate of those falling due after one year. The last two items may appear in the balance sheet rather than in the notes to the accounts.

Where modified accounts are delivered to the Registrar of Companies, the balance sheet must include immediately above the directors' signatures a statement by them that they are entitled to file modified accounts. Modified accounts for a holding company and its subsidiaries may be delivered if the group, as a whole, qualifies as a small or medium-sized company and does not contain an ineligible company.

A greater number of companies will fall into the categories of small- and medium-sized companies when the decision by the EEC Council of Ministers to raise the balance sheet total and turnover limits is introduced into UK legislation.

Audit

The full accounts which must be laid before the shareholders must be accompanied by the auditors' report on them following the normal audit, for which there is no relaxation. *A special auditors' report* must accompany the modified accounts filed with the Registrar confirming the directors' claim of entitlement to file modified accounts. This opinion implies also that the accounts have been properly prepared. The special audit report must incorporate the full text of the auditors' report on the accounts presented to the shareholders, including, of course, any qualification.

SSAPs and modified accounts

Modified accounts need not include disclosures or statements required by SSAPs as the latter apply only to accounts based on the true and fair view formula. Modified accounts by definition will not follow that precept.

This reduction in the standards of reporting for the small company was strongly opposed by the accountancy profession which feared the consequences of the publication of such drastically reduced information. Of the 856,000 registered companies in Britain at the beginning of 1984, only some 18,000 were public companies, so that it is likely that detailed information will be absent in respect of very many companies.

The reduced administrative burden which was said to be among the Government's objectives will not eventuate for these companies; on the contrary, the work will be increased in providing full accounts for the shareholders and modified accounts for the Registrar. There is nothing, of course, which prevents small or medium-sized companies from filing full accounts if they wish.

The choice to file modified accounts, even though accompanied by the mandatory notes mentioned above, may well result in doubts about the companies' financial rating in the minds of people dealing with them, including other small businesses.

Unless the risk is immediately accepted, greater time will need to be devoted to checking on credit references in order to minimise bad debts.

1985 Consultative DTI document

Following on from proposals in a government report '*Burdens on Business*', the Department of Trade and Industry published a consultative document in June 1985 on the accounting and audit requirements affecting *small* companies. Among matters noted as options were the elimination of the audit requirement for small shareholder-managed companies or for all small companies below a certain size; also up for consideration was the exemption for such companies from the need to prepare and present full accounts to its shareholders. The document also considers raising the turnover threshold defining small and medium-sized companies from £1.4 million to £2 million for the former, and from £5.75 million to £8 million for the latter. (See note page 38.)

THE ROYAL MAIL STEAM PACKET CASE

This famous case (*Rex v Kylsant and Morant*, 1931) was referred to earlier in this chapter when noting the major step forward of the CA 1948 in requiring the publication of a detailed profit and loss account. It is ironic that, some half-a-century later, the CA 1981 took disclosure of accounting information a step or two backwards.

For some years the Royal Mail company, although incurring trading losses like many others in the depression years of the late 1920s, had revealed in its published accounts considerable profits available for dividend. This position was brought about by the utilization of tax and other reserves created in the past and no longer required for the purposes for which they were set up. These reserves were 'secret reserves' inasmuch as they were not disclosed in the accounts. The only indication of this action was the information that the 'profits' of the years in question were 'after adjustment of taxation reserves'. It was alleged by the prosecution that the result of such adjustments was to cause shareholders (and investors) to believe that the company was trading profitably, whereas in fact it was making losses.

Criminal proceedings against the chairman and the auditor of the company, alleging that the chairman had issued and the auditor had aided and abetted the issue of false annual reports *with intent to deceive*, failed, but the result of the case was the outlawing of secret reserves through the CA 1948 requirements for a detailed profit and loss account and information on movements on reserves and other provisions. The comments of Mr Justice Wright in his summing up of the case are of interest in relation to the non-filing of a profit and loss account by small companies taking advantage of the provisions of the CA 1981:

> "You may say, referring to every word and every figure, there is nothing false about this or that, but the document as a whole may be false, not because of what it states, but because of what it does NOT state and because of what it implies."

THE CA 1981 ACCOUNTING AND DISCLOSURE REQUIREMENTS (4 Sch. CA 1985)

Section 1 of the CA 1981 amended S149, CA 1948, by the insertion of a new 8th Schedule to the 1948 Act. This new 8th Schedule was set out in Sch. 1 to the 1981 Act. The form and contents of accounts are now governed by Schedule 4 Companies Act 1985 the replacing consolidation law.

Sch. 1 of the 1981 Act implements the provisions of the EEC 4th Directive which is intended to harmonise accounting practices and the format and content of annual accounts in member States. Companies can choose between two balance sheet formats and four profit and loss formats. *Tables 3* and *4* are based on the formats likely to be used by listed companies. The same format must be used every year. If the directors deem a change is necessary, they must give particulars of it and a reason for the change in a note to the accounts. The accounting principles and rules and the required notes to the accounts set out in the CA 1985 4th Schedule have been covered in Chapters 4 and 5, though not exhaustively.

The general requirements for *directors' reports* under company law are dealt with in the next chapter. Any inconsistency between the directors' report and the accounts is to be stated in the auditors' report.

Banks and insurance companies, for which there are to be separate EEC Directives, and shipping companies were not required to comply with the 1981 Act accounting arrangements, and continued to prepare accounts as under the CA 1948. The 1985

Companies Act (SS257–62) sets out the legal requirements covering 'special category companies' which includes these types of company.

The legal changes introduced in 1981 relating to the share premium account and merger accounting, and in respect of share capital including the power given to companies to issue redeemable shares and to purchase and redeem their own shares, are covered in the examples of Chapter 4.

Disclosure of interests in shares

Sections of the CA 1948 allowed the Department of Trade to conduct an investigation into the ownership of a company's shares, and CA 1967 and CA 1976 required disclosure of substantial interests by shareholders, with a threshold at 5%. These provisions were found to prove ineffective against *concert parties*, that is a group of people who vote and act in concert in every way. Holding less than 5% of the shares individually, disclosure of interest was not required.

The CA 1981 restated much of the existing law and extended it to increase its effectiveness. A concert party defined as an agreement, whether legally binding or not between persons acting together to acquire interests in shares in a public company, is obliged to tell the company of its collective holding. Concert parties are now covered by SS204–7 of the Consolidated 1985 Act which contains numerous other relevant sections.

UK AND INTERNATIONAL ACCOUNTING STANDARDS

The first Accounting Standard was issued by the Accounting Standards Committee (ASC) in January 1971 and to date it has been followed by 22 others (*Table 5*). The ASC at present comprises members from all six bodies forming the Consultative Committee of Accountancy Bodies, i.e. the three Institutes of Chartered Accountants (England and Wales, Scotland and Ireland), the Chartered Association of Certified Accountants, the Institute of Cost and Management Accountants, and the Chartered Institute of Public Finance and Accountancy. The standards (Statements of Standard Accounting Practice) are therefore formulated and issued by the profession. Their main aim is to narrow the choice of accounting treatment so that published financial statements are so prepared that they can be clearly understood and are comparable one with another.

Compliance with standards

The respective Councils of the accountancy bodies expect their members who are responsible for the preparation of financial statements for publication to observe the standards. If they are not observed, it is expected that significant departures from them are disclosed and explained in the accounts. Where members of the profession act as auditors, the onus is on them not only to ensure such disclosure and explanation, but also, to the extent that their concurrence is stated or implied, to justify them.

Failure by members of the accountancy bodies to observe the standards exposes them to enquiry and sanction.

If auditors do not concur with a material departure from a standard, then they are required to 'qualify' their report to the company's shareholders.

Audit qualifications could lead to the suspension by the Stock Exchange of the listing of a public company's shares.

While, at present, the standards are formulated by and rely on the skills of the accountancy profession, they are designed for the benefit of users of financial statements – a much wider body than the shareholders, e.g. potential shareholders (private and institutional), lenders of money, suppliers, employees, customers, etc. The widening of the

ASC from September 1982 to give representation to users gave added strength to the process of 'standard making' and in 1983 changes were introduced (see Chapter 1, Section 6).

Enforcement of standards

It is important in the interests of the wider public that standards are complied with, and that exceptions arise only in special circumstances affecting a company where compliance would not allow a 'true and fair view' of the accounts.

The ASC has no power to enforce companies to comply with standards. The qualified audit report is the only real sanction on companies at present, with the possibility of listed companies of the suspension of their listing by the Stock Exchange.

Certain disclosures resulting from SSAPs are now required by the CA 1985, e.g. statement of accounting policies (SSAP 2), depreciation (SSAP 12), development costs (SSAP 13), and extraordinary items (SSAP 6). An audit qualification on the omission of such statutory information will no longer refer to a 'departure from an accounting standard', but will have to state that the accounts do not comply with the CA 1985.

Counsels' opinion (1983) on the relationship of the law, the true and fair view concept and the accounting standards is covered in Chapter 1, Section 6.

International Accounting Standards Committee (ASC)

This body came into existence in 1973 following agreement by the leading professional accountancy bodies of Australia, Canada, France, Germany, Japan, Mexico, the Netherlands, the UK and Ireland, and the USA. Other countries have since become members.

Their laudable object is:

"to formulate and publish in the public interest, standards to be observed in the presentation of audited financial statements and to promote their world-wide acceptance and observance."

Relationship of International to UK standards

A UK standard issued *after* a related international standard will endeavour to comply with the latter, and will end with a clause indicating that compliance with the one will mean compliance with the other. *New* international standards will take cognisance of standards and exposure drafts already issued in member countries.

International standards (*Table 6*) will not override domestic standards. The obligation of members of the IASC is to ensure that where differences exist, or there is a conflict between the two (including differences between the international standard and domestic law), the financial statements and the audit report will indicate in what respects the international standard has not been observed.

THE STOCK EXCHANGE LISTING AGREEMENT

Acceptance of the Listing Agreement is one of the requirements for admission of a company to the listing of its securities. Such companies must provide certain information about their operations promptly, and follow certain administrative procedures (see *Table 7*).

In requesting more information in annual reports and accounts than may be required by legislation, the Stock Exchange expect its own additional provisions to be regarded as a minimum standard, and it strengthens the policing of standards by requiring:

"a statement by the directors as to the reasons for adopting an alternative basis of accounting in any case where the auditors have stated that the accounts are not drawn up in accordance with the standard accounting practices approved by the accounting bodies."

In 1984, the UK implemented three EEC Directives (Admissions, Listings, Interim Reports) aimed at harmonising practices in the community (*Table 7*).

STATUTORY AUDIT

It should be understood that the statutory auditor, that is the person(s) appointed as required by law to report to the shareholders of a company on the accounts examined by him and on the balance sheet, etc., laid before the company in general meeting, has no responsibility as *auditor* for the efficiency or otherwise of the business.

If called upon to do so, it will be outside his remit as auditor and should be the subject of a separate contract between himself and the company.

If he is not asked to undertake such an assignment and he believes from his audit examinations that there are doubts as to the company's continuity, he should consider whether there are any respects in which the accounts should reflect this possibility, for the accounting standards (SSAP 2) imply that as a basis for the preparation of accounts "the enterprise will continue in operational existence for the foreseeable future", i.e. as a 'going concern'. This is covered later in this chapter.

Statutory auditor's duties

The Companies Acts require that the auditor, generally appointed by the *shareholders*, reports to them whether in his *opinion*:
  (i) the balance sheet gives a true and fair view of the company's affairs;
  (ii) the profit and loss account gives a true and fair view of the profit or loss for the year, and
  (iii) the accounts give the information required by the Companies Acts in the manner required.
In addition, he has to report to the shareholders when he is *not* satisfied that:
  (i) proper accounting records have been kept;
  (ii) proper returns, adequate for his purposes, have been received from branches not visited;
  (iii) the accounts are in agreement with the accounting records and returns received from branches, and
  (iv) he has received all the information and explanations he requires.
He also has to have regard to *Auditing Standards* issued by the Auditing Practices Committee of the accounting bodies.

The accounting standard, 'The Audit Report', requires that the auditor should refer expressly in his report as to:
  (i) whether the financial statements have been audited in accordance with approved auditing standards, and
  (ii) whether, in the auditor's opinion, the financial statements including the Sources and Application of Funds Statement (see Chapter 11) give a 'true and fair view'.
An explanatory note on the 'true and fair view' phrase, requires that when the auditor expresses an opinion that the financial statements, etc., meet this precept, he should be satisfied, inter alia, that:
  (i) all relevant SSAPs have been complied with except in situations in which for justifiable reasons they are not strictly applicable because they are impracticable, or exceptionally, in the circumstances, would be inappropriate or give a misleading view.

In this latter respect, it has been noted earlier that the CA 1985* emphasises that the requirement to show a true and fair view overrides all other accounting requirements of the Companies Acts and requires:

(i) any additional information necessary to give a true and fair view must be provided in the accounts, and

(ii) where compliance with the accounting requirements of the Acts would not give a true and fair view and the directors depart from them so as to meet the precept, that particulars of the departure, the reasons for it and its effect must be disclosed in a note to the accounts.

* See Section 6, Chapter 1.

The primary responsibility for presenting accounts showing a true and fair view lies with the *directors*. The auditor's duty is to express his *opinion* to the shareholders on the outcome of that responsibility.

In addition to his main responsibility of reporting on the accounts, the auditor should refer expressly in his report to any matters prescribed by relevant legislation or other requirements (Auditing Standard – 'The Audit Report').

Examples of these additional responsibilities mentioned in this chapter are the special auditor's report accompanying modified accounts filed with the Registrar, CA 1985 (see page 159), and that of S237(6) CA 1985, which requires that any inconsistency between the directors' report and the accounts is to be stated in the auditor's report.

In Chapter 4, in relation to the power of a private company to redeem or purchase its own shares out of capital, it was noted that the directors' statutory declaration of solvency must be accompanied by the company auditor's related report.

The importance of AUDITED accounts

(i) Auditor's duty to third parties

The auditor has no statutory duty to report to users of audited accounts other than the shareholders of the company by whom he is appointed. But he has a professional duty of care in undertaking his task and the recent predilection of 'third parties' to make significant claims in law against accountancy firms alleging negligence adds weight to his responsibilities. As I write, I read of a possible £76 million plus damages claim against a firm of auditors for alleged negligence in the audit of a company's accounts which, said the claimants, induced them to invest in it and occasioned their losses. The auditors deny negligence and will defend any action.

Until recently, a prerequisite of any liability of an auditor to third parties appeared to be that he *knew* or *ought to have known*, that the financial statements were being prepared, or would be used, for the purpose or transaction which led to loss. But the recent cases of *Twomax Ltd* and *Goode v Dickson, McFarlane & Robinson, Gordon v Dickson* and *McFarlane and Robinson* (1982) has presented the audit profession with the responsibility of a much more open-ended liability.

In that case, Lord Stewart held that a firm of accountants were liable to make reparation to three investors who had purchased shares on the strength of accounts which had been negligently audited. His Lordship observed that, 'auditors of a company, public or private must know that reliance is likely to be placed upon their work by a number of persons for a number of purposes. While their contractual and statutory duty may be to the shareholders, their work has repercussions in a wider field.' Accountants would probably agree in general with this truism, but would strongly question 'how wide is wide?' In this respect, Lord Stewart was impressed by the approach of Mr Justice Woolf in the *Jeb Fasteners Ltd* case (1981) for establishing whether a duty of care exists. It was held that in these circumstances, the existence of such a duty could be determined by reference as to whether the defendant knew, or *reasonably could have foreseen* at the time the accounts were audited, that a person might rely on the accounts for the purpose of deciding whether or not to take over the company. Such an approach said the Judge, combines 'the simplicity of the *proximity or neighbour principle* with a limitation which has regard to the warning against exposing accountants' to indeterminate liability.

In the 'whole circumstances' of the *Twomax* case, Lord Stewart considered that the auditor should have foreseen before he certified the accounts that they might be relied on by a potential investor. The 'whole circumstances' included the company being short of capital, a director wanting to sell his shares, and the accounts being available to lenders in that they were lodged with the company's bank.

The proximity of the parties and the circumstances of any particular case will determine auditors' liability to third parties, but the growth of litigation against them and other officers of the company, taken together with the cases discussed above, has added considerable weight to the auditors' responsibilities. And to all this must be linked the potential responsibility of auditors in respect of the *going concern concept* underlining the preparation of audited accounts (SSAP 2), a concept given statutory emphasis in the Companies Act 1981.

(ii) The auditors' considerations in respect of 'going concern'

In the *Twomax* case the tradition position of the company deteriorated to such an extent in the years following the investment in question that it eventually went into liquidation wiping out the investment entirely. That company thus joined the record numbers of companies who have failed in recent recessionary years; in 1984, liquidations were exceeding 260 per week. For each of these failed businesses, the accounts will have been drawn up based on accounting principles including that of the 'going concern'. SSAP 2 defines this concept as meaning that the enterprise will continue in operational existence for the *foreseeable future*. The Companies Act 1981 has underlined its importance, setting out in paragraph 10 of the revised Schedule 8 (CA 1948) – 4 Sch. CA 1985 – as a first accounting principle that 'the company shall be presumed to be carrying on business as a going concern'. If, for example, a company fails nine months after it has issued accounts with a clean audit certificate, with its accounts based on the going concern principle, it follows that there will be people looking for possible redress (see (iii) below) including suppliers, customers missing vital goods or services, employees and others, besides the investing shareholders. While the directors have the prime legal responsibility for the preparation of these accounts, the auditors now know that they too will be in line for criticism and possible litigation.

There is no interpretation in the Standard or the Act as to what 'going concern' means, neither does SSAP 2 delineate the phrase 'foreseeable future', but it is likely that users would assume that going concern based accounts are prima-facie evidence that the company assumes there is no intention or necessity to liquidate or curtail significantly the scale of operation; and that this will be the position at least until the next set of annual accounts are prepared and presented. The implication of this assumption by users of financial statements and the present climate of litigation will lead auditors to be ever more watchful for indications of going concern problems and after due investigation, if they eventually conclude there is reasonable doubt over the survival status, they will qualify their report.

This statement, however, cloaks a number of practical problems. These include the extent to which auditors' have a duty to actively look for going concern problem indicators, how far ahead should they be looking, and how should they word their qualification particularly where the extent of possible difficulties is in doubt and the qualification could become a self-fulfilling prophecy speeding the client company into liquidation? For, of course, the future is always uncertain and the extent to which the *auditor per se* can realistically forecast the future is always limited. With the absence of reasonable forecasting and budgetary systems, many companies rely on feel, intuition and the crystal ball. Predicting future events for more than a few months ahead will be difficult. Auditors will therefore presumably press such company managements to install good systems, but even with good systems, the future often turns out remarkably different to that anticipated!

(iii)   Purposes for which audited accounts are used

The importance of audited accounts, with an indication of persons other than the shareholders who have an interest in them, may be judged from the following list of purposes for which they are used ('*The Audit Report*' – J.C. Shaw (Gee & Co.)):

(i)   to judge managerial effectiveness;
(ii)   to calculate tax liabilities;
(iii)   as a basis for providing and maintaining credit facilities;
(iv)   for investment decisions, including the purchase and sale of shares;
(v)   in assisting the determination of the legality of certain transactions, e.g. borrowing limits, dividend payments, etc.;
(vi)   in determining contractual obligation, e.g. commissions or profit-sharing arrangements;
(vii)   to provide information about the financial stability of the company to those trading with it, including customers and suppliers;
(viii)   referred to in wage negotiation;
(ix)   in assisting the design and implementation of national economic and social policies.

From 1 July 1985 when all four Acts comprising the consolidation of company legislation came into force, auditors' reports must refer to the Companies Act 1985. Section 236 covers the Auditors' Report and Section 237 covers the Auditors duties and powers. See *Table 9* at the end of this chapter.

Table 5

STATEMENTS OF STANDARD ACCOUNTING PRACTICE

	Title	Effective (from)
SSAP 1	Accounting for associated companies (revised)	1 Jan 1982
SSAP 2	Disclosure of accounting policies	1 Jan 1972
SSAP 3	Earnings per share	1 Jan 1972
SSAP 4	The accounting treatment of government grants	1 Jan 1974
SSAP 5	Accounting for value added tax	1 Jan 1974
SSAP 6	Extraordinary items and prior year adjustments	1 Jan 1974 (revised 1986)
SSAP 7	Accounting for changes in the purchasing power of money, a provisional standard, not used	Withdrawn
SSAP 8	The treatment of taxation under the imputation system in the accounts of companies	1 Jan 1975
SSAP 9	Stocks and works in progress	1 Jan 1976
SSAP 10	Statements of source and application of funds	1 Jan 1976
SSAP 11	Accounting for deferred taxation – superseded by SSAP 15	Replaced
SSAP 12	Accounting for depreciation	1 Jan 1978 (revised 1986)
SSAP 13	Accounting for research and development	1 Jan 1978
SSAP 14	Group accounts	1 Jan 1979
SSAP 15	Accounting for deferred taxation	1 Jan 1979 (revised 1985)
SSAP 16	Current cost accounting	1 Jan 1980 (mandatory
SSAP 17	Accounting for post balance sheet events	1 Sep 1980 status
SSAP 18	Accounting for contingencies	1 Sep 1980 withdrawn
SSAP 19	Accounting for investment properties	1 Jul 1981 1985)
SSAP 20	Foreign currency translation	1 Apr 1983
SSAP 21	Accounting for leases and hire purchase contracts	1 Jul 1984
SSAP 22	Accounting for goodwill	1 Jan 1985
SSAP 23	Accounting for acquisitions and mergers	1 Apr 1985

Exposure drafts covered in this text

ED 16   Supplement to extraordinary items and prior year adjustments (1975) absorbed by ED 36.
ED 36   Extraordinary items and prior year adjustments (January 1985).
ED 37   Accounting for depreciation (March 1985).
ED 32   Disclosure of pension information in company accounts (May 1983).
ED 35   Accounting for the effects of changing prices (July 1984).

Table 6

INTERNATIONAL ACCOUNTING STANDARDS (IAS)

	Title	*Effective (from)*	*Related SSAP*
IAS 1	Disclosure of accounting policies	1 Jan 1975	2
IAS 2	Valuation and presentation of inventories in the context of the historical cost system	1 Jan 1976	8
IAS 3	Consolidated financial statements	1 Jan 1977	14
IAS 4	Depreciation accounting	1 Jan 1977	12
IAS 5	Information to be disclosed in financial statements	1 Jan 1977	Note 2
IAS 6	Accounting responses to changing prices superseded by IAS 15	Replaced	—
IAS 7	Statement of changes in financial position	1 Jan 1979	10
IAS 8	Unusual and prior period items and changes in accounting policies	1 Jan 1979	6
IAS 9	Accounting for research and development activities	1 Jan 1980	13
IAS 10	Contingencies and events occurring after the balance sheet date	1 Jan 1980	18
IAS 11	Accounting for construction contracts	1 Jan 1980	9
IAS 12	Accounting for taxes on income	1 Jan 1981	15
IAS 13	Presentation of current assets and current liabilities	1 Jan 1981	Note 2
IAS 14	Reporting financial information by segment	1 Jan 1983	Note 2
IAS 15	Information reflecting the effects of changing prices	1 Jan 1983	16
IAS 16	Accounting for property, plant and equipment	1 Jan 1983	Note 2
IAS 17	Accounting for leases	1 Jan 1984	21
IAS 18	Revenue recognition	1 Jan 1984	Note 2
IAS 19	Accounting for retirement benefits in the financial statements of employers	1 Jan 1985	ED 32
IAS 20	Accounting for government grants and disclosure of government assistance	1 Jan 1984	4
IAS 21	Accounting for the effects of changes in foreign exchange rates	1 Jan 1985	20
IAS 22	Accounting for business combinations	1 Jan 1985	23
IAS 23	Capitalisation of borrowing costs	1 Jan 1986	Note 2
IAS 24	Related party disclosures	1 Jan 1986	Note 2

Note 1: International Accounting Standards do not come into force in the UK and Ireland until equivalent SSAPs exist. The CCAB bodies incorporate wherever practical the provisions of IASs into SSAPs. The UK Stock Exchange requires foreign registered companies to prepare accounts in compliance with IASs.

Note 2:   IAS 5, 13 and 16 are materially covered by Companies Acts requirements. IAS 14 has coverage in the Companies Acts and the Stock Exchange requirements for listed companies. IAS 18 subject matter is met by current generally accepted practice in the UK. IAS 23 and 24 are among projects of the ASC.

Table 7

STOCK EXCHANGE REQUIREMENTS FOR THE DISCLOSURE OF INFORMATION WITH THE ANNUAL REPORT OF THE DIRECTORS

This information from listed companies includes:

1. The reasons why the trading results shown by the accounts for the period under review differ materially from any published forecast made by the company.
2. A statement by the directors of their reasons for any significant failure to comply with statements of standard accounting practice.
3. A geographical analysis of turnover and of contribution to trading results of trading operations carried on outside the UK (this disclosure is now required by the CA 1985).
4. The name of the country in which each subsidiary operates.
5. Particulars regarding each company in which the group equity interest is 20% or more of:
   (i) the principal country of operation;
   (ii) detail of its issued share and loan capital and, unless dealt with in the consolidated balance sheet as an associated company, the total of its reserves.
6. Statements of directors' share interests and of other persons' substantial shareholdings.
7. Detailed information regarding company borrowings.
8. Waivers of emoluments by directors and waivers of dividends by shareholders.
9. 'Close' company and 'investment trust' status.
10. Particulars of any contract of significance between the company or one of its subsidiary companies, and a corporate substantial shareholder.
11. In the case of a UK company, particulars of any shareholders' authority for the purchase by a company of its own shares.

These are *examples* of disclosure requirements contained in the Stock Exchange publication *The Admission of Securities to Listing* which is, of course, revised from time to time. The last revision followed the 1984 Statutory Instrument – *The Stock Exchange (listing) regulations 1984 (SI 1984/176)* which implemented in the UK three EEC directives – the Admission Directive, the Listing Directive and the Interim Reports Directive. Together these aim to harmonise practices in the European Community effective from 1 January 1985. When companies apply for listing, one of the conditions is acceptance of the continuing obligations which will apply following admission. Companies no longer have to sign a listing agreement.

Table 8

EEC COMPANY LAW DIRECTIVES

	Coverage	Comment
1st Directive	Mandatory publication of documents and information (similar to UK 'annual return'). Establishment of company registries in member states. Particulars (company's place of registry and its registered number) on company letters/forms.	Implemented in the UK by the S9 European Communities Act 1972.
2nd Directive	Classification and capital of public and private companies. Formation of public companies – allotment and maintenance of their share capital. Payment of dividends. Restrictions on distributions.	Companies Act 1980.

Table 8 *contd.*

	Coverage	Comment
3rd Directive	Mergers of public companies. Type of merger involved is rare in the UK. Deals with such mergers *within* the same member state. (See 10th Directive.)	Adopted by EEC 1978. DTI consultative document 1982. Likely implementation in 1986 with 6th Directive.
4th Directive	Preparation, content and publication of individual company accounts. Does not cover group accounts, nor those of banking, shipping and insurance companies.	Companies Act 1981.
5th Directive	Structure, management and audit of public companies. Employee participation.	Government and business in the UK are opposed to its introduction. Amended proposals for draft directive issued in 1983. Implementation not expected for considerable time.
6th Directive	Divisions of public limited liability companies ('scissions') to complement those of the 3rd Directive on mergers. The form of merger and division envisaged is likely to have limited application in the UK.	Adopted 1982. To be incorporated in national legislation by 1 January 1986.
7th Directive	The preparation, content and publication of group accounts.	Adopted 1983 to be implemented by the end of 1987. Its provisions need not take effect until 1 January 1990.
8th Directive	Minimum standards for the qualification of auditors, i.e. educational, professional training and examination requirements. Contains only a general statement on the independence of auditors.	Adopted April 1984. Implementation not likely before 1988.
9th Directive	Aims to provide a legal framework within which the behaviour of groups of companies containing public limited companies are managed. It is derived from West German law on combines. It is meant to protect companies which are subject to the control of others. It takes the view that where a dominant/dependent relationship exists, specified legal protection is needed for the shareholders and third parties.	Not yet adopted by EEC. DTI consultative document 1985.
10th Directive	Designed to facilitate and regulate the merger of PLCs governed by the laws of *different* member states. (See Third Directive.)	Adopted January 1985. DTI consultative document 1985.

Table 9

LOCATIONS WITHIN THE COMPANIES ACT 1985 (THE MAIN CONSOLIDATION ACT) OF REFERENCES WITHIN THIS BOOK

	Subject	*CA 1985 Section*	*Topic*	*Source legislation*
Schedule 4	Form and content of accounts	228	Form and contents of individual accounts	CA 48 Sch. 8 (amended) CA 48 S149(1)–(6) amended
		230	Form and contents of group accounts	CA 48 Sch. 8 (amended) CA 48 S152 (amended)
Schedule 5	Form and content of accounts	231	Disclosures in notes to accounts (particulars) of subsidiaries, directors' emoluments and those of higher paid employees	CA 48 S196; CA 67 SS3–8; CA 81 S4 (Other notes to the accounts requirements appear in CA 85 Sch. 4 (above) and Sch. 6 (below)
Schedule 6	Form and content of accounts	232	Loans to directors and connected persons; transactions with directors including loans and quasi loans	CA 80 S54 Regulations about such loans CA 85 S330(1)–(4); (6)(7); CA 85 S332–338; 343
		233	Loans to company officers	CA 80 S56
Schedule 7	Directors' and auditors' reports	235	Directors' report, details of content, etc.	CA 48 S157; CA 67 SS16, 19, 23 CA 81 SS13(1), 14, 16(1)
		236	Auditors' report	CA 67 S14(1)(3)
		237	Auditors' duties and powers	CA 48 S196(8); CA 67 SS6–8, 14; CA 81 S15
Schedule 8	Modified accounts	247	Entitlement to deliver modified accounts	CA 81 SS5(1)–(5), 6(1), 12(7)(9)
		248	Qualification of company as small or medium-sized	CA 81 S8(1)–(3), (9), (11)
		249/50	Modified individual/holding company accounts	CA 81 S8(1)(5)–(7); CA 81 SS9(1)–(6), 10(1)–(3)

Other more specific references:

Requirement to show a *true and fair view* in financial statements CA 85, S228 (above (2) (3), 230 (above) (2) (3) and S258 (special category accounts).

Form and content of balance sheets CA 85 S227(1) Directors duty to prepare annual accounts; S228, S230 (above) 4 Sch. Sch. 9 Special category companies.

Form and content of profit and loss accounts CA 85 S227, 228, 4 Sch. Sch. 9 Special category companies.

Power to issue redeemable shares CA 85 S159(1)(2).

Private company – payment out of capital for redemption/purchase *of own shares* CA 85 S171–7, 504.

Capital redemption reserve CA 85 S170(1) (2)–(4).

Permissible capital payment (redemption) CA 85 S171(3), 181(6).

Power to companies to purchase their own shares CA 85 S162, 170–2.

Rules on distributable profit CA 85 S255, 263, 265, 268–277, *11 Sch.*

Main and alternative accounting rules HCA 4 Sch. S29, 82; CCA 4 Sch. S31 Alternative rules 4 Sch. 29–34.

Definition of public/private companies Public CA 85 S1(3), S735(2) Private CA 85 S1(3), S735(2).

Related companies CA 85 4 Sch. S92.

Disclosure of guarantees and other financial commitments CA 85 4 Sch. S16–28.

Goodwill disclosure CA 85 4 Sch. 21, 66 and Note 3 (balance sheet formats).

Revaluation reserve CA 85 4 Sch. 34.

Share premium account CA 85 S130.

Accounting reference dates CA 85 S224(2)(3)(5), 225.

Disclosure of market value of land 7 Sch. (Directors' report) 1.

Disclosure of 'cost of sales' CA 85, 4 Sch. S228 *Accounting concepts 4 Sch. Accounting policies by way of note* (notes to balance sheet 4 Sch. 37–51, 87, notes to profit and loss account 4 Sch. 52–7) *Turnover* 4 Sch. 52, 54, 55, 95.

Allotment of shares (directors powers) CA 85 S80.

Balance sheet formats – Fixed Assets 4 Sch. S37, 42/44.

                 – Net current assets 4 Sch. S77.

Treatment of dividends in financial statements CA 85 4 Sch. 3(7), 51(3).

Details in financial statements – employees CA 85 4 Sch. 52, 56, 94.

Auditors' duty to check Directors Reports CA 85 S237(6) *on modified accounts* CA 85 8 Sch. 1, 10.

Directors' interest in shares – duty to notify CA 85 S324–325, 328, 732 and 13, 24 Schs.

Directors' report. Changes in Fixed Assets CA 85 7 Sch. 1; *Political and charitable contributions* CA 85 S235(3), 7 Sch. 3–5) *Names of directors* CA 85 S235(3), *Shares of company purchased* CA 85 10 Sch. 1; *Own shares acquired* CA 85 S235(4), 261(5) and 7 Sch. Pt 11.

Directors' interest in shares and debentures CA 85 S328 and 13 Sch.

Directors' powers to pay interim dividends CA 85 Table A Reg. 103.

Interests of members CA 85 S459.

9

The chairman's statement, directors' report and audit report

The annual report of a listed company normally carries a statement by the chairman and must contain a report by the directors. The former is not required by law but is generally expected by shareholders. The latter is subject to legislation which started with the Companies Act 1928 continued through sections of the CA 1948, the CA 1967 and the CA 1981, and is now consolidated in the 7 Sch. CA 1985.

The tendency has developed in post-war years for companies to give detailed information about their operations in the chairman's statement rather than in the directors' report. A typical chairman's statement will probably cover the following:

Give a general review of the year's operations with details of divisional performance within the company.

Summarise the financial results, highlighting particular items, e.g. turnover and earnings per share relative to previous years' figures to indicate a trend.

Comment on any acquisitions and disposals.

Make a statement on dividends paid and proposed.

Refer to the economic, financial, market and political environments mentioning particular aspects that have, or are likely to, affect operations and results.

Refer to changes in the composition of the board of directors. Comment on employees and formally thank them for their contribution. (Increasingly, companies are issuing a separate report to employees – see Chapter 10.)

Look to the future.

On the question of the future, chairmen have a problem as they are speculating about the uncertain future. They have to bear in mind the possible effect of their comment, particularly on the price of the company's shares. They will avoid being too flamboyant. Statements of unsubstantiated optimism will not impress knowledgeable readers who have the ability to analyse the accounts and other information for themselves, or financial commentators who, in addition, have sources of information of their own. Chairmen will obviously avoid, if they can, any 'gloom and doom' comment.

The end result of these considerations is usually a short statement pointing to the likely difficulties but expressing hope and confidence. For example, the chairman of J. Bibby & Sons Ltd (Award-winning accounts) March 1980:

"The improvement in the national economy which I hope will result from the Government's anti-inflation and monetary control programmes will in the longer term benefit your company, but the measures themselves may make our own immediate task of further profit improvement more difficult to achieve. I am, however, confident that your company has the financial and human resources to meet this challenge."

The Directors' Report

This report is by the directors of the company to its shareholders for whom they act as agents and quasi-trustees. In contrast to the chairman's statement, it has tended to become a formal document because of the increasing disclosure requirements of the law. The provision of the CA 1981 – S237 CA 85 – which makes the auditor statutorily bound to examine the directors' report for consistency with the accounts and to report any inconsistencies, is likely to increase the report's formality.

It should be noted that the standard of the auditor's examination is not that of the 'true and fair' standard, the overriding requirement in respect of the accounts, but rather one of consistency.

STATUTORY REQUIREMENTS FOR THE DIRECTORS' REPORT

The law requires that the directors' report be attached to every balance sheet of the company laid before it in general meeting. Directors have statutory responsibility for their report and failure by them to secure compliance with the legal provisions makes them liable on conviction to imprisonment or fine.

The more significant mandatory disclosure requirements of the CA 1981 (S235 CA 85) which has amended and extended previous legislation are:

   (i) A *fair review* of the development of the business of the company and its subsidiaries during the financial year and of their position at the end of it.
  (ii) Principal activities of the company and its subsidiaries in the course of the financial year and any significant changes in those activities during the year.
 (iii) Recommended dividend and transfers to reserves. Waivers of dividends are to be disclosed (Stock Exchange listing requirements).
  (iv) Significant changes in fixed assets during the year; significant differences between the market value of land and buildings held as fixed assets and the book amount, where the directors consider this to be of interest to the members or debenture holders.
   (v) Political and charitable contributions made (amended by statutory instrument as to the cut-off point, i.e. 'more than £200 taken together' SI 1980).
  (vi) Names of directors in office during the year.
 (vii) Particulars of important events affecting the company and its subsidiaries which have occurred since the end of the year.
(viii) An *indication* of the activities of the company and its subsidiaries in the field of research and development.
  (ix) An *indication* of likely future developments in the business of the company or any of its subsidiaries.
   (x) Details of shares of the company purchased by the company during the financial year.
  (xi) Details of the company's own shares acquired by the company, its nominee, or with financial assistance from the company, or shares made subject to a lien or charge.
 (xii) Information on directors' interests in shares or debentures of any company in the group *may* now be given in the notes to the accounts rather than in the Directors' Report.
(xiii) Section 1 of the *Employment Act 1982* requires the Directors' Report of larger companies (more than 250 employees) to contain a statement describing what action has been taken during the year to introduce, maintain, or develop

arrangements aimed at furthering *employee involvement* in the company's affairs. The Act does not require companies to take specific action, merely to state what they have done. (See Chapter 10 on Vredeling proposals and EEC Fifth Directive.)

Notes: Item (ii). There is no explanation in the Act as to what will constitute a *fair* review. In view of the need to protect sensitive information, the legal responsibility of the directors for their report and the Act's audit provision, it is likely that the practice will be for the Directors' Report to give a brief review only of developments, results and position at the end of the year. The Chairman may be prepared to be more expansive in his report. Apart from the obvious need for caution in statements about developments, the Stock Exchange listing requirement for the Directors' Report to explain material differences between operating results and any published forecasts, is likely to mean that the latter will be written in a general way and with reservation.

Item (vii). This item is subject to an SSAP (17) which already requires the disclosure of material post-balance sheet events in the *financial statements*. The legal requirements, however, unlike the standard do not differentiate 'adjusting' and 'non-adjusting' events of this kind. Adjusting events in the context of SSAP 17 provide additional evidence to conditions existing at the balance sheet date, e.g. information affecting the provision for doubtful debts which lead to its adjustment. Non-adjusting events are events which arise subsequent to the balance sheet and concern conditions which did not exist at that time. They do not result in changes in estimates used in preparing financial statements. If they are material, their disclosure is required in 'notes to the accounts' to ensure that these are not misleading. An example is the issue of share capital post-balance sheet date. It is likely that for both adjusting and non-adjusting events, the Directors' Report note would be brief and would refer to the accounting adjustment for the former and the accounting note for the latter. The taxation implications of the non-adjusting event will be disclosed in the notes to the accounts (SSAP 17) and are unlikely to be repeated in the Directors' Report.

Items (viii) and (ix). Both these requirements are affected by the need to protect sensitive information from competitors. Obviously major development planned, and R & D activities will be noted in a general formal way. There is no requirement to provide a forecast. R & D is subject to an SSAP (13) which deals with the accounting treatment thereof. This disclosure requirement is additional. The use of the word 'indication' will allow for the protection of information from rivals.

Certain information previously required in the directors' report must now be given as notes to the accounts (CA 1981):
  (i) Analysis of turnover and profit (or loss) before tax.
 (ii) Issues of shares or debentures during the year, the relevant consideration received and the reason for making the issues.
(iii) Employee information, except for the policy applied by the company in respect of aspects of the employment of disabled persons, which has to appear in the directors' report.

Information on directors' interests in the shares or debentures of any company in the group (CA 1967/Listing Agreement) may now be given in the notes to the accounts rather than in the directors' report.

Close company status

The Listing Agreement requirement for a statement stipulating whether or not the company is a 'Close Company' is often met in the directors' report, though sometimes elsewhere, e.g.

under the heading of 'Financial Information' where, in addition, the market value of the company's shares and debentures on 6 April 1965 are given for the purpose of the capital gains tax. Generally, a Close Company is one under the control of five or fewer persons or their associates, or is under the control of its directors. In such a company, dividends are likely to be restricted because of the personal tax positions of those controlling the company.

Transactions involving directors among others

Insider dealing was briefly covered in the last chapter (page 158). Among persons having 'inside information' about the company are, of course, the directors. The law Company Securities (Insider dealing) Act 1985 is concerned to ensure that no director or his associates should abuse his position of trust for personal gain.

In addition, the disposal of a substantial interest in the company by a director might be taken as an indication of problems and, conversely, an increase in holdings as a favourable omen for the future. However, like any other shareholder, directors have to deal in their shares from time to time for valid personal reasons. In so doing, they must not use 'price sensitive information' illegally.

Loans to directors

The CA 1985 imposes comprehensive requirements relating to loans to directors and others, including certain prohibitions. Disclosure is required of loans (including guarantees or security for loans); quasi-loans (e.g. where expenditure is incurred on another's behalf) and guarantees or security therefor; credit transactions, assignments or rights, obligations etc., or other material transactions, made by the company for a director or an associated person (called 'connected person' in the Act and closely defined, S346 and 6 Sch. 11). This information is additional information *to be given in the accounts* and will not necessarily appear in the directors' report. This applies also to the CA 1985 requirement for disclosure of directors' interests in significant contracts with the company.

Directors' and shareholders' interests, auditors responsibilities

The act of audit is meant to provide an independent reassurance to shareholders of the credibility of financial statements produced by a company's directors as evidence of the outcome of their stewardship responsibilities. The CA 1985 provides for material penalties against directors who fail in those stewardship responsibilities. Statutory provisions require full disclosure of transactions in which directors have interests (see above); and the auditor is required to present such information in his report if it is *not* disclosed in the accounts.

S75 CA 1980 – S459–61 CA 85 – grants *individual* shareholders recourse to the Courts if directors' actions unfairly prejudice their interests. Following the legal case *Prudential Assurance Co v Newman Industries* (1982), this right was extended in a practical way as the Prudential, a minority shareholder, was permitted to bring representative and derivative actions against Newman directors on behalf of the shareholders as a whole. These legal developments aim to enhance the interests of the shareholders relative to the directors and follows damaging revelations by Department of Trade inspectors in successive cases of company failure in recent years.

The Audit Report

The audit report and the statutory auditor's duties have been considered in some detail in the previous chapter. The report must be circulated to every member, debenture holder and person entitled to receive notice of general meetings not less than twenty-one days before the meeting before which they are to be laid. It shall be read before the company in general meeting and shall be open to inspection by any member. The law requires that the balance sheet and accounts on which the auditor reports should show a 'true and fair view' of the state of affairs of the company at balance sheet date and of its profit or loss for the year. This phrase, whose over-riding importance is emphasised by the CA 1985 (see Chapter 1 and previous chapter, page 164), is not defined by law but implies that the content and presentation of the accounting statements has some dependence on matters of judgement.

In giving his opinion as to whether the accounts meet this criterion, the auditor will consider legal requirements, statements of standard accounting practice and auditing standards. Within this framework he will be considering, in general, whether the particular report presents the economic reality of the company. The word 'fair' in this context may be taken as a confirmation that judgement was reasonably exercised by the directors. It might also have relevance to completeness of information. The implication of the word 'true' is that figures and words used are not false.

The comments of Mr Justice Wright in the Royal Mail Steam Packet case, *Rex v Kylsant and Morland* (1931), are relevant to 'truth' and 'falsehood' in relation to published accounts:

> "What exactly does that (written statement known to be false in any material particular) mean? The conclusion I have arrived at is this, that it is not limited to a case where you point to a written statement or account and say 'here are certain figures and words which are false'. I think that is to narrow unduly the words 'in any material particular'. If it is true in that way, it would shut out the type of fraud in connection with written documents and accounts which may be of the utmost importance, the type of fraud where you have a *document, not fraudulent in the sense of what it states, but in the sense of what it conceals or omits*."

If the auditor is unable to report affirmatively on the accounts and balance sheet (page 164), he must *qualify his report*.

The qualified audit report

Qualifications will range from those which start with the words 'subject to', where the auditor effectively disclaims an opinion on a particular matter which is not considered fundamental, through the 'disclaimer of opinion' where he states he is unable to form an opinion as to whether the financial statements give a true and fair view, to the extreme position where he specifically states that, in his opinion, the statements do *not* give a true and fair view.

The latter would, of course, be extremely serious for the company and its directors. The Auditing Standard leaves the manner in which the reasons for qualifying are disclosed as a decision of the auditor in the particular circumstances of each case, but says the overall objective should be clarity, and where this is relevant and practical, the auditor should quantify the effects on the financial statements.

The audit report and the sources and application of funds statement (SSAP 10)

The audit report extends to this statement (see Chapter 11), where unabridged accounts (CA 1985) are required. In the unlikely event of its omission by such a company, the auditor will refer to the fact in his report. Companies offering modified accounts are not bound to publish such a statement.

The audit report and current cost accounts (SSAP 16)

When, in 1985, the *mandatory* status of SSAP 16 was suspended (see Chapter 12), agreed that auditors were no longer expected to refer in their report to any omis current cost accounts. Should current cost accounts be adopted by a company as the n only accounts as they may do in law, then the statutory obligation of the normal audit in true and fair view terms would apply.

The qualified audit report and distributable profits

The legality of a proposed distribution under the provisions of the CA 1980 – S271, 273 CA 85 – (see Chapter 5) is to be determined by the relevant accounts. These are the final audited accounts and should the auditor's report be qualified, he is required to state whether his qualification is material to the determination of the proposed distribution.

Extension of the auditor's basic responsibilities

In the past, the auditor has been required only to report on the truth and fairness of the accounts and monitor the disclosure of directors' remuneration. The CA 1980 and the CA 1981 – S237 CA 85 – have considerably expanded his duties to include:
  (i) a report on the consistency between the directors' report and the accounts;
  (ii) a statement on the legality of a distribution of profits where there is a qualified report;
  (iii) a monitoring of the disclosure requirements in relation to loans and quasi-loans to directors and 'shadow directors';
  (iv) a report to accompany the directors' statutory declaration of solvency where there is a proposed payment out of capital by a private company.
The view has been expressed that these extensions of the auditor's duties need a corresponding expansion of his powers and of his protection, so that he is sufficiently independent of the directors to perform them properly.

The auditor and fraud

The accounting profession regard the fundamental responsibility for the prevention and detection of irregularities including fraud as resting with management. Nevertheless they plan their audits with the reasonable expectation of detecting material misstatements in financial statements resulting therefrom. A famous legal case, 'Kingston Cotton Mill', over ninety years ago affirmed the auditors' duties as *not* requiring him specifically to search for fraud unless required by law or contract. 'Watchdog, yes, bloodhound, no!' aptly paraphrases the Judge's comments in that litigation. Auditors accept that where suspicions of fraud are aroused, they must probe the matter thoroughly to allay their anxieties or qualify their report under their statutory duty (S 237, CA 1985).

Where fraud or possible fraud has been corrected by management, auditors have accepted no specific responsibility to comment in their audit report provided the financial statements published gave a true and fair view despite the occurrence of an irregularity. The duty of confidentiality deters them from reporting such matters publicly without their clients' permission.

However, the Government sees a wider public duty for auditors and set them out in the consultative document published alongside the *Financial Services Bill 1986*, a concomitant of the revolutionary changes taking place in the financial services industry centred on the City of London, the so-called 'big bang'. The Government's aim is to enhance these changes 'while excluding the fraudulent, the dishonest and the insolvent'. It is 'encouraging auditors to take a more positive view of their reporting duties'. This vague statement cloaks a potentially revolutionary change for auditors in their relationship with clients and the supervisory bodies being set up. It is having a cool reception.

177

10

Employee reports, value added statements, interim statements and statistical summaries

Financial Reports for Employees

Although there is at present no legal obligation which requires companies to provide financial and other information in a report to employees, there are signs of this becoming customary for enterprises of size, including listed companies.

Rapid post-war changes in the views of our society have led to employees, at least collectively, regarding themselves as an intrinsic part of their companies, with a similar right to receive information as the owners; a right not only to know what is happening now, but what is likely to happen in the future. And there are those who would also wish to participate in the decisions taken by their company and who would want more detailed information for this purpose.

This latter objective is more likely to involve employees' trade union representatives, who presently have the legal right under S17, Employment Protection Act 1975, to require an employer to disclose, upon request, information, including financial information, for collective bargaining purposes. There are those who believe that advantage would accrue to all parties if more information was given to unions and to employees about the company's performance, economic position and prospects. With more information and understanding of the company's position, it is argued, wage settlements could be more realistic. The statutory accounts are, of course, available to all, including trade unions for their purposes. Notably, in 1977, the Transport and General Workers Union commissioned stockbrokers Phillips and Drew to provide them with "an independent and expert opinion" on the Ford Motor Company's inflation-adjusted current cost accounts for collective bargaining purposes.

The Green Paper, *Company Accounting and Disclosure* (September 1979), noted that many companies were making special efforts to communicate financial and other information to their employees and to monitor the results to ensure that the information was understood. It then stated the Government's philosophy on such reports:

"The process of experimentation and evaluation could be undermined by the introduction of rigid statutory requirements relating to disclosure to employees and the Government propose to treat this matter as one for companies and employees to deal with themselves."

The Companies Act 1985, in dealing with directors' responsibilities, as noted earlier, imposes upon them an obligation in the performance of their functions to have regard not only to the interests of members, but also to 'employees in general'. Section 309(1–2) adds that this duty is enforceable in the same way as any other fiduciary duty *owed to a company* by its

178

directors. The general phraseology of the section allows a wide interpretation of its purpose, and its significance will await future events.

The annual *Survey of Published Accounts* published by the Institute of Chartered Accountants in England and Wales shows that most listed companies issue an annual financial report specifically for employees. The nature and scope of the information contained in these reports varies, and there is the view that employees should get the same information as the members.

A number of companies make their annual report available on request, with the "Employee report" containing a note to this effect. The possible objection that some employees will not understand the information in the annual report is not regarded as a reason for withholding it from those who can.

Example 10.1

Comparison of the information given in the Employee Reports of the two winners of the 1981 *Accountant and Stock Exchange Annual Awards* for the reports and accounts of public companies.

	J. BIBBY & SONS LTD	ERF HOLDINGS LTD
Number of pages	12	4
Chairman's statement	Yes	Yes
(*Note:* Both statements repeated substantially the information given to members.)		
Profit and loss account and Balance Sheet	No	No
Sources and application of funds statement	No	A diagrammatic representation
Value added statement	Yes	Yes
(*Note:* This was a main feature for both companies. See *Example 10.3* for that of J. Bibby & Sons Ltd.)		
Information about the future	In the chairman's statement and in the divisional analyses	Chairman's statement generally

Comment: J. Bibby & Sons Ltd, the larger company, gave detailed information per division in terms of ratios "per employee" (e.g. sales, trading surplus and average capital employed) accompanied by charts. Notable was the absence of the word 'profit' and use of the term 'trading surplus'. This company also gave information on past trends and future developments, on its employee numbers and pay, and detail of the spread of ownership of its ordinary shares. Both companies, as is common practice, used the value added statement as the main feature. Interestingly, the version in the members' annual report was limited to figures, while that in the employees' report repeated the figures but emphasised them with highly effective coloured graphics. See *Examples 10.2* and *10.3*. This reader thought the latter much more effective and pondered on the possible reasons for the differentiation!

When in 1985, the weekly journal *Accountancy Age* in association with the Industrial Society introduced its *Simplified Reporting Awards*, these were aimed primarily at *employee reports*. The judging criteria included 'a clear explanation of current financial position and performance, avoidance of financial jargon, and the use wherever possible of plain English; other information looked for included future prospects and competitive position, description of activities, company objectives and corporate structure.'

179

THE 'VREDELING DIRECTIVE' PROPOSALS AND THE EEC FIFTH DIRECTIVE

The *'Vredeling Directive'* proposals of the EEC, so called since they were originally proposed (1980) by the then European Commissioner for social affairs, Dutchman Henk Vredeling, set out obligations for companies employing more than 1,000 people to provide them with wide ranging information and to consult with them on material issues through employee representatives. The information relates in particular to a company's structure (also company within group), economic and financial situation, probable business development, employment situation and probable trend and investment prospects. The material issues on which consultation with employees is required are those which may have serious consequences for their interests. A revised version of the proposals was approved by the Commission in 1983 after extensive consultations with employers and trade unions and in the light of formal opinions of EEC's consultative bodies and the European Parliament. One of the significant revisions made as far as the UK is concerned is possibly the clause which permits the information and consultation procedures to take place directly with employees, rather than through an 'employee representative'. Late in 1983, the UK government expressed its opposition to the principle of the proposed directive suggesting that the EEC level legislation in the field of industrial relations was inappropriate. While the Vredeling proposals have the support of most EEC member countries with Denmark and the UK speaking out against them, their controversial nature appears to make it likely that they will not be adopted for some time. In the meantime, the UK government is reviewing responses to the consultative document issued jointly by the Department of Employment and the Department of Trade and Industry. This document also covered the proposals of the *EEC Fifth Directive*. This concerns itself with the management and supervisory structure of public companies and with employee participation in company decision making. The Government also prefers voluntary action on these matters rather than EEC prescription. The Fifth Directive has been around for a long time without substantial progress being made. It was first published in 1973 when the UK was joining the EEC, and amended proposals were issued ten years later in 1983. Informed opinion suggests that discussions will continue for some time and implementation is not expected for another decade!

It has been noted that in respect of the 'Directors' Report' of companies with more than 250 employees, the *1982 Employment Act* requires it to contain a statement declaring what action has been taken during the year to introduce, maintain or develop arrangements aimed at furthering employee involvement in the company's affairs. It may be taken that this is the Government's way of fostering voluntary progress in the field of employee participation/information in anticipation of the flexibility for domestic legislation which will be allowed if and when 'Vredeling' and the Fifth Directive are required to be enacted here.

The Value Added Statement

The Corporate Report (see Chapter 1) identified the value added statement (VAS) as a means for "putting profit into a proper perspective as a collective effort by capital, management and employees" and recommended its use.

There is no legal requirement for it, but over recent years a growing number of listed companies have included it in their annual report to members and it is a major feature of employee reports.

Among the advantages claimed and benefits accruing from the VAS are the following:

(i) It may influence employee beliefs and attitudes and through them their union negotiators. It has an educative role to play.

(ii) It may have a beneficial effect on collective bargaining. It may improve industrial relations. Employees may be motivated to greater efficiency.

(iii) It may facilitate the introduction of productivity schemes based on the concept of 'value added'.

(iv) The VAS is said to direct attention to the employees' share thereof and to trends in that share over time. Employees commonly receive the greatest share of the value added of their company and the wider knowledge of this should help combat the inaccurate belief of many that they are exploited and that their efforts unduly benefit the shareholders.

(v) The VAS may symbolise management's acceptance that it has responsibilities to the employees as well as the shareholders and that a statement of this kind showing the creation of wealth by a "team of labour, management and capital, and its disposition, is a better measurement of performance than that of profit to capital employed".

(vi) The VAS draws attention to the relative sharing of the wealth created between employees, providers of capital, and the government.

Professors Gray and Maunders in their research study '*Value Added Reporting – Uses and Measurement*', sponsored and published by the Chartered Association of Certified Accountants (1980), being concerned for the credibility of reports to employees (including the VAS), argue that such reports must be seen to be compatible in content to the formal audited annual report to shareholders, and to this end, if it is deemed useful to have a VAS in the employee report, it should appear also in the members' report. It is notable that few benefits for shareholders are adduced from the publication of these statements to them. Gray and Maunders debate its use as an indicator of the trend of earnings and dividends and of the efficiency of the directors, but as the above list confirms, it is seen to be most useful to employees for internal comparisons specific to the company. Any resulting increase in productivity stemming from its publication will, of course, accrue to all parties.

VALUE ADDED DEFINED

Value added has been variously described, e.g.

> *The Corporate Report* (1975) stated it to be "the wealth the reporting entity has been able to create by its own and its employees' efforts" and comprises "salaries and wages, fringe benefits, interest, dividend, tax, depreciation and net profit (retained)".
>
> *The Government Green Paper – The future of company reports* (1977) defined it as "Turnover less goods and services purchased from outside."

These two definitions complement each other and describe the two sections of the VAS, see *Example 10.2* following.

The Gray and Maunders research study does not offer a *precise* definition of value added, believing tha "adherence to a criterion of usefulness dictates that what is meant by 'value added' can and should vary in different circumstances". For their working definition they took it to represent "in monetary terms and for a particular period, the *net output* of an enterprise, i.e. the difference between the total value of its output (including but not necessarily limited to sales revenue) and the value of the corresponding inputs (materials and services) obtained from other enterprises".

An alternative view of this *net output* is that it also "represents the sum of the monetary amounts arising from the enterprise's activities during the period which may be attributed to employees, providers of capital and governments".

PREPARATION OF VALUE ADDED STATEMENTS

Prior to the CA 1981, because of the absence of certain information, e.g. cost of sales, wages and salaries, in published accounts, external analysts could not produce their own VAS if it was not given by the company. Now they should be able to do so.

Example 10.2

An abbreviated version of the VAS appearing in the Award-winning annual report of J. Bibby & Sons, where it was accompanied by figures for the previous year and explanatory notes. It can be contrasted with the VAS appearing in the company's employee report – *Example 10.3*.

	VALUE ADDED STATEMENT year ended 29 December 1979		
CREATION OF ADDED VALUE		£'000s	£,000s
Sales		188,091	
Cost of materials and purchased services		159,301	28,790
Other income			282
ADDED VALUE			29,072
DISTRIBUTION OF ADDED VALUE			
To *employee:*	Take home pay	10,819	
	Pension contributions	1,393	12,212
To the *government:*	Income tax and social security contributions	4,536	
	Corporation tax	1,426	5,962
To the *providers of capital:*	Lenders	850	
	Shareholders	1,620	2,470
Retained in the business:	To replace fixed assets and stocks at current prices	6,067	
	For expansion	2,361	8,428
ADDED VALUE			29,072

Interim Statements

Listed companies are required by the Stock Exchange Listing Agreement to provide holders of their securities (shareholders/debenture holders) with a half-yearly or interim financial report. Publication in leading newspapers in place of, or as well as, postal circulation is allowed. This must be not later than six months from the date of the notice convening the AGM of the company. The contents of the reports may vary, but the Stock Exchange lays down minimum requirements, and these include: turnover; profit (loss) after tax; UK/Overseas tax; profit (loss) attributable to members of the holding company; extent to which profit (loss) has been affected by special credits/debits including reserve transfers; dividends paid/proposed; earnings per share, together with supplementary information

Example 10.3

Value Added Statement in the Employee Report of J. Bibby & Sons

Company performance 1979

Again our performance is being presented in **Value Added** terms.

Value Added is the difference between the money we receive from sales and the money we pay out for raw materials and services. Its size depends upon our efficiency in **making** our products and our skill in **selling** them.

In **1979**	£
Total sales were	188,091,000
Total costs of raw materials and services were	159,301,000
Value Added from manufacturing and trading was	28,790,000

In addition to this total **Value Added** from manufacturing and trading, we benefited from Associated Companies' profits of £685,000, but used £403,000 to cover costs which are not part of our normal trading. The net effect of these was to increase **Value Added** to **£29,072,000**.

Distribution of Value Added   for every **100p**

Distribution	for every 100p	Total amount £
To employees — Take home pay	37.2p	
Pension contribution by employees	1.3p	
Pension contribution by employers	3.5p	**42.0p** — 12,212,000
To Government — Employees Income Tax and Social Security payments	10.7p	
Company's Social Security payments	4.9p	
Company's Corporation Tax	4.9p	**20.5p** — 5,962,000
To providers of capital — Shareholders' dividends	5.6p	
Lenders' interest	2.9p	**8.5p** — 2,470,000
To the Company — To replace worn out plant etc.	20.9p	
For expansion	8.1p	**29.0p** — 8,428,000
		29,072,000

Elsewhere in this report the term '**Trading Surplus**' is used. **Trading Surplus** is the amount of money left after all operating costs (wages, raw materials, production, transport, etc.) and depreciation have been deducted from total sales. It is a measure of profit usually used to measure the efficiency of operating management. The relationship between the **Value Added** analysis above and **Trading Surplus** can be shown as follows:

Value Added from manufacturing and trading		28,790,000
less		
Take home pay and pension contribution	12,212,000	
PAYE and Social Security payments	4,536,000	
Depreciation	2,172,000	18,920,000
Trading Surplus		9,870,000

There are two figures given for depreciation:
£6,067,000 in the **Value Added** analysis
£2,172,000 in the **Trading Surplus** calculation

Depreciation is the money set aside to replace old, worn out plant, etc. But, it is calculated from the original purchase price of the plant. Because of inflation, a piece of plant bought some years ago costs much more today. So the **Value Added** figure also contains an addition of £3,895,000 to allow for inflation, and bring the replacement costs to their current level.

necessary for a reasonable appreciation of the results. Comparative figures for the corresponding previous period are necessary.

The statements are unaudited and are usually qualified by a statement such as the following:

"and are subject to adjustments which can only be made in the accounts for the full year."

A statement from the chairman accompanying the financial report usually contains a brief note of his expectations for the company in the succeeding half-year or remaining period of the financial year, and the declaration by the directors of the interim ordinary dividend also appears.

Note: Unless excluded by their company's articles of association, company law allows directors to *declare* the interim dividend, but not the final dividend. The latter is given as a recommendation for the shareholders to approve in general meeting. Directors declaring interim dividends have to bear in mind the CA 1985 requirements regarding the determination of legally distributable profits for the financial year. The interim dividend is in effect a payment on account of the total dividends for the year. Directors must ensure that no illegal payment is made, leaving aside any consideration of whether it would be prudent so to do in the absence of adequate profit. In practice, companies declaring dividends in loss-making periods, and directors declaring interim dividends, do so in the knowledge that there are ample reserves of past profits retained.

In a study by Henry Lunt, published late in 1982 by the English Institute of Chartered Accountants, the author noted the virtual absence of accounting standards, audit guidelines, Stock Exchange detailed rules, or statutory regulation on interim reporting. His research showed wide divergencies in its practice and identified a number of areas where the impetus to use a different approach from annual accounts is the greatest. He listed these as taxation, foreign currency translation, current cost accounting (CCA) and prior year adjustments. Shortly after the publication of this research study, the Stock Exchange announced that it was withdrawing its requirement of listed companies to publish CCA adjusted interim figures. The reasons behind this were the fall in the rate of inflation, the rejection by the Inland Revenue of CCA as a tax base and opposition from companies. This anticipated the subsequent disenchantment with, and disregard of, SSAP 16 the CCA standard, by companies within its ambit (se Chapter 12). In 1984, the UK enacted by statutory instrument 'The Stock Exchange (Listing) Regulations 1984 (SI 1984/176)' three EEC directives (see *Table 7*, Chapter 8), one of which was the 'interim reports directive'. These were aimed at harmonising listing regulations and practices in the European community. The operation of these regulations is subject to judicial review to ensure that the Stock Exchange, as 'the competent authority', acts fairly.

Statutory authority thus now overlies the domestic requirement of the Stock Exchange for listed compnies to provide interim financial reports. From 1 January 1985, these are required to be published four months after the end of the period covered, although that date may, of course, be anticipated. Meanwhile to deal with the inadequacies of the present interim reporting practices, the ASC in 1985, listed the subject as a new project to be undertaken. This project will, no doubt, pick up the important features of Mr Lunt's work.

EXTRAORDINARY ITEMS

ED 36 (the revision of SSAP 6) noting that the Stock Exchange requires listed companies to publish preliminary profit statements and half-yearly reports and to include a historical summary in their annual reports, although emphasising that such statements do not form part of audited accounts nor fall within the scope of accounting standards, points out that they, and the trends which they show, can be misleading if they only disclose profit before extraordinary items. ED 36 therefore states that the amount of extraordinary items and their decription should be stated therein. This requirement is extended to exceptional items included in profit or loss on ordinary activities, particularly where, in the case of historical summaries, they have a material effect on the profit trend for the period covered by the summary.

Statistical Summaries

Statistical summaries are not a legal or a listed company requirement, but it is customary for listed companies to provide them. Content varies between companies. Some provide figures over a period of five years (increasingly popular), but many cover ten years. the summaries set out what are regarded as the salient features of the accounts, often accompanied by relevant ratios and illustrations.

Most listed companies also provide early on in their annual report a "Results at a glance" or "Financial highlights" feature with the comparative figures for the previous year. The trend to show both historic and current cost versions of the "results at a glance" has ended following the demise of SSAP 16.

The information provided in five or ten year summaries often highlights a logical progression of important totals, starting with 'sales', through 'profit before tax', 'profit after tax', dividends and retentions, to a final line of 'earnings per share'. Balance sheet information ('employment of capital' and 'funds') are treated similarly and a variety of ratios and/or graphs complete the package.

CAUTIONARY USE OF HISTORICAL SUMMARIES

It is only common sense to observe that during periods of inflation care should be taken over the interpretation of historical summaries. There are also difficulties of comparison when the adoption of new accounting policies, perhaps following the publication of SSAPs, results in material change to 'profit' figures. Companies may only note the change, without making adjustments to the summaries. While certain ratios, e.g. the current and liquid ratios, are reasonably comparable over years, others are not, particularly 'turnover ratios' which are more immediately affected by inflation than asset values and will tend to rise over time even if there is no improvement in efficiency.

Adjustments based on the Retail Price Index (RPI) can be made to figures where there is pertinent. J. Bibby & Sons Ltd, in their Award-winning accounts, made adjustments using the RPI to employee ratios, e.g. sales per employee, and trading surplus per employee.

Similar adjustments, based on the RPI, were also made to the figures for earnings per share.

See also the note above (interim statements) of the requirements of the revision to SSAP 6 (ED 36) in respect of 'extraordinary' and 'exceptional' transactions in relation to historical summaries.

Example 10.4

J. Bibby & Sons Ltd showed their *earnings per share* over a successful five-year period as follows:

	1979	1978	1977	1976	1975	
EARNINGS pence per share	32.68	25.79	17.22	15.69	4.39	

If the year ended December 1975 is taken as the base year, the percentage increases from that base are:

	1979	1978	1977	1976	1975	
EPS% increases	744.4	587.5	392.3	357.4	100	Historic % increases (X)

However, the RPI for December in each of these years was:

	1979	1978	1977	1976	1975	
RPI (December):	239.4	204.4	188.4	168	146	

which adjusted, taking December 1975 as the base year, becomes:

	1979	1978	1977	1976	1975	
RPI (Adjusted):	164.0	140.0	129.0	115.1	100	(Base) (Y)

The percentage increases in the EPS adjusted for the fall in the value of money become:

	1979	1978	1977	1976	1975	
EPS % increases (adjusted)*	450	420	310	310	100	(Base) Real % increases in EPS

*X/Y × 100.

Allowing for an extraordinary item charged against profit in 1975, the 744.4% increase in the *historic* EPS was a notable achievement for the company. It is still very good when adjusted against the RPI to 450% over the five-year period. Between 1976 and 1977, when EPS increased from 15.69p to 17.22p in historical terms, there was no increase in real terms.

Among the proposals for the successor to SSAP 16, whose mandatory status was withdrawn in 1985, a five-year inflation indexed summary of a company's performance, as exemplified by *Example 10.4*, is being considered (see Chapter 12).

11

Statement of sources and application of funds

Statement of Standard Accounting Practice 10 requires that the audited financial accounts for all enterprises (other than those small businesses with a turnover of less than £25,000 per annum) shall include a statement of sources and applicaton of funds for both the period under review and for the corresponding previous period. The funds statement complements the profit and loss account and balance sheet. It is derived from information contained in the current and previous balance sheet and the profit and loss account for the current period which links those two documents (see *Example 11.2*, MANSELTON TRADING plc).

Objective of the funds statement

The objective of the statement is to show the sources from which the business obtained its funds during the year and how those funds were utilised.

The input of funds will be distinguished between those generated internally from operations and those from external sources. The statement should differentiate long and short-term external sources.

The 'application of funds' side of the statement will show the amount of total funds available used for capital investment, the amounts paid out in dividend and taxation, and detail of the increase or decrease in working capital.

The difference between the total input of funds into the business in the year and the expenditure of funds will result in an increase or decrease in net *liquid* funds (cash and cash equivalents, e.g. short-term investments, less short-term borrowings repayable within one year of the balance sheet date, including any bank overdraft) and this will be the final line of the statement.

Uses of the funds statement

Its *general* purpose is to provide users of financial statements with significant information for interpreting the reported operating results and assessing the effectiveness of management in providing and utilising the company's financial resources. Its particular use will vary with the interests of the users, e.g. management, investors, analysts, creditors.

The statement included in the company's annual report is, of course, historic, as are the accounts themselves. Both carry this disadvantage. A *forecast* statement of sources and application of funds can be produced from the balance sheet at the beginning of the planning year, the budgeted profit and loss account and budgeted end of year balance sheet. This would summarise for management the effect of their planned decisions on funds flow and show the net effect on liquidity. It could point, in advance, to a potential *overtrading* position (expansion of business without proper consideration of its financing) and thus lead to its avoidance through the provision of the proper mix of long-term and short-term funds. If overtrading is not recognised in advance and controlled, the historic statement with the accounts at the end of the financial year will show external analysts this weakness of management. At the other extreme, the statement may indicate that the company is holding funds surplus to its needs.

Profitable, but short of funds

The sources and application of funds statement provides clear indications of the reasons why a company whose business is booming may be short of funds.

Among the main reasons are:

(i) Capital expenditure being met from short-term sources of funds.
(ii) The company is overtrading.
(iii) The impact of inflation.
(iv) The length of the working capital cycle.

Ideally, a company should want to provide for growth, in terms of capital investment and the required additional working capital, out of retained profits. Rarely, however, in these days, will profit earned be sufficient to meet tax demands, provide the level of dividend expected by shareholders, and leave sufficient surplus to meet the demands of capital maintenance and growth. Companies therefore, as well as issuing shares, borrow and repay long-term funds on a cyclical basis to meet capital costs plus that part of working capital which is not provided by short-term, trade credit and bank overdraft. Where these long-term funds are not, or not immediately provided, then, with the banks' agreement, overdraft levels will rise.

If a company overtrades, that is, it expands without properly providing finance for extra materials, work in progress, finished goods, debtors, and capital expenditure, etc., the result will include increasing trade creditors, expense creditors, bank overdrafts and other short-term loans, together with increasing interest expense and increasing illiquidity.

If the falling value of money over time has not been fully anticipated, there will be a similar effect to overtrading. The rising inflationary costs through the working capital cycle will increase liquidity problems.

Even with no inflation and no overtrading, it is a common experience for businesses to be short of funds to meet their day-to-day needs of paying suppliers of goods and services, paying wages and salaries and other operating expenses while waiting for the inward flow of cash from sales to customers. The longer the production cycle, the longer the period of financing commitments prior to the receipt of sales income. Manufacturing companies normally deal with this problem by negotiating a level of bank overdraft related to the peak deficiency of cash indicated by the cash budget of the succeeding year. Retailers often have the benefit of income from cash sales being received before their need to pay their suppliers.

The profit and loss account ignores this delay in the recovery of cash outlays for it is prepared on the accruals or matching basis. The statement of sources and application of funds will disclose its effects.

Management control of funds

In the management of an enterprise, decisions have to be taken on the allocation of resources entrusted to it. Capital investment projects are not undertaken without considerable research and estimates of cash outflows and inflows. Working capital requirements to sustain particular levels of turnover call for consideration, *inter alia*, of optimum stock levels, limits of extensions of credit to customers and the cash required daily. These considerations will be buttressed and constrained by the limits of credit available from suppliers of goods and services and short-term borrowings.

The turnover and profit margins have to be adequate to cover the payment of dividends and provide accretions to reserves sufficient to influence the capital markets to provide support for future funding operations.

These decisions are made against a background of varying degrees of uncertainty. It is management's task to reduce this uncertainty to a minimum, and it is on this ability that it stands to be judged.

Cash budgeting, day-to-day determination of variances from estimates of cash flow, and action where these show material divergence from plans, is the planning and control function undertaken for this purpose.

Evidence on which management is judged is presented in the annual report in the profit and loss account and balance sheet, but more *immediately* in the statement of sources and application of funds, for the management of funds is crucial to a company's survival. For survival, a company has to be both liquid and profitable.

The funds statement answers questions

FOR MANAGERS, INVESTORS AND FINANCIAL ANALYSTS

The prime question for this group is: Is there a reasonable balance between the funds, long and short, provided and their use for capital and working capital purposes? If not, is there overtrading, or a material surplus of funds?

Subsidiary questions are:

   (i) How has the business met its needs for cash?

   (ii) How much capital was raised from operations compared with capital raised externally?

   (iii) How much long-term capital was raised from the shareholders compared with that from loans?

   (iv) To what extent did depreciation provisions cover new acquisitions of fixed assets?

   (v) How were the funds from any share issues and from long-term loans spent?

   (vi) What happened to the profits made during the period?

   (vii) What was the profit earned compared with the dividend paid?

  (viii) What was the relative use of funds invested in fixed assets and working capital?

   (ix) How much loan capital was repaid and from what sources?

   (x) Why are dividends not larger in view of the funds available?

   (xi) How can dividends be paid when there was a loss for the period?

   (xii) What is the net effect on the company's liquid position?

FOR CREDITORS

The primary concern of all creditors (trade creditors for supplies, expense creditors for services, banks for overdrafts and loans, debenture holders and others for long-term loans, the Inland Revenue for taxation) is the ability of the enterprise to repay its debts on a timely basis, including any interest due. Since repayment is most often in cash, the ability to repay depends on the generation of the needed funds. The statement of sources and application of funds assists creditors in appraising this ability.

Comparative funds statements covering several accounting periods may give external analysts insights into financing methods and their relative efficiency and, in the extreme, point to potential liquidity crises.

Presentation of the published statement

SSAP 10 does not prescribe any obligatory layout. However, the examples shown in its Appendix are closely followed by listed companies. In the case of groups, the statement must relate to the group and not merely the holding company.

In *Example 11.1*, the previous year's figures given in the company's annual report are omitted.

Example 11.1

J. BIBBY & SONS LTD
Consolidated source and application of funds
year ended 29 December 1979

	£'000s	£'000s
SOURCE OF FUNDS		
Trading profit	9,020	
Adjustment for item not involving the movement of funds:		
Depreciation	2,172	
FUNDS GENERATED FROM OPERATIONS		11,192
FUNDS FROM OTHER SOURCES		
Disposal of fixed assets, subsidiaries and investments		1,197
		12,389
APPLICATION OF FUNDS		
Cost of fixed assets less grants, goodwill and investments	(6,443)	
Dividends paid less received	(1,094)	
Taxation paid	(938)	
Term loans repaid	(500)	
Debentures redeemed	(203)	(9,178)
WORKING CAPITAL		
Inventories	(3,914)	
Debtors	(2,205)	
Creditors excluding provision	2,769	(3,350)
		(139)

MOVEMENT IN NET LIQUID FUNDS

Increase/(decrease) in cash balance		322
(Increase)/decrease in short term borrowings	)	461)
	(	139)

Tutorial comment on the statement

Despite the Chairman's comment in his report that the fixed capital investment programme had been affected by an engineering dispute, some 52% of the total available funds were so invested.

The ability of the group to finance this investment, repay loans, pay tax and provide for working capital needs without recourse to any long-term loans or share issues, resulting only in a marginal increase in net short-term borrowings (bank overdrafts) is an indication of the efficient planning and control of resources.

READERS MAY CARE TO APPLY THE SUBSIDIARY QUESTIONS LISTED ON PAGE 189 TO THE INFORMATION GIVEN IN THE ABOVE STATEMENT AND DRAW THEIR OWN CONCLUSIONS.

Example 11.2

This example illustrates the preparation of the Sources and Application of Funds Statement of the MANSELTON TRADING public limited company for the accounting year 19x2 from its successive balance sheets and its intervening profit and loss account.

(A) *BALANCE SHEETS OF MANSELTON TRADING plc at the end of years 19x1 and 19x2*

	19x1		*19x2*	
	£'000	£'000	£'000	£'000
	Freehold	*Plant and*	*Freehold*	*Plant and*
FIXED ASSETS				
Tangible assets	*Premises*	*Machinery*	*Premises*	*Machinery*
Cost	320	260	320	410
Additions this year	—	150	160	400
	320	410	480	810
less accumulated depreciation	20	170	30	310
		240		500
	300	300	450	450
		540		950
CURRENT ASSETS				
Stock		700		850
Debtors		400		450
Short-term investments		100		150
Cash		105		106
		1,305		1,556

Less
CREDITORS: AMOUNTS FALLING DUE WITHIN
        ONE YEAR

Trade creditors	300		420	
Expense creditors	5		6	
Taxation	80		130	
Proposed Dividends	80		100	
Bank Overdraft	30		60	
NET CURRENT ASSETS	495	810	716	840
		1,350		1,790

CAPITAL AND RESERVES

Called up ordinary share capital	700	800
Share premium account	—	50
General reserves	300	450
Profit and loss account	50	90
	1,050	1,390

CREDITORS: AMOUNTS FALLING DUE AFTER
        MORE THAN ONE YEAR.

Long-term loan	300	400
	1,350	1,790

(B) *SUMMARY PROFIT AND LOSS ACCOUNT OF MANSELTON TRADING plc for the accounting year 19x2*

	£'000	£'000
PROFIT BEFORE TAXATION for the period *after* charging all expenses, *including* depreciation	150	420
less Corporation tax		130
PROFIT AFTER TAXATION		290
add balance of profit unappropriated brought forward from last year		50
		340
less: Proposed dividend	100	
Transfer to general reserve	150	250
BALANCE OF PROFIT RETAINED ON PROFIT & LOSS ACCOUNT CARRIED FORWARD	—	90

PREPARATION OF THE SOURCES AND APPLICATION OF FUNDS STATEMENT OF MANSELTON TRADING PLC

WORKINGS
1. *Extract the differences in balance sheet figures (A), segregating those derived from the profit and loss account:*

Statement of sources and application of funds

		Balance sheet differences (C)		Balance sheet difference derived from P & L A/c (D)
		£'000	£'000	£'000
Fixed assets:	Freehold premises		+ 160	
	Plant and machinery		+ 400	
Depreciation:	Freehold premises			+ 10
	Plant and machinery			+ 140
Current assets:	Stock		+ 150	
	Debtors		+ 50	
	Short-term investments		+ 50	
	Cash		+ 1	
Creditors falling due within one year:				
	Trade creditors		+ 120	
	Expense creditors		+ 1	
	Taxation			+ 50 (80 to 130)
	Proposed dividends			+ 20 (80 to 100)
	Bank overdraft		+ 30	
Called up ordinary share capital		+ 100		
Share premium account		+ 50	+ 150	
General reserves				+ 150
Profit and loss account				+ 40
Creditors falling due after more than one year:				
	Long-term loan		+ 100	

2. Most of the entries for the funds statement are now available from column C.

   The increase in the share premium account derives from the issue of share capital at a premium, the total funds received being £150,000. Funds have also been raised from additional long-term loans £100,000. Any necessary repayment of long-term loans within the succeeding financial year is required to be shown by the CA 1985 within the heading 'Creditors falling due within one year'. In this illustration, there are no sales of fixed assets. Any such event and the amount of the *sales proceeds* would be determined from the accounts and shown as a source of funds.

3. The basic layout of the funds statement starts with the net profit *before* tax. This figure is shown in the summary profit and loss account (B) as   £420,000

   This represents the major part of the funds derived from operations.

   A consideration of the profit and loss account (B) shows that this amount is made up of those balance sheet items listed in column (D) above which are appropriations of profit.

   These are then ignored to avoid double counting in the funds statement.

	£	
They are: Increase in general reserve	150,000	
Increase in profit & loss account	40,000	
Dividend appropriation	100,000	
Taxation appropriation	130,000	£420,000

4. The remaning figures in column D are:

   Depreciation £150,000. This has been set aside from profit earned, and is added to the £420,000 profit before tax to derive the total of 'funds generated from operations' £570,000 in the funds statement.

   Taxation £80,000. This represents *tax paid* and will be shown as an application of funds in the statement. This is a logical conclusion as this amount was shown as a current liability in the previous year's balance sheet. Where balance sheets show deferred taxation in addition to current taxation, the shortfall between the aggregates of these from the two balance sheets after deducting any over-provision or adding any under-provision of past tax estimates, will be the tax paid.

Dividend £80,000. This represents dividend paid in the year and will be shown as an application of funds in the statement. Shown as a current liability in the opening balance sheet, one can conclude that it has been paid by the end of the accounting year.

The funds statement can now be set out:

MANSELTON TRADING plc
Statement of Sources and Application of Funds
for the accounting year ended 19x2

SOURCE OF FUNDS	£'000	£'000	
Profit before tax	420		Previous
Add adjustment for depreciation	150	570	year's
	—	—	figures
FUNDS FROM OPERATIONS		570	would
Issue of ordinary shares	150		normally
Issue of loan capital	100		be given.
	—		
FUNDS FROM OTHER SOURCES	250	250	
	—	—	
		820	
APPLICATION OF FUNDS			
Dividends paid	(80)		
Taxation paid	(80)		
Purchase of Freehold property	(160)		
Purchase of Plant & Machinery	(400)	(720)	
INCREASE IN WORKING CAPITAL		100	
Increase in Stock	(150)		
Increase in Debtors	(50)		
Increase in trade and expense creditors	121	(79)	
	—	—	
INCREASE IN NET LIQUID FUNDS being:		21	
		—	
Increase in cash in hand	1		
Increase in short-term investments	50		
Increase in bank overdraft	(30)	21	
	—	—	

Students who wish to write a short analysis of this statement may check their notes against the commentary which follows.

Commentary on the MANSELTON TRADING plc Statement of Sources and Application of Funds

The profit and loss appropriation account shows the company's conservative dividend policy, leading to high retentions of after-tax profit.

Of the £29,000 after-tax profit, 34.5% went in dividends (only 7.2% on the book value of the shareholders' capital employed, £1.39m) and thus 65.5% is retained.

This policy is reflected in the Funds Statement which shows that:

The new funds arising from operations		£570,000	70%
complemented by new long-term capital			
from shareholders	£150,000		
and from loan sources	£100,000	£250,000	30%
		£820,000	100%
adequately covered			
capital investment	£560,000		68%
and payments of tax and dividends	£160,000	£720,000	20%
and provided increased working capital		£100,000	12%

These working capital funds provided by the company from operations and long-term sources	£100,000
were increased by additional trade and expense credit	£121,000
	£221,000
which supported the increase in stocks and debtors	£200,000
leaving an increase in *liquidity* of	£ 21,000

This indication of a strong control of funds flow provides the analyst with information to complement that given in the profit and loss account, balance sheet, directors' report, notes to the accounts etc., in the annual report and available to him from other sources.

Pointers for the analysis of funds statements

The focal point of the statement is the *change in working capital*. There will always be a change in working capital; whether for the better or the worse requires some consideration. How has the change been brought about?

The major effect of the change will usually be as a result of the *applications* which may be divided into two broad sections: those of a capital nature, i.e. investment in fixed assets, repayment of long-term borrowings including the redemption and purchase of share capital (allowed by the CA 1985), and those of a current nature embracing disbursements by way of dividends and taxation.

Scrutiny of the capital items – the nature of the fixed assets acquired– will give an indication of management's intentions or long-term strategy. For example, investment in land and buildings, and plant and machinery could mean expansion through organic growth, or the purchase of subsidiary companies could mean expansion by acquisition. Both could indicate an intention of the company to diversify.

Turning to sources, how have the applications been financed? The payment of dividends and taxation should, wisely, be well covered by the internally-generated funds, the operating profit. (An improved presentation of the statement might well show such applications as deductions from profit to reveal this more clearly.)

The investments in long-term assets would, preferably, be supported by long-term externally generated funds to complement internal sources. Scrutiny of the sources might reveal an alternative answer if, for example, there are entries indicating the disposal of a considerable amount of plant and machinery or of land and buildings, or even of subsidiary companies. This would suggest that a policy of rationalisation is being implemented with the disposal of obsolete and worn out plant and machinery and the disposal of subsidiaries which do not fit into overall plans.

Returning to the change in working capital, how does this change appear in the light of the analysis made of the generation of funds and the decisions apparently taken in regard to their application? Has the working capital been enhanced or has part of it been utilised towards financing the investments or the distributions or the repayments?

Do the changes to the constituent elements of the working capital appear to be the outcome of thoughtful action? Increases in stocks, debtors and creditors are the expected result of expansion but they may also indicate inefficient management and slackness in control; their relative movements will need to be checked against balance sheet ratio analysis. An improvement in the liquid assets, if accompanied by decreases in stocks, debtors and creditors and little or no movement in the capital applications in the upper part of the statement, may be a sign of unhealthy stagnation or decline in the business, indicating a failure of management to come to grips with the situation.

While it would be wrong to claim that the funds flow statement enables a dogmatic view to be taken of the activities of an enterprise, nevertheless, accompanied by the other information available in the annual report, it provides a fair basis for a preliminary assessment of the capabilities of the enterprise's financial management. For management wanting to assess the effect of its *present decisions in the future*, a forecast source and application of funds statement should be as much a part of its planning equipment as are sales forecasts, expenditure forecasts, cash forecasts and budgets.

Funds flow and cash flow statements

Cash flow statements chart the actual flow of *cash* (including cheques etc. regarded as cash) in and out of the business. The *cash book* (or its computer equivalent) records the *current* daily flow of cash and this information is used for control purposes by management when comparing the actual flow of net cash against that estimated and anticipated in the *cash budget*. That document summarised the timing and effect of current management decisions on future cash flows.

The funds statement considered in this chapter is not a cash flow statement, but is its near-equivalent.

Comparative analysis of funds statements
Exercises for this purpose, for which answers are provided, are included in
Workbook 2: *Exercise 20.* Prudent plc and Profligate plc.
            Exercise 21. A plc and B plc.

12

Current cost profit and loss account and balance sheet

Impact of Inflation on Historic Cost Accounting

An important aspect of the maintenance of historic cost accounting (HCA) in the 1960s and 1970s was the widespread reporting of profits earned at a higher level than was in fact the case when rising replacement costs and the falling value of money were taken into account. While inflation in the 1960s ran at a compound annual rate of 3%, this was regarded as less significant, but when in the early 1970s increases in the Retail Price Index (RPI) reached 10% and quickly accelerated to a peak of 26.5% in 1975, the effect became traumatic. Profits were taxed at a much higher rate than appeared to be the case and, after paying dividends, companies' retained profits were inadequate for the replacement of fixed assets and the maintenance of working capital – and still more inadequate for business expansion.

In 1974, the Government introduced as a 'temporary measure' a 'stock relief'* for tax purposes with the intention of eliminating 'stock profits' from taxable earnings (see *Example 12.2*). This was superseded by a new method of calculating the relief introduced by the Finance Act 1981. This provision together with a 100% tax capital allowance* on certain capital expenditure, offered major relief from over-taxation, but not a solution to the difficulties of companies operating in these inflationary times. And it was increasingly recognised that HCA had become outmoded.

The Accounting Standards Committee responded to the sharp rise of inflation in the 1970s by issuing an accounting standard in May 1974 favouring a system called 'Current Purchasing Power (CPP) Accounting', using the RPI to remove the effects that changes in the *general purchasing power of money* have on accounts prepared under the HCA convention. These CPP statements (profit and loss account and balance sheet) were supplementary to the HCA published accounts and were concerned primarily with the effects of inflation on the measurement of the profits of the company, and on the purchasing power of the investment in the company by the equity shareholder.

The standard was, however, issued as a provisional one (PSSAP 7), for immediately before its publication the Government intervened to set up a committee to enquire into the need for and the method of accounting for inflation. The provisional standard was subsequently withdrawn.

The Government's committee (Sandilands Committee) rejected the ASC's CPP method and recommended a system of value accounting which was labelled 'Current Cost Accounting'. However, the ASC's detailed version of this (ED 18), was rejected as

---

* With inflation then at a much lower rate, the Finance Act 1984 abolished stock relief and withdrew the 100% capital allowance (see Chapter 4).

complicated, impracticable and vague in relation to the definition of distributable profit. But it was probably the proposal to abandon the well-tried HCA system and replace it with CCA accounts (rather than the provision of supplementary statements to HCA) which was the main cause of rejection.

The search for an acceptable alternative started in November 1977 with an interim compromise (the Hyde guidelines), continued with the issue of exposure draft 24 (which took into account submissions and debate on ED 18 and 'Hyde') and ended in March 1980 when an important landmark in the development of accounting in the UK was reached with the publication by the ASC of SSAP 16, which required that listed and 'large' unlisted companies as well as nationalised industries publish mandatorily their current cost accounting information. This new standard was to remain unchanged for at least three years while experience was gained of its operation. The Stock Exchange brought in a requirement for listed companies to draw up accounts in accordance with the CCA criteria and extended this stipulation to interim statements. The latter requirement was subsequently withdrawn as the level of inflation fell (see Chapter 10).

The review of SSAP 16 and the search for its successor

A significant factor affecting the views of the business community on the need for accounting for inflation was the over-riding priority given by the Government to reduce its rate to a minimal level, if not to eliminate it. The rate was indeed dramatically reduced to under 5% although by 1985 it was fluctuating at around 6%. By that time, SSAP 16, although mandatory, had become the most disregarded of all standards providing the danger of discredit to standards generally. Nationalised industries under Government direction were still complying with SSAP 16, but some 80% of the listed and large unlisted companies coming under its aegis were not. This presented difficulties for the Stock Exchange which required companies who were applying for the first time for listing or designation for trading in the Unlisted Securities Market to comply with all accounting standards. Reasons given by companies for not preparing CCA accounts included the views that the time/cost involved was out of proportion with the benefit to shareholders and that they were unnecessary now that the inflation rate had been so much reduced. Following the auditing guideline 'Auditors' reports and SSAP 16, auditors were required to include in their report a suitable 'omission statement' (see page 000) for companies who were subject to the standard but who failed to comply with it: this 'qualification' seems to have been treated with indifference by companies although, no doubt, pressure was placed on auditors not to include it. There is no evidence that it has materially discouraged investors, and dividend decisions appear not to have been affected by small or even negative CCA retained earnings while HCA profits provided justification for paying them.

In 1983, the monitoring working party set up to review the experience of using SSAP 16, while it reported considerable dissatisfaction with the historical cost accounting to be continued, it found little support for the CCA standard. The opposition to SSAP 16 and the problems of applying it to smaller firms led to a recommendation that different methods be allowed for companies within a flexible framework but that, nevertheless, it was necessary for *all* companies to produce accounts to the same standard under the requirements of company law. This recommendation was opposed by those dealing with the affairs of small companies and criticised by those who saw the *flexing* of standards as undermining the stated purposes of the standards programme.

The suggested simple solution of the issue of a short statement requiring all companies to show the effect of changing prices in their accounts without specifying the method of so doing was rejected by the ASC who saw it as being an abandonment of their duty to narrow the allowed standard practices of accounting. In their view, for companies within the scope of the standard, compliance with its recommendations was seen as essential in giving a true and fair view, the concept emphasised by the Companies Act 1985 and over-riding all other accounting provisions of company law. But could small companies be exempted from the standard and still be able to produce accounts showing a 'true and fair view'? And could there then be different versions of 'true and fair' view accounts, those coming within the ambit of a new standard and making adjustments for changing prices, and those outside it who did not? Having taken Counsel's opinion which supported the presence of practical divisions for compliance and stated their view that accounts should always include information which is necessary for a true and fair view but that such information might reasonably be omitted if it could only be provided with significant expense or difficulty, the ASC in July 1984 published *ED 35 Accounting for the effects of changing prices*.

Despite its neutral title, ED 35 prescribed *current cost information* as the *most appropriate method* for use in accounting for the effects of changing prices. The CCA information required was to be given in the main accounts, either *as a note* or as a part of full current cost accounts. Supplementary CCA accounts were to be abandoned. The CCA information to be disclosed included those familiar to SSAP 16, i.e. adjustments for depreciation, cost of sales, monetary working capital, gearing (although two methods additional to that of SSAP 16 were indicated) and others consistent with the current cost convention. The standard deriving from ED 35 was to apply only to public companies, excluding value based companies (e.g. authorised insurers, property-dealing companies, investment, unit trusts and similar long-term investment entities) and wholly owned subsidiaries. The ASC reiterated its view in ED 35 that for these companies, within its scope, compliance was essential to give a true and fair view. The new standard was to be issued in 1985 and to come into effect from 1 January 1985; in the meanwhile SSAP 16 was to remain in force.

ED 35 rejected

ED 35 soon ran into trouble. The essence of the legal opinion obtained by the ASC as to the value of a SSAP to a court which has to decide whether accounts are true and fair (see Chapter 1) is, (i) that it is supported by professional opinion, and (ii) that it is widely followed. As to (i), ED 35 was rejected by professional bodies, members of the CCAB. As to (ii), there were clear doubts that the proposed new standard, seen by many as SSAP 16 in a different guise, would not be disregarded by companies as the latter standard had been. Audit firms argued that the new approach – that compliance is essential to a true and fair view – would be justified if there were general acceptance that CCA information was essential to the true and fair view for larger companies, but not for smaller ones, as the auditor would then have established practice of the profession as a whole to assist him. They pointed out that there was no such general acceptance. In March 1985 ED 35 was withdrawn, leaving ASC with the problem of what was to succeed it, moreover what to do with SSAP 16 which was increasingly being ignored.

SUCCESSOR TO ED 35 AND THE STATUS OF SSAP 16

Clearly the withdrawal of a standard because of widespread non-compliance could lead to the view that any unpopular standard could be killed off in the same way. SSAP 16s withdrawal could also be interpreted as an abandonment by the ASC of current cost principles, which may have a place in any subsequent standard and are, in any event, an acceptable basis for reporting under the CA 1981. The UK has an obligation to reflect International Accounting Standards in domestic ones. This obligation in respect of *IAS 15 'Information reflecting the effects of changing prices'* would not be met if SSAP 16 were to be abandoned before a replacement was ready. These were some of the important issues facing the ASC now under pressure from the Stock Exchange, the Auditing Practices Committee and the increasing non-compliance with SSAP 16 for its withdrawal. It responded with a recommendation which was accepted by the CCAB bodies, that until a new standard was promulgated, that *SSAP 16 should not be mandatory*, although companies and others were encouraged to provide information on the effects of changing prices, or to disclose the fact that they have not done so. As it was likely that the replacement standard would allow a choice of methodology, but include among them that of SSAP 16, companies were encouraged to maintain their current cost records where these had been set up.

Of interest as to the future standard requirement in the UK for accounting for changing price levels is the comment within IAS 15:

> 'There is not yet an international consensus on the subject. Consequently the International Accounting Standards Committee believes that further experimentation is necessary before consideration can be given to requiring enterprises to prepare primary financial statements using a comprehensive and uniform system for reflecting changing prices. Meanwhile evolution of the subject would be assisted if enterprises that present primary financial statements on the historical cost basis also provide supplementary information reflecting the effects of price changes. There are a variety of proposals as to the items to be included in such information, ranging from a few income (profit and loss) statement items to extensive income and balance sheet disclosures. It is desirable that there be an internationally established minimum of items to be included in the formation.'

In a statement published by the Minister for Corporate and Consumer Affairs in April 1985, reacting to the suggestion that statutory support be given to whatever standard may develop, he reiterated government support for the view that the effects of changing prices should be given in the accounts but saw the responsibility for coming to an agreement on and developing a standard as resting with the profession within the framework of company law. He concluded that the Government believe very strongly in the principle of self-regulation by the profession.

The pressure on the ASC to provide a solution acceptable to the profession and to practical usage thus continued, although this had eluded them over a decade of trying. In June 1985, the ASC was considering the conclusions of yet another working party which included:

   (i) that the successor to SSAP 16 should be a standard and not a statement of recommended practice;
   (ii) listed companies should be required to show the effects of changing prices;
   (iii) this would be done either by using CCA adjustments to reflect the *real maintenance of operating capability*, *or* by using CCA with a CPP adjustment for the change in value of shareholders funds, to *maintain financial capital* in real terms;
   (iv) the information should be shown by way of notes to the accounts.

A further proposal for a possible separate ED was being considered covering a five-year inflation-indexed summary of a company's performance (see e.g. *Example 10.4,* Chapter 10).

By February 1986, however, the ASC, while remaining committed in principle to the need to account for the effects of changing prices and the use of CCA for the purpose, admitted that the level of resistance from companies indicated that "achieving general practice of even the modest minimum disclosure was beyond the profession alone". The Committee issued a long statement setting out its policy on the matter reiterating:

   (i) the material effect changing prices can have on reports or results and financial position using the HCA convention adopted by most companies;
   (ii) the major limitations of HCA on reported results, capital employed, ROCE, maintenance of capital and trend statements (see coverage of HCA limitations, page 201 *et seq.*), and noting –

(iii) that the original high level of compliance with SSAP 16 CCA had rapidly fallen with the abatement of inflation rates in recent years.

ASC proposed to the CCAB bodies that *SSAP 16 should be withdrawn* in the interests of "freeing the way" for innovation and development of appropriate disclosures, although they commended the CCA principles as the preferred model. In order to preserve the experience gained over the last decade they intend to publish an official "Handbook of Accounting for Changing Prices". The Committee is consulting with CCAB on the appropriate way to achieve minimum disclosures of the effects of price level changes on accounts, but the latter has ruled out an approach to Government for statutory backing as untimely.

Meanwhile ASC recommends retaining the subject in examination syllabuses in recognition of the fundamental importance of understanding the effects of inflation and price level changes on company accounts, and – noting that historically the cycle of inflation always returns – intends actively to research means of improving cost effective calculation and effectual disclosure of information and to encourage companies to that end.

Limitations of Historical Cost Accounting (HCA)

1. THE GENERAL IMPACT OF INFLATION ON PROFITS

The effect of inflation on the purchasing power of money is not always fully appreciated. Consider *Example 12.1* which sets out the value of the pound at differing time intervals given inflation of 3% (the 1960s), 10%, 20%, 25% (the 1970s) and back to 10% and lower in the 1980s.

Example 12.1

Effect of inflation on the £1

Inflation rate	3%	10%	20%	25%
After 5 years	0.86p	0.62p	0.40p	0.33p
After 10 years	0.74p	0.39p	0.16p	0.11p
After 20 years	0.55p	0.15p	0.03p	0.01p

Even with a compound annual rate of inflation at the relatively low rate of 3%, the general price level will double – or the purchase power of money will halve – in just over 20 years. After only 5 years at 25% inflation, the value of money is only one-third of that at the start of the period. A company would have to triple its profits in that time merely to maintain its position. Unless it has increased its depreciation provisions (of fixed assets) in line with inflation during the period, its financial position will be futher exacerbated. And working capital requirements, even to *maintain* the *same volume* of business, increase pro-rata with inflation.

The UK Government's target of single-figure inflation in the early 1980s is seen as modest after noting that, with inflation at 10%, a company which doubles its historic profits in 10 years has in fact suffered a decline in RPI terms – each original £1 of profit, now £2 on the HCA base, having a purchasing power of only 0.78p.

2. HCA's UNDERLYING ASSUMPTION OF A STABLE MONETARY UNIT

Example 12.1 shows that such an assumption, even at low levels of inflation, is unsafe. At higher levels, any tendency to consider money to be the standard of value and to be a value in itself is a dangerous delusion. The reality of a company's position has been hidden or distorted by the fall in the value of money.

Accounting does nothing to stop or control inflation. Its objective is to convey information about economic events. If that information is incomplete, inaccurate or not understood, decisions based on that information will be wrongly made.

Even worse is the position where the decision-taker believes the accounting information presented to him to be facts, facts which he understands, but which because of inflation are sham. The objective of the Inflation Accounting Steering Group's work which led to the Current Cost Accounting Standard, SSAP 16, was, in essence, to require the publication of improved accounting information. If this leads to better decisions and the more efficient allocation of economic resources, the result will be worthwhile and in itself may contribute to the control of inflation.

3.   FIXED ASSET VALUES ARE UNREALISTIC UNDER HCA

One result of maintaining fixed assets in books of account at historic cost, particularly property, in the 1950s and 1960s was that capital employed remained understated in value and profits reported as a percentage of such capital employed were higher than they would have been following revaluation. Share prices did not fully represent the true underlying value of capital employed and consequently companies were exposed to take-over bidders with more certain knowledge of the current values of properties than the directors or shareholders. Share price offers sufficiently above current market values to attract shareholders but below realistic prices based on the inclusion of the up to date values of the properties, led to large gains for the speculators at the expense of the shareholders. The Companies Act 1967 (Section 16(1a)) – 7 Sch. 1 CA 85 – introduced a requirement of the directors to state in their report to the shareholders whether *in their opinion* there was any significant difference between the book and market value of land (including the buildings thereon) as a counter to the operations of the take-over bidders which when successful were usually followed by asset stripping involving the breaking up of the company to enable undervalued items to be sold at a handsome profit.

4.   DEPRECIATION BASED ON HCA IS INADEQUATE

Under HCA, the aim of depreciation is to spread the cost of the asset as a charge against each year's profit and loss account, over its estimated effect life. Incidentally, profit is retained equalling at the end of this period to the original historic cost. Both aims are undermined by inflation. The annual expense charged for the use of the asset is understated and thus profit is overstated (or loss understated) and as the cost of the fixed assets rise over time, the depreciation provision falls increasingly short of the cost of replacement.

5.   COST OF SALES BASED ON HCA IS UNDERSTATED

Gross profit is arrived at by deducting the 'cost of sales' from 'sales'. In the calculation of 'cost of sales', the value of the closing stock is deducted from opening stock plus purchases (or manufactured goods), e.g.

Example 12.2

Cash transactions
HCA Trading Account of XY Co Ltd

	£			£
Opening stock		Sales		
1,000 units at £1	1,000	1,000 units at £1.50		1,500
Purchases				
1,000 units at £1.20	1,200			
	———			
	2,200			
less				
Closing stock				
1,000 units at £1.20	1,200			
	———			
Cost of sales	1,000			
Gross profit (HCA)	500			
	———			———
	1,500			1,500
	———			———

This example shows that if the historic profit of £500 had been distributed, there would have been insufficient funds (i.e. only £1,000, equal to the cost of the original stock) to replace stock sold. Itis clear that as the replacement stock was purchased for £1,200, only £300 is available for distribution and that this is a more reasonable measure of profit. The remaining £200 is stock appreciation due to the rising cost of replacing stocks.

This measure of a *holding gain* of £200 has assumed for the purpose of the illustration that sales and replacement purchases were made concurrently. The example is based on the commonly-based convention in the UK of valuing stock on the FIFO (First in, First out) basis.

The example shows also that the amount of working capital required to maintain the same *volume* of business progressively increases. The capital maintenance objective of current cost accounting requires a cost of sales adjustment (COSA) to deal with this problem. This is covered later in the chapter.

6. HCA FAILS TO INDICATE GAINS ON HOLDING NET MONETARY LIABILITIES OR LOSSES ON HOLDING NET MONETARY ASSETS

The holding of money, or assets reflecting money values (monetary assets), e.g. debtors, leads to losses in a period of inflation (falling money values). Conversely, the holding of monetary liabilities (e.g. trade creditors) provides gains.

A 'quick ratio' (monetary assets: short-term monetary liabilities) above par derived from historical accounts may be desirable from a conventional liquidity point of view, but the unrecorded purchasing power loss is often overlooked.

The Massey Ferguson (tractors) group of companies had over 600 million dollars outstanding from its customers (debtors) in early 1970s balance sheets, with debts outstanding on average for over 12 months. The quickening pace of inflation saw large, unexpected monetary losses accruing to the group and management moved to modify its credit policy to reduce its losses. Inflation, of course, gives added potency to the need for efficient credit control procedures.

Quick ratios (liquid ratos) below par are, therefore, becoming the norm as the effect of inflation on the net monetary position is appreciated. Many UK manufacturing companies have quick ratios between 0.90 and par.

Holding gains also arise from long-term borrowings of a company which, in an inflationary period, makes repayment at some future time in pounds of reduced purchasing power. Current cost accounting (SSAP 16) introduced a 'monetary working capital adjustment' (MWCA) and a 'gearing adjustment' to deal with these problems, and these are covered later in the chapter.

7. THE RETURN ON CAPITAL CALCULATION IS INVALIDATED

In a period of inflation, balance sheets become out of date as assets are undervalued using the HCA convention (3 and 5 above). Reported profits are overstated by reason of inadequate depreciation (4 above), because in calculating cost of sales the closing stock is deducted at inflated prices (5 above) and because profits are reported in terms of money which itself has declined in value.

Thus, in a comparison of PROFIT on CAPITAL EMPLOYED in ratio analysis, there is a double inflationary effect as the numerator is overstated and the denominator understated.

8. COMPARISONS OVER TIME (INTER-TEMPORAL) AND BETWEEN FIRMS (INTER-FIRM) ARE INVALIDATED

Example 10.4, page 185, showed the effect of adjusting the five-year summary of the 'earnings per share' of J. Bibby & Sons Ltd to take into account the fall in the value of money in the period. Without such adjustment, the *real* increase could not be seen.

Comparisons between companies using HCA accounting (leaving aside problems arising through the use of different accounting judgements, e.g. one company applying a higher rate of depreciation of plant than another) are made more difficult in an inflationary period.

Example 12.3

X Ltd and Y Ltd each show *total assets of £1 million* in their historic cost accounts, and *profit before tax and interest of £300,000*. They report the same *return on capital of 30%*.

However, although each is showing an historic cost figure of £200,000 against its 'land and buildings', X Ltd bought its property in 1970 and Y Ltd made its purchase in 1980. The current market valuation sets the X Ltd property at £1,200,000 and Y Ltd's at £230,000.

Leaving aside any movements in the value of other assets, it is apparent that the reported returns on capital of 30% for each company are unreal. On adjustment, Y's return is marginally reduced to around 29%, but that of X Ltd falls materially to 15%.

Reporting Requirements of the Current Cost Accounting Standard (SSAP 16)

It should be noted that the phrase 'current cost accounting' was introduced as a direct contrast to the traditional concept of historic cost accounting (HCA).

CCA is a system of *value accounting* and is *not* a system of accounting for *inflation*. It has often been said that the historic cost balance sheet is not a statement of value, but merely the end product of the double entry bookkeeping system, i.e. the historical cost balances remaining in the ledgers after accounts representing income and expenditure have been summarised in the profit and loss account. The apparent objectivity of the historic cost balance sheet has been the base of the argument for the system's retention, with implications of widespread subjectivity in alternative inflation and/or value systems. The considerable time and activity in looking at alternative systems of HCA up to March 1980, when the current cost standard was published, were partly symptomatic of the reluctance of the grass roots of the accountancy profession to move from a system which had lasted for several hundred years. There appeared to be an underlying hope that inflation would go away, and with it the associated problems of reporting.

THE SCOPE AND AIMS OF SSAP 16

The standard applied mandatorily* to all annual financial statements of *listed companies, nationalised industries* and *large unlisted companies* (size as categorised by the CA 1981 following the EEC Fourth Directive). Listed companies which are property investment and dealing entities, or investment trust, unit trust or similar long-term investment entities, or authorised insurers, were exempted.

The CA 1981, Sch. 1 – 4 Sch. 29–34 CA 85 – gives companies a choice for their *main method* of accounting and reporting. They can use either historic cost or current cost, but historic cost information must always be available in terms of a historic cost statement. Where *the main accounts* are either historical or current cost based, the CA 1985 valuation rules will apply (see page 70, section 4.6) including the arising of a revaluation reserve.

Most companies chose to report HCA accounts accompanied by supplementary CCA statements during the three year experiential period of SSAP 16, rather than turning to CCA as the principal reporting medium, with the increasing trend towards non-compliance already noted.

The spread of current cost accounting to the vast number of smaller companies outside its ambit depended very much on whether practising accountants and the companies concerned acquiesced to its use, and that decision in turn depended on whether the system is accepted for tax purposes by the Government. By mid-1986 that possibility had disappeared (see page 200).

An objective of SSAP 16 was to provide more useful information than that available from HCA in order to guide management, shareholders and others involved with the business, on its financial viability, i.e. the likelihood of its survival in the short term and its profitable survival in the long term. In addition, it aids decisions on pricing policy, cost control, distribution of profits, and the structure (gearing) of capital. The fundamental concept on which CCA is based is that of *capital maintenance*, i.e. the maintenance of the entity as a going concern. It is only incidentally concerned with the maintenance of financial capital. Operating capability is to be achieved by allowing for the *impact of price changes* on the funds needed to maintain the net operating assets.

* The mandatory status was withdrawn in 1985 during the search for SSAP 16s successor (see page 200).

CAPITAL MAINTENANCE AND THE CCA PROFIT AND LOSS ACCOUNT

The objective of capital maintenance is to be achieved in respect of profits by adjustments leading to the determination of:

1. *Current cost operating profit*

   This is determined as the surplus after allowing for the impact of price changes on the funds needed to continue the existing business and maintain its operating capability, whether financed by share capital or borrowings; it is calculated before interest on net borrowing and taxation.

   It includes adjustments to compensate for the deficiencies of HCA considered earlier, in respect of:

   > Depreciation,
   > Cost of Sales and
   > Monetary Working Capital.

2. *Current cost profit attributable to the shareholders*

   This is determined after taking into account the manner in which the business is financed. As any loans made to the business are fixed in monetary amount, the impact of price changes on operating capability is mitigated and the advantage derived from this borrowing policy is measured by:

   > A *gearing adjustment* set against the interest on the loans.

   This level of profit is finally determined after deduction of taxation and adjustment for any extraordinary items of expense or income. It shows the surplus (or deficiency) for the accounting period after the impact of price changes have been allowed for on the funds required to maintain the shareholders' proportion of the entity's operating capability.

CAPITAL MAINTENANCE AND THE CCA BALANCE SHEET

In the current cost balance sheet, the objective of capital maintenance is met by including the tangible assets at their *value to the business*. This balance sheet is expected to provide a realistic statement of the assets employed in the business and enable the return on capital relationship to be established between current cost profit and the net assets employed.

Normally, the value of an asset to the business is likely to be its *net current replacement cost*, but if a permanent fall below this value is recognised it will be the *recoverable amount*. The recoverable amount is the greater of the net realisable value of an asset and (any) amount recoverable from its further use.

The above general requirement applies to fixed assets, e.g. land and buildings, plant and machinery, furniture and fittings, etc., and to stocks subject to a cost of sales adjustment.

Intangible assets (excluding goodwill) are to be valued at the best estimate of their value to the business, which means in practice that it may be necessary to continue showing these at historic cost. Historic cost will continue as the basis for *current assets* (other than those subject to a cost of sales adjustment) and for *all liabilities*.

Goodwill in group accounts, where it is not already written off, will be shown in the current cost balance sheet, at the excess of the purchase consideration paid for the acquisition of the subsidiary over the *fair value* to the acquiring company of the net assets of the subsidiary. *Investments in associated companies* will be shown either at the applicable proportion of the associated company's net assets on a current cost basis, or where this is not available, at the directors' best estimate, which again is likely to be historic cost. *Other investments*, other than those treated as current assets, will be stated at directors' valuation. Where the investment is listed and the directors' valuation is materially different from the mid-market value, the basis of valuation and the reasons for the difference are to be stated.

The *current cost balance sheet* will contain an additional reserve, the *current cost reserve* which will be:
  (i) credited with any increase in value of fixed assets and stocks, those accounts having been debited;
 (ii) debited with backlog depreciation (see note 1 below) on fixed assets;
(iii) credited with the cost of sales adjustment (COSA) and the monetary working capital adjustment (MWCA) debited to current cost profit and loss account (see note 2 below), and
 (iv) debited with any gearing adjustment (see note 3 below).

Example 12.4

Current Cost Reserve

	£			£
19x2		19x2		
December 31		January 1		
Backlog depreciation		Balance brought down		17,000
(Fixed assets)	1,000	December 31		
December 31		Stock revaluation		1,600
Current cost P & L A/c –		December 31		
gearing adjustment	4,500	Fixed asset revaluation		
December 31		(gross)		6,000
Balance carried down	32,500	December 31		
		Current cost P & L A/c		
		COSA		8,200
		MWCA		5,200
	38,000			38,000
		January 1		
		Balance brought down		32,500

The *current cost reserve* thus takes the contra entries required by the double entry system arising from the current cost adjustments in the fixed asset and stock accounts and those in the current cost profit and loss account. It therefore deals with the four adjustments (above) required to arrive at the current cost profit attributable to shareholders, and also reflects unrealised surpluses and deficits that arise from the difference between the amounts at which fixed assets and stocks are stated in the HCA balance sheet and their value to the business. This reserve is to be regarded as part of the permanent capital of the business, its maintenance ensuring that the entity's operating capability is not impaired.

Note 1. The depreciation adjustment in the current cost profit and loss account
This adjustment allows for the impact of price changes when determining the charge against revenue for that part of the fixed assets consumed in the period. It is the difference between the value to the business of fixed assets consumed and the amount of the depreciation charge in the historical accounts. A depreciation charge based on the *average* current replacement cost for the period will more accurately reflect the value to the business of the assets consumed in the period, but, in practice, many companies base the charge on the current replacement cost *at the end* of the period.
The depreciation adjustments – the amount charged in the current cost profit and loss account and credited to cumulative depreciation provision, and the *backlog* depreciation (see below) – are those amounts which, in addition to the historic cost depreciation charge, must be retained in the business in order to maintain the capital of the business, or in terms of SSAP 16, its operating capability.

Depreciation, whether charged on an HCA or CCA basis, does not provide cash. The funds represented by depreciation (retained profit) are, however, kept in the business and reinvested. To that extent, operating capability is ensured.

Backlog depreciation arises because of the necessity of bringing accumulated depreciation brought forward at the *beginning of the year* up to that amount required following the revaluation of the asset. When the revaluation is based on the gross current replacement cost at the end of the current financial year, the backlog depreciation is known as *prior year backlog depreciation*. The amount (*Example 12.5*) is charged against current cost reserve and does not, therefore, affect the current period's operating results.

Example 12.5

X Ltd operates plant and machinery which cost £20,000 and is being depreciated at £2,000 per annum in the historic cost accounts. At the end of year 5 of its use, the plant's gross replacement cost is indexed at £30,000 with its estimated life unchanged. The accounts would appear:

HCA		CCA		
	£		£	*Difference*
Cost	20,000	Gross replacement cost	30,000	£10,000
Current year depreciation	2,000	Current year depreciation	3,000	£1,000
Cumulative depreciation at the start of the current year	8,000	Cumulative depreciation at the start of the current year	12,000	£4,000
Total cumulative depreciation end of year 5	10,000	Total cumulative depreciation end of year 5	15,000	£5,000
Written down value HCA	10,000	Net replacement cost (NRC) CCA	15,000	

The £10,000 difference between HCA cost and GRC is debited to plant and machinery account and credited to current cost reserve.

The £1,000 difference between the depreciation based on historic cost and the depreciation based on current cost is debited to current cost profit and loss account (*the depreciation adjustment*) and credited to cumulative depreciation provision.

The £4,000 difference between the cumulative depreciation HCA and CCA provisions at the beginning of the year (*the prior year backlog*) is debited to current cost reserve and credited to cumulative depreciation.

In the *current cost balance sheet* at the end of year 5, the entry will be:

Plant and machinery	£30,000	
less cumulative depreciation	£15,000	£15,000

Where the depreciation charge is based on the *average* depreciable value of the asset, instead of on the replacement value at the end of the year, this will give rise to an additional *current year backlog* depreciation charge, made against current cost reserve.

Note 2(i). The Cost of Sales Adjustment (COSA)
It has been shown (*Example 12.2*) that in a period of rising prices, the charge of the historic cost of sales against revenue results in an overstatement of profit; further, that if this 'profit' was wholly distributed there would be an insufficient amount of revenue remaining to replace the stock sold. SSAP 16's objective of maintaining operating capability (real capital) requires a charge in the *current cost profit and loss account* (where prices are rising) of a *Cost of Sales adjustment of the difference between the current cost of sales and the historic cost of sales*.

In the balance sheet (current cost), stock should be stated at its value to the business, normally the lower of the current replacement cost of the asset and its recoverable amount (i.e. net realisable value). An amount equal to the adjustments made for price changes should be credited (or, for falling prices, debited) to the current cost reserve, i.e. where the current cost of sales is greater than the historic cost of sales, the COSA will be charged in arriving at the current cost operating profit and will be added to the surplus arising on the revaluation of the historical cost of stocks to the current replacement cost of stocks at the end of the financial period.

The standard does not prescribe one common method for calculating COSA. It recognises that the differing nature of business activities, varieties of stock, seasonal patterns etc., should be reflected by the development by organisations of methods suitable to them. It could, theoretically, be calculated on an item-by-item base, or on variance information from standard costs. The Guidance Notes to the standard offer practical examples to meet some of the likely situations but the notes, not being part of the standard, are not mandatory. It is probable that many entities will use a single index based on a weighted average of stock.

CALCULATION OF COSA USING THE AVERAGING METHOD

Where sales take place fairly evenly throughout the year and purchases likewise, and the historical cost of stocks (opening and closing) have been calculated on the FIFO basis, the stocks not being stated at average prices for the year are the items in the cost of sales calculation (Opening stock plus purchases less Closing stock) which need adjustment in arriving at the COSA.

Example 12.6

Calculation of COSA using the averaging method

		Historic costs £		*Index Adjustment*		*Current costs* £
19x2	1 January					
	Opening stock	600,000	×	190	=	670,588
				——		
				170		
	Purchases	3,000,000				3,000,000
		————				————
		3,600,000				3,670,588
19x2	31 December					
	Closing Stock	800,000	×	190		779,487
				——		
				195		
	Cost of Sales	2,800,000				2,891,101

COSA = *the difference between historic and current cost of sales, i.e. £91,101.*
Index. 1 January 19x2 = 180; 31 December 19x2 = 200; Average for year = 190.
Assuming Opening stock represents 4 months' purchases, index 31 October 19x1 = 170.
Assuming Closing stock represents 3 months' purchases, index mid-Nov. 19x2 = 195.

The above method is represented by the formula:

$$COSA = (C - 0) - 1a\left(\frac{C}{1c} - \frac{0}{1o}\right)$$

where
0 = Historical cost of opening stock.
C = Historical cost of closing stock.
1a = Average index number for the period.
1o = Index number appropriate to opening stock.
1c = Index number appropriate to closing stock.

Effectively, from the *total* increase £800,000 less £600,000 = £200,000, represented by the first part of the formula, is deducted the *volume* increase, represented by the second part of the formula: £779,487 less £670,588 = £108,899 to give the *price* increase, *the COSA =* £91,101.

STOCK IN THE CURRENT COST BALANCE SHEET

Stock should be stated in the current cost balance sheet at its value to the business. A separate calculation from COSA is necessary.

Example 12.7

Taking the information used in the previous Example:
Historic cost *closing* stock £800,000 is
multiplied by

$$\frac{\text{Index at 31 December 19x2}}{\text{Index for the average purchasing date of closing stock}}$$

$$= £800,000 \times \frac{200}{195} = £820,513 \quad \text{which is}$$

the entry in the current cost balance sheet dated 31 December 19x2.

In the previous year's current cost balance sheet, this year's *opening* stock, historic value £600,000, would have been adjusted by multiplying it
by

$$\frac{\text{Index at 31 December 19x1}}{\text{Index for the average purchasing date of opening stock}}$$

$$= £600,000 \times \frac{180}{170} = £635,294 \quad \text{which was}$$

the entry in the current cost balance sheet dated 31 December 19x1.

In this Example, the rate of price increase slowed between the beginning and the end of the year, which simulates the situation in the UK at the beginning of the 1980s.

The increment on revaluation of the Opening Stock – £35,294 *credited* to Current Cost Reserve – *exceeds* the increment on the revaluation of the Closing Stock, £20,513. A *debit entry* to current Cost Reserve of £14,781 (£35,294 less £20,513) therefore reflects the net change. The *Current Cost Reserve* then holds a credit of £20,513, the difference between the historic and the current cost of closing stock.

Note 2(ii). The Monetary Working Capital Adjustment (MWCA)
It was seen earlier that historic cost accounts fail to indicate gains on holding net monetary liabilities or losses on holding net monetary assets. The MWCA compensates for these deficiencies. It is charged (*net monetary assets*) or credited (*net monetary liabilities*) in the current cost profit and loss account in arriving at the current cost operating profit.

It reflects that most businesses have other working capital besides stock. It allows for the effect of price changes on the monetary working capital needed to support the operating capability. It is equally necessary to the maintenance of a business as a going concern as the depreciation and the cost of sales adjustment. It is axiomatic that more working capital is needed in a period of rising prices. When sales are made on credit, the business has funds tied up in debtors. Conversely, if the suppliers of goods and services to the business allow a period of credit, the amount needed to support working capital is reduced. This monetary working capital is an integral part of the net operating assets of the business and the standard provides for an adjustment in its respect, i.e. the MWCA, within the current cost profit and loss account. It will represent the additional (or reduced) finance needed for monetary working capital as a result of changes in the input prices of goods and services used and financed by the business.

It should be recognised that where a business holds stocks, the MWCA complements the COSA and together they allow for the impact of *price changes* on the total amount of working capital used.

When sales are made on credit, the business has to finance the price changes in its inputs until the sales result in a receipt of cash. The part of the MWCA related to trade debtors in effect extends the COSA to allow for this; conversely, when materials and services are purchased from suppliers on credit, price changes are financed by the supplier during the credit period. To this extent, extra funds do not have to be found by the business and this reduces the need for a COSA and in some cases for a MWCA on debtors. The part of the MWCA related to trade creditors reflects this reduction. The MWCA may, of course, be equally necessary in a business which does not hold stocks.

The logic and necessity of the adjustment being accepted, *how is monetary working capital to be defined and measured for the purpose?* In many companies, for example, overdrafts although shown as current liabilities because of the legal requirement for their repayment, are in nature and reality permanent long-term capital.

Other entities have considerable cash (or near-cash, e.g. short-term investments) retained for expansion purposes. Neither of these examples represent working capital needed to maintain operating capability. The standard suggests that greater objectivity and accuracy will be achieved if the MWCA is limited to trade debtors and trade creditors arising from the operating activities of the business (see later Example of the Current Cost Accounts of J. Bibby & Sons Ltd). While usually, therefore, MWCA would be confined to:

trade debtors, including prepayments and trade bills receivable (plus any stocks not subject to COSA) *less* trade creditors, including accruals and trade bills payable,

in principle, companies can bring in cash floats and any part of bank balances and overdrafts which arise from fluctuations in the volume of stock, trade debtors and trade creditors, i.e. to the extent that they are directly related to the day-to-day operating activities of the business and it would be misleading to leave them out.

CALCULATION OF THE MWCA

Because of its relationship to the COSA, the method used to calculate both adjustments must be compatible. Appropriate indices based on buying and selling prices of stock might be used or a single index for all items including COSA.

Example 12.8

Monetary Working Capital Adjustment

Historic cost balance sheets	*at 31 December 19x1*	*at 31 December 19x2*
	£'000	£'000
Trade Debtors	900	1,100
Trade Creditors	750	920
Opening MWC 150		*Closing MWC* 180

The difference between the opening and closing net monetary working capital, £30,000, represents the *total* increase in monetary terms and includes real and inflationary growth.

The *real* increase in the MWC (*the volume increase*) is determined by indexing, using those from the previous COSA example (*12.6*):

Index 1 January 19x2: 180. Index 31 December 19x2: 200.
Average index for the year: 190.

$$\text{Volume increase} = \left(\text{Closing MWC} \times \frac{\text{Average Index}}{\text{Closing Index}} \right) \text{ less } \left(\text{Opening MWC} \times \frac{\text{Av. Index}}{\text{Op. Index}} \right)$$

$$= \left(180,000 \times \frac{190}{200} \right) \text{ less } \left(150,000 \times \frac{190}{180} \right)$$

$$= £12,667.$$

The *price* increase is the difference between the *total* increase and the *volume* increase, i.e.

$$= £30,000 \text{ less } £12,667 = £17,333 = MWCA.$$

£12,667 is the extent of the real increase of investment in the operating capability of the business. The MWCA of £17,333 represents the amount necessary as a charge against current cost profit and loss account merely to *maintain* the capital of the business.

In the example, debtors exceed creditors and thus *the adjustment is a charge against profit and a credit to current cost reserve*. Where there are net monetary liabilities rather than net monetary assets – as is likely to be the case for retailers buying on credit and selling mostly for cash – and prices are rising, the method will remain unchanged but the adjustment will be a credit to current cost profit and loss account and a debit to current cost reserve. The credit to profit and loss account must not, however, exceed the COSA, the argument being that any excess of net monetary liabilities over stocks is not being used to finance working capital and should not be used in the MWCA calculation.

Note 3. Gearing Adjustment under SSAP 16

The *current cost operating profit* having been determined after adjusting for the deficiencies of HCA in respect of:

Depreciation,
Cost of Sales and
Monetary Working Capital,

it becomes necessary in computing the *current cost profit attributable to the shareholders* to take into account the manner in which the business is financed. If the company is wholly financed by shareholders' capital, no gearing adjustment is required. Where, however, the net operating assets shown in the balance sheet have been partly financed by borrowings, and these borrowings are fixed in monetary terms, it is recognised that the liability to repay is unaffected by changes in the prices of assets which they have partly financed. This provides a benefit to shareholders during a period of increasing prices (or a loss should they decline) which is not brought into current cost operating profit. In determining the current cost profit attributable to shareholders, SSAP 16 requires that this benefit be recognised by a *gearing adjustment*.

This adjustment reduces the total of the adjustments for depreciation, cost of sales, and monetary working capital in the proportion which the net operating assets financed by borrowing bear to the total net operating assets. The calculation (*see Example 12.9*) is based upon the adjustments made when the assets are consumed or sold and complies, therefore, with the prudence concept of SSAP 2 and the CA 1981 (following the EEC 4th Directive) which require that credit should not be taken to profit until realised. Thus the gearing adjustment, subject to interest on borrowing, indicates the benefit (or cost) to shareholders which is realised in the period, measured by the extent to which a proportion of the net operating assets are financed by borrowing. The current cost profit *attributable* to shareholders (see Bibby example, page 217) is therefore the surplus after making allowance for the impact of price changes on the shareholders' interest in the net operating assets, and having provided for the maintenance of the lenders' capital in accordance with their repayment rights. This is the view of the standard despite critics who argued that since the credit (usually) arising could only be distributed if the business were to make further borrowings to maintain its gearing ratio, it should not be treated as attributable to shareholders. This was to confuse the word 'attributable' with 'distributable'. The two are not synonymous. As the Provisional Standard on Inflation (PPSAP 7), now withdrawn, had stated, this argument confused the measurement of profitability with the measurement of liquidity. It had pointed out:

'Even in the absence of inflation, the whole of a company's profit may not be distributable without raising additional finance, for example because it has been invested in, or earmarked for investment in, non-liquid assets.'

SSAP 16 recognised that there are a number of possible methods for calculating a gearing adjustment. It believed, however, that the method defined in the standard is the most appropriate and, on the grounds of the need for comparability between company accounts, *it has been made definitive.*

CALCULATION OF THE GEARING ADJUSTMENT

The *gearing proportion* is the ratio of the average net borrowing to the sum of this and the average shareholders' interest, i.e.

$$= \frac{L}{L + S}$$

where L = average net borrowing and S = average shareholders' interest.

Note: Following the balance sheet equation, L + S is equal to the amount of the net operating assets.

The *gearing adjustment* results from the application of the gearing proportion to the current cost adjustments made to convert historical cost trading profit to current cost operating profit, i.e.

$$= \frac{L}{L + S} \times A$$

where A = the sum of the current cost operating adjustments.

Therefore,

The *gearing adjustment* = the gearing proportion ×
$$\begin{array}{c} \text{Depreciation adjustment} \\ + \\ \text{COSA} \\ + \\ \text{MWCA} \end{array}$$

213

The gearing adjustment is *credited* to current cost profit and loss account, following the line determining current cost operating profit. It is debited to current cost reserve. In essence, it reduces the depreciation, cost of sales and monetary working capital adjustments, and may be regarded as the shareholders' gearing benefit.

Note: Although the gearing adjustment is normally a credit to current cost profit and loss account, it could be a debit if prices fall.

Net borrowing is the excess of the aggregate of all monetary liabilities and provisions (including convertible debentures and deferred tax, but excluding proposed dividends, liabilities included in monetary working capital, and equity capital) over the aggregate of all current assets other than those subject to a cost of sales adjustment and those included in monetary working capital.

Shareholders' interest includes share capital, reserves and proposed dividends (and including preference shares and minority interests where applicable).

Note: Minority interests are treated as part of the shareholders' interest because the current cost profit before taxation is calculated before eliminating the minority interest in the profit, which at that stage is regarded as attributable to the group shareholders including minorities.

Net borrowing and *Shareholders' interest* are determined as the average for the year as shown in the opening and closing current cost balance sheets.

No gearing adjustment is necessary where monetary assets (other than those included in the MWCA) exceed monetary liabilities (other than those in MWCA) as the excess monetary assets are not considered to be part of net operating assets.

Example 12.9 illustrates this narrative description of the calculation of the gearing adjustment.

Example 12.9

Calculation of Gearing Adjustment (SSAP 16)
Current Cost Balance Sheet at 31 December

	19x1 £'000s	19x2 £'000s	
Share capital plus reserves*	1,500	2,000	E
Debentures	500	500	ML
Deferred Tax	100	150	ML
Current liabilities			
Trade creditors	300	350	MWC
Non-trade creditors	70	60	ML
Bank overdraft	100	110	ML
Current tax	90	100	ML
Proposed dividends	200	200	E
	2,860	3,470	
Fixed Assets	2,245	2,665	NMA
Current assets			
Stocks	200	250	NMA
Debtors	350	500	MWC
Cash	65	55	MA
	2,860	3,470	

E = Shareholders' interest. ML = Monetary liability.
MWC = Monetary working capital. NMA = Non Monetary Asset.
MA = Monetary asset.

* When this gearing adjustment is being calculated, the shareholders' total interest is at an amount which remains unchanged when subsequently the gearing adjustment is credited to current cost profit and loss account and debited to current cost reserve.

1. *Net borrowing*   860 ML − 65 MA   920 ML − 55 MA
                              795   865

      Average = L   =   830

2. *Shareholders' interest*   1,700 E   2,200 E
   Average = S   =   1,950

   L+S = Net operating assets =   2,780

3. *Gearing proportion* $= \dfrac{L}{L + S} = \dfrac{830}{2,780} \times 100 = 29.9\%$

4. *Gearing adjustment* 29.9% × £200,000** = £59,800

** It has been assumed that the current cost adjustments made to convert historical cost trading profit (before interest) to current cost operating profit (i.e. the depreciation adjustment, COSA and MWCA) totalled £200,000.

Only trade debtors and trade creditors were included in the MWCA calculation.

ED 35 GEARING ALTERNATIVES

The ill-fated ED 35 allowed two further choices of gearing adjustment in addition to the definitive SSAP 16 version described above. The *first alternative* was an extension of SSAP 16 gearing. It comprised of those parts of the *total adjustments* made to allow for the impact of price changes on the net operating assets and on the net surplus on the *revaluation of assets* arising during the period that may be regarded as associated with items that are financed by net borrowing. Thus, while the SSAP 16 definitive version was based on the additional charges taken up in the profit and loss account, this alternative gearing adjustment may be calculated on balance sheet changes. This reflects the way banks and other lenders look at a company, assuming that in the long-term, the business would seek to maintain approximately the same gearing proportion. ED 35 suggested that if operating capability was to be maintained, an amount equal to this gearing adjustment could be borrowed leaving the gearing ratio unchanged. The *second alternative* of gearing adjustment is calculated by applying the rate of increase in *general prices* (i.e. a CPP/inflation type adjustment) to the average net borrowing (or net monetary assets other than those included in the monetary working capital) of the business during the year. This amount modifies the net charge or credit for interest paid or received during the year from the nominal to the real rate.

These alternatives represented attempts by the ASC to respond to criticism of the SSAP 16 definitive gearing adjustment. While the method selected was to be applied (and explained) consistently by individual entities, comparability of one company's results with another would be reduced. Current cost profit would lack standard definition. Another problem was that the alternative choices effectively brought unrealised gains into the profit and loss account or into the adjusted figures shown in the notes. The SSAP 16 method was definitive not only in the interests of comparability and prudence, but because it anticipated that the Companies Act 1981 would legislate to prevent unrealised gains being included in profit. That Act's general valuation rules – 4 Sch. 29–34 CA 85 – contain the requirement that 'only profits which are realised profits at balance sheet date may be included in the profit and loss account'. This requirement would not inhibit companies who disclose CCA information by way of note from using the alternatives. However, any company presenting full CC accounts would need to consider carefully how they would meet the needs of the 1981 legislation if they chose either of the ED 35 alternatives.

EXAMPLES OF PUBLISHED CURRENT COST STATEMENTS

The Consolidated Current Cost Profit and Loss Account and the Consolidated Current Cost Balance Sheet from the published accounts of J. Bibby & Sons Ltd which won *The Accountant* and Stock Exchange Annual Award in 1981, appear on the following pages and show the SSAP 16 current cost adjustments. Below is a brief commentary.

COMMENTARY ON CURRENT COST STATEMENTS OF J. BIBBY & SONS (pages 217–219)

Profit and Loss Account

The *current cost operating adjustments*, explained by notes 1, 2, and 3, total £4,599,000 and reduce the 'Trading Surplus' shown in the historic profit and loss account from £9,870,000 to the *current cost operating profit* of £5,271,000. These adjustments are mitigated by the *gearing credit* (note 4 of the account) of £704,000. The net adjusting charge of £3,895,000 is the amount that is estimated to be needed to be retained, using SSAP 16 requirements, to maintain the operating capability of the group.

The *current cost profit attributable to (parent company) shareholders* is consequently reduced from £7,876,000 (historical accounts) to that shown in the current cost statement, i.e. £3,981,000. *Earnings per ordinary share fell from 32.68p (historical accounts) to 16.83p (current cost accounts).*

Although the transfer to reserves shown in the historical accounts (£6,029,000) has been reduced to 'profit retained' in the current cost accounts of £2,134,000 by the net adjusting charge of £3,895,000, it will be appreciated that the latter amount, credited to current cost reserve, has also been retained but is now regarded as a capital reserve, i.e. as part of the capital of the group needed to be retained for capital maintenance.

Balance Sheet

Note 1 of the balance sheet shows the make up of the 'reserve' figure and includes the credit for £3,895,000 for 'capital maintenance'. The revalued fixed assets and inventories are the only other items in the balance sheet which show different amounts from those in the historic statement.

The net effect of the changes is to increase 'total shareholders' funds' by £12,634,000.

Because of the *increase* in the shareholders' funds and the *decrease* in the profit attributable to shareholders, the return of profit after tax and preference dividend to the ordinary shareholders' funds falls from 18.3% (historic accounts) to 7.0% (current cost accounts). On the other hand, the net asset value attributable to each ordinary share (historic accounts) of £1.73p rose to £2.25p (current cost accounts). The market value of each ordinary share some 18 months after the date of these accounts stood at £2.86p.

DISTRIBUTABLE PROFIT AND CURRENT COST ACCOUNTS

SSAP 16, in stating that 'the current cost profit attributable to shareholders does not necessarily measure the amount that can be prudently distributed as dividend', reasoned that *with all systems of accounting* the amounts that can be prudently distributed depend not only on profitability, but also on the availability of funds. When determining distribution policy, consideration must be given to factors not reflected in profit, such as capital expenditure plans, changes in the volume of working capital, the effect on funding requirements of changes in production methods and efficiency, liquidity, and new financing arrangements. Although the impact of price changes on the shareholders' interest in the net operating assets has been allowed for in the determination of the current cost profit attributable to shareholders, these other factors still need to be considered. Even if the effect of such factors is neutral, a full distribution of current cost profit attributable to shareholders may lead to the necessity of arranging additional finance (equal to the gearing adjustment) to avoid the erosion of the operating capability of the business. Of course, an increase in the value of the business of its assets may provide increased cover for such financing.

Consolidated Current Cost Statement
Profit and Loss Account
Year ended 29 December 1979

		1979	
	Notes	£000's	£000's
Profits			
Sales			188,091
Trading Surplus as shown in historical Profit and Loss Account			9,870
Less adjustments:			
Depreciation	(1)	2,496	
Cost of Sales	(2)	1,118	
Monetary Working Capital	(3)	985	4,599
Operating Profit			5,271
Interest		850	
Gearing Adjustment	(4)	(704)	146
			5,125
Share of Profits of Associated Companies	(5)		685
Current cost profit before taxation			5,810
Taxation			1,588
Current cost profit after taxation			4,222
Extraordinary Items			(241)
Current cost profit attributable to Parent Company Shareholders			3,981
Appropriations			
Dividends			1,620
Debenture Stock Redemption Reserve			227
Profit Retained			2,134
			3,981
Earnings per Ordinary Share			16·83p

Notes:
1. The depreciation adjustment is the difference between:–
   (a) the current year's depreciation charge, recalculated by
       (i) using an appropriate index of price movement, or
       (ii) reinstating fully depreciated plant at net current replacement cost and
            providing further depreciation over revised residual lives, and
   (b) the historical cost depreciation charge before investment grant credits.
2. The cost of sales adjustment is the difference between the historical cost of
   sales and the current cost of the goods sold, based largely on the average
   arrival prices of replacement raw materials.
3. The monetary working capital adjustment has been calculated, using an
   appropriate index, on the average level of debtors and creditors.
4. The gearing adjustment is the proportion of the depreciation, cost of sales
   and monetary working capital adjustments that the net monetary liabilities
   bear to the total funds of the business on a current cost basis. The average of
   the opening and closing positions has been used for this calculation.
5. Current cost statements have not been prepared by the associated companies
   and their results are included on the historical cost basis.

Consolidated Current Cost Statement
Balance Sheet
29 December 1979

	Notes	1979 £000's
Capital Employed		
Share Capital		14,291
Reserves	(1)	42,921
Total Shareholders' Funds		57,212
Minority Interests		9
Investment Grants	(2)	1,910
Loans		4,682
		63,813
Represented by		
Current Assets		
Inventories	(3)	20,662
Debtors		22,670
Bank and Cash Balances		431
		43,763
Current Liabilities		
Creditors		18,122
Taxation		3,026
Proposed Final Dividend		1,045
Short Term Borrowings		1,545
		23,738

Net Current Assets		20,025
Other Assets	(2)	2,555
Fixed Assets	(4)	41,233
		63,813

Notes:

1. Reserves

	Historical £000's	Capital Maintenance £000's	Total £000's
Balance at 30.12.78	28,162	5,210	33,372
Capitalisation	(4,105)	—	(4,105)
Valuation adjustment	(26)	—	(26)
Revaluation during 1979	—	7,424	7,424
Debenture Redemption	227	—	227
Adjusted retained profit for year	2,134	—	2,134
Net Adjustments	—	3,895	3,895
	26,392	16,529	42,291

2. The value of investment grants, investments in associated companies and deferred expenditure have not be adjusted.
3. Inventories have been included in the balance sheet at their value to the business at 29 December 1979.
4. Fixed assets are included in the balance sheet at their depreciated replacement current cost at 29 December 1979. Those assets which were fully written off under the historical cost convention have been reinstated at their depreciated replacement cost using revised residual lives. Fixed assets which it is not intended to replace have been included at their estimated residual value.

CURRENT COST 'STATEMENT OF SOURCES AND APPLICATION OF FUNDS'

SSAP 16 required that the annual report and accounts should provide a statement of sources and application of funds compatible with the *main accounts*. A mandatory current cost statement of this kind need not, therefore, be provided where current cost accounts are given as *supplementary* to the historical accounts.

CURRENT COST ACCOUNTS AS A BASIS OF TAXATION

Although the acceptance of current cost accounts for taxation purposes by the Government would have provided a need for their adoption by the estimated 99% of registered companies who were outside the mandate of SSAP 16, there was never any sign of this happening. Whatever system of accounting for price level changes succeeds that standard, whether CCA-based or otherwise, no change in the Governments' stance is likely. The system of corporation tax which included relief for stock profits and the 100% first year capital allowances did not result in the general over-taxation of companies. Indeed the Government's Green Paper on corporation tax, published in January 1982, revealed that in any year only 40% of all companies earn sufficient profits to pay mainstream corporation tax. Although the Green Paper devoted some five chapters to a consideration of current cost accounts for tax purposes as one of the options discussed, it made the basic comment that 'fiscal compensation for the effects of inflation is inconsistent with the primary objective of bringing down the rate of inflation, i.e. 'inflation accounting is inflationary'. This view overlooked the fact that current cost accounting is not a system of accounting for inflation *per se*, but was consistent with the Government's refusal in 1981 to implement Section 22 of the Finance Act 1977 which required indexing of personal income tax allowances to the Retail Price Index. In 1984, the Government made material changes to the corporation tax system (see Chapter 4). It is plain that the Government has rejected the option of allowing tax relief in the corporate sector for the effects of inflation.

CURRENT COST ACCOUNTING STATEMENTS AND THE AUDITOR (see page 177)

THE INTERPRETATION OF CURRENT COST ACCOUNTS

Stockbroking analysts estimated that on the introduction of current cost accounting, pre-tax profits of UK quoted companies under CCA could fall by 40/45% (those of J. Bibby fell by 40%) and that dividend cover would fall on average to 1.1 times (J. Bibby's dividend cover, historic 5 times and CCA 2.6 times, is strongly above average).

Average figures cloak the reality for individual companies and the view was that some sectors of the market would be clear beneficiaries from CCA, but that the majority would be losers. Hardest hit sectors were expected to be those groups employing large amounts of plant and equipment and carrying large stocks, exemplified by textiles, motors, mechanical engineering and shipping. Retail and service sectors were likely to suffer less for although (e.g. in retailing) the cost of sales adjustment would be high (reflecting high stocks), they would be able to offset the main impact because most of their sales are for cash and many retail chains obtain large amounts of credit from their suppliers.

It has been noted (with the J. Bibby accounts) that revaluation of asset adjustments will increase net asset backing per share, but it also is the case that where CCA adjusted earnings are substantially *lower*, price earning ratios will become correspondingly *higher*.

By mid-1981, enthusiasm among companies for CCA was still muted, particularly among non-listed companies large enough to come within the ambit of SSAP 16. A survey by Deloitte Haskins and Sells found that 66 (26%) out of 255 such companies had not, or did not intend to, publish CCA information. These companies, mainly owned by a limited number of shareholders engaged in the running of the business, considered CCA was of no value, or a waste of money. The Secretary of the ASC believed this attitude was short-sighted. He said that bankers were showing a keen interest in CCA information because of their concern that companies which borrow funds can generate sufficient returns to repay the loans. CCA, they believed, is a good indication of a company's ability to generate cash. Another 1981 report from a firm of City stockbrokers stated that of the 23 (out of 30) companies in the FT Share Index which had provided CCA information, six had negative CCA earnings at their last accounting date, a further three had their dividend uncovered and some PE ratios reached as high as 54.4.

The *Survey of Published Accounts 1981/82*, published by the ICAEW, reported that only 7% of the companies required to comply with SSAP 16 failed to do so. By 1984, the ICA survey reported that of their sample of 300 companies, 64% of the large, unlisted companies, 10% of the medium-sized and 8% of the large, listed ones were failing to comply with

SSAP 16. In the majority of cases, directors of listed companies who failed to comply with SSAP 16, gave reason for their non-compliance, no doubt in deference to Stock Exchange and audit pressure, but over two-thirds of the unlisted companies gave no reason for the omission. By 1985, this trend towards non-compliance had worsened, leading to the events recorded earlier in this chapter. The CCA system had, of course, been introduced into the UK during a period of economic recession with high levels of liquidations of companies being reported. It is perhaps understandable, if not acceptable given the known deficiencies of the HCA system, that many companies preferred not only to give the thumbs down to SSAP 16, but made little attempt to estimate the effect of changing prices on their results and financial position for the benefit of their shareholders, if no-one else.

THE FUTURE OF THE SYSTEM

By mid-1986, the future of accounting for price level changes was in the melting pot. The complete abandonment of the topic emotively suggested by some, is unlikely, considering the widespread acceptance of the severe limitations of HCA in inflationary times, the Government's favourable outlook on the use of CCA within the nationalised industries, and our international obligations.

Although Professor Myddleton has pointed out,

'CPP uses homogeneous constant purchasing power of units of account which are more relevant than money in times of inflation, which allow proper comparisons over time and correctly report monetary gains and losses . . . [it] retains the objective verifiability of historical cost accounting, is relatively simple to prepare, is acceptable to accountants and to businessmen, and is comprehensive and applies to all businesses and financial calculations and has no serious disadvantage.'[1] (Myddleton (1981))

given the American experience noted below, it is unlikely that the abandoned provisional standard (PSSAP 7) will be revived, although we may see the use of the RPI in company five-year trend reports. The development of a non-mandatory SORP is also unlikely as it would probably lead to a repeat of the SSAP 16 experience with few companies complying, which was the experience in Australia with their non-mandatory standard.

In the USA, where FASB Statement 33 *Financial reporting and changing prices* (1979) requires information both about the effects of inflation and about specific price changes on corporate operation (i.e. both CPP and CCA type statements) to be provided as supplementary to the basic accounts, a recently reported (1984) comprehensive review of its operations concluded that the resulting *inflation adjusted* information had not been widely used. It still believed, however, that 'the most important *effects of changing prices* should be presented as relevant information for users'. In a new exposure draft, it has recommended continued experimentation with inflation accounting disclosures, but with the elimination of the current purchasing power requirements.

In the UK, a study by Kay and Mayer of the Institute of Fiscal Studies (1984) warned that complacency resulting from lower inflation rates was far from warranted. Their research demonstrated that the magnitude of the corrections which have to be made for price level changes are considerable and showed that inaccuracies involved in relying on HCA are not merely confined to periods of high inflation. Their conclusions, however, as we have noted (page 200) are not accepted by companies; it has been shown that it is far easier to promote the value of accounting for inflation than to provide and implement an appropriate and acceptable system for so doing!

[1] **Professor D. R. Myddleton (1981) 'Neglected merits of CPP accounting'** in *British Accounting Standards, the first ten years*, Leach and Stamp. Woodhead, Faulkner, U.K.

PART THREE

Interpreting published company accounts

13

Users and their needs

Whatever their limitations may be in the eyes of users, the published reports and accounts of companies remain the single, regular source of detailed financial information available to them. In the decade of the 1970s, as a result of the accounting standards programme, the quality and comparability of this information improved considerably. While it is accepted as impracticable to establish a code of standard rules sufficiently elaborate to cater for all business situations and every exceptional or marginal case, nevertheless the programme has succeeded in narrowing the likely range of subjective judgement on accounting matters and in requiring the disclosure of the policies adopted. The Companies Acts requirements in respect of explanatory notes to the accounts are more extensive than ever and the Companies Act 1981 – S227, 228 245, 742 and 4 Sch. CA 1985 – provides the framework for standardisation and comparability of published accounts throughout the EEC. The 'true and fair view' concept has been given greater emphasis by this latest Act, and any departure from its accounting requirements seen as necessary by the directors to provide such a view has to be disclosed, with an explanation of the reason for it and its effect on the company's financial position.

More information is now provided – significantly, the statement of sources and application of funds and, for specified companies, current cost information to show the impact of rising prices on the profitability and financial position of the reporting entity.

The accounting information is subject to independent audit and report as to its truth and fairness. The CA 1981 has added to the auditors' responsibilities that of reporting on the consistency of the directors' report with the audited accounting statements. While the legal recipients of this report are the company shareholders, the auditors are keenly conscious of its wider readership and their possible liability to third parties. The leading case of *Hedley Byrne & Co Ltd v Heller & Partners* (1964) indicates that actions for professional negligence may arise if financial loss is suffered by persons as a result of their reliance on the professional skill and judgement of others with whom they had no fiduciary or contractual relationship. A negligent, albeit honest, misrepresentation which results in financial loss may give rise to action for damages by a third party if the accountant knew or ought to have known that the third party was one who might be shown to rely on the accounts in question. The basis of liability to third parties has been extended by the *Twomax* case where it was held that the accountant *reasonably could have foreseen*, given the proximity of the parties, that the audited accounts might be relied on by the third party in question. With the present high level of company liquidations, that liability may be seen to be further extended in relation to company failures whose accounts, based on the 'going concern' concept, were given a clean audit certificate (see Chapter 8).

These potential increases of responsibility in law are now keenly understood by accountants who prepare accounts and by those who audit them, it also will be a material consideration of the latter when reporting to the shareholders.

Satisfying the needs of a wider readership

The *Corporate Report* (see page 22) also envisaged a wider readership of the published report and accounts than the shareholders and saw the objective of published financial information as communicating economic measurements of, and information about, the resources and performance of the company which would be useful to all users.

This stated objective led to a view that the one income statement and its related balance sheet addressed to the shareholders would not satisfy the needs of a wider readership. Additional statements were called for. The statement of value added is one which is provided by many listed companies within the corporate report and/or an accompanying employee report. Others such as a statement of transactions in foreign currency have not appeared. As for the traditional financial statements, the difficulty in arriving at a dual-purpose measurement of performance and capital maintenance raised problems in the application of accounting concepts. The feasibility of producing and publishing multi-column reports was to be researched. An ASC research report in 1981 from a working party chaired by Professor Macve of Aberystwyth University concluded that an agreed conceptual framework for financial accounting and reporting, as being prepared in the USA, is unlikely to serve the UK profession's need. Further research aimed at identifying how accounting information can adapt to meet the needs of the various users of accounts did not produce any tangible result. Paradoxically, while this research proceeded in respect of the listed and larger companies, the CA 1981 radically reduced the reporting requirements of the 'small' company, as we have seen.

Readers are referred to the suggested list by Shaw (page 166) of the many purposes for which audited accounts are used. Accepted that the annual report and accounts will not meet all the specific needs of the variety of users, it is nevertheless likely that *all* will be concerned about the likely *continuity of the business*. This outlook underlines the major limitation of the available information, that is that the accounts, whether historic or current cost based, are about the *past*, whereas the concern is for the *future*.

The objective of continuity (survival) holding primacy, subsumes the interest of users of the accounts in the *liquidity* of the enterprise, i.e. its ability to meet its current financial obligations; in its *solvency*, i.e. its ability to meet its longer term liabilities (liquidity is a time aspect of solvency); and in its *profitability*.

It may be noted that profitability is essential to survival in the long term. A company may be unprofitable in the short term provided it has ample reserves and a strong enough asset position, and/or a future growth/profit potential to attract funds.

Different Users and their Interests

INLAND REVENUE AND CUSTOMS AND EXCISE

As Departments of Government, they should be keenly interested in a company's survival as a provider in the broader sense of economic wealth. They should be concerned about profitability in general – the more profit, the more tax (corporation tax, income tax, VAT, capital gains tax, etc.). Essentially, however, the Inland Revenue will have a direct interest in the published accounts only as the base from which company tax liability is determined. In practice, companies render a separate computation of the taxable profit. Once the liability has been stated, the Revenue will, of course, become creditors of the company and will have the interest of a creditor in the company's ability to pay the amount due.

TRADE CREDITORS

Trade creditors of the recipient company are trade debtors of the supplying company. Suppliers' credit control may start *before* the goods are despatched (or services given) through the assessment of the creditworthiness of the customer. The published accounts of the customer may form part of this assessment, although dated when obtained and therefore of restricted value. They may be analysed in advance of contracting or supplying to give indications of the company's financial position, liquidity, solvency and profitability. Once the goods or service have been supplied, the emphasis shifts to the company's ability to pay promptly.

Research into reasons for company liquidations has indicated that the trend towards illiquidity was apparent from a ratio analysis of the accounts. In addition to the liquidity ratios, a realistic assessment of the break-up value of the company's assets and the cover available for the suppliers' debt, after allowing for secured and likely preferential creditors, can be made. The tendency of a company overtrading to make increasing use of trade credit and bank overdrafts can also be noted. Allied to the suppliers' own experience of dealing with the company and its propensity to pay promptly or otherwise, together with details from other sources like credit agencies, information of value, however limited, may be obtained from the published accounts.

BANKERS

Experience indicates that in recent inflationary times, companies generally have tended to place greater reliance on bank lending than hitherto. Bank overdrafts and the company's gearing ratio rise; liquidity ratios fall. Overtrading, too, leads to the same results. It is noteworthy that many large listed companies include as current liabilities, year after year, sizeable bank overdrafts which from the company's viewpoint have the practical nature of longer term loans, but remain as current liabilities because of the legal nature of the loan, i.e. that it can be recalled in the short term. Banks have become concerned that these 'hard-core' overdrafts have been used by companies to fund long-term assets, e.g. plant and property, leading to a deficiency of working capital and to the company sustaining a liquidity problem. Balance sheets would confirm this unsatisfactory situation from the banks' viewpoint. Thus term lending schemes have grown in importance where investment in new assets is financed under repayment schedules related to the cash flow expected to be generated by the project, with security provided for the bank.

The Rolls-Royce company's crash of 1971, unprecedented for a 'blue chip' company, brought home to banks the risk of unsecured loans including overdrafts and they have generally modified their lending policy, shifting a good deal into medium or even longer term forms with security. This was confirmed in recent evidence to the Wilson Committee showing that, by the end of 1977, medium-term lending covered some 42% of domestic advances to businesses. The crash of large and important companies like Rolls-Royce usually has a ripple effect on the financial position of other companies, for example the liquidity of suppliers. Rolls-Royce balance sheet creditors were £62.3 million in the 1969 balance sheet, probably spread over hundreds of creditors' own balance sheets and appearing at the time to be bad debts although ultimately recovered. Bank borrowing, looking largely unsecured in the final balance sheet, stood at £37 million. This experience for the banks probably led to other blue chip companies getting a close scrutiny from their bankers who had in the past lent them money secure in the belief that bankruptcy was out of the question.

As far as new borrowers are concerned, banks would probably ask to see and have substantiated the applicant company's budgets, particularly the cash budget, and would require as a condition of the loan the provision of sufficient security.

227

If this security takes the form of a fixed charge on property, a professional valuation would be regarded as more important than the balance sheet entry therefor. If, on the other hand, the security was a floating charge, then the balance sheet, historic, current cost (where available) and budgeted would enable a view to be taken of the cover provided by the generality of assets after accounting for any prior secured charge. The banks, assuming they service the current and other accounts of the company, can, of course, plot their own view of the company's actual cash flow and compare it with budget. The profitability and liquidity ratios derived from the published accounts will support an established view of the financial position of the company.

DEBENTURE CREDITORS

The debenture contract is the written acknowledgement of a long-term loan to a company under seal, setting out its terms as to level of interest, dates of payment of interest, dates and terms of repayment, security and the agreed action should the terms not be met. The great majority of corporate debentures of listed companies are provided by the financial institutions including the pension funds. Normally, a trustee is appointed to act on behalf of the general body of lenders to look after their interests and act as their agent when contract terms are not met. For example, this might include the appointment of a receiver and manager when the company is insolvent, to protect the interest of the lenders. In some cases the company would survive its period of trouble. In others, liquidation would follow.

Generally, a debenture lender, e.g. a pension fund manager, would want to limit the risk to his capital and would thus be selective in the choice of borrowing company and would call for adequate security. He would also be looking for a steady, almost certain stream of interest payments, to meet his own obligations of regular, certain pension payments. His scrutiny of the company's published accounts prior to making the loan, and during its continuance, will therefore be concerned with the cover of the profit before interest and tax for the interest payments and the trend of that ratio, as well as with the cover provided on an estimated break-up value of the assets securing the loan.

The informed debenture holder is aware that shareholders can increase their investment return if a larger proportion of the total long-term funds comes from lenders at rates of interest which allow the company to 'earn a turn' on them (what the Americans call 'trading on the equity'). This policy of higher gearing would increase the risk to the shareholders of losing their investment since the interest charges and repayment of capital on long-term loans are fixed obligations. Falling profitability could lead to falling liquidity, and the failure to pay interest on due dates could end in liquidation for the company. Both debenture holders and shareholders will therefore wish to measure the relative risk involved and ratio analysis of published accounts will aid this.

In recent times of high inflation, the level of return required by lenders to cover both the cost of inflation plus the 'real' interest (even allowing for the tax relief available to the borrowing company) has been so high as to make such loans less common. Articles of Association normally give directors power to issue debentures, but restrict the amount borrowed to the amount of the issued share capital unless the company by ordinary resolution overrides the limit.

PREFERENCE SHAREHOLDERS

The preference shareholder is prepared to accept a fixed and normally lower dividend in return for his preferential status vis-à-vis the ordinary shareholder. Like the debenture holder, he is looking for a reasonably certain stream of income. Unlike the debenture holder, his dividend is not a fixed obligation of the company in the absence of profit. Even though his preference shares may be cumulative in character, in the absence of profit, or where not recommended by the directors, he will not get his dividend. The preferential character of his capital investment relative to the equity shareholder is of limited value in an enforced liquidation as he rates after all creditors, preferential secured and unsecured, and his priority over equity is unlikely to be meaningful in most cases as each category may lose its capital.

His investment, like those of the debenture holder and the ordinary shareholder, involves a comparison of available alternative investments. The role of the investment adviser (financial analyst) is considered later. As with debentures, the institutions – notably the pension funds and the insurance companies – hold a high proportion of the preference shares of listed companies. Because of the higher risk of the investment, lacking as it does a legal form of security, the trend of profits after-tax available to the whole body of shareholders and the cover of such profits for the preference dividend will be plotted keenly. For the reasons adduced above, the capital cover will be of lesser, albeit important, interest. The redeemable preference shareholder will, of course, be more concerned for the cover for his capital, particularly as the date of redemption approaches when his appraisal of the published accounts will be directed to the company's ability to repay. If the preference shares are quoted, the dividend yield and the market price will allow comparisons of alternative investment possibilities.

TRADE UNIONS AND EMPLOYEES

The "Employment Report" envisaged by the *Corporate Report* is not yet a reality. It was conceived that it would:

> "detail the size and composition of the workforce relying on the enterprise for its livelihood, and the work contribution of employees and the benefits they had earned.
>
> It would assist users in assessing the performance of the entity, evaluating its economic function and performance in relation to society, assessing its capacity to make reallocations of resources and evaluating managerial performance, efficiency and objectives."

Whether such a report will ever see the light of day will presumably depend on the changing views of society and of its elected government. Even if such a report was given the green light to go ahead, there are evident problems of producing soch a document. Meanwhile, as we have seen in an earlier chapter, the published reports and accounts of many listed companies are being accompanied by an "Employee Report".

The extent to which individual employees are interested in or sophisticated enough to want or be able to unravel published accounts is probably quite limited. Their representative trade unions should have the competence to analyse the report on behalf of the members and there is at least one recorded recent instance of a union employing financial analysts to provide evidence from published accounts to assist wage negotiations. Employee share ownership fostered by the successful British Telecom share issue may give fresh impetus to Employee Reports.

In so far as the funds provided to financial institutions come from the public at large including trade unionists (e.g. money with banks, insurance companies, building societies and pension funds) and a large part of these funds is channelled through the stock market, it must be in the interests of such a pluralistic society for information in published accounts to be widely available and for the implications of 'profit earning' to be understood.

Possible future developments affecting consultation with and the provision of information to employees, arising from the EEC Fifth Directive and the Vredeling proposal directives (Chapter 10) should be noted.

INSTITUTIONAL INVESTORS

The institutions hold nearly all the debentures of listed companies and about two-thirds of the ordinary shares. At December 1980, the Stock Exchange Shareholder Analysis showed the following relative holdings of shares weighted by market value:

Insurance companies	18%	
Investment/Unit trusts	13%	64%
Pension funds	18%	
Other institutions	15%	
Individuals		36%

The importance of 'institutional investment' is clear. The knowledge of 'who are the shareholders' could, with advantage to society, be made more widely known. Working together, the institutional investors can exert great influence on the companies in which they invest. They have not as yet done so to any great extent. In January 1982, they moved to protect their interests when the Post Office Pension Fund, which invests £3,500 million for its employees and those of British Telecom, sought an injunction against the Associated Communications Corporation to prevent a "golden handshake" of £75,000 being paid to a company executive; this action was taken on behalf of all the pension funds who were shareholders in ACC under powers contained in S459–61 of the Companies Act 1985 for the Court to grant relief against a company 'where members are unfairly prejudiced'.

Institutional investors will have available to them professional financial expertise with the ability to analyse the corporate report, a company's position in an industry, and that industry's place in today's dynamic environment.

MANAGEMENT

The top management of listed companies produce the annual report and accounts for their own shareholders as part of their stewardship or custodial responsibilities. The requisite documents are filed with the Registrar of Companies and the report and accounts are made generally available. They show the shareholders and other interested people the outcome of management operations in financial terms. Management will be concerned with the reaction of readers of these statements as it may impinge on the future of the company. Beyond that, they will be concerned with the final outcome of the financial year as compared with the estimated position set out in the company's internal master budget statements. The master budgets are the formalised operational plans for the oncoming year. They comprise the budgeted profit and loss account, the budgeted balance sheet and the budgeted cash flow statement. These documents summarise the outcome of the detailed estmates of income and expenditure in all areas of the business. The actual experience of operations will have been compared regularly throughout the year with that budgeted and the exceptions from the norm will have provided information for management decision.

As the management accounts used will have been integrated with the financial results, management will have been aware by the end of the year of the outcome of their plans sometime before the annual report and accounts are prepared and published. Management's internal analyses of results coud include a consideration of the significant financial ratios starting with the primary ratio – operational earnings before interest and tax related to operating capital employed.

In addition to making valid ratio comparisons with past results and with budget, management should want to compare its own performance with that of other companies. It can obtain the published results of other concerns for this purpose, or obtain summaries of detailed financial information in respect of them from an agency, e.g. Extel Statistical Services Ltd. Computer-based systems accessed to subscribers' own VDUs (visual display units) are an alternative, e.g. Datastream International Ltd provides such a service to financial and investment institutions, including the profit and loss account, balance sheet and other pertinent financial information of all major UK companies.

Comparisons between companies within the same group can be facilitated through the use of the same accounting bases and policies. Comparisons between independent companies require that differences are compensated for, and even then it would be preferable if the comparisons were made between the results of concerns with similar operating characteristics. While the accounting standards programme has narrowed the range of acceptable options, difference in accounting practices can still occur, e.g. where depreciation policy is significantly different, these would need to be noted or adjusted for in comparative exercises.

CENTRE FOR INTERFIRM COMPARISONS

This organisation, which provides a means for companies to make valid comparisons of the whole range of operating ratios between themselves on a confidential basis, is sponsored by the British Institute of Management and the British Productivity Council.

Using methods adopted by the Centre, interfirm comparisons have been carried out in nearly 100 different industries, trades and professions in the UK and international IFCs are now in being. Companies enter into an interfirm comparison group on the understanding that they will remain anonymous, that they agree to use a common set of definitions for measuring their costs, profits and assets and that they must pool their figures with the central organisation which collects, collates and interprets them for the companies. Ratios are used for anonymity and clarity. A typical comparison will have some thirty companies taking part and each will be able to view its overall (ROCE) performance, its profit margin and its turnover of assets (the secondary ratios), against those of others on a valid and objective base.

From the primary ratio and the secondary ratios, the derivatives of cost and assets can be shown as subsidiary ratios in a pyramid form.

A pyramid of ratios
A typical pyramid similar to those used by the CIFC would appear:

(A)
THE PRIMARY RATIO

$$\frac{\text{Operating profit* before interest and tax}}{\text{Total operating assets (current costs)*}} \quad (11.43\%)$$

ROCE

equals $\quad$ (B) $\dfrac{\text{Profit as defined*}}{\text{Sales}}$ (9%) $\qquad$ *multiplied by* $\quad$ (C) $\dfrac{\text{Sales}}{\text{Operating assets as defined*}}$ (1.27 times)

$\qquad\qquad$ *THE PROFIT MARGIN* $\qquad\qquad\qquad\qquad$ *TURNOVER OF ASSETS*

It will be appreciated that (A) the 'return on capital employed' will increase if either (B) 'the profit margin' and/or (C) 'the turnover of assets' is increased. The derivatives of (B) will indicate the ratios of the relative costs whch together with profit make up the selling price. (B) can, therefore, be increased either by reducing costs in any of the areas involved and/or by increasing the selling price. Comparisons can be made of these ratios with those of other companies to give indications of relative efficiency. They may point, for example, to 'purchasing costs' as being materially out of line with those of competitors. If, in addition, material costs are a large percentage of total cost, this analysis could lead to the determination that the importance of the purchasing function had been underestimated and an awareness that a relatively small percentage increase in efficiency in this area could have a significant effect on profit and ROCE.

The pyramid deriving from (B) *would appear:*

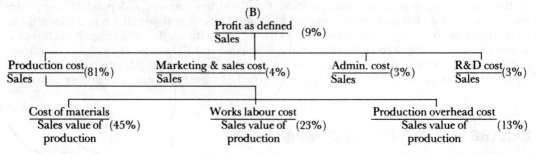

This example poinpoints 'production cost' as the most significant component of 'sales' (100%) with the cost of materials and labour highlighted. Only the production cost has been extended in this example. And, of course, it is possible to continue, showing ratios for significant sub-costs making up the figure for 'cost of materials'. It must be noted that these 'cost ratios' are not available to external appraisers, the detailed information not being published.

However, most of the ratios deriving from the other secondary ratio (C) 'the turnover of assets (capital)' can be calculated from information in a company's annual report.

The pyramid deriving from (C) *would appear:*

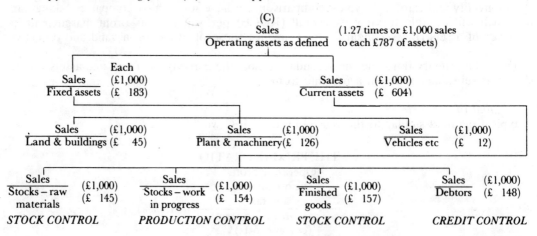

In this example, the company can gain useful information regarding the relative efficiency of its stock, production and credit control functions in comparison with its own previous experience, its budgeted expectations, and with other similar companies through its membership of the CIFC. With £604 of current assets against £183 of fixed assets tied up for every £1,000 of sales, these are the areas highlighted for investigation.

Interfirm comparison may show that the company is very high in the league in stock and production control and very low in credit control, pinpointing this latter function as one for first consideration. Any resulting increase in efficiency will lead to a higher turnover of assets (C) figure, and in turn a higher ROCE (A).

ORDINARY SHAREHOLDERS

Earlier, it was noted that all parties having an interest in the business would be concerned with its continuity – with its survival. No more so is this the view of the equity (ordinary) shareholder. He, as the ultimate owner of the business, is aware that he undertakes the greatest investment risk, that in an enforced liquidation, being last in line of those hoping for some return of capital, he may well end up with nothing. On the other hand, as the carrier of the highest risk, he has expectations of the highest reward. He looks, therefore, to the management of the enterprise to maximise earnings at levels which allow both the payment of dividend commensurate with the price paid for his shares, and for the retention of the residue to provide greater financial strength as a springboard for growth. He is interested in the published accounts as they provide indications of the degree of success of management in meeting his present expectations and his future hopes. It is the future which is his greatest concern. He will be looking at the report and accounts for clues to future performance. If he is an institutional investor, he will have the expertise to make judgements of the likely trend of the future performance of the company. If not, he may turn to a professional adviser to undertake this service for him.

FINANCIAL ANALYSTS

The main tasks of the financial analyst consist of comparison and prediction. He is concerned with the variables which determine the market price of a share as it presently stands. He is required to judge the future movement of that price, the related movement of earnings and thereby the yield expectable. Future earnings and dividend-paying prospects take primacy.

He calculates and analyses past movements of relevant indicators, makes comparisons of alternative investments and extrapolates significant trends into the future. Among the principal indicators are the EPS (earnings per share) and the PER (price-earnings ratio) (see Chapter 5). While he may be hampered by the problem of changing price levels and – despite the accounting standards programme – the variety of acceptable accounting practices, he has the expertise to make adjustments. His concern is for the greatest disclosure of information which will enable him to make adjustments and judgements. For example, analysts calculated their own sources and application of funds statements before these became a mandatory requirement of SSAP 10. The funds statement offers him a clear insight into a company's financial policies and the future outlook for earnings and dividends. He is more interested in the quantum of current investment in long-term capital assets and a confirmation of its proper funding from long-term capital than he is in the balance sheet value of the fixed assets.

A good current example of the adjustments made by analysts, following their view of an accounting practice, relates to the prime measure of comparison used by investors, the PER, i.e. the price per share divided by the earnings per share. Their calculation often differed from that based on the published accounts and that published in the *Financial Times* because they ignored the provisions of SSAP 15 and included deferred tax in arriving at 'fully-taxed' earnings; until the 1984 Finance Act, this reduced the need for their adjustment. Invariably this meant higher PERs (lower earnings per share). This they regarded as a realistic judgment.

Another example of inconsistent practice requiring adjustments by analysts was highlighted in the responses to the discussion paper leading to the proposed revision of SSAP 6 'Extraordinary items and prior year adjustments' by ED 36 (January 1985) (see Chapter 5). Evidence showed that brewery companies treated the profits arising on the sale of licensed properties in different ways, three determined the transaction to be 'extraordinary' and thus dealt with below the line of 'earnings', and a further three determined the transaction *not* to be extraordinary. The inconsistency was ignored by the auditors, including those who audited accounts involving both treatments. Hopefully, the more stringent definitions of what constitutes an 'extraordinary item' in the revision to SSAP 6 will reduce inconsistencies in this area, if not entirely eliminate them.

The analyst in carrying out his tasks will make use of a wide range of information about the environment in general (political, economic, technical, social, national and international – see Chapter 1); about the environment in particular, i.e. that affecting the company and industry under review; indeed, about anything and everything which points to past or current performance, or which aids the prediction of the future.

The analyst's main source of information concerning a particular company or group centres around the published report and accounts. In interpreting this information he will calculate relevant ratios and look for trends.

14

Trends and ratios

The interests and needs of the various likely users of the published corporate report and accounts have been discussed in the previous chapter; any financial analysis should obviously have regard to the particular requirements of the recipient of the information. An *investment analyst*, concerned to give advice for investment decision, will have regard to the degree of risk acceptable to his client and the latter's propensity towards earnings/dividends or increase in value of his shares, or a combination of both.

There are differing views about the objectives of a company. Owner/managers are assumed to want to maximise earnings and the return to themselves. Ownership and management are generally divorced for listed companies, even though directors will hold shares. There is a view that management will aim for that level of profits which will satisfy the shareholder and that this level will be below maximisation. Whatever the truth of the matter, it has been suggested that most parties will have an interest in the company's:
- Survival.
- Liquidity and solvency.
- Profitability.
- Future potential (growth).

And that information by way of ratios and in other ways will be sought to satisfy that interest.

Ratios in perspective

A number of financial ratios have been discussed in earlier chapters to which reference can be made in a particular context. Here, ratios will be considered in relation to the four areas of interest mentioned above. It is important, however, to note some limitations in their use and to keep them in perspective.

RELEVANCE AND LIMITATIONS OF RATIOS TO FINANCIAL ANALYSIS

1. Their calculation is simple, their meaning often elusive.
2. Their principal value as an analytical tool is to suggest questions which need answering. Significant changes are brought into focus.

3. The analysis rarely provides the answers to the questions.

4. An unfavourable comparison between the latest ratio and a previous one, or other comparative, should lead to an investigation into what may be wrong. The comparison will not determine the cause of the difficulty.

5. Ratios are best used in support of, or in conjunction with, other information.

6. They are likely to be more valid when made within one company, or group, when common accounting policies are followed. Comparisons with other enterprises will be difficult, unless made by an organisation like CIFC (Chapter 13).

7. Accounting standards and the publication of accounting policies should aid external analysts in their use of ratios, but there will never be absolute standards for comparison.

8. Compliance with SSAP 6 principles and the separate publication of extraordinary items (Chapter 5), reduce areas of possible incompatibility.

9. Over a period of years, internal changes in accounting bases, following the introduction of a new accounting standard or the enactment of a new Companies Act or Finance Act, need to be adjusted for.

10. Over a period of years, external changes in the value of money and/or rising prices need to be adjusted for. (*Example 10.4*, page 184).

11. Ratios alone cannot give financial control. They can, however, indicate to management the areas where stricter control might be needed. They can be used, starting with ROCE (return on capital employed), when preparing plans and policies; they can act as a target and as a useful means of communication.

12. Absolute figures can be misleading unless compared with a standard. A ratio enables comparisons to be made while at the same time summarising and simplifying the figures. Once a pattern has been revealed for a business or industry for the different ratios, changes to the pattern can be monitored, providing information for decision.

Tests of profitability

Profitability is linked with efficiency and with the return on capital employed. It is a requisite for survival in the longer term.

ROCE

It has been shown that the balance sheet provides information on the structure and value of total capital employed: how much is provided by the shareholders, how much through loan capital and how much in short-term funds from current creditors including the banks. As these three main sources of funds together equal total funds and as total funds equal total assets, various levels of capital employed starting with 'total assets' can be considered against requisite levels of profit derived from the profit and loss account:

1. TOTAL ASSETS : PROFIT BEFORE TAX AND INTEREST
   (If 'total assets' include investments, then with the exclusion of these and investment income from profit, ratio 2 is determined.)

2. TOTAL OPERATING ASSETS : OPERATING PROFIT BEFORE TAX & INTEREST
   (NB. Intangible assets, e.g. goodwill, can be excluded, although if the item arises from the purchase of a subsidiary (as is usual), some would include it.)

3. LONG-TERM CAPITAL : PROFIT BEFORE TAX AND INTEREST
   (Shareholders' funds and long-term loans.)

4. SHAREHOLDERS' FUNDS : PROFIT AFTER TAX AND BEFORE EXTRA-
   ORDINARY ITEMS
   (With the deduction of any preference share capital from shareholders' funds and
   the preference dividend from profit after tax, ratio 5 is determined.)

5. EQUITY FUNDS : THE ATTRIBUTABLE LEVEL OF PROFIT = 'EARN-
   INGS' = PROFIT AFTER TAX AND PREFERENCE DIVIDEND BUT
   BEFORE EXTRAORDINARY ITEMS
   (Equity Funds comprise Ordinary share capital plus reserves.)

6. EARNINGS PER SHARE is derived from 'Earnings' (ratio 5) divided by the
   number of ordinary shares (Chapter 5). Any 'minority interests' would be deducted
   in the case of group accounts.

7. PER (PRICE : EARNINGS) being the market price per ordinary share divided by
   'earnings per share' (Chapter 5).

This progression of ROCEs and ROIs (return on investment) is illustrated in *Example 6.1*
for the GROWSTRONG COMPANY where enhancement of the return to equity
through the use of gearing (borrowing and earning 'a turn' on loan capital) is calculated
net of the tax benefit arising in respect of the loan interest.

The ratios 1, 2, and 3 can be computed net of taxation and if it is accepted that
management's financial decisions may limit the tax bill, the after-tax figures will provide a
better measure of their efficiency. However, it is usually considered that management
performance should be measured separately in respect of its operating functions
(efficiency in the use of operating assets – ratio 2 above) and its financing functions
(raising and structure of capital, control of funds. and financing decisions including the tax
factor). The efficient use of long-term funds in the interests of the equity shareholder and
the effect on EPS is fully illustrated in Chapter 4. The comparison of the return on capital
ratios 3 and 4 incorporates the results of gearing.

The various measures of capital employed can be computed as at the end of the
financial year, or if there have been material shifts of capital during the year, more
properly as a weighted average. Historical and/or current cost accounts may be used. For
historical accounts, their limitations (particularly point 7, page 204) should be borne in
mind.

It has been noted that ROCE based on operating capital can be improved by an
increase in the profit margin (operating profit: sales) and/or the turnover of assets (sales:
operating assets). The derivative 'cost : sales' ratios and the 'sales : assets' ratios are set
out in the pyramid of ratios, and their ultimate potential effect on ROCE can be seen
(Chapter 13).

Prior to the Companies Act 1981 (4 Sch. CA 85), not all the information in the following
example of a statement useful for vertical analysis was available to external users.

Example 14.1

Summarised profit and loss account of
ABC plc for the years ended

	19x2		19x1	
	£'000	%	£'000	%
SALES, net of return of sales	500	100	400	100
less manufactured COST OF SALES	400	80	310	77.5
GROSS PROFIT	100	20	90	22.5
less non-manufacturing expenses, e.g. administration, marketing, sales, distribution	55	11	60	15.0
OPERATING PROFIT BEFORE INTEREST AND TAX	45	9	30	7.5
less Interest	10	2	10	2.5

OPERATING PROFIT BEFORE TAX	35	7	20	5.0
less Taxation provision	10	2	8	2.0
NET OPERATING PROFIT BEFORE TAX	25	5	12	3.0

The common comparative scale used in this example is more useful for analysis than a consideration of the absolute amounts. After making allowance for the rate of inflation in the period, management may be satisfied with the 25% increase in turnover. Their satisfaction will be determined by considering the increase against that planned and against any unforeseen conditions experienced in their market. The increased percentage of manufactured cost of sales and the consequent fall in the gross profit percentage is generally unsatisfactory and should lead to an enquiry internally to pinpoint the matters for management action. This increase has been offset by a reduction of non-manufacturing expense of 4% of sales, the reasons for which should be adduced. It could be, for example, that in 19x1 there was extra expenditure on marketing, the 'pay-off' for which was delayed until 19x2 resulting in increased turnover in the latter year. These brief comments confirm the view (item 2, page 235) that the principal value of ratio analysis is to suggest questions which need answering, with significant changes being brought into focus.

Following the CA 1981 (44 Sch. CA 85) the above analysis is open to external users of the accounts of large and listed companies, the *cost of sales* and *gross profit* figures – invariably published in North America – now being disclosure items in the UK. There are views that in the production of future accounting standards, emphasis should be given to *disclosure* requirements since all *measurement* standards rest on this need.

GROSS PROFIT PERCENTAGE

This figure, which is the difference between sales and cost of sales expressed as a percentage of the selling price (called mark-up when the gross profit is expressed as a percentage of cost of sales), is a key measure of profitability for management and a key comparative figure in relation to competitors. It is also an important test for auditors and for the Inland Revenue concerned with the validity of the accounts. A material change in it between accounting periods could indicate errors or fraud in the figures of sales, stock, purchases or manufactured cost of sales. Leading cases of fraud have involved the falsification of closing stock values to 'raise' profits (see Chapter 1, page 15 *et seq*).

OPERATING PROFIT BEFORE INTEREST AND TAX : SALES

Until the CA 1981 (4 Sch. CA 85) requirement for certain companies to publish their gross profit percentage, this ratio was regarded by analysts as the profit margin on sales as it was the key profit figure publicly available. It can be compared internally and externally with figures for previous periods and within a particular industry or trade. Forecasts of future profitability are judged from its application to budgeted (or projected) sales.

It should be appreciated that while a 9% margin as used in *Example 14.2* below could apply for a company in the manufacturing sector, it is untypical for, say, a supermarket where the margin could be as low as 1%. Supermarkets can, of course, operate on such small margins because of their ability to manage on a much smaller investment of funds per £ of sales (asset turnover) than manufacturers.

Example 14.2

	Supermarket £	Manufacturer £
A. Sales	50,000,000	50,000,000
B. Trading/Operating profit before interest and tax	500,000	4,500,000
Profit margin B : A	1%	9%
C. Trading/Operating assets	2,500,000	40,000,000
Asset turnover A/C	20 times	1.25 times
ROCE (Operating capital) B as a % of C	20%	11.25%

The manufacturer's margin is nine times that of the supermarket, but the latter's ability to turn over that profit 20 times compared with the manufacturer's 1.25 times, leads to a much higher ROCE for the supermarket operation.

Put another way the supermarket's investment (£2.5m) is considerably less than that of the manufacturer (£40m) and this is reflected in the comparative returns on capital:

	ROCE	=	Margin	×	Asset turnover
Supermarket	20.00%	=	1%	×	20
Manufacturer	11.25%	=	9%	×	1.25

The commentary on the pyramid of ratios (Chapter 13) noted that ROCE can be increased:

either by increasing 'the profit margin' or the 'asset turnover', or both, . . . that the margin can be increased by raising the price mix of products and/or reducing costs, and that asset turnover can be improved by increasing sales and/or increasing the efficiency of the use of assets.

While internal analysts acting for management can track changes or proposed changes in ROCE through all levels of both sides of the hierarchy of ratios, many of the subsidiary cost ratios are not available to external analysts. Commentary is therefore directed at the 'turnover of assets' ratio and the more important subsidiary operating ratios.

SALES : OPERATING ASSETS

If this ratio is based on historical accounts, a comparison with previous periods should account for any revaluation of assets during the period and note that the depreciation of assets will reduce the net asset values included in the denominator. If 'sales' takes an earlier account of inflationary rises than such effect on asset prices, that too can distort the picture. Over time, current cost figures are likely to be more comparable. While a rising figure of asset turnover may well mean an improvement in performance. it is well to note that it could also indicate overtrading (increasing turnover without regard to the need for additional supporting capital expenditure and working capital) considered later in relation to liquidity/solvency.

DEBTORS : SALES

This is a credit control indicator ultimately affecting asset turnover and ROCE. It is also important as a measure of the liquidity of the company. The cash flowing in from debtors, i.e. sales revenue, is clearly of utmost importance to the company's ability to pay its way. In an inflationary era, with the value of money falling over time, additional impetus is given to the efficient collection of debts. In effect, a debt represents the situation of a company financing customers while it is outstanding, the cost being the cost of capital plus the cost of inflation. These factors should have been included in the considerations of the company's pricing policy, but in practice, the cost of capital, the pattern of payments and the pace of inflation may have been wrongly estimated.

The '*Debtors' ratio*' is calculated and expressed as 'debtors as a percentage of sales' or by stating the average number of days the debts are outstanding, e.g.

Example 14.3

Debtors as stated in the balance sheet	£600,000
Sales as stated in the profit and loss account	£3,600,000

The *Debtors/sales* percentage is   16.6%

The average number of days the debts were outstanding is

$$\frac{600,000}{3,600,000} \times 365 \text{ days} = 61 \text{ days}$$

The period of 61 days is comparable over time between companies in the same line of business. It is directly comparable as a standard of efficiency of credit control with the contractual period of credit given to customers, e.g. 30 days after delivery. However, 61 days is not unusual in practice against one month's credit; delivery time, delay in despatching invoices and tardy payers being among the reasons for the gap between the two figures which management must try to reduce, if not close.

Sending out invoices with the goods is one way of improving the position. Another way is to endeavour to identify tardy payers and potential bad debts *before* any goods are despatched. One well-known company of size, on daily receipt of its own computer-based, pre-printed order forms from customers, feeds the data into its computer to update debtor (customer) accounts to show the balance outstanding should the orders be met. The computer then compares these debtor balances with a tape record of the credit level allocated to each customer, and prints out a management-by-exception tabulation of those customers whose balance, should today's orders be met, will exceed the limit. The credit control manager then has to decide whether to stop or delay the order while he attempts to extract payment from the customer. A falling collection period normally indicates improved credit control if sales levels are maintained. A change to a policy of factoring debts (effectively selling them to a collection agency for a commission) would, of course, significantly change the ratio.

STOCK : SALES

The CA 1981 – 4 Sch. CA 85 – requirement for listed and large companies to disclose 'cost of sales' figures will allow external analysts to calculate 'stock turnover' ratios based on those figures rather than on the value of 'sales' as hitherto.

The stock turnover ratio is calculated and expressed as 'average stock' as a percentage of 'cost of sales' or as the number of days of stock held. Greater efficiency in stock control will have the effect of increasing 'asset turnover' and ROCE.

Stock control policy is directed, on the one hand, to ensuring a sufficiency of stocks of raw material to keep production flowing and of finished goods to meet the needs of customers, and on the other hand to ensuring that stocks are at a realistic level which minimises the cost of capital involved. Clearly, stocks on shelves in stores or in salesrooms represent idle capital on which no return is being earned. Of course, stocks may be bought in advance of anticipated rising prices, if the item or commodity is a significant part of production, or bought in advance if a shortage is anticipated, with an apparent adverse effect on stock turnover ratios. Obviously, manufacturing stocks turn over much more slowly than those of retailers and like must be compared with like.

Example 14.4

Calculation of stock turnover ratios
X Manufacturing plc

	Year 19x1 £'000	Year 19x2 £'000
Finished goods		
Opening stock	2,500	3,000
Closing stock	3,000	3,500
Average stock	2,750	3,250
Cost of sales	7,000	10,000
Average stock: COS	39.3%	32.5%
Number of days' stock	144 days	119 days

Note: $\dfrac{2,750}{7,000} \times 365 = 144$ days $\qquad \dfrac{3,250}{10,000} \times 365 = 119$ days

For this company, which has increased its sales above the level of inflation, the trend of the stock turnover ratio is favourable.

WORKING CAPITAL: SALES

In so far as working capital equals net current assets (current assets less current liabilities), a realistic level for this ratio is determined by the optimum levels of each of the underlying categories of current assets, i.e. the optimum stock turnover ratios, debtors' ratio and the minimum cash (cash for manufacturers should be virtually 'Nil') offset by the acceptable level of trade creditors (see creditors' ratio, later), necessary bank overdraft (determined by cash budgeting) and other current liabilities. The particular ratio determined for a company will indicate the level of working capital needed to support a given level of sales. A falling trend of this ratio could indicate overtrading and a rising trend, overcapitalisation (see later). The ratio will vary considerably between the supermarket (cash sales, credit purchases and quick turnover) and the manufacturer needing to support operations over a much longer working capital cycle.

FIXED ASSETS : SALES

Proper balance must be maintained by management of the amount of funds invested in fixed assets and the amount invested in working capital in relation to a given level of sales. Improvement in the investment/sales ratios will improve ROCE. Fixed assets are long-term investments and control is best instituted *before* funds are committed in this area and will result from an effective capital budgeting system and investment appraisal. Lease or buy (hire or purchase) decisions should form part of this control. If the business under consideration is large with numbers of divisions and/or subsidiaries, then disposal of those parts with low profitability/high investment outcomes may be indicated. The possible distortion effect for comparisons over time of "sales" in an inflationary period tending to rise, set against the falling depreciated historical cost of fixed assets, resulting in improving ratios even though there is no real gain in efficiency, needs emphasis and points to the option of using current cost accounts.

Tests of Liquidity

It has been noted that liquidity is more immediately important to business survival in the short term than profitability. Unless companies are able to pay their debts as they become due, i.e. be liquid and solvent, to be able to pay immediately or in the foreseeable future, they will not survive. A survey of business failures in England and Wales, sampling one hundred private companies which failed, showed that the main causes of failure in the opinion of the Official Receivers were:

1. Mismanagement.
2. Insufficient capital.
3. Insufficient working capital.

Perhaps not unnaturally, the directors of the companies ignored attribute (1) and listed 'insufficient capital/working capital'. It may be agreed that if the prime cause of failure was lack of capital, it probably followed from a lack of, or inefficient, budgetary planning and control. The failures presumably arose not only through a lack of capital and an inability to raise it, but also through an inability to anticipate the need for it.

While liquidity ratios are an indication of a company's ability to meet its obligations as they become due and falling trends are danger signals, it is necessary to keep their limitation in view. Like the balance sheet itself, they show the position at one moment of time and as cash flows the position is continually changing. Immediately following the date of the balance sheet is a period in which, for many companies, the tax bill has to be paid. At balance sheet date, the company may have a large amount of cash in hand recently raised to meet early projected capital expenditure. The level of the agreed bank overdraft facility is not disclosed in the accounts. The company's *ability to raise funds* is an important factor in assessing liquidity. This, in turn, hinges on the level of profitability and the strength of the assets to provide security for loans. The sources and application of funds statement will be useful to the external assessor in tracking the company's control over the outcome of its plans and their effect on its liquidity.

A banker asked to raise overdraft levels or provide a loan would be as much interested in substantiated budgets, particularly the cash budget, as in ratios deriving from the last available accounts. Nevertheless, they would probably be considered as part of the available information.

CURRENT RATIO (ALSO KNOWN AS THE WORKING CAPITAL RATIO)

This ratio measures the relationship between current assets and current liabilities and the ability of the company to pay its way in the short term. Text books often quote a general norm of 2 : 1, probably derived from statistics over a long period, but it has been earlier noted that during the inflationary 1970s the general ratio fell to around 1.5 : 1 as bank overdrafts particularly and trade creditors rose. Manufacturers can be expected to have higher ratios than retailers, the latter being financed by trade creditors and with cash sales often predominant. Rising current ratios should not necessarily be taken as indicating increasing strength. In fact, following an analysis of stock turnover and debtors' ratios they may point to inefficient stock and credit control. A current ratio of less than par would normally be regarded as unhealthy, it would indicate a deficit of working capital, or looked at another way, of short-term creditors financing long-term assets.

The optimum level of this ratio varies with the nature of a company's business and of its underlying current assets. In interpreting and comparing current ratios, consideration must be given to the proportions of the underlying current assets. Two companies might have the same current ratio, one having much more cash and the other more stock. The latter's stock level may be optimum, expressing the minimum needed for an ongoing manufacturer, the former may be a retailer naturally more liquid, or alternatively a manufacturer with idle cash.

LIQUID RATIO (ALSO KNOWN AS THE QUICK RATIO, OR THE ACID TEST)

This ratio attempts to show the ability of a company to meet its immediate obligations out of those current assets which are in cash or near-cash form (e.g. realisable debtors, short-term investments). Manufacturers' stocks which obviously would not be turned into cash for some time would be excluded from the calculation, which for them would be:

Current assets less stocks : current liabilities.

The theoretical norm is par (1 : 1), but in practice ratios for manufacturers are found between 0.90 : 1. This probably follows the recent trend in an inflationary period to use more bank credit on overdraft or short-term loan. For retailers, 0.40 : 1 may be normal and is accounted for by the fact that retailers have high levels of cash sales while dealing with their suppliers on a one month's (or more) credit basis.

Bank overdrafts are sometimes excluded from current liabilities in the calculation so that the ratio shows the position without reliance on that source of funds. A good liquid ratio in these circumstances would be an indicator of extra strength – that residing in the perhaps untapped source of bank credit. In practice, most companies rely, some over-rely, on banks. It would be a useful extra source of information if companies gave some indication of the extent of the facility unused. In assessing the likely liquidity state of the company in the immediate future, analysts would note the proximity of tax payments, comments in the report and accounts about future capital expenditure plans and the more immediate contracted capital expenditure, plans to raise long-term funds and information on the maturity dates of loans, redeemable capital and on any contingent liabilities.

The *debtors' ratio* and the *stock turnover ratios* have been considered not only as to their potential to increase ROCE, but also as to their importance in a consideration of liquidity.

The Working Capital : Total assets ratio, i.e. net current assets : total assets, is related to the ideal capital structure – that is, the amount of funds optimally invested in both fixed assets and working capital. The higher the ratio, the greater the likelihood of a higher turnover of capital; alternatively, this could be an indication of an inefficient build-up of stocks and/or debtors.

In general, liquidity ratios provide a useful means of monitoring changes in balance sheet items, although they give no indication of the causes of such changes. *The funds statement* provides a summary of the changes in successive balance sheets and an analysis of the impact of the changes in the liquid assets and the short-term borrowings of a company.

RELATIONSHIP BETWEEN DEBTORS AND CREDITORS

Once established for a company or industry/trade, this relationship should remain steady. The terms of trade are not generally known to external analysts. If creditors have to be paid within one month and debtors take or are given two months or more to pay, an adjustment to the liquidity ratios should be made to reflect the changed cash flow; alternatively, as in the case of retailers considered earlier, the differences between the credit given (if any) and taken can be reflected in the determination of the acceptable norms for the ratios.

OVERTRADING

The dangers which may ensue from overtrading, that is the expanding of turnover without the provision of the necessary support capital, have been referred to. Not having properly planned the required increased funding, the company will turn to the first available sources – often to the bank, with overdraft levels rising, and to suppliers for extra credit with perhaps delayed settlements. In so far as some of these short-term funds eventually are supporting fixed asset investment, a deficit of working capital arises and current and liquid ratios fall. Interests costs increase. Marginal overtrading, where deficits are temporary and flexible budgets have anticipated long-term funding needs which are being provided for, are not dangerous. Where, however, a company over-stretches itself, its inability to meet current liabilities may lead first to cessation of supply of materials and credit, and action by creditors to recover amounts due, ending with the liquidation of the business.

OVER-CAPITALISATION

This is the opposite phenomenon to overtrading. It means that a company is not earning a sufficient return on its cpaital and may indicate inefficient management of working capital. Pointers to over-capitalisation are:

Working capital: Sales. A rising trend over a period of time and in relation to the norm for the industry/trade.

Current and liquid ratios. Ratios in excess of say 2 : 1 and par respectively, and the rising trend of cash or/and short-term investments.

Stocks, debtors' and creditors' ratios. Excessive turnover periods for the various levels of stocks, i.e. raw materials, work in progress and finished goods. Internally these should be compared with purchases, cost of production and cost of sales per annum. A rising debtors' ratio and a falling creditors' ratio.

Over-capitalisation (undertrading) may be temporary or seasonal, in which case, surplus liquidity is usually invested short-term to provide some return to offset the cost of capital and the cost of inflation. When it is apparent that over-capitalisation is more permanent, perhaps because the maximum share of the market has been obtained and the market has stabilised at a particular level, management options to deal with the situation include the paying of higher dividends (lower retentions) to shareholders, the purchase or redemption of the company's own shares, a formal scheme for the reduction of capital, or diversification into fields different from, but allied to, the main business, for example, the Imperial (Tobacco) group diversified into the food and drinks industry. Over-capitalisation leads to a lower ROCE. Clearly, the excess funds lying idle must be invested so as to earn an adequate return against the cost of capital and inflation, or must be returned to the shareholders.

CREDITORS : SALES

This is the measure of the trend in the credit allowed or taken. In so far as it does not compare like with like, it is not satisfactory. 'Creditors' in the ratio should be confined to 'trade creditors' and ideally should be compared with the 'cost of purchases' to give the average payment period, i.e.

$$\frac{\text{Average trade creditors}}{\text{Cost of materials}} \times 365 \text{ (days)}$$

The cost of materials is not normally available to external analysts.

244

A rising trend of either of these ratios may be an indication of shortage of cash and of overtrading. Suppliers, as unsecured trade creditors, are keenly concerned with the credit standing of their customer company and with its liquidity position. They, together with the banks, will usually be among the first to want to take action to safeguard their position. Their first (reluctant) action would be to stop supply or refuse credit.

Tests of Solvency

Tests of liquidity are also tests of solvency, but whereas liquidity refers to current obligations, solvency relates to the ability of a company to pay its way over the longer term – mainly to repay at maturity date long-term loans. The structure of capital, that is the relationship of shareholders' funds plus long-term loans to the investment in fixed assets and working capital respectively, and the relationship of shareholders' funds, long-term loans and current liabilities to each other have an important impact on solvency.

Readers are referred to page 34 and *Illustration 2.1* which gives a visual impression of the looked-for relationship between long and short-term funds, and between the funds and assets. It is interesting in this respect to consider these relationships in *Example 14.5*, where are set out the averages for all listed companies in the UK in a recent year:

Example 14.5

Balance sheet relationships – all UK listed companies

FUNDS			ASSETS		
Ordinary shares	18%				
Reserves	29%				
	—				
Shareholders' funds	47%	47%	*Fixed assets*		43%
	—				
Long-term loans	13%				
Other long-term funds	4%	17%			
	—				
Total long-term funds		64%			43%
Short-term funds			*Current assets*		
Creditors	21%		Stocks	24%	
Other current liabilities	7%		Debtors	25%	
Overdrafts	8%	36%	Cash	3%	
	—		Investments	5%	57%
		100%		—	100%

While average statistics conceal any wide divergencies, *Example 14.5* shows an acceptable relationship between "shareholders' funds" and "fixed assets", the former completely providing for the latter and the excess of these plus other long-term funds providing some 21% (working capital) of the investment in current assets, the remainder coming from short-term fund sources.

SHAREHOLDERS' FUNDS : TOTAL ASSETS

This is a basic test of solvency, measuring the margin of safety provided by the shareholders' funds for unsecured creditors in an enforced liquidation of the company. Taking the figures in the above example (*14.5*), 47% of the book value of the assets must be lost before the position of the unsecured creditors would be affected. The actual position would vary according to the realisable value of the assets in the situation envisaged. If 'goodwill' figured among 'fixed assets', it would be excluded therefrom and also from the reserves, as it would probably be worthless in a compulsory liquidation.

This ratio, known as the *proprietary ratio*, is therefore important to unsecured creditors – the higher it is from their point of view, the better.

DEBT : EQUITY

The phrase 'debt capital' sometimes describes long-term loans only, sometimes current liabilities are included. From a company viewpoint, debt capital however defined is more risky than 'equity', for if creditors are not paid (interest and/or amount owed), they can take action leading to the company's liquidation. 'Equity capital' is less risky because dividends are not a legal obligation and directors may recommend in certain circumstances (e.g. falling profitability) that they should not be paid. For this extra risk compared with that accepted by long-term lenders, equity shareholders expect to get a higher return. It follows, therefore, that although from the creditors' and the company's points of view, the higher the equity the less the risk involved in meeting fixed obligations, higher equity involves a higher overall cost of capital. Conversely, the efficient use of borrowed funds where the return to equity is enhanced by the excess of the earnings deriving from the funds over the net of tax interest payable, leads to higher debt : equity ratios. The debt : equity relationship is illustrated in the gearing examples on page 73 *et seq*.

COVER FOR VARIOUS CLASSES OF CAPITAL

Security cover is indicated by the following ratios:

Interest cover. Profit before interest and tax : interest (see page 73). This ratio is a measure of the level to which profit could decline without affecting the company's ability to meet its fixed interest obligations. In so far as 'profit' does not equate to 'cash', the company must have the ability to provide the latter.

Preference share dividend cover. Profit after tax : preference dividend (page 56). This ratio is a measure of the level to which after-tax profit could decline before the preference dividend would be threatened. However, it should be borne in mind that, unlike interest, there is no legal obligation to pay dividends. The directors may recommend that dividends should be passed in the interest of the company as a whole, where profitability has diminished or is non-existent.

Equity dividend cover. Profit after tax and preference dividend and before extraordinary items : equity dividend; or earnings : dividend (E/D ratio) (see page 140). This ratio measures the security afforded by 'attributable profit' to the equity shareholders' dividend.

The *Pay-out ratio*, in a normal situation for corporation tax, is the reciprocal of the equity dividend cover.

Growth and Future Potential

Most likely users of the corporate report and accounts have an interest in the survival and profitable continuity of a company. A limiting factor of most of the information available is that it is about what has happened in the past, whereas concern is concentrated on the future. While other parties dealing with a company are interested in its growth, e.g. major suppliers for whom the business may be of vital interest (the critical effect on supplying companies of the liquidation of Rolls-Royce in 1971 is an example), as are the company's management and staff (it may affect their livelihood and careers), the information derived from published accounts and extrapolated as *future potential* is mostly absorbed and analysed by the investor – private or institutional.

Readers are referred to the commentary in the context of the GROWSTRONG business on the relationship between the market price of a company's ordinary shares, the price-earnings ratio and the net asset value of the shares (pages 129/30).

MARKET PRICE OF THE ORDINARY SHARES

This is the stock market's estimate of the value of the shares based, theoretically, upon the expected flow of earnings and dividends related to those shares. The price will change as it reacts to various influences judged to affect the company's future prospects. Examples are Budget changes to corporation tax, personal tax, VAT etc., level of interest rates, level of inflation, factors affecting the company's products and markets, e.g. new technology, competition and social change, or news of, or rumours about, take-over/merger activity. Such factors impinge on estimates of future profitability, and market prices are geared to forecast earnings.

A ratio which may be related to the market price of the ordinary shares is the book value of net assets per share.

NET ASSET VALUE (NAV) PER ORDINARY SHARE

The book value of the ordinary shareholders' funds is usually shown as a sub-total in the balance sheet. Dividing this figure by the number of ordinary shares in issue at the end of the year gives the NAV per share (see *Example 5.5.8*, page 130).

It is equal to the book value of the gross assets less all liabilities, including preference share capital, divided by the number of ordinary shares. Using current cost accounts, if available, will give a more useful NAV per share.

The difference between the market price of the ordinary share and its net asset value is some indication for the investor of (1) the risk of the investment and (2) of the earnings potential of the company as seen by the market. If the stock market price is below NAV, then either the share is attractively priced (if the investor so judges profit potential) or is realistically priced (as the market judges future potential). The investor must decide whether to back his own judgement.

In looking at NAVs, any goodwill in the balance sheet should be excluded. Goodwill normally appears in the balance sheet only when it has been *paid* for, and is the result of the double entry reflecting the excess of the purchase price paid for an acquired company over a fair market value of the latter's net assets.

Example 14.6

A plc acquired all the ordinary shares in B Ltd for £10m, settling the purchase price by the issue of eight million of its own ordinary shares, nominal value £1 each. The shares were thus issued at a premium of £2m. The agreed net asset value of B Ltd was £9m.

Extract of the consolidated balance sheet entries of this transaction:

	£m		£m
Ordinary share capital	8	Net assets	9
Share premium account	2	Goodwill	1
	—		—
	10		10
	—		—

Presumably A plc paid more for B Ltd than the market worth of its net assets because it considered it could earn its desired return on the £10m investment. The £1m included in the price is the sum paid for goodwill judged to exist at the date of the transaction. It relates to A plc's management expectation to earn profits in excess of the desired return on the £9m net assets acquired. This excess, sometimes called super-profits, is therefore related to the price paid for goodwill.

Example 14.7

If B Ltd's (*Example 14.6*) operating profits before tax in the past few representative years have averaged £1m per annum and are expected at least to be maintained, and A plc plans, say, a return of 10% on the investment, then the simple capitalisation of the earnings is:

$$\frac{£1m \times 100}{10} = £10m$$

and therefore makes the business worth the amount paid for it.

This basic computation is made on the assumption that past profits will be maintained in the future. Many circumstances, some presently unforeseen, including the relative efficiency of the new management to the old, may cause the expected profits to remain unrealised. It is apparent, therefore, that the payment for goodwill was made for a value determined (by negotiation which might have affected the outcome purchase price) at a particular date and that this value will change, i.e. increase or decrease with the passage of time. The balance sheet value of goodwill should be excluded from the calculation of the NAV of the ordinary share. When in doubt, leave it out! (see pages 88/9).

INVESTMENT RATIOS

Those ratios which relate a company's *last reported earnings* with the *current market price* of the ordinary shares, and therefore link the past with the future, are:

Price-earnings ratio (PER): Market price per ordinary share/earnings per ordinary share.

Earnings yield: Earnings per share × 100/market price per ordinary share.

Dividend yield: Dividends per ordinary share × 100/market price per ordinary share.

Commentary and examples of these ratios for the GROWSTRONG enterprise appear in Chapter 5 (5.5 and 5.6).

These ratios focus on earnings and dividend per share – two of the factors which influence the investor. Growth of earnings leading to a rising share price is effected by the company management and workforce and will reflect the company's financial and operating efficiency. With growth of earnings will normally come rising dividends. But some boards of directors are more conservative over dividend policy than others. The investor will make his investment decision based on his own criteria for risk, including dividend and potential capital gain on the disposal of the investment. The dividend yield ratio and dividend cover would be important to the investor who seeks a regular cash flow of a desirable level from his investment. High earnings should mean high market prices, but if the company's dividend policy is conservative because it needs high retentions of earnings to support new investment, it could attract investment from those looking for capital gains but not from those wanting regular cash flows. The institutional investor, e.g. the pension fund manager, is among those who are normally likely to give preference to investment in companies with generous dividend policies, and less weight to possible capital appreciation.

COMPARISONS IN ANALYSIS

The analysis of the *trend* of results of a company over several years, sometimes called *horizontal analysis*, must account for the effects of changing price levels and any changes in accounting policies. The longer the time span of analysis, the greater the likely difficulty of comparison. *Example 10.4*, page 186, showed the 'earnings per share' of J. Bibby & Sons Ltd over a five-year period adjusted for inflation after restating the figures.

An example of *vertical analysis* is that given in *Example 14.5*, page 245, where each balance sheet item was expressed as a percentage of balance sheet totals. Similarly, profit and loss account items can be expressed as a percentage, e.g. of sales, see *Example 14.1*, page 237. Trends over time of the results of a company are more apparent using a common comparative scale and eliminating absolute amounts. *Inter-firm comparisons* co-ordinated from the centre (see last chapter) benefit from this technique.

The corporate report and accounts is an historical document even though it may be expressed in current cost terms

While the analyst is more interested in current and likely future happenings, nevertheless the information available in the report and accounts is important to his work. He can consider the trend of the performance of the one company over a period of time and he can compare the performance of different companies in the same line of business, one with another. This is best done through the inter-firm comparison schemes, but such an arrangement is limited to the internal managements of the partaking companies. These managements can also compare the results shown by the latest accounts with those budgeted. The external analyst must make do with the information available to him and besides the accounts, historic and current cost (if given), he will consider the chairman's statement, divisional summaries, and the sources and application of funds statement published within the report. He will gather and use as much other information about a company as he can obtain, e.g. about its products, and their market potential, and about the industry/trade in which it is placed. He will tend to become a specialist and expert in a particular field, be it the oil, electronics or food industry, for example.

He will be constantly on the search for answers to questions such as:
1. What type of business is it? What is the economic/market outlook for the trade/industry in which it is engaged? Is the sector relatively stable or subject to rapid change and innovation?
2. What is the level of risk involved? What is the competition at home and abroad?
3. What is the industrial relations position? What is the likelihood of strikes?
4. What are the trends of earnings and dividends per share and how do these

compare with alternative investments?

5. What is the structure of capital? Is the relationship between ordinary shares and loan capital profitable for equity? Or is the company too highly geared in relation to potential profit levels and the cover for loan interest?

6. Is there a reasonable relationship between long-term funds and investment in fixed assets leaving a reasonable surplus for working capital? What is the liquidity position?

7. Does the sources and application of funds statement evidence a properly funded and developing capital expenditure programme? Are there any material contingent liabilities and/or leasing commitments not shown in the balance sheet?

8. Is the company overtrading or, alternatively, over-capitalised? What action is being taken to deal with such situations?

9. What does the chairman report and do his comments complement the accounts and other information available?

10. Is the audit report clean; if not, what is the significance of the qualification?

15

A worked example of ratio analysis with examination hints

International Industrial plc

Interpretation and analysis questions in the examinations of the professional accountancy bodies vary in length and content, as those included in WORKBOOK 3 indicate. As for all questions, the time available to complete an answer will be determined by the mark allocation. The question exemplified in this chapter, relating to International Industrial plc,* carried 28 marks in a 100 mark, 3 hour financial accounting paper. The time available was therefore 28% of 3 hours, being just over 50 minutes. This would include reading time.

Examination candidates have a natural inclination to start writing immediately and tend not to give sufficient time to the prerequisites of (i) reading and understanding the question and (ii) thinking about the answer. READ, THINK, then WRITE is the logical progression.

Examination hints

1. Take a sheet of answer paper and, when reading and thinking about the question, write a list of short pointers to the answer. This sheet can be headed 'working paper for question X' and included with the submitted answer.
2. Thought should then be given to the framework, sub-headings and detail of the answer. The pointers to the answer (1 above) should be numbered so that they fall into a logical sequence within determined sub-heads.
3. Answer sub-headings for this type of question *invariably* will include (i) liquidity, (ii) profitability, (iii) capital structure, (iv) future potential, with other heads as indicated by the requirements of the particular question, e.g. (v) special features.
4. As the information available to the candidate is limited (often to two succeeding balance sheets and extracts from profit and loss accounts) and historical (even where current cost information is included, see 5 following), he should briefly note for the examiner in a preface to his answer the *limitations of ratio analysis* (see Chapter 14). Candidates should therefore have prepared this information *before* the examination.
5. Special features (3 above) would include product/market, industry and other environmental features affecting the company and currently must note *the effect of inflation* on the analysis. General comment on this can be prepared *before* the examination.

---

* This example is based on an examination question set by the author for the Chartered Association of Certified Accountants.

Candidates will not adjust figures for inflation unless specifically asked, with relevant (e.g. retail price) indices being made available.

6. Candidates will have considered *before* the examination the ratios to be included in the analysis under the various sub-heads. Using a sheet of examination paper suitably headed, e.g. 'Appendix to Financial Report', the selected ratios, the basis of the ratio calculation, the figures used and the arithmetical result should then be listed, e.g. (as taken from International Industrial plc following):

> *Liquidity*
> 1. *Liquid ratio*   Current Assets (less all stocks):
>   Current Liabilities (excluding bank overdrafts)

19x4	*19x5*
555 : 355 = 1.56 to 1	335 : 285 = 1.17 to 1

This working paper can then be used as the basis of the report on the financial position of the company usually requested and, being referred to in and attached to that report, will suitably impress the Examiner of the candidate's professional approach.

The advantage to the candidate of setting out the information in this way is that it enables the Examiner to allocate marks according to whether the ratio description is relevant, the base figures are correctly extracted from the accounts and the end result properly computed. Very many candidates, in the author's experience, restrict themselves to, for example:

> *Liquid ratio*   19x4   (1.84)   19x3   (1.46)

This presentation, with incorrect figures under any valid computation of the Liquid Ratio, does not tell the Examiner whether the candidate can correctly describe the ratios, whether he has selected the correct base figures but made a wrong calculation, or whether he selected the wrong base figures. He can only award NIL marks.

7. When writing the report within the framework determined (2 and 3 above), additional points entering the mind, unless relevant to the paragraph being written, should be added to those available (1 above) for later consideration, so that the current trend of thought is not interrupted. These additional points can be written into the report subsequently even though they may be out of logical sequence. The Examiner understands that within the time available it is not possible to present that standard of report which could be produced in practice (often after amending first drafts).

8. Invariably the limited information available to the Examinee leaves him with a number of unanswered questions important to the analysis. For example, 'To whom is the report addressed and for what purpose is it to be used?' While many features of the report would be common, there could be different emphasis if written for internal management, or for a bank asked to extend loan facilities. Other questions unanswered might be When are the debentures repayable? Are they covered by a fixed or floating charge? What is the current value of property? Is the bank overdraft secured? It is recommended that candidates do NOT provide assumed answers. The best course is to indicate that the answer is a preliminary report, listing in the conclusion questions to be answered before a more detailed report can be given. This provides the Examiner with knowledge of the candidate's ability to formulate such questions.

Question

INTERNATIONAL INDUSTRIAL plc
The summarised consolidated accounts of the INTERNATIONAL INDUSTRIAL plc

group of companies for the years 19x3 and 19x4, together with certain additional information including a number of calculated ratios, follow:

Consolidated Balance Sheets as at 31 October

	19x4		19x3	
	£'000	£'000	£'000	£'000
Gross funds employed				
Share capital INTERNATIONAL INDUSTRIAL plc, authorised, issued and fully paid.				
1 million (19x3 – 750,000) ordinary shares of 50 pence each		500		375
Reserves				
Share premium account	125		100	
General reserve	110		80	
Fixed assets revaluation reserve	60		17	
Profit and loss account	20	315	18	215
Group shareholders' funds		815		590
10% Debentures	500		500	
10% Mortgage on Freehold Property	100		—	
Minority interests in subsidiaries	52		48	
Deferred Corporation Tax	70	722	55	603
Long-term capital employed		1,537		1,193
Trade creditors	280		235	
Bank overdrafts	8		2	
Current Corporation tax	50		30	
Proposed ordinary dividend	25		20	
Current liabilities	—	363	—	287
		1,900		1,480

	19x4		19x3	
Assets in which gross funds are invested	£'000	£'000	£'000	£'000
Fixed assets				
Freehold land and buildings, after depreciation		450		385
Plant and machinery, equipment, vehicles and loose tools, after depreciation		425		375
		875		760
Goodwill and other tangibles		130		125
Unquoted investments at cost		50		50
		1,055		935
Current Assets				
Stocks of raw materials, work in progress and finished goods	290		210	
Trade debtors	400		325	
Bank balances, and cash balances	155	845	10	545
		1,900		1,480

Notes:
1. International Industrial plc acquired the whole of the share capital of Midland Engineering Limited on 1 May, 19x4. The purchase price was satisfied by the issue of International Industrial ordinary shares. 250,000 ordinary shares, nominal value 50 pence each, were issued at a total market value of £150,000.
2. Freehold land was revalued during the year and the enhancement was credited to revaluation reserve.
3. The £500,000 10% debentures are redeemable at par 20 to 22 years hence. They are secured by a floating charge.
4. The £100,000 mortgage on freehold property is repayable on 31 December, 19x8. The security in case of both the debentures and the mortgage relates only to the assets of the parent company. The mortgage was raised on 1 May, 19x4.

Extract from the Consolidated profit and loss accounts
for the year ended 31 October

	19x4		1	9x3
	£'000	£'000	£'000	£'000
TURNOVER		2,500		2,000
Net trading profit		220		160
Income from Unquoted investments		6		6
Net profit before interest and taxation		226		166
less interest on:				
Debentures	50		50	
Mortgage	5		—	
Bank overdraft	1	56	—	50
Net profit before tax		170		116
Corporation tax (50%) on this year's profit		73		58
Net profit after tax		97		58
less Minority interest in this year's profit		7		4
		90		54
less Extraordinary expenses after eliminating minority interest proportion and adjustment for taxation		8		4
Profit (net) attributable to International Industrial plc shareholders		82		50
less appropriations:				
Ordinary dividends – paid	25		20	
Ordinary dividends – proposed	25	50	20	40
		32		10
Transfer to General reserves		30		7
		2		3
Profit and loss account balance brought forward		18		15
Profit and loss account balance carried forward		20		18

Notes:
1. The Net trading profit is after charging all "ordinary" operating expenses. Tangible fixed assets excepting freehold land (no depreciation) and loose tools (revalued) are depreciated on the straight line bases over their estimated operating lives. Such depreciation in 19x4 amounted to £110,000.
2. The trade creditors of the Group generally allowed one month's credit and the Group's policy is to ensure prompt payment to maintain goodwill.
3. Capital commitments at 31 October, 19x4, amounted to £180,000.
4. The quoted market value of the International Industrial plc ordinary share on 1 November, 19x4, is £1.40.

Calculating accountancy ratios	19x4	19x3
1. *Liquid ratio:*	1.56	1.17
Current assets (less all stocks): Current liabilities (excluding bank overdrafts)		
2. *Current ratio*	2.05	1.89
Current assets: Current liabilities		
3. Working capital: sales	70 days	47 days
4. Debtors: sales	58 days	59 days
5. The proprietary ratio –		
Shareholders' funds: total assets	0.42	0.38
(after adjusting for minority interest and goodwill)		
6. Group floating assets: debentures	3.3 times covered	2.7 times
7. Sales: fixed plus current assets	1.35 times	1.39 times
(based on closing balance sheet values)		
8. Sales: fixed assets	2.48 times	2.26 times
9. Net trading profit as a percentage of sales	8.80%	8.00%
10. Net trading profit as a percentage of fixed plus current assets	11.88%	11.19%
11. Profit before tax and interest as a percentage of long-term capital employed	14.64%	13.91%
12. Profit before interest and after tax as a percentage of long-term capital employed	8.10%	6.80%
13. Pre-tax earnings attributable thereto as a percentage of group shareholders' funds	19.14%	18.30%
14. After tax earnings attributable thereto as a percentage of group shareholders' funds	11.04%	9.15%
15. Capital gearing ratio – Debentures plus mortgage: shareholders' funds	0.69	0.78

You are required to:
   (i) **Calculate and state** *for the year ended 31 October, 19x4 only,* **the following information:**
     (a) Book value of net assets attributable to each ordinary share.
     (b) Capital gearing based on the market capitalisation of International Industrial plc ordinary shares.
     (c) Earnings yield.
     (d) Dividend yield.

                                    (4 marks)

  (ii) **Discuss** *briefly,* **as a foreword to your answer to (iii) below, the relevance and shortcomings of accounting ratios to such an analysis.**

                                    (9 marks)

 (iii) Write a report USING THE INFORMATION AVAILABLE analysing the liquidity, the profitability and the potential of the INTERNATIONAL INDUSTRIAL group.

(15 marks)

(28 marks)

A Candidate's View of the Question

1. It is a good plan to read the REQUIREMENT of the question, usually emphasised with heavy print, *before* reading the detail of the question. Thoughts on reading it are then properly directed.
2. The candidate will note the three parts of the requirement and the marks allocated to each part. He will note (with satisfaction, if he has pre-prepared the answer) that 9 marks are available for the 'relevance and shortcomings of accounting ratios'. If this requirement had not been specified, the limitations of ratio analysis would, nevertheless, have been a needful preface to the answer.
3. Having read the question, the candidate will have noted that the examiner has provided a list of 15 ratios for the two years covered by the information. The implication may be that he considers the *calculation* of the ratios less relevant than their *appraisal*. These ratios, plus the additional four arising from the answer to part (i) of the question will form the basis of the report.
4. Nearly half of the marks for the question are available for parts (i) and (ii) with a time available of 23 minutes, leaving 27 minutes for part (iii). However, some 10 minutes (say) may have been fruitfully used for the reading of this relatively long question and for initial thoughts and notes. The candidate may thus decide to allow around 15 minutes for parts (i) and (ii), and 25 minutes for the report.
5. Should a candidate take a longer time than the available 50 minutes? The choice of each candidate will be based on the following considerations:
   1. Taking more time than 50 minutes will mean less time for other questions.
   2. Will marks be gained more certainly in any additional time taken for this question than in *some* of the time remaining? Put another way, are there other questions, or parts of such questions in the paper which the candidate will find difficulty in answering?
   3. If, at the 50 minute stage, the candidate cannot easily provide additional points for his report, he should move to a fresh question. The answer to the interpretation question should not be ruled off as it may be possible to return to it towards the end of the examination when reviewing answers, when new ideas may come to mind.

The notes to the balance sheet and profit and loss account

Note 1 to the balance sheet explains the increase in the ordinary share capital (£125,000) and the increase in the share premium account (£25,000) arising in the consolidated balance sheet. The increase in the issued capital was not to provide increased liquidity, but for the purchase of the net assets of the acquired company incorporated in the group balance sheet. The material increase in the number of ordinary shares half-way through the financial year will affect the calculation of earnings per share and earnings yield (see answer i(c) following).

Note 2 tells us that the security cover for the various securities provided by the assets includes for freehold property a realistic assessment of current value.

Note 3 tells us that the group has some considerable time to provide for the repayment of the debentures which, if inflation continues at recent levels, will mean a considerably reduced burden for the group in real monetary terms.

The £100,000 mortgage on freehold property (*Note 4*), however, is repayable in just over four years and this is to be noted in the appraisal of liquidity and the capital structure of the group. The calculation of the capital cover for both the Debenture and Mortgage Loan cannot be realistically assessed (they are secured on parent (holding) company assets) as the relevant assets value is not available.

Note 1 to the profit and loss account indicates that the net profit from trading (or operating) is properly determined and tells us the amount of annual depreciation provided under the historical cost convention. This figure may be related to capital commitments (*Note 3*) in an assessment of the group's ability to maintain or enlarge capital investment from 'profit'. The retentions of profit would need to be taken into account in this respect. The candidate should make a note to refer in his answer to the usefulness of a Sources and Application of Funds Statement in respect of both capital investment and liquidity appraisal. In the time available, the production of such a statement would have been difficult. It is likely that this information will be either provided or required to be produced for analysis in some future questions in this area.

Note 2 to the profit and loss account is important to the calculation of current and liquid ratios. The candidate will note the group's policy of prompt monthly payment to creditors against the (near) two months taken to collect debts (ratio 4 – given in the question).

Note 4 is needful to the calculation of the yields (answer i(c) and (d)) and to the alternative method of calculating capital gearing (answer i(b)) based on market capitalisation of ordinary shares.

A Suggested Answer

INTERNATIONAL INDUSTRIAL plc

(i)(a) *Book value of net assets attributable to each ordinary share*
£815,000 (net assets) divided by 1 million (number of ordinary shares) = 81.5 pence per share.

Alternatively, if the book value of 'Goodwill and other intangibles' is excluded, the net tangible assets have a book value of £685,000 = 68.5 pence per share.

Tutorial note: 'Net assets' equals 'Gross assets less gross liabilities'. Competent students understand, however, that 'net assets' equals 'shareholders' funds', a figure invariably given as a sub-total in all modern balance sheets. It is given in this question: 'Group shareholders' funds £815,000'. The Examiner, having made the end of year ordinary share number 1 million, provides a simple mental calculation needing only a moment of examination time.

(i)(b) *Capital gearing based on the market capitalisation of International Industrial plc ordinary shares*
Debt : Equity ratio, i.e. Debentures plus Mortgage £600,000 : Market capitalisation of equity 1m × £1.40 = £1.4 million = 43%
Debt : Debt plus Equity (Gearing ratio), i.e. £600,000 : £2 million = 30%
(It would be preferable to use the market value of all securities but those for the loan capital are not given.)

(i)(c) *Earnings yield* equals Earnings per share/market price per share × 100. 'Earnings' equals 'Earnings per ordinary share before extraordinary items' = £90,000.

Number of shares in the EPS calculations is in this case based on a weighted average to account for the new issue of 250,000 shares mid-way through the financial year, and is:

750,000 × ½ plus 1,000,000 × ½ = 875,000.

EPS equals £90,000 divided by 875,000 = 10.28 pence per share.

Earnings yield equals 10.28 × 100/140 = 7.34% per annum.

(*Tutorial note:* the Price-earnings ratio is the reciprocal of the earnings yield, or 140 : 10.28 = 13.6 (to 1)).

(i)(d) *Dividend yield* equals Dividend per share/market price per share × 100. Ordinary dividend paid and proposed equals £50,000, which for 1 million shares equals 5 pence per share.

Dividend yield equals 5p × 100/140 = 3.57%.

(ii) *The relevance and shortcomings of accounting ratios to financial analysis*
Readers should refer to pages 235 and 236.

(iii) *Report on the liquidity, profitability and the potential of the International Industrial group using ratio analysis*

Liquidity

(1) Overtrading occurs when a business attempts to expand its turnover to a level where the working capital employed is insufficient to finance trading. There is evidence that the group was overtrading in the year ended 31 October 19x3.

(2) The liquidity ratio appears favourable but it is calculated on the assumption of the same credit period for both debtors and creditors. The average period of credit allowed to (or taken by) customers is nearly 2 months. If the group maintained its policy of prompt payment of trade creditors within an average period of one month, only (say) half of the debtors would be collected within that time and an adjustment for this reduces the liquidity ratio to a critical level of 0.60 (from 1.17).

(3) The 19x3 current ratio (1.89) below two, and the working capital ratio representing 47 days sales, are further pointers to overtrading (under-capitalisation).

(4) The over-reliance on borrowing (for an industrial group) is indicated by the proprietors' ratio (0.38) well below an optimum of 0.5. Only 38% of the book value of the tangible assets need to be lost on a forced liquidation for the position of unsecured creditors to be affected. There is confirmation of the over-high level of debt from the gearing ratio at 0.78 when based on book values. However, this judgment of too high a gearing is modified on consideration of capital gearing based on market capitalisation when the ratio drops to 0.43, (i)(b) above.

Tutorial note: The incentive to the company of using loan capital with tax relief on the interest to increase the return to equity has been dealt with earlier. Financial management should want to maximise the market value of all its securities through finding the optimum relationship between equity funds and borrowing. It must not increase the latter to that point where the cover afforded the lenders' principal and interest is eroded so that the risk (for them) is not acceptable. Where there is a clear enough view of continued expansion, there is room for higher gearing as has happened in Japan in recent years; however, if the optimism about expansion is not borne out, higher gearing can be dangerous to the company's survival.

(5) Tangible asset cover afforded to the debenture loan in 19x3 (2.7 times) appears adequate, but this based on the group assets is invalid to the extent that there is a legal claim only against the parent company assets.

(6) The liquidity position improved in 19x4 mainly through borrowing £100,000 on mortgage (the preparation of a Sources and Application of Funds Statement and its analysis would give a clearer indication of the flow of funds). The liquidity ratio (as

adjusted (2) above) reached par. Current ratio improved to 2 and the working capital ratio rose to represent 70 days sales. An optimum figure is not known, but the ratio is probably still low in relation to the cash cycle of an industrial group and may well prove inadequate if sales continue to increase as in 19x4 (25% in historic terms).

(7) The proprietor's ratio has increased (0.42) but is still well below 0.5. The capital gearing ratio based on book values has marginally improved in the year despite the extra borrowing, following the increase in equity and the revaluation of freehold land.

(8) Capital commitments, £180,000, are well above the year's depreciation provision but there has been an increase in the profits retained in General Reserve.

(9) It may be concluded that the group's liquid assets are barely adequate to meet known commitments (current tax, dividends, capital commitments, trade creditors) and expansion and further cash capital, ideally from its ordinary shareholders, is needful. Continuing inflation will enhance the need for further working capital (even in the absence of expansion). Despite the attraction of loan capital in a period of inflation, it is likely that lenders would build in compensation for loss of monetary value by requiring high interest rates.

Profitability

(1) The turnover ratios (7 and 8) show little change. As turnover is more directly affected by inflation than asset value, these ratios should improve each year even in the absence of real gain in efficiency. In addition, it should be noted that revaluation of assets upwards (this occurred for Freehold Property) causes the ratios to fall. Average figures for the various "capital employed" denominators would have been more realistic, particularly as both the share capital and the loan capital were increased halfway through the year.

(2) Profitability ratios have risen encouragingly. The expansion in sales, with the fixed element of cost probably not rising proportionately, has been a factor in the increase of net *trading* profit.

(3) Pre-tax return on long-term capital in 19x4 rose to 14.64% (8.10% after tax) compared with the loan capital cost at 10% (5% after tax). This favourable "trading on the equity" factor, linked with high capital gearing, sees the return on equity rising in 19x4 to over 19% pre-tax (11.04% after tax) – an excellent return.

Potential

(1) The market price of the equity, £1.40 per share, is well above the book value of the net assets attributable thereto (81.5p). It is more than double in value if Goodwill is excluded from the latter calculation (68.5p). See answer (i)(a).

(2) The high book gearing, although modified when based on the market value of the equity, is at a level where any fall in trading profit would lower the cover for both the interest and the current level of ordinary dividend. A fall of 25% or more would leave the dividend uncovered by current profit.

(3) The yields (dividend and earnings) are moderate for an industrial group by current standards. Potential investors would, if investing long term, be looking for growth of earnings, dividend and share price – all reliant on a growth of trading profit. The stock market sets high value on the group's future profitability (1) above. Information on present and future market environments (economic, technical, social and political) would be needed to consider the extent to which such future potential had been discounted in the market price of the ordinary shares.

(4) The group's need for cash, preferably from ordinary shareholders, is likely to lead to a rights issue being offered to current members. Alternative investments in fixed interest securities currently yielding high interest with less risk would no doubt be considered. However, given agreeable environmental conditions and the continuance of the recent increase in turnover and profitability, it is reasonable to infer that yields could grow to the level of an acceptable long-term rate for equity investment.

WORKBOOK 1

Understanding the terminology of accounting: exercises and discussion assignments
also
recapitulation questions including multi-choice

Understanding the terminology of accounting – exercises and discussion assignments; also recapitulation questions including multi-choice

The object of the first section of Workbook 1 is to test the reader's understanding of the accounting terminology used in the book and described in detail in Part One.

For each of the 150 items listed below in related groups of five, a concise description should be written.

For the individual working alone, they may be regarded as SELF-TEST QUESTIONS. Within a teaching situation, they may be used over a period of time within TUTORIAL DISCUSSION; alternatively, tutors may request written answers.

Checks may be made against the *brief* answers given in Appendix 1. These are pointers to fuller answers and do not repeat any of the detail of the text. Individuals, particularly if they are not satisfied with their own attempts, should REVIEW and RESEARCH the text to ensure understanding. Alternatively, tutors may wish to elaborate the answers themselves.

The second part of the Workbook 1 takes the form of tutorial discussion assignments.

The third section of Workbook 1 lists 33 recapitulation questions including multi-choice ones offering 100 (maximum) marks. Test your understanding before turning to the answers in Appendix 1.

GROUP 1
1. Profit and Loss Account
2. Trading Profit
3. Gross Profit percentage
4. Mark-up
5. Cost of Sales

GROUP 2
1. Trading Account
2. Stock in Trade
3. Turnover
4. Revenue Expenditure
5. Provisions

GROUP 3
1. Net Profit
2. Appropriation account
3. Appropriations of profit
4. Retained Profit
5. Taxable Profit

GROUP 4
1. Extraordinary income/expenditure
2. Prior Year item
3. Proposed dividend
4. Interim dividend
5. Advance Corporation Tax

GROUP 5
1. Ordinary dividend
2. Preference dividend
3. Earnings
4. Dividend cover
5. Dividend percentage

GROUP 6
1. Franked Investment Income
2. Unfranked payment
3. Corporation tax
4. Deferred taxation
5. Overseas taxation

GROUP 7
1. Loan interest payable
2. Profit before tax and interest
3. Profit before tax
4. Profit after tax
5. Profit brought forward

GROUP 8
1. Balance Sheet
2. Fixed Assets
3. Current Assets
4. Current liabilities
5. Shareholders' funds

GROUP 9
1. Net worth
2. Net assets
3. Book value
4. Net Asset Value of an ordinary share
5. Equity

GROUP 10
1. Long-term funds
2. Loan capital
3. Total funds
4. Gross Assets
5. Mortgage Debentures

GROUP 11
1. Capital employed
2. Preference share capital
3. Cumulative preference share
4. Redeemable preference shares
5. Ordinary share capital

GROUP 12
1. Reserves
2. Capital reserve
3. Statutory capital reserve
4. Share premium account
5. Capital redemption reserve

GROUP 13
1. Revenue reserve
2. Working capital
3. Net current assets
4. Creditors
5. Debtors

GROUP 14
1. Bank overdraft
2. Liquidity
3. Cash flow
4. Overtrading
5. Capital structure

GROUP 15
1. Current ratio
2. Liquid ratio
3. Capital gearing
4. Leverage
5. Highly geared

GROUP 16
1. Return on capital employed
2. Primary ratio
3. Secondary ratios
4. Profit margin
5. Turnover of capital

GROUP 17
1. Capital expenditure
2. Capital commitments
3. Deferred revenue expenditure
4. Write off
5. Depreciation provision

GROUP 18
1. Price earnings ratio
2. Market price of equity
3. Dividend yield
4. Earnings yield
5. Earnings per share

GROUP 19
1. Goodwill
2. Research and development expenditure
3. Contingent liabilities
4. Short-term investment
5. Investment in subsidiary

GROUP 20
1. Holding company
2. Parent company
3. Subsidiary
4. Wholly-owned subsidiary
5. Minority interest

GROUP 21
1. Associated company
2. Public limited company
3. Limited liability
4. Private limited company
5. Listed company

GROUP 22
1. Historic cost accounts
2. Current cost accounts
3. Accounting concepts
4. SSAP
5. EEC Directives

GROUP 23
1. Authorised capital
2. Issued capital
3. Paid up capital
4. Called up capital
5. Nominal value

GROUP 24
1. Fully paid up shares
2. Fixed interest capital
3. Institutional investors
4. Floating charge
5. Fixed charge

GROUP 25
1. Rights issue
2. Bonus issue
3. Convertible debentures
4. Liquidation
5. Unsecured creditors

GROUP 26
1. Double entry book-keeping
2. True and fair view
3. Prudence concept
4. Going concern concept
5. Statutory audit

GROUP 27
1. Memorandum of association
2. Articles of association
3. Directors' statutory declaration*
4. Permissible capital payment*
5. Realised profit

*as related to the redemption or purchase by a private company of its own shares out of capital.

GROUP 28
1. Statement of Intent (SOI)
2. Statement of recommended practice (SORP)
3. Franked SORP
4. Exposure draft (ED)
5. International Accounting Standard (IAS)

GROUP 29
1. Finance lease
2. Capital lease
3. Operating lease
4. Off-balance sheet item
5. Hire purchase contact

GROUP 30
1. Acquisition accounting
2. Merger accounting
3. Pooling of interests
4. Vendor rights
5. Vendor placings

Tutorial Discussion Assignments

The following discussion topics are based on material in Part One of the book. Their purpose is to consolidate and develop understanding of financial matters relating to the company report and accounts. They may be used in tutor-led group discussion within courses or by the student working alone for research and review purposes. Alternatively, tutors may request written answers from students.

1. Discuss the importance of *The Corporate Report* 1975 and assess its impact on company reporting to the present time.
2. Discuss the statements:

    'The enactment by member countries of the EEC Directives will do much to harmonize company reporting and auditing standards within the community.'

    'The publication of domestic Accounting Standards based on independent programmes in individual countries is not only wasteful duplicaton of effort and therefore cost, but also results in conflict of ideas. All this should be stopped so that the agreed Standard can be issued internationally.'

3. Many listed companies show sizeable bank overdrafts in excess of £1 million in successive balance sheets as current liabilities. Should not these funds be shown as long-term debt?

4. Explain the importance of the valuation of stock to the determination of a 'true and fair view' of profit.

5. Consider recent developments in the company reporting environment and their impact on the direction and development of reports and accounts.

6. Discuss the relative importance of liquidity, solvency and profitability to the survival of a company.

7. Show, using your own figures, the relationship between long-term funds and fixed or non-current assets, and between short-term funds or current liabilities and current assets. Link both relationships to working capital.

8. The Creditable Limited (Case 1, Table 5(b)) ordinary shareholders, on reading the Balance Sheet (5) set out, comment that their 'net worth' according to this statement is £11,112. Discuss their concept of 'net worth'.

9. Discuss the proposition that 'depreciation, being an amount set aside from profit, is a source of funds'.

10. 'There is little point in carrying forward any credit balance on profit and loss account; all retained profit should be transferred to and contained in a reserve account.' Comment on the logic of this statement.

11. Discuss the accounting concepts of prudence and consistency in relation to a company chairman's view that 'all our research and development expenditure should be carried forward in the balance sheet and written off against profit over a period of time'.

12. A shareholder asks the board of a company listed on the Stock Exchange – 'we are making very large profits and they are increasing every year, yet the figure for "goodwill" shown in our group's balance sheet is being reduced each year. Will you explain this paradox please?" Discuss the explanation which might be given.

13. Mrs Smith, a widow, was delighted to receive a communication from the company in which she owned ordinary shares, enclosing one extra *bonus share* for every three shares she held. Her son shared her delight, saying 'Mother they've given you some free shares', until he saw a few days later that the market price of the shares had fallen considerably. 'I don't understand it,' he tells his mother sadly. Explain the situation to them.

14. What is a 'capital redemption reserve' and what has it to do with the concept of limited liability?

15. 'I don't understand it,' says the employee, keenly interested in his company's balance sheet after receiving company shares as part of a profit sharing scheme. 'The management are telling us that it is short of cash for operations and that we should go easy on our wage claim, but this balance sheet shows we have millions of pounds in reserves. They have some explaining to do.' Make the explanation on behalf of management.

16. Preference shareholders and debenture holders receive a 'fixed interest' return, but there the similarity ends. Discuss the important differences between these two methods of funding a business.

17. 'And now,' says the company chairman at the board meeting, 'bearing in mind the level of our profits and our expansion plans, not to mention inflation, what amount of dividend should we recommend for our ordinary shareholders?' Discuss the importance of dividends from the point of view of the company and of its individual shareholders. How has the Companies Act 1980 affected the position?

18. Is there any truth in the suggestion that the excess of the market value of a company over its net asset value as derived from its balance sheet is a measure of the value of goodwill?

266

19. Describe the taxation of a company under the Imputation System.
20. What is the importance of the price-earnings ratio to 'take-over' transactions where the purchase consideration is met by an exchange of shares between the parties?
21. 'The change to showing a current estimate of the value of property in the balance sheet from the previous custom of showing its cost came too late to prevent some companies from being taken over. Many boards of directors and many accountants were caught napping. And the Companies Act 1967 requirement in this respect is not strong enough. Still, current cost accounting should solve the problem, though I see some boards are not keen on the idea of CCA supplementary accounts.' Comment on these statements and include an explanation of the events underlining them.
22. 'By the time the shareholders get the report and accounts it is of very little use, and with inflation as it is, even the current cost statement is historical.' Discuss.
23. The Companies Act 1981 has added emphasis to the overriding importance to published accounts of the true and fair view concept and has given legal backing to the accounting standards programme. Discuss.
24. Discuss the protection given by the Companies Act 1981 to shareholders and others dealing with a private company proposing to purchase its own shares out of capital.
25. How has the Companies Act 1981 definition of 'realised profits' clarified the Companies Act 1980 rules on 'distributable profits'?
26. Discuss and illustrate the effects of the Finance Act 1984 on corporate and deferred taxation.

Note: The originating companies legislation noted in these questions is now consolidated in the CA 1985.

Recapitulation questions including multi-choice

Tackle the following 33 questions as a recapitulation exercise before checking your performance within the 'answers to Workbook 1'. The marks available total 100.

True and fair view

1. Explain the meaning of the 'true and fair view over-ride'.   3 marks
2. In respect of the 'true and fair view over-ride' what new requirements did the CA 1981 introduce compared with the 1948 legislation?
                                        3 marks × 2 requirements   6 marks
3. What is the status of the true and fair view concept in relation to 'modified accounts' to be filed with the Registrar of Companies by small and medium-size enterprises, as designated by the CA 1981?   3 marks
4. What is the status of SSAPs in relation to the true and fair view concept?   3 marks
5. What is the value of an SSAP to a Court which has to decide whether accounts are true and fair?   3 marks

Note: The currently familiar originating legislation noted in these questions on the 'true and fair view' is consolidated in SS228, 230, 258 CA 85.

Audit

6. Set out the contents of the audit report required under the CA 1981 (S173(5) CA 85) to support the 'directors' statutory declaration' in respect of the redemption or purchase of its own shares out of capital by a private company.   3 marks

7. What is the auditors' responsibility in law in respect of the directors' report? 3 marks

8. How does SSAP 2 define 'the going concern concept'? What is its importance to the auditor? 3 marks

Companies Acts 1980 and 1981

9. State both the *general* and the *particular* requirements of the CA 81 – 4 Sch. 36 CA 85 – in relation to accounting policies. 2 marks × 2 4 marks

10. The definition of 'realised profits' is fundamental to the CA 1980 rules on distributable profit. The CA 81 – 11 Sch. CA 85 – sets out a definition of 'realised profit'. What is that definition? 3 marks

11. How does a capital redemption reserve arise? 3 marks

12. Under the terms of the CA 80, a public company may only make a distribution provided this does not reduce the net assets to less than the aggregate of its called-up share capital and its undistributable reserves. In this context, define (a) net assets and (b) undistributable reserves.

2 marks for (a) 4 marks for (b) 6 marks

13. State the conditions under which a company may issue shares which are to be redeemed at the option of the company or the shareholders (CA 81 S45) – S159(1–2) CA 85. 6 marks

14. What is the essential requirement of SSAP 17 Accounting for Post-balance sheet events? 3 marks

15. What is the essential requirement of SSAP 19 Accounting for investment properties? 3 marks

16. In the context of SSAP 20 Foreign currency translation, briefly define the 'net investment concept' related to the preparation of the consolidated financial statements of a company and its foreign subsidiaries. 3 marks

17. What is the requirement of SSAP 13 Accounting for Research and Development in respect of pure and applied research expenditure? 3 marks

18. What are the stringent circumstances set out in SSAP 13 Accounting for Research and Development expenditure which allows the deferment of development expenditure to future periods? 3 marks

19. What uses are allowed by the CA 1948 S56 (CA 85 S130(1)–(3)) for the Share Premium Account? 3 marks

20. Which method is the prescribed method of 'accounting for deferred tax' (SSAP 15) – the deferral method or the liability method? Briefly define both methods. 3 marks

21. What is the objective test contained in SSAP 23 Accounting for Acquisitions and Mergers which determines whether or not a business combination may be treated as a merger? 3 marks

22. What methods are allowed under SSAP 4 for accounting for government grants? 2 marks

For the following questions based on SSAP 22, Accounting for Goodwill, tick the statements which are correct and those which are incorrect. Take one mark for each correct or incorrect statement identified.

Correct Incorrect

23. The standard applies only to the accounts of individual companies and not to groups.

24. Inherent goodwill is not to be recognised in accounting statements.
25. The preferred accounting treatment of positive purchased goodwill is:
    (i) immediate write off against profit and loss account;
    (ii) immediate write off on acquisition against reserves;
    (iii) amortisation against profit over 5 years;
    (iv) amortisation against profit over 20 years.
26. Where a policy of amortisation of purchased goodwill is followed, it is:
    (i) written off against profit as an extraordinary item over a period of years;
    (ii) written off systematically against profit as an extraordinary item over its economic lifetime;
    (iii) systematically amortised against profit and loss account in arriving at profit or loss on ordinary activities over its useful economic life.
27. Purchased goodwill may, if considered too large an amount to write off:
    (i) be carried permanently on the balance sheet;
    (ii) be combined with other intangible assets in the balance sheet, e.g. patents, trade marks.
28. Companies *must* choose a policy *either* of write off immediately against reserves *or* amortisation against profit and loss accunt for *all* acquisitions, ie. the policy must be consistent.
29. SSAP 22 is based on the concept in the UK Companies Acts that *purchased* goodwill has a limited useful life, so that ultimately its elimination *must* constitute a *realised loss*.
30. What is a *related company* for the purposes of the CA 1985?   3 marks
31. How does SSAP 9 require that long-term contract work in progress be valued?   3 marks
32. How does the CA 1981 (4 Sch. CA 85) relate to the requirements of SSAP 9 in respect of long-term contract work in progress (Q.31) and what disclosures in the notes to the accounts are needed?   3 marks
33. What are the conditions under which a contingent liability should be brought into the accounts rather than being disclosed by way of a note?   3 marks

WORKBOOK 2

Financial statements – analysis and interpretation: graded exercises

Financial statements – analysis and interpretation: graded exercises

Workbook 2 contains 21 graded exercises which have the objective of testing the reader's ability to understand, classify, analyse and interpret financial statements.

A number of questions are in sequence, building on each other:

  (i) Questions 1 to 6 are interconnected.

 (ii) Questions 7 and 8 are interconnected.

(iii) Questions 9 and 10 are interconnected.

Questions 20 and 21 require the analysis of comparative Sources and Application of Funds statements.

Students should attempt answers to the questions without reference to the text, and then check with the suggested answers given in Appendix 2.

Note: Questions 1 to 6 are interconnected.

1.   Write a two-sided balance sheet from the following balance sheet sub-totals, entering the total of Shareholders' funds as a sub-total:

	£
Fixed Assets	209,000
Current liabilities	140,000
Current assets	236,000
10% Mortgage Debentures	45,000
Shareholders' funds	?

2.   What is the balance sheet value (Question 1) of 'total funds' and 'gross assets'?

3.   Rewrite the balance sheet (Question 1) and show the balance sheet value of 'long-term funds' and of 'working capital'. Use the vertical form of statement.

4.   The total list of balance sheet items (Question 1) is given below:

	£
Stock at the year end	76,000
Sundry debtors	116,000
Sundry creditors	75,000
Issued Ordinary £1 shares fully paid	200,000
Land & Buildings	50,000
10% Mortgage Debenture	45,000
General revenue reserve	50,000
Profit & Loss account (credit balance)	10,000
Current taxation	45,000

Proposed dividend to Ordinary Shareholders	20,000	
Plant & Machinery (book value)	126,000	
Patents (book value)	33,000	
Cash in hand and with bank	44,000	

Required:
(i) Write alongside each item its classification as either Fixed Asset, Current Asset, Current Liability, Long-term Liability or Shareholders' fund.
(ii) The Authorised Ordinary Share Capital is £250,000 in £1 Shares. From this information and that given above, prepare a vertical form of balance sheet.

5. Using the balance sheet prepared in answer to Question 4, calculate:
(a) The current ratio.
(b) The liquid ratio, assuming Debtors and Cash as liquid assets.
(c) The net asset value based on the balance sheet of one ordinary share.
(d) The Dividend percentage.
(e) Given that the market value of one ordinary share is £1.50, calculate the Dividend yield.
(*Note:* (d) and (e) assume that no interim dividend has been paid.)

6. The profit and loss account for the company whose balance sheet was outlined in Question 4 is as follows:
Profit and Loss account for the period ended at Balance Sheet date

	£	£	%
Sales		650,000	100.00
Cost of Sales		390,000	60.00
Gross profit on sales		260,000	40.00
Administrative expenses	58,500		
Selling & Distribution	71,500	130,000	20.00
Net Operating Profit		130,000	20.00
Debenture Interest		4,500	0.69
Net Profit before tax		125,500	19.31
Taxation		45,000	6.90
Net Profit after tax and before Extraordinary items		80,500	12.41
Extraordinary items – expenses		2,500	
		78,000	
Proposed Ordinary dividend	20,000		
Transfer to General Reserve	50,000	70,000	
Net Profit Retained		8,000	
Retained profit beginning of year		2,000	
Retained profit at end of the year		10,000	Credit balance on P & L account

Using the balance sheet in answer to Q.4, and the above
Required:

Compute –
(a) The rate of return on total assets.
(b) The number of times total assets were 'turned over'.
(c) The rate of return to turnover (sales).
Show –
(d) The reconciliation of the answers (a) (b) and (c).
Compute –
(e) The rate of return, after taxes, to shareholders' funds at year end.
(f) The earnings yield.
(g) The earnings per share.
(h) The price-earnings ratio.
(i) The number of times profit before tax and interest covered the debenture interest.
(j) The rate of turnover of stock.
(k) The average collection period of debtors.
(l) The dividend cover.
Comment briefly on –
(m) The profitability of the company for the year.
(n) The company's dividend/retention policy.
Note: Questions 7 and 8 are interconnected.

7. BLOUGH LIMITED has the following year-end Balance Sheet:

Funds	£	Assets	£
100,000 Ordinary Shares of £1	100,000	Premises	75,000
100,000 6% Preference shares of £1	100,000	Machinery less depreciation	110,000
Revenue Reserves	60,000	Stock	55,000
Profit and Loss account balance	30,000	Debtors	32,000
Trade creditors	34,000	Cash	68,000
Proposed ordinary dividend	10,000		
Proposed preference dividend	6,000		
	340,000		340,000

Required:
(a) What is the net book value of the business?
(b) What is the net asset value of one ordinary share?
(c) What is the working capital?
(d) Redraft the balance sheet in vertical form with appropriate sub-headings and sub-totals.

8. Using the BLOUGH LIMITED Balance Sheet (Question 7), revise it to show the 'state of affairs' of the company after the completion of the following four transactions:
(a) The payment of the proposed dividends (ignore tax considerations).
(b) Receipt of £12,000 from debtors and the payment of £14,000 to creditors.
(c) The purchase of additional machinery for £50,000, for which £10,000 was paid as a deposit, with the remainder still owing.
(d) The company issues 50,000 ordinary shares of £1 each at a price of £1.50p per share. All the shares were taken up and fully paid.
Draft your revised balance sheet in vertical form with appropriate heads and totals.
Note: Questions 9 and 10 are interconnected.

9. The summary balance sheet of WORKSTONE Ltd is as follows:

Shareholders' funds	£		£
400,000 Ordinary £1 shares	400,000	*Fixed assets*, including Land	
Reserves, including profit &		and Buildings	500,000
loss account balance	50,000	*Net current assets*	250,000

	450,000	
Long-term loans	300,000	
	750,000	750,000

(a) The Land & Buildings included at cost among the Fixed Assets at £100,000 is revalued to £200,000.
   Required: Incorporate the revaluation in the summary balance sheet.
(b) After incorporating the revised revaluation of the Land & Buildings, the company makes a bonus issue of 1 ordinary share for every four held, utilising the reserve arising on the revaluation for the purpose and thus consolidating it as permanent capital.
   Required: Redraft the balance sheet resulting from Q.9(a) to account for the bonus issue.

10. WORKSTONE Ltd, as part of its expansion programme, and subsequent to the bonus issue (9(b) above) makes a 1 for 5 rights issue to its ordinary shareholders at a price of 150p a share. All the rights are taken up and cash received in full.
   Required: Amend the balance sheet resulting from Q.9(b) to account for the rights issue and set it out in appropriate form.

11. *Comparison X Ltd and Y Ltd.*

Trading and Profit and Loss Accounts for the year ended 31 March 19x1

	X Ltd	Y Ltd		X Ltd	Y Ltd
	£	£		£	£
Opening Stock	15,000	5,000	Sales	100,000	100,000
Purchases	80,000	86,000	Closing Stock	25,000	11,000
Gross Profit	30,000	20,000			
	£125,000	£111,000		£125,000	£111,000
Overhead expenses	21,900	12,800	Gross Profit	30,000	20,000
Net Profit	8,100	7,200			
	£30,000	£20,000		£30,000	£20,000

Balance Sheets as at 31 March 19x1

	X Ltd	Y Ltd		X Ltd	Y Ltd
	£	£		£	£
Share Capital	50,000	50,000	Fixed Assets	60,000	49,000
Profit & Loss A/c	40,000	10,000	Current assets:		
Shareholders'			Stocks	25,000	11,000
capital employed	90,000	60,000	Debtors	10,000	7,500
Current liabilities	10,000	11,000	Cash at bank	5,000	3,500
	£100,000	£71,000		£100,000	£71,000

Required:
1. Compute – (a) the current ratio, (b) the liquid ratio, (c) the rate of stock turnover, (d) gross profit as a percentage of sales, (e) the mark-up, (f) net profit as a percentage of sales, (g) overheads to sales, (h) the net profit as a percentage of shareholders' capital employed at 31 March 19x1, (i) sales to shareholders' capital employed at the same date.

2. Describe briefly the limited conclusions to be drawn from a comparison of the above ratios and percentages, relating those of X Ltd to those of Y Ltd.

12. P Ltd has a capital of £100,000 divided into shares of £1 each, plus accumulated reserves of £100,000. Q Ltd has a capital of £150,000 divided into shares of £1 each, plus accumulated reserves of £50,000. P Ltd pays a dividend of 20% on its share capital and Q Ltd a dividend of 15% on its share capital. Which firm's dividend is more profitable to its shareholders?

13. Assuming the market value of one P Ltd ordinary share (Q.12) was £2.10p and the market value of one Q Ltd ordinary share was £1.50p, which offered the best yield?

14. Using your own figures, draw up the balance sheet of a limited company engaged in manufacturing and incorporate the following features:
    (i) preference and ordinary share capital
    (ii) capital and revenue reserves
    (iii) mortgage debentures
    (iv) a long-term investment (in an associated company); reflect the following ratios:
    (v) a current ratio of 2–1
    (vi) a liquid ratio of 1–1
    (vii) a fixed assets to loan ratio of 3–1 and from your figures insert sub-heads showing:
    (viii) the book value of the shareholders' funds
    (ix) the long-term capital employed
    (x) the working capital.
    (Adapted from a question – Certified Diploma in Accounting and Finance.)

15. From the following figures, draw up a balance sheet of XYZ company limited as at March 31 19x1. Comment on the position disclosed thereby and say what further information you would require before you could go beyond your preliminary comment.

	£		£
Debtors	750	Trade investment	3,000
Motor Van (cost)	2,000	Depreciation (Van)	1,600
General reserve	3,000	Bank Overdraft	1,500
Creditors	2,500	Stock	2,400
Cash in hand	250	Plant & Machinery (cost)	20,000
Depreciation (Buildings)	6,000	10% Debentures	20,000
Depreciation (Machinery)	8,000	Buildings (cost)	30,000
Profit & Loss A/c (Debit balance)	4,200	Authorised and Issued capital, fully paid 10,000 £1 Ordinary shares	10,000
		10,000 8% £1 cum. preference shares	10,000

16. Construct a hierarchy of ratios starting at the apex with the primary ratio (profit : capital employed), through the two secondary ratios to the subsidiary ratios. Use the hierarchy to indicate to the management of a company (manufacturing) the possible ways in which the primary ratio may be improved.

17. The summarised accounts of CITY LIMITED for the year ended 31 December 19x5 are:
    PROFIT AND LOSS ACCOUNT for the year ended 31 December 19x5.

	£	£
Sales		350,000
Trading profit		85,000
Interest	5,000	
Operating expenses	45,000	50,000

Profit before tax		35,000
Tax	15,000	
		————
Profit after tax		20,000
Dividend		12,000
		————
Retentions		8,000
		————

BALANCE SHEET as at 31 December 19x5

	£		£	£
Ordinary £1 shares fully paid	60,000	Fixed Assets		88,000
Reserves including P & L balance	24,000	*Current Assets*		
	————			
Shareholders' funds	84,000	Stock	62,000	
Long-term loan:		Debtors	45,000	
10% Debenture 19y5	50,000	Cash	5,000	
			————	
			112,000	
			————	
		Less *current liabilities*		
		Taxation	15,000	
		Creditors	39,000	
		Dividend	12,000	
			————	
			66,000	46,000
	————		————	————
Capital employed	£134,000	*Net Assets*		£134,000
	————			————

Required:
Compute the following ratios and describe each one (see first example).
  (1) Profit before interest and tax : Capital employed. (Description : Return on long-term capital employed.)
  (2) Net operating profit : sales
  (3) Sales : long-term capital employed
  (4) Profit after tax : shareholders' funds
  (5) Long-term debt : capital employed
  (6) Current assets : current liabilities
  (7) Liquid assets : current liabilities
  (8) Profit after tax : dividend
  (9) Profit before interest and tax : interest
 (10) Shareholders' funds : gross assets.

Required:
Answer the following questions:
  (1) What yardstick could be used to judge the ratios calculated?
  (2) What alternative measures of capital employed could be used?
  (3) Do you agree with the description of 'net assets' against the total of £134,000?
  (4) What alternative is there to the description 'net current assets' and what is its amount?
  (5) The Managing Director wants to include a value for 'Goodwill' in the accounts. What is your view on this? If agreed, what would be the 'double entry' effect on the balance sheet?
  (6) What is the relationship between ratios 1, 2, and 3?

18. Companies A, B and C have the same long-term capital employed, i.e. £500,000, but different capital structure being:

	A £	B £	C £
Ordinary £1 shares	100,000	200,000	300,000
Reserves	200,000	200,000	200,000
Shareholders' funds	300,000	400,000	500,000
10% Loan	200,000	100,000	—
Long-term capital	500,000	500,000	500,000

The Earnings before interest and tax (EBIT) as a percentage of long-term capital was for each company 20% in 19x1, but dropped for each company to 6% in 19x2. Assuming that the capital structure and the long-term capital of each company remained as above for both years, all after-tax profits having been distributed as dividends, *set out for comparison and brief comment* the following information with the relevant figures inserted:

Assume tax at 50%.

	A		B		C	
	19x1 £	19x2 £	19x1 £	19x2 £	19x1 £	19x2 £
EBIT						
Interest						
Profit before tax						
Tax (50%)						
Profit after tax						
1. Return on Long-term capital	20%	6%	20%	6%	20%	6%
2. Percentage return on Shareholders' funds						
3. Number or times interest covered						
4. Earnings per share						

19. On 1 January 19x2, Parent (P) Ltd acquired 60% of the Ordinary Share Capital of Subsidiary (S) Ltd for £140,000. This purchase price was settled by the issue of 80,000 P Ltd Ordinary Shares which were quoted at £1.75 to S Ltd. At 31 December 19x1, immediately before the acquisition, the balance sheets of the two companies were:

	P Ltd £	S Ltd £
Issued Ordinary Shares of £1	280,000	100,000
Reserves	180,000	40,000
Shareholders' funds	460,000	140,000
Long-term loan	140,000	60,000
	600,000	200,000
Invested in:		
Fixed Assets	480,000	140,000
Net Current Assets	120,000	60,000
	600,000	200,000

Required:

(a) Show the balance sheet of P Ltd after effecting the double entry on the acquisition of S Ltd.

(b) Show your workings leading to, and the consolidated balance sheet of, P Ltd and its subsidiary S Ltd on completion of the transaction on 1 January 19x2.

Note: The object of this exercise is to enable readers to follow through the outcome of an acquisition transaction, first, on the separate balance sheet of the parent company and, secondly, the basic book-keeping which leads to the preparation of the consolidated balance sheet and (in this case of a part, though controlling, interest) the arising of 'Goodwill' and 'Minority Interest'.

The solution in the appendix is accompanied by tutorial notes explaining the outcome.

20. *Prudent plc and Profligate plc.*

You are required to write a commentary following a preliminary analysis of the following statements of Sources and Application of Funds of the two companies comparing their funding activities.

In practice, this analysis would be made in conjunction with other information available, e.g. the final accounts, chairman's statement and directors' report etc. and you may want to make reference thereto in your commentary.

Statement of Sources and Application of Funds
for the year ended 31 December 19x1
(Previous year's figures are not given)

	Prudent plc £'000	Prudent plc £'000	Profligate plc £'000	Profligate plc £'000
SOURCES				
Profit before taxation (*note*)		2,050		2,800
Add items not involving movement of funds:				
Depreciation		100		35
Funds from operations		2,150		2,835
Issue of ordinary shares (cash)	1,000			
Debenture loans (cash)	500	1,500		—
		3,650		2,835
APPLICATION				
Purchase of Plant and Machinery	1,800		1,950	
Loan repaid	200		375	
Dividends	200		450	
Taxation	370	2,570	590	3,365
INCREASE IN WORKING CAPITAL		1,080		
DECREASE IN WORKING CAPITAL		—		530
Represented by:				
Increase in stocks		350		280
Increase in debtors		780		370
		1,130		650
Increase in creditors		240		420
		890		230

Increase in net liquid funds	70			
Decrease in net liquid funds		180		
Decrease in bank overdraft	120			
Increase in bank overdraft		190	120	300
		1,080		530

Note: The profit and loss accounts show current tax provisions of £450,000 (Prudent) and £680,000 (Profligate).

21. *A plc and B plc.*
    Comparative Statements of Sources and Application of Funds
    You are the deputy to the chief accountant of a group of companies making your routine quarterly visit to the offices of one of the subsidiary companies in the group. This subsidiary is contemplating the award of a major long-term contract to one of two companies A plc and B plc, both of which have submitted similar tenders for that contract. An important requirement of the contract is the need to ensure the reliability and continuity of the contractor.

    The subsidiary's contracts manager has obtained, but mislaid, copies of the last year's published final accounts of the companies. He is, however, able to show you the following Sources and Application of Funds Statements received from the companies. He asks you to interpret them for him since he is to meet representatives of the two companies on the following afternoon:

	A plc		B plc	
Sources of Funds	£'000	£'000	£'000	£'000
From Operations (Turnover A plc £3.2m)				
(Turnover B plc £3.7m)	505		560	
Add Depreciation	100	605	20	580
Less Dividends paid	40		160	
Taxation paid – Corporation tax	164		140	
Taxation paid – ACT	20	224	80	380
		381		200
From External Sources				
Equity share issue	100			
Loans – 20 year term	200			
Loans – 5 year term			40	
Plant sales (Obsolete and superfluous)	59			
Sales of Investments (at a loss of £15,000)		359	45	85
		740		285
Application of Funds				
Purchase of New Factory	100		110	
Purchase of New Plant	182		170	
Redemption of Short-term loan	100			
Redemption of Long-term debentures		382	60	340
		358		(55)
Change in Working Capital – Increase/(Decrease)				
Stocks	120		140	
Debtors	254		300	
	374		440	

Cash at bank	39		(200)	
	413		240	
Creditors	55	358	295	(55)

You are required:

(a) to analyse the Funds Flow Statements and comment briefly to the contracts manager, separately in respect of A plc and B plc, on any information they contain which is significant for the award of the contract;

(b) to suggest four items of additional information for which the contracts manager should ask at his meeting on the following day.

WORKBOOK 3

Past examination questions from the papers of
selected professional bodies

Past examination questions from the papers of selected professional bodies

1. Workbook 3 contains 35 selected examination questions from past papers of:
   The Certified Diploma in Accounting and Finance.
   The Chartered Association of Certified Accountants.
   The Institute of Chartered Accountants in England and Wales.
   The Institute of Cost and Management Accountants.
   The Institute of Bankers.

2. Nineteen of the questions require short, essay-type answers demonstrating an *understanding* of the company report and accounts.

    Apart from one question which requires calculations of ratios only, the remaining sixteen are of variable length and require of the candidate not only understanding but the ability to *interpret* financial and other information and *to write lucid commentary*.

3. Notable recent trends in this type of question are the inclusion of Sources and Application of Funds Statements as well as, or in place of, the more usual financial accounting information (Q.17, Q.20 and Q.31), and the inclusion of such information in model answers (to Q.14).

    Current Cost information is also now being provided (Q.7).

4. Unlike Workbooks 1 and 2, where answers to all the questions have been provided in the appendices, Workbook 3 has 29 questions for which answers do not appear. The questions to which answers are given are 6, 7, 14 23, 28 and 31. Tutors can thus use the 'essay-type' questions to provide examination practice for their students and the longer 'interpretation' type of question can be used alternatively as a 'mini case study'.

5. Students should attempt Questions 6 and 7 *before* turning to Appendix 3 to check the quality of their efforts. In the Appendix, the author sets out a feature which potential examination candidates will find to their advantage. *It is a novel tutorial approach to the answer* in which candidates are advised always to read the *requirement* of the question before reading the question itself. Then, on reading the question, candidates should note points of importance on a 'worksheet for answer x' which can be used as the basis of the submitted answer, being submitted itself when time is short. The approach to the answers to Questions 6 and 7 using this examination technique appear in the Appendix.

6. *A full model answer* to Question 14, written by the author as examiner, together *with full tutorial comment*, appears in Appendix 3. A full answer with tutorial comment is also given for Questions 23, 28, and 31.

Understanding and Interpretation

1. With regard to the capitalisation of a public limited company, distinguish between:
   (a) a preference share
   (b) an ordinary share, and
   (c) loan stock
   as to general characteristics and their relative advantages as methods of raising capital.
   (Certified Diploma in Accounting and Finance)

2. Discuss how the following terms differ in meaning and how they are treated in financial statements:
   (a) Market value.
   (b) Book value per share.
   (c) Par value.
   (d) Authorised share capital.
   (e) Issued share capital.
   (Certified Diploma in Accounting and Finance)

3. *The summarised trading and profit and loss account of Apex Ltd for the year 19x2 was as follows:*

	£		£
Stock, 1 January	16,000	Sales	120,000
Purchases	94,000	Stock 31 December	20,000
Gross Profit	30,000		
	140,000		140,000
Overhead expenses	19,200	Gross profit	30,000
Net profit	10,800		
	30,000		30,000
Proposed dividend	7,000	Net profit	10,800
Undistributed profit at		Undistributed profit at	
31 December	23,900	1 January	20,100
	30,900		30,900

You are given the following information:
   (i) Issued share capital is £50,000.
   (ii) In the balance sheet the only reserve was the undistributed profits. There were no investments or intangible assets and no liabilities other than trade creditors of £11,850 and the proposed dividend.
   (iii) No new capital was issued during 19x2.
   (iv) Ignore taxation.
   CALCULATE:
   (a) The average net capital employed during 19x2.
   (b) The following ratios and percentages:
       (i) gross profit as a percentage of sales;
       (ii) Net profit as a percentage of average net capital employed;
       (iii) net profit to dividend ratio;
       (iv) rate of stock turnover.

(c) The gross capital employed at 31 December 19x2.

(Certified Diploma in Accounting and Finance)

4. The balances in the books of account of Anglia Ltd after the preparation of the profit and loss account for the year 19x2 were as follows:

	£
Share capital (authorised and issued) 200,000 ordinary shares	100,000
Share premium account	10,000
Balance of undistributed profit	6,000
General reserve	35,000
9% Debentures (secured on freehold property)	20,000
Freehold property, at cost	110,000
Equipment, at cost	30,000
Vehicles, at cost	18,000
Provisions for depreciation – Equipment	11,000
– Vehicles	16,800
Stock in trade	48,200
Trade debtors	19,000
Bank overdraft	800
Trade creditors	9,600
Proposed dividend	16,000

Sales for the year amounted to £152,000 and purchases to £115,200 all being on a credit basis.

REQUIRED:

(a) On the basis of the above figures, calculate the following:
  (i) the average period of credit allowed to trade debtors;
  (ii) the average period of credit taken from suppliers;
  (iii) the par value of an ordinary share;
  (iv) the net asset value of an ordinary share;
  (v) the break-up value of an ordinary share, given that equipment would fetch only £1,000 if sold piecemeal, but other values would be as above.
(b) Outline the differences between a share premium account and a general reserve.
(c) Calculate the current ratio and the liquid ratio and comment on the liquid position of Anglia Ltd at 31 December 19x2.

(Certified Diploma in Accounting and Finance)

5.

ABC Limited Balance sheet as at
30 September 19x4

	£'000	£'000		£'000	£'000
Issued share capital		936	Fixed assets at cost	3,044	
Reserves		585	less: depreciation	1,165	1,879
Profit and Loss Account					
At 1 October 19x3	470		*Current Assets*		
Profit for the year	850		Stocks	1,002	
	——		Debtors	817	
	1,320		Cash	38	1,857
Less: corporation tax	420	900		——	
	——				
		2,421			
Bank loan		430			
Corporation tax		420			
Current liabilities (including					
current taxation)		465			
		——		——	
		£3,736		£3,736	

Sales for the year to 30 September 19x4 amounted to £5.8m.

REQUIRED:

(a) Calculate five ratios which might be of assistance to the management of ABC Limited, and explain the significance of each of the ratios used.

(b) By what standards would the ratios be compared?

(Certified Diploma in Accounting and Finance)

6. Fairfield Ltd, a food canning firm, is one of twelve member companies of a Trade Association.

In the year ended 31 March 1981, Fairfield Ltd has made a profit of £186,000 but has closed the year with a bank overdraft of £183,000.

The board of the company has indicated to its bankers that the overdraft is likely to show only a modest decrease in the year ended 31 March 1982. This forecast is based upon the following information:

	£
Planned sales for the year ended 31 March 1982 evenly spread over the year, and identical to the sales achieved in the year ended 31 March 1982	1,200,000
Planned profit	176,000

Budgeted cash flow statement for the year ended 31 March 1982.

Sources

Profit	176,000
Depreciation charges	63,000
	£239,000

Application

Dividends paid	35,000
Stock increases	84,000
Capital expenditure	109,000
	£228,000
Reduction in bank overdraft	£ 11,000

Your attention is now drawn to two documents.

First, a memorandum dated 11 May 1981 from the Managing Director of Fairfield to all senior managers:

I have today been notified by the company's bank that they are not prepared to allow our overdraft to continue at its present level, and our early proposals for its reduction to £50,000 by the end of the financial year are requested. I have already indicated that I do not believe that the time is right for a capital issue of either equity or debt.

Would you therefore consider possible approaches to overdraft reduction before our next meeting.

Second, a summary of financial statistics collected, summarised and issued by the Trade Association, Fairfield Ltd is identified by the code letter 'C'; and 'A' and 'B' are considered to be the two other Trade Association members having most similarities with Fairfield. The statistics relate to the year ended 31 March 1981.

Company	*A*	*B*	*C*
Profit as a % of sales	14.0	15.0	15.5
Sales/capital employed (net assets)	1.6/1.0	1.5/1.0	1.2/1.0
Profit as a % of capital employed	22.4	22.5	18.6
Current ratio	2.5/1.0	3.0/1.0	2.8/1.0

Sales/Fixed Assets	3.5/1.0	3.0/1.0	2.5/1.0
Sales/Debtors	4.0/1.0	4.0/1.0	3.0/1.0
Sales/Stocks	3.1/1.0	4.0/1.0	2.4/1.0

REQUIRED:

Write a memorandum to your Managing Director indicating lines of worthwhile investigation in seeking to reduce the level of bank borrowing.

Indicate clearly any conclusions drawn from the information supplied.

(Certified Diploma in Accounting and Finance, Paper 3 Financial Management, June 1981)

SEE SUGGESTED OUTLINE ANSWER IN THE APPENDIX AND THE TUTORIAL NOTE IN RESPECT OF THIS QUESTION.

7. *The following data reflect the accounts of three companies in a segment of the cosmetics industry.*

  (i) *Balance sheets at 31 December 1980 – Current Cost basis*

	Schwarz	Weiss	Blau
	£m	£m	£m
Fixed assets (net)	2.9	3.3	1.5
Stocks	0.6	1.5	0.8
Debtors and prepayments	0.8	2.9	0.3
Bank balances (overdraft)	(1.3)	0.2	(0.2)
Creditors	0.7	1.7	1.9
Ordinary shares £1, fully paid	1.4	0.7	0.4
Preference shares 10% £1, fully paid	—	1.0	—
Debentures 15%	—	2.0	—
Retained profit (including current cost reserve)	0.9	2.5	0.1

  (ii) *Profit for year ended 31 December 1980 – Current Cost basis*

	£m	£m	£m
Sales	5.0	13.0	4.0
Profit before interest and tax	1.1	3.0	0.1
Debenture interest	—	0.3	—
Bank interest – net paid	0.5	—	—
Gearing adjustment (negligible)	—	—	—
Taxation (rebate)	0.2	0.4	(0.2)
Dividends – Preference	—	0.1	—
– Ordinary	0.4	0.8	0.5
(iii) Market share – sales volume %	15	39	12

Schwarz and Weiss are independent public companies and Blau is a wholly-owned division of a vertically integrated multinational.

REQUIREMENT:

(a) Compute the following four ratios using the information from Schwarz's accounts:
  (i) Return on capital employed.
  (ii) Current ratio.
  (iii) Debt : equity ratio.
  (iv) Debtor turnover. (8 marks)
(b) For each ratio comment briefly on any computational problems and limitations in using this ratio and identify the 'key area of performance' to which it relates.
(6 marks)
(c) Explain and illustrate any limitations in using the ratios from (a) in performance comparison between Schwarz, and Weiss and Blau. (6 marks)
(20 marks)

(Certified Diploma in Accounting and Finance, Paper 1, Financial Accounting, June 1981)

SEE SUGGESTED OUTLINE ANSWER IN THE APPENDIX AND THE TUTORIAL NOTE IN RESPECT OF THIS QUESTION.

8. (a) What do you understand by the statement 'The company's capital is highly geared?' In such a company, what is the effect of a rise or fall in total profits on the return to the Ordinary Shareholder? Why is it common for the capital of a property company to be highly geared?

   (b) Define 'Working Capital'. What will be the effect in a manufacturing company of a lack of working capital during a period of expanding sales? In what ways can the accountant of such a company ensure that working capital remains at an effective level?

   (*Chartered Association of Certified Accountants, Professional 2 Examination, Accounting 4, June 1980*)

9. You are required to comment BRIEFLY on the meaning and practical application of the following ratios:

   (a) Capital gearing ratio.
   (b) Shareholders' funds : total assets (the proprietary ratio).
   (c) Percentage of net trading profit to turnover.
   (d) Liquid ratio.
   (e) Yields.

   (*Chartered Association of Certified Accountants, Professional 2 Examination, Accounting 4, December 1975*)

10. You are required to write adequate notes explaining your understanding of:

    (a) 'A company being over-capitalised'. How can the situation arise, and what are the consequences thereof?

    (b) 'A company overtrading'. What are its causes and consequences, and what warning signals can be determined from an analysis of its profit and loss account and balance sheet?

    (*Chartered Association of Certified Accountants, Professional 2 Examination, Accounting 4, June 1978*)

11. You are required to give ONE example of a ratio representative of each of the following headings and to comment on its construction and usefulness:

    (a) Primary ratio.
    (b) Secondary ratio.
    (c) Solvency ratio.
    (d) Capital ratio.

    (*Chartered Association of Certified Accountants, Professional 2 Examination, Accounting 4, December 1977*)

12. From the following information extracted from the accounts of Robin Company Limited as at 31 December 19x8, you are required:

    (a) to draw up a vertical form of Balance Sheet with suitable sub-headings, and in a form suitable for analysis, and

    (b) to comment on the position disclosed thereby.

    Your comments in (b) should include the additional information you may require and any action you may consider the company needs to take.

	£		£
Bank overdraft	15,000	Plant and Machinery at cost	200,000
Sundry Creditors	25,000	Provision for depreciation –	
Sundry Debtors	7,500	on Land and Buildings	40,000
General Reserve	2,500	on Motor Vehicles	16,000
Goodwill	40,000	on Plant and Machinery	88,000
Investments at cost	22,500	Profit and Loss Account –	
Land and Buildings at cost	110,000	debit balance	42,500

Motor Vehicles at cost	20,000	Stock at valuation	24,000
6% Mortgage Debentures		Share Capital, Authorised and	
19y4/19y6	40,000	Issued –	
		100,000 5% Preference shares of	
		£1 fully paid	100,000
		140,000 Ordinary shares of £1	
		each fully paid	140,000

(Chartered Association of Certified Accountants, Professional 2 Examination,
Accounting 4, December 1978)

13. The summarised balance sheet of MacSuit and Coat Limited, together with extracts from its revenue account for the year ended 31 March 19x6, are given below:

MACSUIT AND COAT LIMITED
Balance Sheet as at 31 March 19x6

	£	£
Share Capital – Ordinary Shares of £1 fully paid		3,000
Profit and Loss account		500
		3,500
Loans by Directors		5,500
Current Liabilities		
Accrued expenses	5,000	
Trade Creditors	55,000	60,000
		£69,000
Fixed Assets		
Plant and Machinery (cost less depreciation)		10,500
Motor Vehicles (cost less depreciation)		1,500
Goodwill		1,800
		13,800
Current Assets		
Cash at bank	11,800	
Trade debtors	17,000	
Stocks and work in progress	23,500	
Prepayments	2,000	
Preliminary expense	900	55,200
		69,000

Extracts from the *profit and loss account* for the year ended 31 March 19x6 –
   Sales   £230,000.   Purchases of stock   £140,000.

	£
Profit for the year (after all expenses including those below)	4,550
Provision for Corporation Tax	Nil
Provision for depreciation of Fixed Assets	1,800
Provision for Directors' remuneration	6,400

This small company manufactures clothing and is managed by two young, capable, energetic directors with a good knowledge and experience of the trade.

They have made loans to the company to the full extent of their personal resources and currently require funds to finance a large contract worth £60,000 from reputable first class buyers for a quantity of suits.

They have applied to their bank for an unsecured overdraft limit of £15,000 to finance the contract. They have offered the bank manager their personal guarantees and postponement of their own loans. They do not wish to offer a secured debenture as they feel this would precipitate action from the company's creditors.

You are employed by the bank in its regional office as accountant adviser to bank managers in the region in respect of requests such as this.

YOU ARE REQUIRED to write a report to the bank manager –

(a) analysing the information available to you, in the context of the request made, and

(b) advising him of the risk to the bank in granting the overdraft.

(*Chartered Association of Certified Accountants, Professional 2 Examination, Accounting 4, June 1976*)

14. The summarised balance sheets of Cedar plc for the years ended 31 December 19x7 and 31 December 19x8 follow:

CEDAR PLC   BALANCE SHEETS

	Years ended 31 December	
	19x7	19x8
	£'000	£'000
Issued Share Capital in £1 Ordinary Shares, fully paid	1,200	1,200
General Revenue Reserve	240	260
Profit and Loss Account	572	510
8% Debenture Stock	—	600
Corporation Tax (payable 1 January 19x8)	148	—
Corporation Tax (payable 1 January 19x9)	178	178
Corporation Tax (payable 1 January 19y0)	—	62
Proposed Dividend	180	180
Sundry Creditors	738	1,080
	£3,256	£4,070
	£'000	£'000
Plant, at cost	1,620	1,990
Less: Depreciation	616	736
	1,004	1,254
Freehold Property	400	480
Goodwill	300	300
Stocks	990	1,276
Sundry Debtors	484	736
Bank	78	24
	£3,256	£4,070

The following information is relevant to the profits for the years ended 31 December 19x7 and 19x8:

	Years ended 31 December	
	19x7	19x8
	£'000	£'000
Sales	6,000	6,600
Net profit before Corporation Tax	560	200

Among the items charged in the calculation of net profit before Corporation tax were:

	Years ended 31 December	
	19x7	19x8
	£'000	£'000
Depreciation of plant	100	120
Bad debts	46	164
Directors' emoluments	50	52
Advertising and sales promotion	216	324

Cedar plc shares have been quoted on the London Stock Exchange since January 19x6. It had started business some 20 years ago and has had a continuous expansion record under the control of its Chairman and major shareholder, Mr Gohead. Currently, the main business is the manufacture of high quality furniture of which 45% is exported. In February 19x9, the Chairman asked the company's bankers for overdraft facilities of £400,000 during the succeeding twelve months (the overdraft limit in the year ended 31 December 19x8 had been £100,000).

In making this request, the Chairman indicated:

(1) That in the year ended 31 December 19x8, the company had expanded its production capacity and the sales organisation was extended by the acquisition of retail distribution outlets in Europe.

(2) Initial difficulties with the European acquisitions and increasingly severe competition in both home and overseas markets were the cause of the fall in profits in the year ended 31 December 19x8.

(3) These were unprecedented setbacks, but his board were hopeful that conditions would prove more favourable in the coming year.

(4) The requested overdraft facility is necessary if the company is to continue to offer delivery and credit terms comparable with its competitors in the export market.

YOU ARE REQUIRED as an investigating accountant in the bank's regional office:

(a) to draw up a memorandum for the bank manager commenting on the financial condition of Cedar plc as disclosed in the above statements, and

(b) to set out matters on which you would require further information before making a recommendation in respect of the proposed overdraft level.

(*Chartered Association of Certified Accountants, Professional 2 Examination, Accounting 4, June 1979*)

SEE FULL ANSWER IN THE APPENDIX TOGETHER WITH TUTORIAL NOTE IN RESPECT OF THIS QUESTION.

15. The latest Balance Sheet and Profit and Loss account summary of Sunlight plc, a manufacturing company, is as follows:

SUNLIGHT PLC BALANCE SHEET AS AT 31 MARCH 19x9

	£			£
Authorised Share Capital –		*Fixed Assets*		
400,000 £1 Ordinary Shares	400,000	Freehold Property (book value)		240,000
Issued and fully paid –		Plant and Machinery (cost less		
200,000 £1 Ordinary Shares	200,000	depreciation		400,000
Capital Reserves	100,000	Motor Vehicles (cost less		
Revenue Reserves	400,000	depreciation)		100,000
Shareholders' funds employed	700,000	Office Furniture (cost less		
Loan capital		depreciation)		100,000
200,000 10% £1 Debentures				
(secured on Freehold Property –				840,000
repayable 19z1)	200,000	*Current Assets*	£	
		Stocks	500,000	
Book value of Long-term funds	900,000	Debtors	200,000	
Current liabilities	£	Investments	60,000	760,000
Trade Creditors	119,200			
Bank Overdraft (secured)	439,200			
Current taxation	88,000			
Dividend payable	53,600	700,000		
	£1,600,000			£1,600,000

Summary Profit and Loss Account for the year ended 31 March 19x9

	£
Sales (all on credit)	2,000,000
Profit after charging all expenses except debenture interest	220,000
Less: Debenture Interest (gross)	20,000
Profit before taxation	200,000
Less: Corporation tax on the taxable profit for the year	88,000
Profit after taxation	112,000
Less: Ordinary dividend proposed	53,600
Retained profits transferred to revenue reserve	£58,400

Notes: Purchases for the year were £1,080,000. Cost of sales for the year was £1,500,000. The market price of a Sunlight plc ordinary share at 31 March 19x9 was £4.00. Income tax is to be taken at 33%. ACT is ignored. The company estimates the current value of its Freehold property at £440,000. The Managing Director has suggested that a figure representing the company's goodwill be computed and included in the Balance Sheet under that heading with the Shareholders' funds increased by its value.

YOU ARE REQUIRED:
(a) to compute the following ratios:
   (i) Primary ratio (using the BOOK value of total assets as capital employed).
   (ii) Secondary ratio – the profit margin.
   (iii) Secondary ratio – the turnover of capital.
   (iv) Current ratio.
   (v) Liquid ratio.
   (vi) Debtors ratio.
   (vii) Stock turnover ratio.
   (viii) Dividend yield.
   (ix) Price Earnings ratio and its reciprocal.
(b) to write a brief comment on the *liquidity* of Sunlight plc, stating the reference points to which relevant ratios can be compared.
(c) to write a memorandum to the Managing Director explaining the nature of goodwill from an accountant's point of view, and stating, *with reasons*, whether or not you recommend the inclusion of a figure for goodwill in the Balance Sheet.

(Chartered Association of Certified Accountants, Professional 2 Examination, Accounting 4, December 1979)

16. The following are the summarised revenue accounts and balance sheets of Aix Limited:
Revenue Accounts for years ended 31 December

	19x8		19x9	
	£'000	£'000	£'000	£'000
Sales		800		1,100
Less: Opening Stock	110		130	
Costs of production	500		700	
Closing stock	(130)		(170)	

Cost of goods sold	480		660	
Running expenses (including interest charges)	260	740	362	1,022

Net profit	60	78
Proposed dividend	—	40
Retained profit	60	38

Balance Sheets as at 31 December

	19x8 £'000	19x9 £'000
Ordinary share capital	200	200
Retained profit	100	138
12% debentures, issued 1 January 19x9	—	200
Bank overdraft	10	—
Dividends	—	40
Creditors	110	120
	420	698
Fixed assets	170	338
Stock	130	170
Debtors	120	160
Bank	—	30
	420	698

No dividends were paid during either 19x8 or 19x9.

REQUIRED:
(a) A calculation of the following accounting ratios and percentages for 19x8 and 19x9 presented in the following tabular format:

	19x8	19x9
Liquid ratio		
Average rate of stock turnover		
Net profit as a percentage of sales		
Earnings as a percentage of long-term capital employed		
Net earnings for ordinary shareholders as a percentage of equity		
Ratio of sales to long-term capital employed		

For the purpose of your calculations equity and long-term capital employed are to be included at their estimated figures at 30 June in each year, assuming no seasonal variations in the level of business activity.
(b.) Comment on the implications of the differences between the above ratios and percentages between the two years.
  Ignore taxation.
(*Institute of Bankers, Banking Diploma Examination, Part 2 Stage 2, Accountancy, April 1980*)

17. Cardbox plc is an unquoted public company in which the directors own in total less than 20 per cent of the issued share capital. Its business activities are concerned primarily with manufacturing and printing packaging materials. The draft accounts for 19x9 include the following information:

Balance sheets as at 31 December	*19x8*		*19x9*	
	£'000	£'000	£'000	£'000
Uses of capital				
Fixed assets at book value		690		726
Trade investments at cost		61		61
		751		787
Current Assets:				
Stock valued at the lower of total cost and net realisable value	685		625	
Debtors	421		397	
Cash balances	5		5	
	1,111		1,027	
Current Liabilities and Provisions:				
Creditors	375		420	
Bank overdraft	126		149	
Dividends	21		—	
Taxation	89		—	
	611		569	
Net Current Assets		500		458
		1,251		1,245
Sources of Capital				
Share of capital		700		700
Capital reserves		200		200
Revenue reserves		276		270
		1,176		1,170
Deferred Taxation		75		75
		1,251		1,245

Profit and Loss Account extracts, Year to 31 December

	19x8	*19x9*
	£'000	£'000
Sales (all on credit) – Home	1,906	2,014
– Overseas	520	3
	2,426	2,017
Gross Profit – Home	630	664
– Overseas	172	1
	802	665
Running costs	629	671
Net profit (loss) before tax	173	(6)
Taxation	80	—
	93	(6)

Funds Flow Statement, Year to 31 December 19x9

	£'000	£'000
Sources:		
Loss on trading		(6)
Depreciation		92
Funds generated from operations		86
Application:		
Purchase of fixed assets		128
		(42)
Increase (decrease) in working capital analysed as follows:		
Stock	(60)	
Debtors	(24)	
Creditors	(45)	
Bank	(23)	
Dividends	21	
Taxation	89	(42)

The directors consider their trade investments to be worth £72,000 at the end of 19x9. The bank overdraft is secured on freehold premises, which are used for business purposes. The premises were purchased in 19w6 and remain in the books at cost, £120,000. The auditors drew the shareholders' attention to the company's failure to depreciate freehold buildings, in their report on the 19x8 accounts. A similar qualification is likely to be made in the report on the 19x9 accounts.

On 2 January 19x9, overseas sales ceased as a result of the introduction of import restrictions by the government of the country to which goods had previously been exported.

The company has an overdraft facility with its bank, which has been fixed at £150,000 for each of the last three years. The managing director of Cardbox plc wrote to the bank on 10 January 19y0, requesting renewal of the overdraft facility for a further year and enclosing a copy of the draft accounts. The letter includes the following comments:

'It is true that the extent of my company's activities has been reduced because of the loss of our overseas market. However, you will see from the accounts that we have succeeded in increasing our home sales during 19x9 and the gross margin on home sales remains the same as in 19x8, at 33 per cent. We are hopeful that a similar increase in sales will be achieved during 19y0, and this may result in a small net profit for the year. At any rate we expect a return to profitability in 19y1 at the latest. Your continued support will be much appreciated during this difficult period.'

REQUIRED:

A full discussion of the past progress, financial position and future prospects of Cardbox plc from the viewpoint of the company's bank. You should support your answer with relevant accounting ratios and numerical calculations.

(*Institute of Bankers, Banking Diploma Examination, Part 2 State 2, Accountancy, April 1980*)

18. Accounts prepared for the benefit of shareholders are now so complex that they hinder the shareholders' understanding and therefore defeat their own purpose.
    Discuss.
    (*Institute of Chartered Accountants in England and Wales, Professional 2, Auditing, July 1980*)

19. The following is an extract from *Accountancy*, March 1977, p.50:

    "Take profit before tax divided by current liabilities; current assets as a proportion of total liabilities; current liabilities as a proportion of total tangible assets; take into account the no-credit interval; mix them in the right proportions and you can tell whether a company will go bust."

    The no-credit interval is defined as (current assets – current liabilities) divided by (operating costs excluding depreciation).

    The following are the summarised accounts of Go-go Products Ltd and Numerous Inventions Ltd for the years ended 30 April 1977 and 1976:

	Go-go Products		*Numerous Inventions*	
	1977	1976	1977	1976
	£'000	£'000	£'000	£'000
Turnover	30,067	25,417	9,734	8,044
Costs: depreciation	311	284	331	195
other	28,356	24,198	8,313	6,571
Profit before tax	1,400	935	1,090	1,278
	30,067	25,417	9,734	8,044
Intangible assets	918	937	—	—
Fixed assets	4,644	5,228	1,950	1,530
Stock	6,243	6,773	986	1,257
Debtors	4,042	4,580	3,234	2,236
Bank	516	184	2,578	1,366
	16,363	17,702	8,748	6,389
Creditors	5,261	5,144	1,297	972
Current taxation	312	379	483	321
Short-term borrowing	2,357	4,447	2,577	1,174
Long-term loans	1,409	1,168	55	38
Capital and Reserves	7,024	6,564	4,336	3,884
	16,363	17,702	8,748	6,389

You are required to:
(a) Calculate three of the stated factors for the two companies and two others you consider relevant to their going-concern status.
(b) Compare the two companies stating clearly which of your calculated ratios have moved in an unfavourable direction, and
(c) Describe and discuss the limitations of ratio analysis as a predictor of failure.
    (*Institute of Chartered Accounts in England and Wales, Professional 2 Examination, Financial Accounting 2, July 1977*)

20. The summarised balance sheet, profit and loss account and statement of sources and application of funds for Northern Manufacturing plc follow:

	31 December	
	1979	*1978*
	£'000s	£'000s
Balance Sheet		
Fixed Assets	1,900	1,400
Current assets		
Stocks	1,000	600
Debtors	800	500
Cash	—	40
	3,700	2,540
Share capital – Ordinary shares of £1	1,000	600
Reserves	600	300
Convertible 8% loan	500	500
12% Loan repayable 1990	600	600
Current liabilities		
Trade creditors	700	350
Overdraft	300	190
	3,700	2,540
Profit and Loss account		
Turnover	7,000	5,000
Trading profit before depreciation	800	500
Depreciation	600	400
Advance corporation tax paid and written off	60	33
Dividends paid, as interim and only one for year	140	67
Retained	—	—
Statement of sources and application of funds		
Profit before taxation and depreciation	800	500
Share issues	700	—
Increase in creditors	350	100
	1,850	600
Purchase of plant	1,100	200
Dividends paid	140	67
Advance corporation tax paid and written off	60	33
Increase in debtors	300	100
Increase in stock	400	200
	2,000	600
Increase (Decrease) in net bank and cash balance	(150)	

The overdraft has been renewed every three months since 1 January 1970. Since that time the maximum overdraft each year has varied between £750,000 and £250,000. The 8% loan is convertible into ordinary shares at the rate of 1 ordinary share for each £1 of loan stock on 31 December 1985.

There was an issue of new shares to existing shareholders on the basis of 4 new shares for every 6 held at a price of £1.75 each on 1 May 1979.

The 1979 accounts were published on 31 May 1980 and since that date the share price has fluctuated between £2.00 and £1.10. The current price is £1.80.

No taxation is provided as planned expansion of activities indicates that none will be payable in the foreseeable future.

YOU ARE REQUIRED TO:

(a) Calculate earnings per share as disclosed in the accounts of 1978 and 1979.

(b) Calculate the current PE ratio and the range of the ratio since 31 May 1980.

(c) Calculate three ratios based on the accounts of 1978 and 1979 appropriate to an assessment of the liquidity of the company, and

(d) Comment on the liquidity position of the company at 31 December 1979.

(*Institute of Chartered Accountants in England and Wales, Professional 2 Examination, Financial Accounting 2, July 1980*)

21. There are given below the activities of eight companies, and information from the companies' balance sheets expressed as percentages of net assets employed.

You are required to state *with reasons* which balance sheet you consider identifies with each of the companies. Marks will be allotted for *reasons* only and not for the matching of correct pairs.

The respective areas of activity of the companies are:

    A. General engineering
    B. Investment in properties for rental
    C. Estate development and house builders
    D. Whisky distillers and blenders
    E. Brewers
    F. Retail stores
    G. Conglomerate with various activities
    H. Insurance brokers

The assets and current liabilities shown as percentage of net assets employed are:

Reference	1. %	2. %	3. %	4. %	5. %	6. %	7. %	8. %
Land and property	83	31	2	32	72	81	11	147
Other fixed assets	13	28	3	22	23	7	9	3
Stock and work in progress	8	43	111	45	—	11	75	—
Trade debtors	11	36	36	56	436	4	18	7
Cash/temporary investments	4	5	1	3	91	7	1	1
	119	143	153	158	622	110	114	158
Trade creditors	(19)	(34)	(35)	(47)	(509)	(10)	(9)	(9)
Bank overdraft	(—)	(9)	(18)	(11)	(13)	(—)	(5)	(49)
Net assets employed	100	100	100	100	100	100	100	100

(*Institute of Cost and Management Accountants, Professional 1 Examination, Financial Accounting 2, May 1978*)

22. It is suggested that some of the problems of the accounting profession arise from the fact that different classes of users each attempt to obtain information particular to their own needs from the same statements.

Whom do you see as the major groupings of users of accounts?

What requirements does each group have from published financial statements?

Do you consider that these requirements are now being satisfied?

(*Institute of Cost and Management Accountants, Professional 1 Examination, Financial Accounting 2, May 1980*)

23. You are required to list and discuss four possible reasons why companies in the same type of business have different Price-Earnings (P/E) ratios. A recently published article referred to the P/E ratio as 'an attempt to value a company in terms of its earnings' and suggested that, from the point of view of an individual investor, this attempt involved a basic fallacy. In your answer comment on these views.

    (Institute of Cost and Management Accountants, Professional 3 Examination,
    Financial Management, November 1980)

    SEE APPENDIX TO WORKBOOK 3 FOR A MODEL ANSWER TO THIS QUESTION.

24. A strong likelihood exists that you will shortly be appointed to the main board of Branscombe Enterprises plc. It is probable that one of the first decisions you will be involved in will be the determination of the final ordinary dividend in respect of the financial year nearing its conclusion.

    REQUIRED:

    Identify and discuss in turn, FOUR factors of importance in arriving at a dividend decision.

    (Certified Diploma in Accounting and Finance, June 1982)

25. Experience with current cost accounting (CCA) since the issuance of SSAP 16 *Current Cost Accounting* (1980) suggests that it may not have been a success, and that the standard may have to be drastically modified, or even abandoned.

    YOU ARE REQUIRED:

    (a) to suggest ways in which SSAP 16 may have failed to justify the expectations with which it was launched; and

    (b) to point out weaknesses in the conception and in the practice of CCA which may have contributed to its failure in commending itself to the business community.

    (Chartered Association of Certified Accountants, Level 3,
    Advanced Financial Accounting, December 1984)

26. The setting of mandatory accounting standards by a semi-official body representative of the accountancy profession began in the UK and Ireland in 1970. Doubts have recently been expressed about the practical workings of the standard setting process, and about the usefulness of standard setting in general.

    YOU ARE REQUIRED:

    (a) to set out arguments *both* for *and* against the setting of mandatory accounting standards by bodies representative of professional accountants; and

    (b) to appraise the 1983 proposals of the Accounting Standards Committee for the issuing of *statements of intent* (SOI) and *statements of recommended practice* (SORP), in addition to the documents already issued by the ASC.

    (Chartered Association of Certified Accountants, Level 3,
    Advanced Financial Accounting, December 1984)

27. Certain accounting theorists have made suggestions for the amplification of published financial statements, in a manner calculated to increase their interest and usefulness to, among other persons, a company's employees. Such changes are also recommended by the Accounting Standards Committee in *The Corporate Report (1975)* and again by the UK Government in their Green Paper – *The Future of Company Reports (1977)*.

    YOU ARE REQUIRED:

    (a) to outline (but *not* to illustrate) the functions and formats of two additional statements, viz, the value added statement and the Employment Report, not at present required in the UK or Ireland by law or by any Accounting Standard, which would be helpful to a company's employees as distinct from its shareholders; and

(b) to appraise the usefulness of the said two statements for their ostensible purposes.

(*Chartered Association of Certified Accountants, Level 3,*
Advanced Financial Accounting, June 1982 – adapted)

28. (a) State what you understand by the term 'capital maintenance' and give examples of *two* capital maintenance concepts.
    (b) Outline the practical reasons for mesuring and reporting profit.

(*Chartered Association of Certified Accountants, Level 2,*
Regulatory Framework of Accounting, December 1984)

SEE APPENDIX TO WORKBOOK 3 FOR A MODEL ANSWER TO THIS QUESTION.

29. (a) What do you understand by the terms – accounting concepts, accounting bases and accounting policies? Explain the inter-relationship between them.
    (b) Why is the disclosure of accounting policies by quoted companies considered to be desirable?

(*Chartered Association of Certified Accountants, Level 2,*
Regulatory Framework of Accounting, December 1984)

30. The Companies Act 1981 has amended the reporting requirements for directors' reports by introducing new disclosure requirements and deleting some items required under previous legislation.
REQUIRED:
    (a) What additional items, not required under previous legislation, need to be disclosed in the directors' report under the Companies Act 1981?
    (b) Why do you consider certain items have been deleted from the directors' report, and how might this improve financial reporting?

(*Chartered Association of Certified Accountants, Level 2,*
Regulatory Framework of Accounting, December 1983)

31. The following data has been prepared for the managing director of a small packaging company as part of the planning process shortly after the financial year end.
Summarised financial data relating to Penryn Limited Financial year (of 52 weeks)

Year end balance sheet data	1980–1	1981–82	1982–83
	£'000s'£'000s	£'000s	
	Actual	*Actual*	*Forecast*
Net fixed assets	120	130	150
Stocks	107	124	170
Debtors	230	341	491
Bank loan (repayable in equal instalments)	59	49	39
Current liabilities (mostly trade payables)	100	203	150
Shareholders' capital	200	200	200
Retained profit	128	158	?
Cash position	30	15	?
Other information for these years			
Fixed asset acquisitions (negligible disposals)	15	34	46
Turnover	1,300	1,587	1,988

The company has in the past paid out 40% of its profits as dividends and the managing director intends to continue this practice and has already forecast £32,000 as dividends for the financial year 1982–83. The managing director has now asked for a preliminary appraisal of the forecast on the company's cash flow, and at the first stage will ignore the impact of taxation as it has been of negligible importance in the past.

YOU ARE REQUIRED:
(a) to prepare a budgeted statement of source and application of funds for the year ended 31 May 1983 in a format suitable for presentation to the managing director.
(b) to provide a statement of the explanations and implications of the results shown in (a).
(c) to provide an analysis of two options available for improving the cash flow assuming the company is unwilling to raise further long-term debt finance.

(*Certified Diploma in Accounting and Finance, June 1982*)

SEE APPENDIX TO WORKBOOK 3 FOR A MODEL ANSWER TO THIS QUESTION.

32. (a) How would you define goodwill?
    (b) Three accounting treatments of goodwill are:
        (i) retain goodwill as an asset to be amortised over its estimated useful life;
        (ii) retain goodwill as an asset indefinitely;
        (iii) write off goodwill to reserves at the time of acquisition.
    Discuss briefly the principles underlying each of these approaches.

(*Chartered Association of Certified Accountants, Level 2,*
Regulatory framework of accounting, December 1983)

Note: SSAP 22 Accounting for Goodwill was published (1984) shortly after the above question tested students knowledge of contemporary issues. So:
        (iv) qualify your answers to the sub-parts of question 32 by reference to SSAP 22.

33. The Corporate Report states that accounting information should be useful.
    REQUIRED:
    (a) Identify the characteristics of useful information and discuss each briefly.
    (b) Explain whether or not you consider that identification of desirable characteristics helps to improve financial reporting.
    (c) It has been suggested that corporate reports which possess these desirable characteristics sometimes recognise the economic substance of a transaction in preference to its legal form.
    Describe two examples of where this may occur.

(*Chartered Association of Certified Accountants, Level 2,*
Regulatory framework of accounting, June 1983)

34. The purchase by a company of its own non-redeemable shares was declared illegal by an English court decision of 1887, and specifically forbidden by the Companies Act 1980, S35, but is now permitted by the Companies Act 1981, S46–61.
    YOU ARE REQUIRED:
    (a) to set out the main arguments FOR and AGAINST permitting the practice mentioned above;
    (b) to outline *two* situations in which a company's directors might reasonably desire the company to purchase some of its own non-redeemable shares; and
    (c) to state, in each case, how the transaction would be recorded in the company's accounting records.

(*Chartered Association of Certified Accountants, Level 3,*
Advanced Financial Accounting, December 1983)

35. Fast Developments Ltd is a rapidly expanding company which during the last eighteen months has trebled its turnover. The majority of this increase in the company's sales is due to the successful penetration of a number of export markets. The internal monthly accounts have shown that profits have continually advanced. Throughout this period the net profit percentage has declined from 9.1% of sales in October 1981 to 5.4% of sales in March 1983. It was expected that profitability would have to be sacrificed in

order to achieve an increase in turnover. What was not anticipated was neither the size of the increase in sales nor the amount of the reduction in profitability.

However, as the actual profits are well ahead of the plan, the Board of Fast Development Ltd are not unduly worried. The one major concern of the Board is the ever-increasing bank overdraft – which has now reached the limit agreed with the bank. Furthermore, the company's gearing is relatively high and there is no real scope for reducing it. What is worrying the Board even more is that there are plans to double the turnover next year even though the company's margins will have to be trimmed even further.

Attached is a summary of Financial data for Fast Developments Ltd for the last three years.

WOULD YOU BE HAPPY ABOUT THE COMPANY'S FUTURE PROSPECTS? (Ignore taxation).

Fast Developments Ltd
Summary of Financial data from Past Accounts
£'000s

Year ended 31 March	1981	1982	1983
Sales	90.0	170.0	460.0
Gross profit	19.8	34.4	69.2
Net profit	6.4	17.5	28.1
Dividends	—	9.0	15.0
Equity capital	28.0	36.5	49.6
Long-term loans	16.2	31.1	53.0
Fixed assets	30.0	42.3	64.7
Current ratio	2.7	2.6	1.6
Liquid ratio	1.5	1.6	0.8

(*Certified Diploma in Accounting and Finance, June 1983*)

APPENDIX 1

Answers Workbook 1

Answers Workbook 1

The brief answers given in this appendix are intended to indicate to readers whether their own attempts are satisfactory or whether they need to review and research the text. They should be regarded as pointers to fuller answers which may be required and also double as a *glossary of accounting terms*.

Understanding the Terminology of Accounting

1.1 *Profit and loss account.* A summary of the revenue income and operating expenses of a business for an accounting period, showing also the tax charged against profit, the appropriation of after-tax profit in dividends and the balance retained.

1.2 *Trading profit.* A description used in *published* profit and loss accounts, usually indicating the profit earned from trading (or operating) activities. It is the gross profit less operating expenses.

1.3 *Gross profit percentage.* The excess of sales over cost of sales expressed as a percentage of sales.

1.4 *Mark-up.* Gross profit as a percentage of cost of sales.

1.5 *Cost of sales.* The value of opening stock plus purchases for the accounting period less closing stock.

2.1 *Trading account.* A summary account showing the sales and cost of sales for the accounting period from which the derived gross profit (or loss) is carried down to the profit and loss account.

2.2 *Stock in trade.* An account in which the accepted value of the stock at the end of the accounting period is recorded as an asset. The contra double entry credited to Trading account forms part of the cost of sales calculation.

2.3 *Turnover.* A synonym for the value of sales in an accounting period.

2.4 *Revenue expenditure.* All expenses incurred in maintaining the fixed assets of a business, in operating, selling, and administration activities undertaken towards earning revenue.

2.5 *Provisions.* An amount charged against profit to provide for the depreciation of fixed asset or retained to provide for a known or expected liability the amount of which cannot be stated with substantial accuracy, e.g. provision for doubtful debts.

3.1 *Net profit.* The excess of the value of all revenue (sales plus investment and any other income) for an accounting period over all revenue (or operating) expenditure including provisions. Usually infers the net profit before tax.

3.2 *Appropriation account.* Although tax is regarded as an appropriation (rather than a charge) of profit, this account is usually accepted as that starting with the (net) profit after tax within which dividends and appropriations to reserve are made.

3.3 *Appropriations of profit.* Interim dividends paid, final dividends proposed by the directors and transfers to reserves.

3.4 *Retained profit.* The excess of the net profit after tax over dividends paid and proposed.

3.5 *Taxable profit.* The net profit of a business assessed for tax according to tax law. It is not the same as the accounting net profit.

4.1 *Extraordinary income/expenditure.* Income and expenditure of a material value arising from circumstances or transactions *outside* the ordinary activities of the business. SSAP 6 requires their separate disclosure within the profit and loss account below the line 'net profit after taxation', any tax element arising being stated.

4.2 *Prior year item.* Material adjustments to *previous* year's profits arising from e.g. a change of accounting policy or a correction of a fundamental error, required by SSAP 6 to be adjusted against the balance of retained profits brought forward into the current profit and loss account.

4.3 *Proposed dividend.* The amounts recommended to be paid by the company directors to shareholders, charged in the profit and loss appropriation account and appearing as current liabilities in the balance sheet.

4.4 *Interim dividend.* Payments on account of a full year's dividend made at the discretion of the directors and empowered by the company's articles of association.

4.5 *Advance corporation tax.* The amount (three-sevenths of the dividend, with basic rate tax at 30%) currently payable to the Inland Revenue consequent upon the payment of a dividend as part of the payment of, but in advance of the normal due date of, corporation tax.

5.1 *Ordinary dividend.* The amount of profit distributed or proposed for distribution to the ordinary shareholders.

5.2 *Preference dividend.* The fixed dividend payable under the articles in priority to other classes of dividend. The dividend is a fixed percentage of the paid up value of the share. Like all dividends it may be paid only if profits exist.

5.3 *Earnings.* Defined in the context of earnings per share, earnings yield, or the price earnings ratio as the net profit after tax, preference dividend (if any), and minority interest (in case of a group) and before extraordinary items attributable to the ordinary shareholders (equity). SSAP 3 'Earnings per share' refers.

5.4 *Dividend cover.* The number of times the attributable earnings cover the dividend.

5.5 *Dividend percentage.* The dividend expressed as a percentage of the nominal paid up value of a share.

6.1 *Franked investment income.* Dividends received on shares in other companies which are exempt from corporation tax since they were paid out of profits which had already borne such tax.

6.2 *Unfranked payment.* A payment, e.g. interest on a debenture loan, which is an allowable expense against corporation tax. It is unfranked income in the hands of a recipient company, i.e. received from a source which has not borne corporation tax.

6.3 *Corporation tax.* Taxation on a company's income and capital gains first introduced by the Finance Act 1965 and modified in 1973 on the introduction of the imputation system of tax.

6.4 *Deferred taxation.* (Formerly called tax equalisation.) The amount a company may be liable to pay at some future time but not in the reporting year, resulting from 'timing differences'. Mainly a sum equal to the difference between the corporation tax actually payable on the taxable profit and the tax that would have been payable if the capital allowances had equalled the depreciation in the accounts.

6.5 *Overseas taxation.* Tax in other countries on a company's profits earned there, often attracting some measure of 'double taxation relief' by way of reduction of the charge to UK corporation tax.

7.1 *Loan interest payable.* The amount payable under the loan contract or debenture deed, or the amount of it outstanding and unpaid at the end of an accounting year and shown as a current liability in the balance sheet.

7.2 *Profit before tax and interest.* That level of profit which is the relevant measure against capital employed where the latter includes loan capital.

7.3 *Profit before tax.* That level of profit which is set against shareholders' funds when this is a desirable measure of return on capital employed.

7.4 *Profit after tax.* The profit (after adjusting for any extraordinary items) which accrues to the shareholders and, after payment of (any) preference dividend, to the ordinary shareholders. The proportion paid as an ordinary dividend and the residue retained as additional funds is a matter for directors' recommendation.

7.5 *Profit brought forward.* That amount of previous year's profit not appropriated as a dividend or transferred to reserve but carried forward to this year's P & L account.

8.1 *Balance sheet.* A summary of the balances of the ledger accounts of assets, liabilities and shareholders' funds remaining after the preparation of the profit and loss account, listed as the funds of the business and the employment of those funds at a specified date.

8.2 *Fixed assets.* These are the long-term assets of the business held to produce its goods or services and not intended for sale in its ordinary operating activities.

8.3 *Current assets.* Assets in which the business deals, acquired for subsequent conversion into cash within twelve months from the date of the balance sheet.

8.4 *Current liabilities.* Liabilities due to be paid within twelve months from the balance sheet date.

8.5 *Shareholders' funds.* The nominal value of paid up preference share capital (if any) plus the nominal paid up value of ordinary share capital and all reserves. Synonymous with book value of net assets.

9.1 *Net worth.* Usually synonymous with 'shareholders' funds' and 'net assets' but sometimes restricted to the balance sheet value of paid up ordinary share capital plus reserves.

9.2 *Net assets.* The book value of total assets less total liabilities, equalling the book value of shareholders' funds.

9.3 *Book value.* The value recorded in the books of account of assets, usually historic cost in HCA but property is often shown at an estimate of current market value.

9.4 *Net asset value (NAV) of an ordinary share.* Net assets after deducting the balance sheet value of (any) preference capital (or, and equally the balance sheet value of paid up ordinary share capital plus reserves) divided by the number of ordinary shares on issue at balance sheet date.

9.5 *Equity.* Usually taken to mean the issued *ordinary* share capital, but strictly includes any other share capital which has a right to participate beyond a fixed amount in a capital or revenue distribution (e.g. participating preference shares).

10.1 *Long-term funds.* Shareholders' funds plus long-term loans and deferred liabilities.

10.2 *Loan capital.* Usually long-term loans to a company subject to the terms of a loan contract.

10.3 *Total funds.* Shareholders' funds, long-term loans, deferred and current liabilities. Synonymous with gross assets.

10.4 *Gross assets.* Fixed assets, plus (any) long-term investments plus current assets.

10.5 *Mortgage debentures.* Long-term loans subject to contract (the debenture) and secured by a charge on the company's assets (specifically land and buildings).

11.1 *Capital employed.* That value of a company's capital judged to be appropriate in planning or calculating 'the return on capital employed', e.g. long-term funds; shareholders' funds; total funds.

11.2 *Preference share capital.* Share capital whose holders are entitled to a fixed dividend and/or repayment of capital in priority to other classes of shares.

11.3 *Cumulative preference shares.* Shares with the right to a fixed percentage dividend on the paid up amount each year and the right, where a dividend is not paid in any year, for the arrears to be paid out of future profits in priority to other dividends.

11.4 *Redeemable preference shares.* A class of shares repayable during the life of a company, redeemable at or before a date specified when issued.

11.5 *Ordinary share capital.* Also described as 'equity capital' and usually the major proportion of a company's capital. Entitled to the surplus profits after preferential rights have been met and in a liquidation to the residual capital (if any) after the repayment of all creditors and preference capital. The voting capital of the company and thus holding the control.

12.1 *Reserves.* The profit retained after providing preferential and ordinary dividends. It accrues to the ordinary shareholders and forms part of the ordinary shareholders' funds. Reserves also arise on the issue of shares at a premium (share premium account), the upward revaluation of assets and in other rarer circumstances.

12.2 *Capital reserves.* Reserves which by law (statutory capital reserves) cannot be distributed to the shareholders as dividends, e.g. share premium account, or which so designated by the directors are *legally* distributable but are *regarded as* non-distributable.

12.3 *Statutory capital reserves.* See 12.2.

12.4 *Share premium account.* That part of the issue price of a share being the excess over its nominal value must be credited to this account and is regarded as part of the capital of the company not free for distribution as a dividend. Its use is restricted by law (S130, CA 1985), hence its designation as a statutory capital reserve.

12.5 *Capital redemption reserve.* When redeemable equity or preference share capital is repaid out of funds representing profits, the law (S170, CA 1985) requires that a sum equal to the nominal value of the redeemed shares be transferred from distributable reserves to the non-distributable capital redemption reserve so that in effect capital is not reduced.

13.1 *Revenue reserves.* Reserves available for dividend.

13.2 *Working capital.* The excess of current assets over current liabilities, or the excess of long-term funds over long-term assets.

13.3 *Net current assets.* Synonymous with 'working capital'.

13.4 *Creditors.* Persons and businesses to whom amounts are owing.

13.5 *Debtors.* Persons and businesses from whom amounts are due, usually for supplying goods or services on credit.

14.1 *Bank overdraft.* The amount overdrawn on a current bank account and due on demand. A current liability in the balance sheet.

14.2 *Liquidity.* The measurement of a company's ability to meet currently due liabilities.

14.3 *Cash flow.* The measurement of the *flow* of cash through the business.

14.4 *Overtrading.* The expansion of sales to a level where the available working capital is insufficient to support such expansion.

14.5 *Capital structure.* The composition of long-term funds raised or provided to finance capital expenditure and working capital.

15.1 *Current ratio.* The ratio of current assets to current liabilities.

15.2 *Liquid ratio.* The ratio of those current assets in liquid or near-liquid form to current liabilities.

15.3 *Capital gearing.* The relationship of shareholders' funds and loan capital.

15.4 *Leverage.* The term used in the United States to describe the debt : equity ratio.

15.5 *Highly geared.* A capital structure where borrowed capital is significant in proportion ot the whole.

16.1 *Return on capital employed.* A comparison of the 'profit' regarded as relevant to the defined 'capital employed', e.g. profit before interest and tax to total funds (=total assets).

16.2 *Primary ratio.* Defined 'profit' to defined 'capital employed', the apex ratio in a pyramid of ratios.

16.3 *Secondary ratios.* The two ratios (profit margin), (turnover of capital) which multiplied together produce the primary ratio.

16.4 *Profit margin.* The secondary ratio measuring profit (as defined in the primary ratio) to sales.

16.5 *Turnover of capital.* The secondary ratio measuring sales against capital (as defined in the primary ratio).

17.1 *Capital expenditure.* Expenditure on (long-term) assets for use in the business and not for sale, or expenditure on *improving* the operating capacity of assets.

17.2 *Capital commitments.* Capital expenditure contracted for (but not provided for in the accounts) or authorised by the directors to be shown by way of note or otherwise in the published accounts (CA 1985).

17.3 *Deferred revenue expenditure.* Expenditure not resulting in the acquisition of a capital (fixed) asset, but is revenue in character, material in amount and expected to benefit succeeding accounting periods, e.g. advertising. That proportion regarded as relevant to future periods is carried forward in the balance sheet to be written off over time.

17.4 *Write off.* An amount, expense or loss charged against (debited to) the current year profit and loss account, e.g. a debtor account balance regarded as irrecoverable – a write off of a bad debt.

17.5 *Depreciation provision.* An amount charged against profit representing the proportion of the cost of a fixed asset regarded as used up during the current accounting period (i.e. akin to an expense for the use of the asset) and resulting in the retention of profit (where profit is earned) which might otherwise be distributed. Its necessary charge where losses are made will increase the loss, reduce reserves or when reserves do not exist, reduce capital.

18.1 *Price-earnings ratio.* The relationship of the (daily) market price of an ordinary share and the attributable earnings per ordinary share as determined in the most recent published profit and loss account.

18.2 *Market price of equity.* The daily stock exchange price of a listed ordinary share.

18.3 *Dividend yield.* The percentage of the dividend paid and/or proposed in the most recent financial year to current market price of the related share.

18.4 *Earnings yield.* The percentage of the attributable earnings per ordinary share as determined in the most recent profit and loss account to the current market price of that share. The reciprocal of the price-earnings ratio.

18.5 *Earnings per share.* The attributable earnings per ordinary share as determined in the most recent profit and loss account divided by the number of ordinary shares in issue at the end of the year (or the weighted number in specific circumstances).

19.1 *Goodwill.* In accounting terms, the excess of price paid for the controlling interest in a business over the agreed market value of the net assets acquired. This definition of *purchased* goodwill contrasts with that of SSAP 22 which embraces any goodwill inherent in a business whether purchased or not. This states "goodwill as the difference between the value of the business as a whole and the aggregate of the fair values of its separable net assets."

19.2 *Research and development expenditure.* Expenditure on research undertaken to gain new technical knowledge (pure research) directed to a specific practical application (applied research) or expenditure using technical knowledge to produce new products, etc (development). Except for development expenditure meeting criteria stated in SSAP 13 which may be deferred to later periods, all R & D should be written off as incurred.

19.3 *Contingent liabilities.* Liabilities which may arise as a condition in existence at balance sheet date where the outcome is dependent upon the happening, or failure to happen, of an uncertain future event or events. Excluded from this definition are uncertainties relating to accounting estimates. Material contingent liabilities expected to arise should be provided for in current accounts, otherwise if the arising of a liability is other than remote (no action) the accounts should contain a note. (SSAP 18.)

19.4 *Short-term investment.* Such an investment may be made using temporary surplus cash and thus earn some return pending its realisation so that the proceeds may be used by the business. Designated as a current asset if it is expected that it will be realised within twelve months of balance sheet date.

19.5 *Investment in subsidiary.* The purchase of a majority (partly owned subsidiary) or all the controlling voting shares in another business.

20.1 *Holding company.* (Also known as parent company.) The company purchasing the majority or all the controlling voting (ordinary) shares in a subsidiary. Where, in turn, the majority of its shares (or all of them) are held by another company, the latter is the ultimate holding company and the others are designated subsidiary and sub-subsidiary companies respectively.

20.2 *Parent company.* See 20.1.

20.3 *Subsidiary.* See 20.1. *Note:* in addition to the usual circumstances in which the holding-subsidiary relationship arises, it may also arise where the holding company is a member of the subsidiary and controls the composition of its board of directors.

20.4 *Wholly owned subsidiary.* Where the holding company holds all of the equity share capital of a company it is 'wholly owned'.

20.5 *Minority interest.* Where the holding company holds more than half of the equity capital but less than all of that capital, the net asset value attributable to the remaining (outside) shareholders is designated the minority interest in the consolidated accounts of the group.

21.1 *Associated company.* One company is defined (SSAP 1) as an associated company of another, if, whilst not being a subsidiary, the other (investing) company is (1) effectively involved as a partner in a joint venture; or (2) its interest is long term, not less than 20%, and it can exercise significant influence.

21.2 *Public limited company* (PLC). A public company is one limited by shares, the memorandum of which states that it is to be a public company and which has been registered as such (1(3), 735(2), CA 1985). Its capital must not be less than 'the authorised minimum' (£50,000, alterable by statutory instrument). Minimum members are two. It can raise money from the public at large, e.g. by issue of shares or debentures.

21.3 *Limited liability.* The concept that the liability of a member of a registered company is limited in the case of a company limited by shares to the amount *unpaid* on his shares.

21.4 *Private limited company.* Unless a company is specifically registered as a public company, it will be private, with the consequence that it must not offer its shares or debentures to the public (1(3), 735(2), CA 1985).

21.5 *Listed company.* A company whose securities have been granted a listing on a recognised stock exchange so that a market is made for them.

22.1 *Historic cost accounts* (HCA). Accounts in which substantially all entries are recorded at actual monetary cost or monetary income, or based thereon. The more recent practice of including some fixed assets, principally property, at a valuation, led to the description 'basic accounts'.

22.2 *Current cost accounts.* A phrase first suggested by the Sandilands Committee for their recommended system of value accounting, meant to provide a direct contrast to HCA. Now appended to the SSAP 16 system.

22.3 *Accounting concepts.* The well established basic assumptions which underlie the periodic financial accounts of business enterprises, principally, (1) the going concern concept, (2) the accruals concept, (3) the consistency concept, and (4) the prudence concept.

22.4 *SSAPs.* Statements of Standard Accounting Practice describe methods of accounting for particular transactions approved by the professional accounting bodies and obligatory on their members to observe or to justify departures therefrom.

22.5 *EEC Directives.* Company law directives which, after adoption by the Council of Ministers, are required to be incorporated into the domestic laws of member countries.

23.1 *Authorised capital.* The full amount of capital which a company is authorised to raise as stated in its Memorandum of Association; also called its nominal capital.

23.2 *Issued capital.* That part of the authorised capital which has been issued to the shareholders whether paid up or not.

23.3 *Paid up capital.* That part of the issued capital which has been paid up by the shareholders. The sum actually received in cash or other consideration.

23.4 *Called up capital.* That part of the issued capital which the company has called up. It is not bound to require the full nominal amount of each share to be paid immediately, but can call up such parts as it requires.

23.5 *Nominal value.* The nominal value of a share is its face value, which is not necessarily the price at which it is issued. It is the amount recorded in the share capital account of the company, any excess over nominal value being credited to share premium account. Shares may no longer be issued at a discount, i.e. for less than their nominal value (100, 112, 114 CA 1985).

24.1 *Fully paid up shares.* Issued shares upon which the issue price has been fully paid so that consequently the member has no further liability.

24.2 *Fixed interest capital.* Share capital (preference shares) carrying the right to a fixed dividend, or loan capital (e.g. debentures) carrying the right to a fixed rate of interest. The latter is an obligatory expense of the company but the former may only be paid where profits exist.

24.3 *Institutional investors.* For example, pension funds, insurance companies, banks, etc., as investors in company shares and debentures and elsewhere.

24.4 *Floating charge.* A charge on the assets of a company given by a debenture or trust deed in order to secure money borrowed by the company, and having the characteristics: (1) it is a charge on a class of assets of a company, present and future; (2) which class is, in the ordinary course of business, changing from time to time, and (3) it is contemplated by the charge that, until the holders of the charge take steps to enforce it, the company may carry on business in the ordinary way as far as concerns the class of assets charged.

24.5 *Fixed charge.* This is a mortgage of ascertained and definite property and prevents the company from realising that property without the consent of the holders of the charge.

25.1 *Rights issue.* New shares being offered to existing shareholders in proportion to their existing holdings and at a discount to the current market price.

25.2 *Bonus issue.* Also known as a scrip issue or capitalisation issue; a free issue of new shares to existing shareholders, made by capitalising reserves.

25.3 *Convertible debentures.* More usually convertible unsecured loan stock which allows the holders the right to take shares of the company on stated conversion terms during a given period in the life of the loan as an alternative to cash within the redemption period.

25.4 *Liquidation.* The legal termination of the life of a company, either voluntary – initiated by resolution of the company in general meeting – or compulsory, i.e. by the Court initiated by petition to the Court.

25.5 *Unsecured creditors.* Those persons or businesses having an unsecured claim on the assets of a company for goods provided or services rendered, who in a liquidation rank after secured creditors, liquidation costs, preferential creditors and debenture holders secured by a floating charge.

26.1 *Double-entry book-keeping.* The system of recording financial transactions based on the fundamental principle of equating the resources held by an enterprise with the claims against the enterprise in respect of those resources. The earliest published source of the technique is the work of a Franciscan friar, Luca Pacioli – Summa de Arithmetica, Geometrica, Proportione et Proportionalita, 1494.

26.2 *True and fair view.* A company's legal obligation (S228, 230 and 258, CA 1985) in respect of its published profit and loss account and balance sheet is that the accounts should give a true and fair view of the profit (loss) for the financial year and its state of affairs at the year end. The use of the phrase 'true and fair' instead of the word 'correct' in this context implies that given different judgements in respect of figures to be recorded, different sets of accounts could be produced – the essence of the phrase being that the judgement made should be based on the consistent application of current accounting practice to show as objective a picture as possible.

The CA 1985 restates the 1948 provision that the requirement to give a true and fair view overrides all other accounting requirements of the Companies Acts. Where necessary, additional notes must be provided in the accounts to meet the legal obligation, and where the directors depart from an accounting requirement so that a true and fair view is the result, they must give information on the departure and its effects.

26.3 *Prudence concept.* One of the broad, basic assumptions which underlie the periodic financial accounts, implying that no profit or income is anticipated, but that all known liabilities are brought into account.

26.4 *Going concern concept.* Another of the fundamental accounting concepts and is the assumption that the financial accounts have been compiled on that basis with no intention or need for the business to go into liquidation.

26.5 *Statutory audit.* The work to be undertaken by auditors recognised for the purpose by the Companies Acts and appointed by the company to enable them to report to the members (the shareholders) whether, in their opinion, the profit and loss account and the balance sheet, and any group accounts, have been properly prepared in accordance with law and give a true and fair view of the profit (loss) and state of affairs of the company or group. There are other duties connected with the statutory audit of the accounts, for example, a duty is placed on the auditors to consider whether the information given in the directors' report is consistent with the accounts. Inconsistencies must be reported in the auditors' report.

27.1 *Memorandum of association.* This is the document forming the constitution of the company and defining its objects and powers.

27.2 *Articles of association.* These are the rules for the company's operation; they define the rights of the members and the powers and duties of the directors.

27.3 *Directors' statutory declaration.* This is required to be given by the directors of a *private* limited company proposing to make a payment out of capital for the redemption or purchase of its own shares. (S170–7 CA 1985.) It will state their opinion of the continuing solvency of the company. It will be accompanied by an auditors' report confirming the reasonableness of the declaration and stating that the permissible capital payment (see 27.4) specified in the declaration has, in their view, been properly determined in accordance with the Act.

27.4 *Permissible capital payment* (see 27.3). This is the amount which may be paid by a private company out of capital for the redemption or purchase of its own shares. It will be equal to the price of redemption or purchase after deducting the distributable profits of the company *and* the proceeds of any fresh issue of shares made for the purposes of redemption or purchase.

27.5 *Realised profit.* For the purposes of references to the phrase 'realised profits' in the 1980 and 1981 legislation, para 91, 4 Sch. CA 1985, in respect of profits available for distribution etc., these are such profits of the company treated as realised for accounting purposes in accordance with generally accepted accounting principles at the time the accounts were prepared.

28.1 *Statement of intent* (SOI). A public statement by the ASC setting out in a brief summary how it intends to deal with a particular accounting matter.

28.2 *Statement of recommended practice* (SORP). An authoritative pronouncement on an important accounting issue which does not meet all the criteria for an accounting standard. There are two types (1) prepared and issued by ASC dealing with matters of widespread application but not fundamental importance, and (2) prepared and issued by, subject to ASC approval, for example a specific industry on matters of limited application.

28.3 *Franked SORP.* The seal of approval given by ASC to the type 2 SORP noted in 28.2.

28.4 *Exposure draft.* The public exposure of the full text of a proposed accounting standard, including, to stimulate comment, details of the background to the subject matter and some of the arguments for and against the proposals.

28.5 *International accounting standard* (IAS). An accounting standard formulated and issued in the world-wide public interest by the International Accounting Standards Committee, aimed at promoting generally accepted and observed international reporting rules in the presentation of audited financial statements.

29.1 *Finance lease.* This is defined in the context of SSAP 21, 'Accounting for leases and hire purchase contracts', as a lease that transfers substantially all the risks and rewards of ownership of an asset to the lessee.

29.2 *Capital lease.* The term is synonymous with finance lease (29.1).

29.3 *Operating lease.* This is defined by SSAP 21 as any lease other than a finance lease. It is a short-term lease of some physical asset, usually cancellable at short notice and without material penalty. The rights and obligations of ownership subsist with the lessor.

29.4 *Off-balance sheet item.* The term indicates an asset, liability or other transaction pertaining to a view of the company's value which was not required by law or practice to be noted or shown in the company report and accounts. Prior to the requirements of SSAP 21 to capitalise (the rights in) the asset and the obligations to the lessor under a finance lease, such information was an example of an off-balance sheet item.

29.5 *Hire purchase contract.* A contract for the hire of an asset which contains a provision giving the hirer an option to acquire legal title to the asset upon the fulfilment of certain conditions stated in the contract.

30.1 *Acquisition accounting.* The method commonly used for accounting for business combinations where the results of the acquired company are brought into the group accounts only from the date of acquisition. Assets acquired are stated at cost to the acquiring group (SSAP 23).

30.2 *Merger accounting.* An alternative to 30.1, where, conversely, the financial statements are aggregated and presented as if the combining companies had always been together (SSAP 23).

30.3 *Pooling of interests.* An alternative description of merger accounting noted also in IAS 22 as a 'uniting of interests'.

30.4 *Vendor rights.* A method of financing a business combination aimed at allowing a transaction, in essence a takeover, to be accounted for as a merger in order to gain attendent benefits.

30.5 *Vendor placing.* This is similar to and has the same objective as vendor rights. Whereas in vendor rights the shares of the acquiring company issued as the purchase consideration for the acquisition are subsequently bought back by the rights agreement, in vendor placing they are purchased through an institutional placing.

Recapitulation Questions Including Multi-choice

1. Accounts prepared under the requirements of the CA 81 (SS228, 230, 258 CA 85) must give a true and fair view of the company's state as at the end of its financial year, and of its profit or loss for that year. This requirement over-rides all other accounting requirements of the Companies Acts as to matters contained in the company's accounts or notes to the accounts. *And see the Answer to Q.2.*

2. The new requirements of the CA 81 were:
    (a) any additional information necessary to give a true and fair view *must* be provided in the accounts; *and*
    (b) in special circumstances where compliance with the requirements of the Companies Acts 1948–81, now consolidated in the CA 85, would *not* give a true and fair view (even if additional information as required by (a) was given), the directors *must* depart from that requirement. Where they do so, particulars of the departure, the reasons for it and its effect, must be disclosed in a note to the accounts.

3. Modified accounts to be filed with the Registrar (as opposed to the accounts to be presented to the shareholders) are not intended to give a true and fair view and this is especially the case for small companies. *And see the Answer to Q.4.*

4. SSAPs apply to all financial statements intended to give a true and fair view of the financial position and the profit or loss. They are declarations by the accountancy profession that save, in exceptional circumstances, accounts which do not comply with a standard will not give a true and fair view. Modified accounts filed with the Registrar are not intended to give a true and fair view; hence, although based on the shareholders' accounts which must comply with SSAPs, the modified accounts need not include disclosures or statements required by SSAPs. Thus, for example, no statement of source and application of funds is required.
    Note: The concept of a true and fair view is dynamic, whereas statutory and standard requirements are static, at least during the period they are in force.

5. It represents professional opinion about the standards which readers may reasonably expect in accounts which are intended to be true and fair, *and* because accountants are professionally obliged to comply with a SSAP, it creates in the reader's mind an expectation that the accounts will be in conformity with the standards. This is in itself a

reason why accounts which depart from the standard *without adequate explanation* may not be true and fair.

6. The Directors' Statutory Declaration specifies the amount of the permissible capital payment and their opinion of the solvency and going concern status of the company. The audit report attached to the declaration must state that: (a) they have inquired into the company's state of affairs; (b) the permissible capital payment as specified in the declaration has, in their view, been properly determined in accordance with the Act (CA 81 S54/SS170, 171, 172, CA 85); and (c) they are not aware of anything to indicate that the opinion expressed by the directors in the declaration is unreasonable.

7. The CA 81 (S237, 261, CA 85) places a duty on the auditor of a company (with the except of banking, insurance and shipping companies) to consider whether the information given in the Directors' Report relating to the financial year in question is *consistent* with the company's financial statements for the period. If he considers that any of the information given is inconsistent, he *must* state that fact in his report. Otherwise, no reference need be made by the auditor to the Directors' Report.

8. SSAP 2 defines 'the going concern concept' as meaning that the enterprise will continue in operational existence for the *foreseeable future*. The CA 81 underlined its importance (4 Sch. CA 85) stating as a first accounting principle that, 'the company shall be presumed to be carrying on business as a going concern'. There is no interpretation in the Standard or the Act as to the precise meaning of the term 'going concern', neither does SSAP 2 delineate the phrase 'foreseeable future', but it is likely that users would assume that going concern based accounts are prima-facie evidence that the company assumes there is no intention or necessity to liquidate or curtail significantly the scale of operation; that this will be the position at least until the next set of annual accounts are prepared and presented. Auditors will appreciate the significance of this assumption to their responsibilities not only to the shareholders of a company, but also to third parties, and in the present climate of litigation, will be watchful for indications of going concern problems.

9. In general, the accounting policies adopted in the determination of profit or loss and the preparation of the balance sheet for the period, *must* be stated in the notes to the accounts. In particular, the Act requires that the policies are explained in respect of (a) foreign currency translation, and (b) depreciation and the diminution in the value of assets.

10. '. . . references to realised profits in relation to a company's accounts are references to such profits of the company as fall to be treated as realised profits for the purposes of those accounts *in accordance with the principles generally accepted for accounting purposes at the time when those accounts are prepared.*' The precise determination of accounting principles and, therefore, profits is left to the profession. What is regarded as acceptable accounting practice will be acceptable in law.

11. Where redeemable equity or preference share capital is repaid out of funds representing profits, the CA 81 (S170 CA 85) requires that a sum equal to the nominal value of the redeemed shares shall be transferred from distributable reserves to the non-distributable capital redemption reserve, so that in effect capital is not reduced. Similarly, where a company, empowered by its articles, purchases its own shares (whether designated redeemable or not) wholly or partly out of distributable profit, a transfer to capital redemption reserve is required.

12. 'Net Assets' are defined as total assets less liabilities and provisions. The 'undistributable

reserves' are (a) the share premium account, (b) the capital redemption reserve, (c) the excess of current unrealised profits less unrealised losses (*Note:* the CA 81 Revaluation Reserve (4 Sch. 34 CA 85)) and (d) any reserve, the distribution of which is prohibited by the company's memorandum or articles.

13. (a) The company must be so authorised by its articles;
    (b) No redeemable shares (equity/preference) may be issued unless there are shares in issue which are not redeemable;
    (c) Redeemable shares must be cancelled on redemption;
    (d) No redemption may take place unless (i) the shares are fully paid, (ii) the shares are redeemed out of distributable profits or out of the proceeds of a fresh issue, *and* (iii) any premium payable on redemption must be paid out of distributable profits of the company, except where it is paid out of the proceeds and the shares redeemed were *issued* at a premium. In this case, the premium on redemption may be provided out of the share premium account to the extent that it does not exceed the *lesser* of (i) premiums received on the *issue* of the shares being redeemed and (ii) the balance on the share premium account.

14. Financial statements should be prepared on the basis of conditions existing at the balance sheet date. Material events after balance sheet date should be *disclosed* where this is necessary to enable users to reach a proper understanding of the financial position. The Standard refers to such events as non-adjusting events. Adjusting events are those of material effect, e.g. the insolvency of a large (amount) debtor or changes in taxation as happened to the system of deferred tax following the Finance Act 1984. In these cases the accounts are adjusted to prevent a misleading view.

15. Properties held as investments, rather than for use in a manufacturing or commercial enterprise, should not be depreciated but should be revalued annually and the valuation incorporated in financial statements.

16. The net investment concept in the context of SSAP 20, 'Foreign currency translation', recognises that the investment of a holding company is represented by the 'net worth of the foreign business enterprise' rather than by the direct investment in its individual assets/liabilities.

17. SSAP 13 requires that pure and applied *research* costs be written off in the year of expenditure. (*Note:* The CA 85 stipulates that research costs may not be treated as an asset.)

18. *Development* expenditure may be deferred to future periods only:
    (i) where there is a clearly defined project; and
    (ii) the related expenditure is separately identifiable; and
    (iii) the outcome of the project has been assessed with reasonable certainty as to its technical feasibility and to its ultimate commercial viability (in the light of stated factors);
    (iv) if further development costs are to be incurred on the same project, the aggregate of such costs together with related production, selling and administration costs are reasonably expected to be more than covered by related future revenues; and
    (v) adequate resources exist, or are reasonably expected to be available, to enable the project to be completed and to provide any consequential increases in working capital.

19. The Share Premium Account may be used:
    (i) to provide for the paying up of shares for distribution as a bonus issue; or

(ii) to write off the expenses of forming a company, the expenses and commissions of issuing share or loan capital, or to provide for the premium on the redemption of redeemable shares or loan capital;

(iii) where a private company purchases or redeems its own shares out of capital, the share capital and undistributable reserves (share premium account included) will be reduced by the permissible capital payment.

20. On the issue of the revised SSAP 15 (1985) 'Accounting for deferred tax', the liability method became the prescribed method. The liability method of accounting for deferred taxation requires the balances on that account to be maintained at the rate of corporation tax current in the year of account. The deferral method involves the recording of deferred taxation applicable to original timing differences at the rate of tax then current and their reversal at the same rate.

21. The objective test contained in SSAP 23 is to determine whether or not a business combination may be treated as a merger and whether or not material resources have left one or other of the combining companies. If an acquisition involves a material cash payment by the acquiring company (more than 10%) then the conditions for merger accounting have *not* been met because resources have left that company. Alternatively, if the acquirer issues its own shares of not less than 90% of the fair value of the total consideration, only limited resources will have left the company and merger accounting would be appropriate.

22. Government grants may (i) be deducted from the capital cost of additions (fixed assets) during the year, effectively spreading the benefit of the grant over the life of the assets as the annual depreciation charge is reduced; (ii) the grants may be credited to profit and loss account as deferred income over the life of the assets. The net effect of either method is the same.

Questions 23 to 29 inclusive based on SSAP 22

Q.23 incorrect; Q.24 correct; Q.25 (i) incorrect; Q.25 (ii) correct; Q.25 (iii) incorrect; Q. (iv) incorrect; Q.26 (i) incorrect; Q.26 (ii) incorrect; Q.26 (iii) correct; Q.27 (i) incorrect; Q.27 (ii) incorrect; Q. 28 incorrect; Q.29 correct.

30. For the purposes of the CA 1981 (4 Sch. 92 CA 85) a related company is one in which the investing company holds on a long-term basis a 'qualifying capital interest' for the purpose of securing a contribution to its own activities by the exercise of any control or influence arising from that interest. 'Qualifying capital interest' means the holding of equity share capital with the right to vote. Where that interest is 20% or more of all nominal value equity shares carrying voting rights, there is a presumption that the company in question is a related company.

31. SSAP 9 requires that long-term contract work in progress should be valued at cost plus any attributable profit, less any foreseeable losses and progress payments received and receivable. If, however, anticipated losses on individual contracts exceed the cost incurred to date, less progress payments received and receivable, such excesses should be shown separately as provisions.

32. The CA 81 – 4 Sch. CA 85 – valuation rules do not permit the inclusion of profit in the valuation of a current asset. Consequently when profit is included in the valuation of long-term contract work in progress so as to meet the over-riding need for the accounts to show a true and fair view, particulars of the departure from the legal provision, the reasons for it and its effect, must be disclosed in a note to the accounts.

33. The contingent liability should be brought into the accounts when (i) the future event related to it is probable; (ii) it will result in a loss; (iii) the amount of the loss can be assessed with reasonable accuracy; and (iv) the amount is material.

APPENDIX 2

Answers Workbook 2

Answers Workbook 2

1.

Balance sheet as at the financial year end

Funds	£	Assets	£
Shareholders' funds (balancing figure)	260,000	Fixed Assets	209,000
10% Mortgage Debentures	45,000		
Current liabilities	140,000	Current Assets	236,000
	£445,000		£445,000

2. Total funds at book value £445,000 are represented by Gross assets of £445,000.

3.

Vertical form of Balance sheet as at the financial year end

Long-term Funds		£
Shareholders' funds		260,000
10% Mortgage Debentures		45,000
Book value of long-term funds		£305,000

Invested in:		
Fixed Assets		209,000
Working capital	£	
Current Assets	236,000	
less Current Liabilities	140,000	96,000
		£305,000

Note: This form of balance sheet shows that the long-term funds cover the whole of the investment in the long-term (fixed) assets and provide £96,000 for working capital.

4. The items listed in Question 4(i) are classified in the balance sheet below given as the answer to Question 4(ii). The 10% Mortgage Debentures are long-term liabilities in balance sheet terms provided that their repayment date(s) are more than 12 months later than the balance sheet date.

*Vertical form of Balance Sheet as at
the financial year end*

	£	£	
*Authorised Share Capital**			*Not part of the
250,000 £1 Ordinary Shares	250,000		balance sheet totals
Issued Share Capital			
200,000 £1 Ordinary Shares fully paid	200,000		
General revenue reserve	50,000		
Profit & Loss Account (credit)	10,000	260,000	*Shareholders' funds.*
10% Mortgage Debentures		45,000	
		305,000	*Long-term funds.*
Current liabilities			
Sundry creditors	75,000		
Proposed dividend	20,000		
Current taxation	45,000	140,000	
		£445,000	*Book-value total funds.*
Fixed Assets			
Land & Buildings	50,000		
Plant & Machinery	126,000		Book value.
Patents	33,000	209,000	Book value.
Current Assets			
Stock	76,000		
Sundry debtors	116,000		
Cash in hand and at bank	44,000	236,000	
		£445,000	*Gross Assets.*

Note: An alternative form of this balance sheet would be a detailed elaboration to answer (3).

5. (a) *Current ratio* (assuming the same credit period for debtors and creditors)
    £236,000 : £140,000 = *1.69 to 1.*
    (b) *Liquid ratio* (assuming the same credit period for debtors and creditors)
    £160,000 : £140,000 = *1.14 to 1.*
    (c) *Net Asset value of one ordinary share* based on balance sheet values. Shareholders'
    funds = Net Assets = £260,000 (given as a sub-total in the balance sheet answer 4
    (above)).
    Proof: Gross Assets £445,000 less (Current liabilities £140,000 plus Long-term
    liabilities £45,000) = £260,000.
    Net Assets £260,000 divided by the *number* of Ordinary Shares,i.e.
    200,000 = Net Asset Value (NAV) per Ordinary Share = *£1.30.*
    (d) *Dividend percentage* (assuming no interim dividends)
    Dividend £20,000 as a percentage of the *nominal* value of the ordinary shares i.e.
    of £200,000 = *10%.*
    (e) *Dividend yield* (assuming no interim dividends)
    Dividend £20,000 as a percentage of the *market* value £1.50 of the ordinary shares,
    i.e. of 200,000 × £1.50 = £300,000 = *6.66%*
    or Dividend percentage $\times \dfrac{\text{nominal value}}{\text{market value}} = 10\% \times \dfrac{£1.00}{£1.50} = 6.66\%$

6. (a) The appropriate 'rate of return' on total assets is the 'net operating profit'

$$\frac{£130,000}{£445,000} \times 100 = 29.2\% \text{ (one form of a 'return on capital employed').}$$

(b) The 'turnover' of capital (total assets) is shown by Sales : Total Assets

$$\frac{£650,000}{£445,000} = 1.46 \text{ times}$$

(c) The appropriate 'rate of return' to Sales is again the 'net operating profit'

$$\frac{£130,000}{£650,000} \times 100 = 20\%.$$

NB: The end of the year figure of 'total assets' is used in the absence of the opening (of the period) balance sheet which would have allowed for the calculation of the more appropriate 'average total assets'.

(d) The reconciliation of the answers (a) (b) and (c) is based on the equation:

Return on Capital (Total Assets) = Return on Sales × Turnover of Capital
= (a) 29.2%   = (c) 20% ×   (b) 1.46 times.

(e) The 'Net profit after tax but before extraordinary items' to 'Shareholders' funds

$$= \frac{£80,500}{£260,000*} \times 100 = 30.9\%.$$

*The average of the 'Shareholders' funds' for the year would be more appropriate.

(f) The earnings Yield is 'the net profit after tax and before extraordinary items' to the market value of Equity Shares

$$= \frac{£80,500}{£300,000*} \times 100 = 26.8\%.$$

*200,000 shares × £1.50p.

Note: Answer (e) 30.9% exceeds (f) 26.8% because the book value of the Ordinary Share (see 5(c)) £1.30p, is less than the market value £1.50p.

(g) Earnings per share is 'the profit *attributable* to the ordinary shareholder divided by the number of ordinary shares in issue.

In this exercise, as there are no preference dividends, it is that figure used in (f) £80,500 divided by 200,000 shares = 40.25 pence per share.

Note: It has been assumed that the number of ordinary shares remained unchanged during the year.

(h) Price − Earnings Ratio (PER) is the market price of the ordinary share divided by attributable 'earnings per share':

150.00p divided by 40.25p = 3.73 to 1.

(i) The cover provided for the debenture interest by the profit before interest and tax is:

£130,000 divided by £4,500 equals 29 times.

(j) Strictly, the rate of turnover of stock cannot be calculated from the figures given. Assuming the company was a manufacturing company the figure for 'stock' in the balance sheet would include stocks of raw materials, work in progress, and finished goods. The 'stock turnover' would be given by 'cost of sales' divided by 'average finished goods stock'.

On the figures given, 'Cost of Sales' £390,000 divided by 'Closing Stock' £76,000 = 5.1 times.

(k) Average collection period of debtors (taking end of year debtors in place of average debtors) is:

Debtors $\dfrac{£116,000}{£650,000} \times 365$ (days) = 65 days.

(l) Dividend cover. Attributable earnings divided by dividend = £80,500 divided by £20,000 = 4 times.

(m) *Profitability*

To make any reasonable comment on the company's profitability, comparative information would be needed:

e.g. (a) Industry statistics, (b) the company's own budgeted targets, (c) the company's previous year's record, (d) other market, economic information.

  (i) The 'operating profit' to 'sales', 20%, is high for a manufacturing company, the 'sales/total assets' figure is average, so that the 'operating profit' to 'total assets' of 29.2% is good.

  (ii) Earnings per share of 40.25 pence is an excellent result. The earnings yield (26.8%) and its reciprocal the PER (3.73) are dependant on the market's view of the value of the share. At £1.50 it is not a great deal above the Net Asset Value per share of £1.30, and it appears that the market is not convinced of the company's grcwth potential, its product/market position and its dividend policy. The market's view may also be a reflection of a 'general slump' position. If the company can maintain this year's results, then it is likely that its share price is undervalued by the market.

(n) *Dividend/Retention policy*

There were no 'Reserves' prior to this year, the whole £50,000 being appropriated out of this year's profit. Only £2,000 stood on Profit and Loss account at the beginning of the year.

Its dividend policy is therefore conservative, dividend being covered 4 times. The strong retention policy may reflect recent poor profits (check with previous year's results) or a budgeted policy decisions. If the latter is the case it is added evidence of the underpricing of the share. High retentions towards growth are attractive to investors looking for capital appreciation and ordinarily the share price should rise. However, investors looking for high income potential and a higher percentage distribution of 'attributable earnings' would find the policy unattractive.

7. (a) £290,000 (see answer 7(d)).
    (b) £190,000 Ordinary Shareholders' funds divided by 100,000 (shares) = £1.90.
    (c) £155,000 Current Assets less £50,000 Current Liabilities = £105,000 or £290,000 Long-term (Shareholders') funds less £185,000 Long-term (Fixed Assets) = £105,000.
    (d)

BLOUGH LTD Balance Sheet as at year end

	£	£
100,000 6% £1 Preference Shares fully paid		100,000
100,000 Ordinary £1 Shares fully paid	100,000	
Revenue Reserves	60,000	
Profit and Loss account balance	30,000	190,000
Net book value of the business		£290,000
Fixed Assets		
Premises	75,000	
Machinery less depreciation	110,000	185,000
Current Assets		
Stock	55,000	
Debtors	32,000	
Cash	68,000	
	155,000	

Current liabilities	£		
Trade creditors	34,000		
Proposed ordinary dividend	10,000		
Proposed preference dividend	6,000	50,000	105,000
			£290,000

8. Effect of transactions (a) to (d) on accounts listed in BLOUGH LTD balance sheet:

(a) Debit – Dividend accounts (reduced to zero)   Credit – Cash at bank £16,000
       Proposed ordinary £10,000   (Cash paid out)
       Proposed preference £6,000

(b) Debit – Cash (received from debtors) £12,000   Credit – Debtors' accounts £12,000
                                                   (Reducing balance due)

    Debit – Creditors' accounts £14,000   Credit – Cash at bank £14,000
       (reducing balance due)   (Paid to creditors)

(c) Debit – Machinery account £50,000   Credit – Cash at bank £10,000
       (increasing balance sheet value)   (Paid as deposit)
                                                   Credit – Creditor account
                                                   £40,000 (amount still owing)

(d) Debit – Cash (received from shareholders)   Credit – Ordinary share capital
       £75,000   £50,000 (Nominal value)
                                                   Credit – Share Premium account
                                                   £25,000 (Premium received)

REVISED BALANCE SHEET reflecting above changes
       BLOUGH LTD Balance Sheet after above transactions

	£	£
100,000 6% £1 Preference shares fully paid		100,000
150,000 Ordinary £1 shares fully paid	150,000	
Share Premium account	25,000	
Revenue Reserves	60,000	
Profit and loss balance	30,000	265,000
Net book value of the business		365,000
Fixed Assets		
Premises	75,000	
Machinery less depreciation	160,000	235,000
Current Assets		
Stock	55,000	
Debtors	20,000	
Cash	115,000	
	190,000	

Current liabilities	£		
Trade creditors	20,000		
Creditor (Machinery)	40,000	60,000	130,000
			£365,000

9. (a) *Summary Balance Sheet of WORKSTONE PLC*
after revaluation of Land and Buildings

	£		£
Shareholders' funds			
400,000 Ordinary £1 shares paid	400,000	*Fixed Assets* including Land	
Capital Reserve	100,000	and Buildings	600,000
Reserves including profit and		*Net Current Assets*	250,000
loss account balance	50,000		
	550,000		
Long-term loans	300,000		
	£850,000		£850,000

(b) *Summary Balance Sheet of WORKSTONE PLC*
after the 1 for 4 Bonus Issue

	£		£
500,000 Ordinary £1 shares paid	500,000	*Fixed Assets* including Land	
Reserves including profit and		and Buildings	600,000
loss account balance	50,000	*Net Current Assets*	250,000
	550,000		
Long-term loans	300,000		
	£850,000		£850,000

10. *Summary Balance Sheet of WORKSTONE PLC*
after Rights Issue of 1 for 5 at £1.50 per
share is received in cash in full

	£		£
600,000 Ordinary £1 shares paid	600,000	*Fixed Assets* including Land	
Share Premium Account	50,000	and Buildings	600,000
Reserves including profit and		*Net Current Assets*	400,000
loss account balance	50,000		
	700,000		
Long-term loans	300,000		
	£1,000,000		£1,000,000

11. *Comparison of X Ltd and Y Ltd*

		X Ltd	Y Ltd
1.	(a) Current ratio	4 – 1	2 – 1
	(b) Liquid ratio	1.5 – 1	1 – 1
	(c) Stock turnover ratio	3.5 times	10 times
	(d) Gross Profit as a % of sales	30%	20%
	(e) The Mark-Up (Gross profit as a % of cost of sales)	42.8%	25%
	(f) Net profit as a % of sales	8.1%	7.2%
	(g) Overheads to Sales	21.9%	12.8%
	(h) Net profit as a % of shareholders' capital employed	9.0%	12.0%
	(i) Sales to shareholders' capital employed (turnover of capital)	1.11 times	1.66 times

2. Since it is not stated that the two businesses are engaged in the same trade in

similar circumstances, it is doubtful whether detailed comparison of the ratios and percentages will serve much useful purpose. Certain broad differences can be pointed out, however. Y Ltd turns over its stock almost three times as frequently as X Ltd and will be a material factor towards Y Ltd's better turnover of capital. Y Ltd's sales turnover is the same as that of X Ltd, but the gross profit earned is only two-thirds as great, 20% compared with 30%. The overhead expenses of Y Ltd are somewhat lower than those of X Ltd, being 12.8% of sales compared with 21.9%. This leaves the net profit to sales percentage of Y Ltd only 0.9% less than that of X Ltd despite the much greater gross profit margin of the latter.

Both the current and liquid ratios of Y Ltd are lower than those of X Ltd. It is possible that X Ltd may be overstocked. But the disparity between the stock turnover ratios and the mark-ups make it doubtful that the companies are in the same line of business. If Y Ltd is a retailer, as seems likely, then its lower current and liquid ratios are not a cause for concern. The fixed assets of Y Ltd are rather lower than those of X Ltd but a comparison is invidious in the absence of a breakdown of their make-up and dates of purchase, with depreciation policies. However, the capital employed of Y Ltd is in fact considerably less than that of X Ltd, so that the slightly smaller net profit of Y Ltd represents a rather higher return on the capital employed.

$$\text{Net profit/capital} = \text{Net profit/sales} \times \text{sales/capital}$$

X Ltd	9.0%	=	8.1% × 1.11 times
Y Ltd	12.0%	=	7.2% × 1.66 times

In the absence of a market value of the shares and details of the relative risks involved, it would be rash to state that one company is more successful than the other.

12. The expression, dividend of 20% on a company's share capital, means 20% on its nominal (issued) share capital. For P Ltd, 20% on £100,000 share capital, i.e. £20,000, is equivalent to only 10% on the book value of the shareholders' capital employed (£200,000). For the shareholders of Q Ltd, the 15% on its nominal (issued) share capital of £150,000, i.e. £22,500, is equivalent to 11.25% on the book value of the shareholders' capital employed (£200,000). Q's dividend is therefore the better return when expressed as a relationship of the book value of shareholders' capital.

The dividend yield, however, will relate to the particular market price paid by an individual shareholder, and there could be material differences between the yields of holders of the same £1 share.

13. The dividend yield is the relationship of the dividend paid to the market price paid for his share by the individual shareholder. In the financial press it will be related to the price of the share at the end of the previous day's dealings on the stock market.

Given the nominal value, the market price and the dividend percentage,

$$\text{Dividend yield} = \frac{\text{Nominal value of share}}{\text{Market value of share}} \times \text{Dividend percentage.}$$

$$\text{P Ltd dividend yield} = \frac{£1}{£2.10p} \times 20\% = 9.52\%$$

$$\text{Q Ltd dividend yield} = \frac{£1}{£1.50p} \times 15\% = 10.00\%$$

Q Ltd's dividend yield is therefore superior to that of P Ltd.

14.

MANUFACTURING plc
Balance Sheet as at 31 March 19x5

	£
Authorised Share Capital	
750,000 8% Preference Shares of £1 each	750,000

3,000,000 Ordinary Shares of 50 pence each		1,500,000
		£2,250,000

Issued Share Capital

500,000 8% Preference Shares of £1 each fully paid		500,000
2,400,000 Ordinary Shares of 50 pence each fully paid	£1,200,000	
Capital Reserve: Share Premium Account	500,000	
Revenue Reserve: General	250,000	
Profit and Loss Account	25,000	1,975,000

BOOK VALUE OF SHAREHOLDERS'		
FUNDS		2,475,000
Loan Capital: 8% Mortgage Debentures		800,000
LONG-TERM CAPITAL EMPLOYED		£3,275,000

applied in:		£
Fixed Assets: Freehold Land and Buildings at valuation		750,000
Plant and Machinery cost less depreciation		1,400,000
Fixtures and Fittings cost less depreciation		100,000
Motor Vehicles cost less depreciation		150,000
		£2,400,000

Investment in Associated Company (cost plus share of retained profits)	£150,000

Working Capital

Current Assets	£	less *Current liabilities*	£	
Stocks	725,000	Proposed Pref. dividend	40,000	
Debtors	600,000	Proposed Ord. dividend	120,000	
Short term investment	125,000	Current tax	150,000	
		Trade creditors	250,000	
		Bank Overdraft	165,000	
	1,450,000		725,000	725,000
				£3,275,000

15. *XYZ COMPANY LIMITED as at 31 March 19x1*

Authorised share capital	£	£	£
10,000 8% £1 cum. preference shares			10,000
10,000 £1 ordinary shares			10,000
			20,000

Issued share capital	£	£	£
10,000 8% £1 cum. preference shares fully paid			10,000
10,000 £1 ordinary shares fully paid		10,000	
General reserve	3,000		
Profit and Loss account (Dr)	4,200	(1,200)	8,800

BOOK VALUE OF SHAREHOLDERS' FUNDS (NET ASSETS)	18,800
Long-term loan – 10% Debentures	20,000

BOOK VALUE OF LONG-TERM FUNDS   £38,800

invested in:

Fixed Assets

	Cost	Depreciation	
	£	£	£
Buildings	30,000	6,000	24,000
Plant and Machinery	20,000	8,000	12,000
Motor Van	2,000	1,600	400
			36,400
Trade Investment			3,000
Current Assets			
Stock	2,400		
Debtors	750		
Cash	250	3,400	
Current liabilities			
Bank overdraft	1,500		
Creditors	2,500	4,000	(600)
			£38,800

Comment. It would be foolish in practice to make an isolated study of the balance sheet. There is a need to consider profitability, rates of dividend paid and retention policy over a number of accounting periods and in addition to obtain a good deal of non-accounting information as well as answers to questions posed by the accounts themselves.

However, certain information can be derived from the balance sheet and certain questions asked.

1. There is an indication of recent losses (i.e. debit balance on P & L account).
2. There is a deficit of working capital.
3. The liquid ratio £1,000/£4,000 = 0.25 is a critical figure indicating technical insolvency. If the trade investment is saleable and realisable then the position is temporarily eased. However, budgets will need to be seen and assessed to take a view on future profitability, liquidity and survival.
4. The market value of the trade investments, the reason why they are being held (the implication is of some linked trading benefit) and the return therefrom should be considered relative to the possibility of sale and the more useful employment of the funds in the business.
5. There is no full capital cover for the ordinary shareholders. On the basis of balance sheet (book) values, they have already lost part of their investment. Net asset value per ordinary share (nominal value £1) = £8,800/10,000 = 0.88p.
6. The Buildings (? Land and buildings,? Freehold? Leasehold) may well have a value in excess of cost which would enhance both the net asset value per ordinary share and provide greater security for loans. Could they be sold and leased back?
7. The Motor Van is nearly fully depreciated and may need to be replaced immediately. Funds, difficult to come by in the present situation, will be required unless the asset is leased. A new van in the present inflationary economy is certain to cost much more than £2,000.
8. The relationship of stock to sales should be considered, i.e. stock turnover ratios should be calculated. Are the stocks too high, optimum or low? This question is bound up with questions on the order book. What are the reasons for the likely fall in profit? *What kind of business is it?* What is the market? What is the company's

product/market position? Has it declined? What is the competition? Is there a future for the company?

9. The company is under-capitalised in relation to its loan capital. Further long-term and working capital funds are needed. A further issue of shares may be difficult in view of the erosion of the present equity share capital. Current shareholders may come in (are they owner/managers?) with further investment if a reasonable future prospect can be shown, rather than lose their present capital (in whole or part) on a forced liquidation.

10. With regard to debenture holders. Who are they? Do they include majority shareholders? What are the terms of the debenture deed in respect of security, repayment of principal, penalties on non-payment of interest? If they are secured by way of a 'floating charge' their capital cover on book values is 2.14 times (£42,800/20,000), even higher if the buildings have a value above cost. If the loan is covered by the security of 'buildings', the cover is much less at 1.2 times on book values. It is unlikely that they are unsecured; if they are, they will rank equal with the trade creditors and the bank (if also unsecured) and the cover is reduced even further. Presumably the debenture interest has been paid and does not appear among the creditors? It may be noted in connection with the gearing of capital that the company's articles may prohibit the raising of loan capital beyond the amount of issued capital. This is the current position as the result of losses. The loan at 10% with the interest as a charge against profit for tax purposes is quite cheap and with inflation rates at or around 5% (mid-1980s), the *real* cost is *circa* 2% only..

11. It is not known whether the preference dividend is in arrear and to what extent. IF it is, it is likely that the company's articles will allow preference shareholders a vote alongside that of equity shareholders in company meetings. The shares are cumulative. The capital cover on book values 18,800/10,000 = 1.88.

12. There is no information on taxation or dividends. There may be tax losses available. Finally, have the accounts and balance sheet been audited?

13. The key to immediate survival is the attitude of (1) the bank (2) suppliers in respect of the company's future and the security of their involvement in the company.

16. A hierarchy of ratios as requested by this question is shown in the text (Chapter 13).

The diagram shows that the size of the primary ratio, return on assets, is dependent on the size of the detailed cost ratios shown on its left and the asset ratios on its right. Any improvement made in the ratios at the foot of the pyramid, and those above reacting to those improvements, is reflected in the size of the ratio at the top.

The secondary ratio – the profit margin – can, of course, be improved by raising selling prices if market conditions allow, or by reducing the cost of sales, or by a combination of the two. Or by introducing new products with improved profit margins, or changing the mix of products for sale. If, for example, on the cost of sales side, a company (e.g. British Leyland) spends £1 million (or more) per day on materials, a five per cent efficiency in materials management over (say) 300 working days per annum would improve pre-tax profit by £15 millions and would be reflected in a higher ROCE resulting from the improvement in the ratio on the bottom left-hand side of the pyramid. Similarly, on the right-hand asset side, improvements in the efficiency of stock control, production control, credit control and cash control would increase each of the bottom line relationships with sales, combine to increase the secondary ratio, sales : total assets, and thus the primary ROCE ratio.

17. *Description*
(1) Return on capital employed.   Profit before interest and tax : Long-term capital employed £40,000/£134,000 = 29.8%.

(2) Profit margin. Net operating profit (Profit before interest and tax) : sales £40,000/£350,000 = 11.4%.

(3) Turnover of capital. Sales : Long-term funds £350,000/£134,000 = 2.6 times.

(4) Return on Equity (NB. There are no preference shares). Profit after tax/Ordinary shareholders' funds £20,000/£84,000 = 23.8%.

(5) Gearing ratio (Debt ratio). Long-term debt : Long-term capital employed £50,000/£134,000 = 37.3%.

(6) Current ratio. Current assets : Current liabilities £112,000/£66,000 = 1.7 to 1.

(7) Liquid ratio (Acid test). Liquid assets : Current liabilities £50,000/£66,000 = 0.76 − 1.

(8) Dividend cover. Profit after tax/dividend £20,000/£12,000 = 1.66 times.

(9) Interest cover. Profit before interest and tax/interest £40,000 : £5,000 = 8 times.

(10) Proprietary ratio. Shareholders' funds/Gross Assets £84,000/£200,000 = 42%.

Questions:
(1) The Master budget profit and loss accounts and balance sheets based on company forecasts.
Previous years' results.
Inter-firm comparisons.
(2) Shareholders' funds (ratio 4).
Gross (Total Assets).
Current Cost versions of these and that used in ratio 1.
(3) The description 'Net Assets' as shown in the question against £134,000 is used in some texts, but logically:

Net Assets = Gross Assets less Gross Liabilities = Shareholders' funds.
   i.e. £84,000   = £200,000   less £116,000   = £84,000

NB: Net Asset per share an important comparison against market value per share = £84,000/60,000 = *£1.40.*
(4) 'Working capital' is an alternative to 'Net current assets' and the figure in the question is £46,000 (£112,000 less £66,000).
   Because of the double entry equation 'Working capital' is also the excess of the Long-term capital employed (£134,000) over the long-term (fixed) assets (£88,000) = £46,000.
(5) Goodwill exists only if profits in excess of the expectable norm for the business (super profits) are being and will be earned in the future.
   As the future is uncertain, the accounting concept of conservatism/prudence is followed and it is not the practice for a continuing business even if successful to make such an entry. If, however, the successful business is offered for sale, the vendor will want to be paid a sum in excess of the mutually agreed value of the net tangible assets on offer for the goodwill of his business, crystallising all those factors (e.g. prime site, high share of market, favourable contracts, progressive R & D etc) which lead to the earning potential of super profits.
   If such an entry were to be made, it would be to debit Goodwill account which would appear on the asset side of the balance sheet with the Fixed Assets and to credit a capital reserve which would increase the ordinary shareholders' funds.
(6) Primary ratio = Profit margin × asset turnover, i.e. Ratio 1 = Ratio 2 × Ratio 3
29.8% = 11.4% × 2.6 times.

18.

	A		B		C	
	19x1	19x2	19x1	19x2	19x1	19x2
	£	£	£	£	£	£
EBIT	100,000	30,000	100,000	30,000	100,000	30,000
Interest	20,000	20,000	10,000	10,000	—	—
Profit before tax	80,000	10,000	90,000	20,000	100,000	30,000
Tax (50%)	40,000	5,000	45,000	10,000	50,000	15,000
Profit before tax	40,000	5,000	45,000	10,000	50,000	15,000

	A		B		C	
	19x1	19x2	19x1	19x2	19x1	19x2
1. Return on Long-term capital	20%	6%	20%	6%	20%	6%
2. Percentage return on shareholders' funds	13.33%	1.67%	11.25%	2.5%	10%	3%
3. Interest cover	5 times	1.5 times	10 times	3 times	—	—
4. Earnings per share	40p	5p	22.5p	5p	16.7p	5p

Comment: This question illustrates that ordinary shares in a highly geared capital structure are more speculative than in other cases. Company A which is highly geared (a high proportion of loan capital in its capital structure) sees its earnings per share drop 8 times following a fall of 3.33 times in EBIT. For Company B, lowly geared, its EPS falls only 4.5 times following the same 3.33 times fall in EBIT. Company C which has no loan capital has the same 3.33 times fall in EPS as in its EBIT which equals its profit before tax. The effect on Company A of the fall in profitability exemplifies the situation of many such highly geared UK companies in the early 1980s recession. At the higher level of profit, Company A does best, earning the highest 'turn' on its borrowed funds, for:

In addition to earnings of 20% (before tax and interest), being 10% after tax (and before interest) on its funds (shareholders) of £300,000 = £30,000 (as for C Shareholders),

it earned for the shareholders on the borrowed funds a net of tax additional	£10,000	*
Taking its shareholders after tax profit to	£40,000	(13.33%)
* 10% net was earned on borrowed funds of £200,000 =	£20,000	
of which was paid as interest net (of tax) =	£10,000	
Excess to Shareholders' return =	£10,000	

It will be noted that at the level of £30,000 EBIT, the effect of gearing is neutral, all three companies returning an EPS of 5p.

19. The double entry made in the ledger accounts of P Ltd recording the acquisition of a controlling (60%) interest in S Ltd is:

	£
Debit: Investment in S Ltd Account (60,000 shares in S Ltd at cost)	140,000
Credit: Issued Ordinary Share Capital (80,000 £1 shares – nominal value)	80,000
Credit: Share Premium Account (Premium on 80,000 £1 shares issued at £1.75 each)	60,000

The balance sheet of P Ltd resulting from these entries is:
Balance Sheet of P Ltd after investment in S Ltd

	£
Issued Ordinary Shares of £1	360,000
Capital Reserve – Share Premium	60,000
Revenue reserves	180,000
Shareholders' funds	600,000
Long-term loan	140,000
Long-term capital employed	740,000
invested in:	
Fixed Assets	480,000
Investment in S Ltd (at cost)	140,000
Net Current Assets	120,000
	740,000

Tutorial note:
In preparing the consolidated balance sheet of P and S Ltd at the date of acquisition, a 'cost of control' account using double entry principles sets the purchase price (£140,000) represented by the 'Investment in S Ltd account' in the P Ltd balance sheet above, against the 60% of the net assets of S Ltd acquired (60% × £140,000) £84,000, indicating that £56,000 (£140,000 less £84,000) had been paid for 'goodwill'.

The net assets of S Ltd (Fixed Assets plus net current assets less long-term loan) £140,000 equates to and is the investment of S Ltd's Shareholders' funds (Share Capital and Reserves). It is 60% of the latter which is set off against Investment in S Ltd account in the 'Cost of Control' account entries.

Cost of Control account P Ltd in S Ltd (60%)

Dr			Cr
	£		£
Investment in S Ltd	140,000	Share Capital S Ltd	
		60% × Nominal value £100,000	60,000
		Reserves S Ltd	
		60% × £40,000	24,000
		(Shareholders' funds (60% acquired))	84,000
		Balance down	56,000
	140,000		140,000
Balance brought down*	56,000		

*Goodwill = the excess of the purchase price paid for a (share of) business over the value of the net assets acquired.

The remaining 40% of the Shareholders' funds of S Ltd, i.e. 40% × (£100,000 plus £40,000) = £56,000 represents the investment of the remaining (outside the group) shareholders of S Ltd who are shown in the Consolidated balance sheet as a 'Minority Interest'.

These entries in the Cost of Control account and the Minority Interest account eliminate the Investment in S Ltd account in P Ltd's books and the Share Capital and Reserve accounts in the books of S Ltd. All the remaining accounts in the respective balance sheets are entered in the Consolidated Balance Sheet, aggregated where necessary:

Consolidated Balance Sheet P Ltd and S Ltd
as at the date of acquisition of a 60% interest in S Ltd

	£	£
Issued ordinary Share of £1	360,000	
Capital Reserve – Share Premium	60,000	
Revenue Reserves	180,000	600,000
Long term loans (140 plus 60)		200,000
Minority Interest		56,000
		856,000
Goodwill		56,000
Fixed Assets (480 plus 140)		620,000
Net Current Assets (120 plus 60)		180,000
		856,000

20.

Prudent plc and Profligate plc
Comparative Statements of Sources and Application of Funds
Commentary after preliminary analysis

An examination of the statements reveals that both companies appear to be pursuing a policy of expansion, borne out by the purchase of plant and machinery and the increase in operating assets. The plant and machinery is deemed to be additional as there is no evidence of sales of these assets which might indicate that the purchases were mere replacement of worn out or obsolete equipment. It may be concluded that the extra plant is intended to increase the companies' productive capacity, in order to support an expansion of turnover (reference to the notes to the balance sheet showing the *movements on fixed assets* as required by 3 Sch. 5 Companies Act 1985 will provide confirmation or otherwise of this assumption).

Further support for the theory is provided by the changes in operating assets. Expansion of manufacture would be expected to be followed by expansion of turnover (again, verfiable by reference to the profit and loss account) and this in turn would be expected to result in an increase in stocks and debtors.

Reference to the funds flow statements of both companies shows this to be so. Increased investment in both fixed and working capital raises the question – where have the supportive resources come from?

The funds may arise from *internal* or *external* sources or both. The funds statement provides the answer.

Prudent plc, in recognition that long-term investment (fixed assets) requires financial support from the long-term funds, has floated both a share issue and debentures.

Profligate plc, on the other hand, has not shown that its management understands that funds may not flow from a capital investment until some time after that investment has been made; that until the investment does begin to generate a flow of funds into the enterprise then it will be necessary to provide resources to permit daily operations to continue. This at a time when very probably the enterprise resources have been depleted by that very investment.

Profligate plc's purchase of the fixed assets and its expansion have clearly been financed out of the cash flows generated by its annual profit, heavy dependence upon the goodwill of its creditors and reliance upon short-term borrowings from its bankers. Doubtless, a check on the current and liquidity ratios derived from the balance sheet of the company would also reveal dangerous trends in these areas. An important figure in the statement is the very revealing change in the working capital.

As has already been indicated, a policy of expansion of selling and productive activity demands a commensurate increase in working capital and in the case of Prudent plc this has been acknowledged and the requisite action taken. The increase in stocks and debtors, £1,130,000, has been partially financed by increased indebtedness to the creditors of £240,000, but the balance of £890,000 and the improvement in liquid funds have been funded out of the annual profit.

The purchase of the fixed assets and the redemption of the loan, together totalling £2 million, have been funded by the issue of shares and debentures plus the depreciation, together with some help derived from the delay arising from the settlement of the *current* year's tax (reference to the profit and loss account will give the amount), all amounting to £2.05 million; the excess of £50,000 going towards the increase in working capital and the ultimate improvement in liquidity.

The evidence shows that the management of Prudent plc, having decided upon a policy of expansion, was aware of the financing needs of that policy and took the necessary decisions and actions to ensure that its objectives were achieved.

The statement of Profligate plc reveals a very different picture. It has been shown that their purchase of fixed assets has not been financed out of long-term funding and must, therefore, have been provided either out of current profits or at the expense of working capital, or both. The situation has been exacerbated by its distribution policy. It has paid out dividends, which means an outflow of cash not only in respect of the dividends, but also the related ACT, at a higher rate than that of Prudent plc.

The depreciation provision, too, is widely at variance between the two companies. The exact relationship to capital invested in fixed assets and the depreciation policies of each company would need to be ascertained from the annual accounts, but in absolute terms raises yet another question concerning the quality of decisions taken by the management of Profligate plc. In contrast to the management of Prudent plc, the evidence of the Funds Statement is that there was little understanding of the consequences of pursuing a policy of expansion and that decisions and actions were taken that may jeopardise the future of the company.

A precise comparison is inadvisable, as it is not known if the companies' activities can allow this (except that they are both manufacturers); they could, for example, be operating in different markets. Nevertheless, the statements in one case provide a basis for confidence, while in the other they give cause for concern.

21.   *A plc and B plc*
Comments made to the contracts manager would include:
From the restricted information available, it would appear that the underlying policy of both companies is that of expansion.

In both instances, investment in Fixed Assets has been considerable and Stocks and Debtors have increased – prima facie indications of increased turnover. Company A appears to have understood that increased productive capacity alone is not sufficient to ensure increased turnover and profits, but that support in the form of additional working capital is vital. To this end, it appears to have rationalised its capital structure by replacing short-term borrowings with longer term borrowings in the form of 20 year loans and additional equity capital, and at the same time converting unwanted or unused assets into cash.

The expenditure on Fixed Assets has been well covered by the additional long-term capital introduced and the retention of funds in the form of a substantial provision for depreciation. This company has also retired obsolete and superfluous plant, implying a planned reorganisation, leaving only sophisticated modern plant – but do they have enough spare capacity for our contract? It also appears to be pursuing a more conservative dividend policy than Company B, which when coupled with a share issue, suggests confidence on the part of investors. Sensible use of suppliers' funds is being made without damaging the company's reputation and affecting the goodwill of those suppliers.

Company B, whilst aiming at the same objective, does not generate as much confidence as Company A. The increase in Fixed Assets has been financed out of income and a reliance on short-term borrowings, which has resulted in a considerable reduction in liquidity. Increases in Stocks and Debtors appears to have been achieved at the expense of the suppliers with a possible damaging effect on their goodwill towards the company. Increased turnover may have been obtained by a relaxation of the credit control polcy and this, coupled with the need to find funds for the investment in Fixed Assets, has added to the liquidity deterioration. It would appear that at some stage during the year liquidity became an acute problem forcing the company to dispose of investments at a loss. The redemption of long-term borrowings in the form of debentures has exacerbated the situation. Notwithstanding the liquidity difficulties, the company has distributed large dividends and the concomitant payment of Advance Corporation Tax has caused a further outflow of funds. A change in overdraft policy by its bank could embarrass Company B. Another worrying sign is that although the expansion in Fixed Assets is similar to that of Company A, the depreciation provision would seem to be relatively inadequate. This could imply that B has less plant than A with which to undertake the contract.

From the foregoing, it appears that Company A has planned its expansion, in contrast to Company B which appears to have proceeded haphazardly. On this score, Company A would appear to be the safest and its financial management more efficient. It must be understood, however, that a conclusion based on the study of one year's funds flow is quite inadequate and a thoroughgoing ratio analysis of the revenue accounts and balance sheets from which the statements have been compiled should be carried out. Particular attention should be directed to the capital structure and gearing, the shareholders' and working capital ratios, together with detailed analyses of the constituent elements of stock and debtors. Over-reliance on outside short-term finance is a sign of weakness, so how strong is the goodwill of trade creditors who supply raw materials to Company B?

Some further pertinent questions
All this information, however, relates only to the past and in awarding the contract our company must be concerned with the future. It would be important, therefore, that answers should be obtained to some searching questions as to each company's future policies and proposed actions with regard to, inter alia:
 (i) Future short and long-term financing. How much is owed to the bank, the suppliers and the Inland Revenue?
 (ii) The condition of the Companies' order books – is there spare capacity for our contracts?
 (iii) Dividend and profit distribution policies. Credit and stock control policies.
 (iv) Are fixed assets secured against liabilities?

APPENDIX 3

Tutorial answers to Questions 6, 7, 14, 23, 28 and 31 in Workbook 3

Tutorial answers to Questions 6, 7, 14, 23, 28 and 31 in Workbook 3

Examination Question 6

Tutorial Comment for Outline Answer

1. It will be noted that this question is in a Financial Management paper. Most of the other examples are from Financial Accounting papers. The lesson for students is that they can take information across the boundaries of examination papers.

2. This question carried 20 marks with a reading and completion time of 36 minutes for the 100 mark, 3 hour paper. When reading, therefore, it is worthwhile writing your thoughts as comments on a 'working paper' which you should not hesitate to submit to the Examiner. He is looking for any evidence with which to assess your performance and will welcome such an approach. Your comments, although likely to be brief, may well be to the point and should be tabulated neatly.

3. Always read the 'requirement' before reading the question, so that your considerations may be properly directed. The requirements tells us that bank borrowing is to be reduced. The crux of the question is how?

4. (a) Bank overdraft stands at £183,000 at the beginning of the year. The reduction to £50,000, i.e. by £133,000, is proportionately a sizeable task.
   (b) The summary sources and application of funds statement, which is erroneously labelled 'budgeted cash flow statement' in the question, indicates that 'capital expenditure' (£109,000) is to be financed completely from internal funds. This, if achieved, is extraordinary in today's conditions but highly commendable, providing 'working capital' is not to be bled. The other 'applications' show no change for 'debtors' and 'creditors' (see note below) and we see that tax is ignored. The result is an expected reduction in the overdraft by £11,000. This is, on the face of it, excellent, but the MD's target reduction is well away. He has confirmed the budget projection that no external long-term funds are to be raised.
   (c) The comparative ratios of Fairfield and its competitors A and B must be the key to the requirement of the question, i.e. the further drastic reduction of the bank overdraft.
   (d) We can observe the primary ratio (Profit/capital) with Fairfield's the lowest of the three, despite the best profit margin (Profit/sales). The rogue is therefore the secondary ratio 'turnover of assets' i.e. Sales/capital employed, and we should now

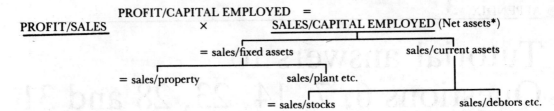

be visualising the right hand side of the hierarchy of ratios (shown in full elsewhere in this book):

(e) We see confirmation for this in the question, where these subsidiary ratios are listed, with Fairfields being in every case the poorest. We will need to refer in our report to the possibility of reviewing the capital expenditure programme and increasing the utilisation of our present fixed assets. Clearly, if Fairfield can increase its sales/capital employed ratio to the level of its competitors, improve its stock control (and production control of stocks of work in progress) and its credit control, and also consider the leasing instead of purchase of fixed assets, then the cash flow problem as related to the bank overdraft will be eased.

(f) We now have the solid core of the answer, which can be improved, given time, by making calculations using the more favourable ratios of Fairfield's competitors against projected sales to show the specific effect on the overdraft.

Note: The comment in the question that the planned sales will be identical to sales achieved in the previous year, £1,200,000, could mean, if inflation has not been accounted for in arriving at that figure, that sales revenue in real terms will fall, which will worsen the cash position.

*Although 'net assets' is used in the question to represent 'capital employed', there are other alternatives, e.g. (and preferably) 'total assets'.

Examination Question 7

Tutorial Comment for Outline Answer

1. The question carried 20 marks in a 3 hour, 100 mark paper. 36 minutes are available for reading and writing the answer.

2. Requirement (a) asks for computation of ratios – surprisingly from Schwarz's figures only, until we see that requirements (b) and (c) ask us about computational problems and limitations of using ratios in a comparison such as that with Weiss and Blau.

3. The marks are given for each segment of the three-part answer. With 36 minutes to do all three, time should not be wasted calculating finely the division over the parts.

4. Having read the requirements (a) (b) and (c) we should not be surprised to find that each of the three companies has a different financial structure. S has no long-term loans but a bank overdraft of a size which is the norm for many companies these days. Its appearance as a 'Current liability' year after year indicates only its legal status as a 'short-term borrowing' but realistically it is long-term in nature. W has both preference shares and debentures and is highly geared. B has no loans and a smaller relative overdraft than S.

The best ROCE base will be that which is common to all three – 'Profit before interest and tax' to 'Total Assets'.

ROCE (Schwarz only).   Earnings before interest and tax/total assets = 1.1/4.3 = 26%

Current ratio.   Current Assets : Current liabilities = 1.4 : 2.0 = 0.7

Debt : Equity.   Bank Overdraft*/Ordinary Share Capital plus Reserves. 1.3/2.3 = 0.6

*It is not possible for external analysts to separate that part of the bank overdraft which is of a long-term nature and that part which is not. Students are advised not to make assumptions but to refer to the difficulty. In this case, the reference is a desirable part of the answer to part (b).

Debtors turnover.   Sales/Debtors 5.0/0.8 = just over 6 times per year or a 2 months' collection period.

Tutorial Note: Observe how the ratio answers are first described in narrative, then the comparative figures are stated, and finally the ratio (answer) itself. Always do this, rather than merely write in the ratio (answer) which you may have determined using a calculator. There are two benefits. If you make a wrong calculation from correct comparative figures and only show the former, the Examiner can only give you zero marks. If you show the comparative, he will give you marks for that which is correct, deducting a margin only for your careless error. Secondly, if you use a ratio base which, while different from that used by the Examiner in his model, is nevertheless an acceptable alternative, he can give you full marks.

5. (b) A list of the limitations of ratio analysis is given elsewhere in this book. Sometimes, as in this question, the Examiner requires you to write about them, but in every 'interpretation question using ratios' a short paragraph on limitations is relevant and is an example of information candidates can take into the exam room. A comment on the alternative definitions of capital employed should be made; also that the use of current cost information rather than HCA information makes the ratios more realistic. The key area of performance to which ROCE relates is that of overall effectiveness.

   Ratio a(ii) gives an indication of the ability of the company to pay its way in the short term. Although text books talk of a 2 : 1 norm, this is a generalisation and, in practice, the effective level of the current ratio will be set by the optimum underlying stock ratios, debtor ratios and any cash ratios. At 0.7 it appears low and with a liquid ratio of 0.4 points to a liquidity problem and may be to overtrading.

   Ratio a(iii) concerns a gearing relationship where the loan is a bank overdraft, and the computational problem in this respect has been referred to. Gearing ratios give an indication of the relative risk taken by lenders and the likely volatility of earnings per ordinary share set against different levels of profit.

   Ratio a(iv) indicates the effectiveness of credit control. It can be directly compared to the credit period given to customers. Many businesses which give one month's credit average two months for collection. While the debt is uncollected the business is using its own (costly) funds to finance its customers. Inflation exacerbates the position. We assume all 'sales' used in the computation are credit sales and that there will be no bad debts.

6. (c) Here we should refer to the problems of inter-firm comparison. For strict comparison, the companies should be in comparable businesses, at the same level, adopting the same accounting policies in respect of, for example, depreciation, treatment of R & D, stock valuation etc. While accounting standards have done much to ease the problems of comparison, there are still areas where individual, acceptable judgments will make comparisons difficult. W is taking the largest share

of the market and this could lead to a price advantage following the absorption of its fixed costs over the greater sales. B, being a subsidiary of a vertically-integrated multinational, will have its policies determined elsewhere and its 'sales value' may be influenced by inter-group transfer prices. B's liquidity must be assessed differently from that of S and W. Although it is a separate legal entity from its holding company, the latter may be able to provide guarantees for overdrafts and it would be necessary to segregate inter-company debtor/creditor balances for true comparisons.

We have already referred to W's highly geared capital structure which is not present in S or B. The risks for creditors/ordinary shareholders are different in W than in S or B. B's shareholders are the shareholders of the parent company and will be concerned more with group profitability than with that of B itself.

Examination Question 14

Suggested Answer

(a)   Memorandum to The Manager, XYZ branch, Financing Bank Ltd.
From: The Regional Accountant.   20 March 19x9

Request by Cedar plc for increased overdraft facilities
Cedar plc obviously had difficulties in the year ended 31 December 19x8. The central point at issue is whether it is strong enough in its operations and finances to withstand this and any future setbacks.

Its short-term assets cover was thin. Current ratio at 1.4 to 1 for both years would generally be regarded as low for a manufacturing company, although it is in fact in line with industry figures. But the liquid asset cover of 0.53 to 1 for both years is dangerously low. These relationships for the two years remained fairly stable because of the substantial fund raising by way of debentures.

The funds from trading were in fact insufficient to meet the tax and dividend payment as is indicated in the following summarised funds statement:

	£'000s	£'000s
Flow of Funds (In)		
Funds from trading including depreciation	320	
Debentures	600	920
Flow of Funds (Out)		
Plant purchases	370	
Property purchased	80	
Tax payment	148	
Dividend payment	180	
Increase in net current assets including the change in the liquid position	142	920

The following primary and secondary ratios are revealing (previous year in brackets):
Primary ratio equals : Profit/Total Assets : equals 200/4.070 : equals 4.92% (17.2%).
Secondary ratios
   Profit margin equals : Profit/Sales : equals 200/6,600 : equals 3.03% (9.34%) : multiplied by
   Asset turnover : equals Sales/Total Assets : equals 6,600/4,070 : equals 1.62 times (1.84).

The relations of stock, creditors and debtors to sales (purchases were not given) all indicated a slowdown in the turnover of resources in the year ended 31 December 19x8 compared with the previous year, although the rates of turnover do not appear unduly low even in the latest year. For example, debtors ratio has fallen from 29 days to 41 days, but the latter compares well with the industry average of 63 days. However, such a situation where rapid turnover can no longer be maintained in the face of levelling sales (after accounting for inflation) must inevitably put a strain on the company's liquid resources.

The substantial increase in advertising and sales promotion and the near four-fold increase in bad debts are clearly items which depressed last year's profits. Information should be sought as to the effect of the increased advertising and sales promotion on current year sales. The company having been trading for some three months of the current year, the actual figures for that period can be compared with the company's budgets.

The source of the bad debts should be determined. Presumably it relates to either the European extensions, or home sales if the company uses the Exports Credit Guarantee Department for normal exports.

The selling policy of the company should be reviewed since 25% of the extra turnover in 19x8 has been lost to bad debts.

(b) There is considerable evidence in the accounts to cast doubts on the overdraft application and I would not recommend a favourable decision without information on a number of matters including the following:

(1) How would seasonal requirements affect the use of the overdraft? Immediate payments of £358,000 (Corporation tax and proposed dividend) were due at the end of the last financial year and would absorb the bulk of the proposed borrowing. It would be necessary to assume a substantial inflow of funds early this year if the company is to have the resources to meet any significant fluctuations in its funds requirements and it may be that the proposed overdraft level is inadequate. A check should be made of the cash budget for the current year against the actual cash flow to date.

(2) In connection with the proposed dividend, the company's need for funds appears so pressing that it might have been expected to take priority over the objective of maintaining the share price.

(3) What are the future expectations of sales in Europe and at home? 'Hopes' of more favourable conditions are insufficient. Clearly the study of detailed budgets, particularly the cash budget with the evidence to support assumptions therein, together with results of actual operations so far this year, is needful.

(4) What security for the proposed overdraft is offered? Are the debentures secured as a prior claim on Freehold Property? What is the current value of the Property?

(5) Does the company have adequate insurance, including loss of profits insurance, to ensure proper cash flow in the event of fire?

Tutorial Comment on this Question and Answer from an Examination Point of View

The marks available for these sample examination questions have not been given, for the reasons set out in the preface to the questions. This one carried 25 marks in a 3 hour, 100 marks paper. The time available to complete an answer (including reading time) was 45 minutes. This period could have been exceeded by candidates who considered it worthwhile so to do in terms of the additional marks which could be gained compared with tackling another question. How reasonable is it, therefore, to expect such an answer as given above (written by the author as the Examiner in question) in such a time?

The response must be that while many candidates would be hard pressed to do so, such an answer is possible from the well prepared student. A candidate who covered the salient points on liquidity/solvency, profitability, immediate cash flow expectations as evidenced by budgets compared with the actual experience of the *current* year, and the special features of the question, would have scored the majority of the marks. With an assumed overall 50% pass mark for the whole paper, this would be very valuable. Students who had followed the 'Examination hints' in Chapter 15 would have prepared and submitted a 'Working Paper' showing under suitable heads relevant ratios with their calculations,

e.g. *Liquidity* : Current ratio, Liquid ratio, Debtors ratio.

Profitability: : ROCE, Primary and Secondary ratios.

and comment on these in the report could be made without repeating the detail of the workings, as in the printed answer.

The use of the summary Funds Flow Statement in the answer assumes the candidate's knowledge of the Standard (10) and an ability to prepare such statements quickly. *It is a noticeable and likely trend that Examiners will increasingly include such statements as part of the material given in interpretation questions, or use them separately for this purpose as in the examples given elsewhere in this book.*

Two other features of the answer would have been in the mind of a practically-minded student:

(1) The use in practice of budgets in the appraisal of liquidity where these can reasonably be expected to be available for external viewing, as in the case of a lending banker.

Future cash flow is a critical part of his considerations.

(2) The brief but important reference to inflation ('levelling sales after accounting for inflation').

Note: Should Cedar plc, as a public limited company, have chosen not to give current cost information (following ASC's 1985 decision to make the application of SSAP 16 non-mandatory) nor to offer notes on the effect of inflation/price level changes – given the current level of inflation – then banks would have certainly required the provision of an analysis of its effects on HCA statements. Students would be wise to refer to this likelihood in answers to questions based on historical cost information, particularly applying in detail to HCA's limitations as necessary in the question context.

In the answer, reference is made twice to the industry (ratio) figures. The Examiner would not expect candidates to memorise a range of industry figures (which are in any event dynamic) but would expect comment that absolute ratios are not much use and comparatives are needed. He would expect students to refer to the theoretical norm of par for the liquid ratio of manufacturing companies with actual experience showing between 0.90 and par.

Most students would have dealt with the 'special features' of the question, e.g. the rise in bad debts (19x8) and the appreciable 'deferred revenue expenditure' on advertising and sales promotion. The good student would have picked up the point that the proposed dividend was not covered by the after-tax profit, and the dilemma for the directors of deciding between maintaining the market price against cash flow considerations.

Finally, is the model answer complete? Those readers who have tackled the question before considering the model may well have comments not covered therein. Are they valid? The answer is 'Yes, they may well be'.

The author's experience as teacher and examiner is that most 'interpretation' questions because of their very nature of limited information, when used as classwork (case study) material over time with different groups of students, do in fact tend to elaborate beyond the model answer. So other (valid) points will be acceptable to the Examiner. An example here is that nothing has been said about the gearing effect on future profit and cash flow of the debenture loan raised in 19x8, and such comment would have been very relevant.

Examination Question 23

PRICE-EARNINGS RATIO – SUGGESTED ANSWER

The Price-Earnings ratio (PER) is the relationship of the Share Price divided by Earnings per Share (EPS). Although historical EPS are static, being based on the attributable earnings of the last published profit and loss account, investors are concerned with *prospective* EPS. PERs of different companies within the same type of business will therefore vary with any event/information/indication which investors (private and institutional) interpret as affecting future earning potential and which influence their decision to buy, sell or hold the companies' shares.

The policy of each company on the amount of the attributable earnings it will distribute in the form of dividends is also a material factor influencing PERs. From the above general comment, many reasons may be listed explaining variable PERs, of which the following four are examples:

1. The companies have different historical earnings (earnings after tax attributable to ordinary shareholders) patterns and expectable earnings for any number of reasons, e.g.
   (a) more or less efficient management of R & D, buying, production, marketing/selling, finance and general direction.
   (b) Gains/losses flowing to equity resulting from different gearing structures.
   (c) The companies' capital expenditure programmes and related depreciation policies/allied tax planning.
2. Variable dividend policies. Companies retaining a high proportion of earnings to help finance growth attract shareholders looking for share price rises, preferring to receive their income in capital gains. On the other hand, institutional investors tend to invest in companies distributing as dividends a high proportion of their earnings. The ordinary share prices of these latter companies tend to stand higher in the market than the former.
3. Variable Net Asset Values (NAV) of the companies' ordinary shares. These values tend to underpin the investment as its basic security.
4. A company within an industry is the target of a take-over bid. Where a company has a lower than average PER, often indicating a low expectable rate of growth, it may be a prospect for take-over. It may have, or appear to have, idle capital in the form of surplus cash, higher than reasonable amounts of debtors and other factors depressing its PER so that it is attractive to the potential acquiring company possessing a higher PER.

Theoretically, the share price may be regarded as a capitalisation of future earnings. If, and only if, the historical EPS is maintained, PER would indicate the number of years over which an investor would be repaid his investment, on the assumption that all earnings were distributed. The quotation in the question is presumably based on this reasoning.

However, some indication has been given of the many variables which could affect future earnings and therefore the price. The stock market reaction to variables is not finely tuned and, in addition, general market swings have had traumatic effects on share prices and PERs. From the top of a Bull market with the *Financial Times* 500 PER around say 20, falls over a relatively short period to say 4 at the bottom of the Bear market have been recorded.

It would be unwise, therefore, to regard PERs in any general sense as indications of the value of companies.

Tutorial Note: This question carried 15 marks in a 3 hour, 100 mark paper. The above answer is representative of the answer which could have been produced in the 27 minutes available.

Examination Question 28

SUGGESTED ANSWER

This question carried 20 marks, with equal marks for (a) and (b).

Tutorial Note: The term *'capital maintenance'* is a familiar one for economists, and given the 'theory' side of the ACA syllabus for their 'Regulatory framework paper', all reasonably prepared students should have been prepared to write of the now well-known views of Hicks and Fisher. Accountants, as opposed to economists, generally first acknowledged the phrase 'capital maintenance' as it attained prominence within the concepts of current cost accounting of the Sandilands Committee (1973) and more lately in SSAP 16.

Pointers for an answer to part (a) therefore include:
1. Hicks' concept of 'well-offness' (capital maintenance) as fundamental to income measurement and asset valuation.
2. The focus of current cost accounting on the maintenance of the business entity as a going concern.
3. Hicks definition of income as consumption in the period in addition to changes in the value of capital; since income is derived from capital, then the measurement of income and the concept of capital maintenance are inter-related.
4. The objective (2) of CCA required that system to reflect the impact of specific price changes on the business when determining profits for an accounting period and preparing the balance sheet. Adjustments (e.g. cost of sales, additional depreciation, gearing) are made by arriving at the current cost profit attributable to shareholders, and in the current cost balance sheet the objective of capital maintenance is met by including assets at 'their value to the business'.
5. Fisher's approach to the measurement of income was to argue that income is simply consumption, ignoring the concept of capital maintenance.
6. An alternative accounting view of capital maintenance is the need to maintain financial equity capital in general purchasing power terms as underlined by PSSAP 7. This is significantly different to the CCA view of capital which is based on the total assets of the business and their valuation.

(b) *Practical reasons* for *measuring* profit include:
1. In general, to indicate to shareholders, managment effectiveness in carrying out its stewardship function.
2. To provide comparisons with budgeted plans, budgeted profit targets and return on capital employed, enabling timely management action on variances and control data.
3. To assist joint consultation, decisions on levels of labour/staff remuneration.
4. To assist pricing decisions.
5. As a base for tax planning, computation, assessment.
6. To measure the effectiveness of the use of borrowed funds.
7. To be the base for the dividend/retentions decision.
8. To determine the level of 'retained profits' as a major source of finance, an offset to inflation and a provision for growth.

Practical reasons for *reporting* profit include:
1. To provide pertinent information:
    (a) required by company and other legislation;
    (b) to meet the needs of shareholders, investors, suppliers, lenders and people dealing with the company, employees and their representatives, financial markets, financial institutions and government.

Examination Question 31

SUGGESTED ANSWER

(a) Preparation of Sources and application of funds statement, (b) analysis thereof, and (c) comments on options for improving cash flow without further borrowing.

Tutorial Note: The question totalled 26 marks, apportioned 13 for (a), 8 for (b) and 5 for (c), and allowing for approximately 47 minutes to complete the whole answer. The 23 minutes for (a) was an adequate amount of time for the numerics of that part. However, if that had proved troublesome, completion of that part could have been deferred while attempts were made for the 50% of the overall marks available for parts (b) and (c). Indeed part (c) could have been independently tackled, e.g. in circumstances where time was not left to complete the whole question.

(a) Workings: *Profit (budgeted) 1982/83.* Forecast dividend = £32,000 = 40% of after-tax
(1)   profit. After-tax profit is therefore = £80,000, i.e. £32,000 × 100/40.
        Profit (actual) 1981/82. Retained profit = £158,000 less £128,000 = £30,000 = 60% of after-tax profit. After-tax profit is therefore = £50,000, i.e. £30,000 × 100/60.
        Note: Tax is ignored.

Workings: *Depreciation (budgeted) 1982/83.* Net difference between closing fixed assets
(2)   and opening fixed assets is £20,000, i.e. £150,000 less £130,000. Acquisitions of fixed assets in 1982/3 = £46,000. Therefore, depreciation = £26,000, i.e. £46,000 less £20,000.
        Depreciation (actual) 1981/82. Net difference between closing fixed assets and opening fixed assets is £10,000, i.e. £130,000 less £120,000. Acquisitions of fixed assets in 1981/2 = £34,000. Therefore, depreciation = £24,000, i.e. £34,000 less £10,000.

Statement for the Managing Director Penryn Ltd, comparing budgeted funds statement for 1982/3 with the actual funds statement for 1981/2

		1982/83		1981/82		
		£'000s	£'000s	£'000s	£'000s	
Sources of funds						
	Profit for the year		80		50	Workings (1)
ADD	Depreciation adjustment		26		24	Workings (2)
	Internal funds from operations		106		74	
	External funds		Nil		Nil	(see *Note 3*)
			106		74	
Application of funds						
	Dividends paid	32		20		
	Taxation	—		—		
	Bank loan repaid	10		10		
	Purchase of fixed assets	46	88	34	64	
			18		10	
Increase in working capital						
being:	Increase in debtors	(150)		(111)		
	Increase in stocks	(46)		(17)		
	Increase (decrease) creditors	(53)	(249)	103	(25)	

		(231)	(15)
leaving:	Decrease in liquid funds		
	Opening cash balance	15	30
therefore:	Closing cash balance	(216)	15

Note 3: this small company covered its growth in turnover and the financing of fixed assets without recourse to longer term external borrowing.

(b) (i) Rise in turnover 1981/82 (actual) = 22% less (say) 6% inflation = 16%
Rise in turnover 1982/83 (budget) = 26% less (say) 6% inflation = 20%

    (ii) Working capital increases in debtors and stocks in 1981/2 were substantially (and only) covered by an increase in trade creditors of £103,000 (103%). Operations cash flow in the year £74,000 covered dividend, repayment of longer term loan, and capital expenditure leaving only £10,000 to support the financing of working capital. The liquid position was largely maintained through the heavy reliance on trade credit.

  (iii) In the budgeted year this reliance on creditors finance is to be reduced. But as the excess of operations cash flow over dividend, bank loan repayment and capital expenditure provides only £18,000 towards working capital, the financing of increased debtors and stocks, together with the repayments to trade creditors, has the alarming effect of causing a budgeted decrease in liquid funds of some £231,000!

(c) Budgeted debtors ratio (1982/83) is 91 days (debtors/sales × 365) compared with actual debtors ratio (1981/82) of 78 days.

One way of improving cash flow is by tightening credit control. If the terms of trade average, say, 30 days net, a credit control target of 60 days might be realistic taking into account time lag for invoicing, although that target could be reduced.

However, at 60 days target, the budgeted 91 days is 31 days adrift and a cause for concern. The cost of financing customers to this extra extent (and the potential saving), assuming 20% interest on borrowed cash (with inflation taken into account that cost could be higher at 25% say), is approximately £33,500 (£42,000 at 25%).

A second way of improving cash flow is to factor the debts, the calculation of which would account for the terms of the contract as to timing of payment by the factors to the company, their charge and the daily investment in debtors inherent in the above figures, i.e. *circa* £5,000 per day in the budget year (£491,000/91 days).

It is clear that apart from improved credit/stock control, the company needs an injection of long-term funds (shareholders/loan capital).

Index

Note: Items defined in the 'terminology of accounting' are referenced in italics